BUILDING PARADISE

A sweeping historical study, *Building Paradise* seeks to construct a garden ethic for the design arts. It is an ethic predicated on the idea that, with our recent ecological and biological insights, we can build more intelligently than the status quo of current design practices. The paradisiacal instinct is the motivation behind every artistic impulse. From its theological origins to the present, the idea of paradise—the garden as a place of peace, beauty, and happiness—has acquired numerous meanings. It was a motif expounded in the earliest cultures of Mesopotamia, Egypt, and the Indus Valley, and it later became a dominant feature of Buddhist, Judeo-Christian, and Islamic practices. It informed Greco-Roman mythologies and the design of a Japanese garden; it was a motivation for the Renaissance humanists, and was complicit in visions of a New Arcadia within the landscapes of the Americas. This book, underscoring how the built and urban environments shapes culture, takes a biophilic approach and draws upon the major advances of the human sciences of the last few decades to argue on behalf of a design ethic centered squarely on human needs and aspirations. Written for students and academics within architecture and all related fields, this book focuses on the efforts to build paradise in a material way.

Harry Francis Mallgrave is a Distinguished Professor Emeritus from Illinois Institute of Technology and an Honorary Fellow of the Royal Institute of British Architects. He received his PhD in architecture from the University of Pennsylvania, and over the years he has enjoyed a career as teacher, scholar, editor, translator, and architect.

BUILDING PARADISE

Episodes in Paradisiacal Thinking

Harry Francis Mallgrave

Routledge
Taylor & Francis Group

NEW YORK AND LONDON

First published 2022
by Routledge
605 Third Avenue, New York, NY 10158

and by Routledge
2 Park Square, Milton Park, Abingdon, Oxon, OX14 4RN

Routledge is an imprint of the Taylor & Francis Group, an informa business

Library of Congress Cataloging-in-Publication Data
Names: Mallgrave, Harry Francis, author. | Havik, Klaske, 1975- writer of supplementary textual content.
Title: Building paradise : episodes in paradisiacal thinking / Harry Francis Mallgrave.
Description: New York, NY : Routledge, 2022. | Includes bibliographical references and index. |
Identifiers: LCCN 2021013627 (print) | LCCN 2021013628 (ebook) | ISBN 9781032014012 (hardback) | ISBN 9781032014029 (paperback) | ISBN 9781003178460 (ebook)
Subjects: LCSH: Architecture—Philosophy. | Design—Philosophy. | Paradise.
Classification: LCC NA2500 .M2768 2022 (print) | LCC NA2500 (ebook) | DDC 720.1—dc23
LC record available at https://lccn.loc.gov/2021013627
LC ebook record available at https://lccn.loc.gov/2021013628

ISBN: 9781032014012 (hbk)
ISBN: 9781032014029 (pbk)
ISBN: 9781003178460 (ebk)

DOI: 10.4324/9781003178460

Typeset in Bembo
by Apex CoVantage, LLC

To Susan's Jardin d'hiver

CONTENTS

ILLUSTRATIONS

FOREWORD

In the Beginning . . . Stories of Human Experience and Imagination

Was there ever a paradise, a perfect place, a good world, in the beginning? And can we construct paradise in the reality of our contemporary world? Architects and literary writers alike have attempted to construct ideal worlds—both mental and built ones. Through their designs and stories, they have depicted alternative worlds, sometimes oneiric mental constructions of lush vegetation and richly decorated palaces, populated by mythical humans and gods, sometimes more mundane ones, that offered models for places of shelter, contemplation, or delight.

In many of these mental constructions of paradise, the boundaries between seeming dichotomies fade: freedom and enclosure, body and mind, sacred and mundane, wildness and order all come together in these key stories of human experience. From an architectural perspective, an interesting field of tension that appears in the stories of paradise is the simultaneous idealization of nature and the presence of architectural ordering.[1] The distinction between what is real and what is imagined becomes blurred as well. Is paradise by definition an imagined and idealized place, or could it also be perceived, and even built, in the real world? Whereas some of the paradisiacal episodes presented in this book are situated in the realm of myth and dreams, others have existed in reality or have been attempts to create an earthly paradise by means of architecture.

Perhaps we should stop thinking in terms of such distinction, and acknowledge that there does not exist any space in the real world of human experience that is not also imagined. Likewise, our imagined spaces could be argued to be by definition responses to those spaces and situations we know in the real world. To do justice to the multiple perspectives from which places can be experienced and imagined, Edward W. Soja spoke of real-and-imagined places, arguing that Lefebvre's notion of lived space could be seen as such a space that is simultaneously real and imagined, a combination of real (perceived) and imagined (conceived) space.[2] If lived spaces are simultaneously real and imagined, we could argue the same for spaces in literature, for these offer us an imaginative perspective on our existing human world.

The attention to human experience has long been relatively absent in mainstream architectural discourse. Harry Francis Mallgrave has been one of the few strong voices that has insisted, through multiple books, to bring the human dimension of architecture to the fore and to plead for an architectural approach that takes into account the experiential qualities of architecture. His writings have addressed the complexity of human perception, human consciousness, the workings of body and mind, and have brought insights from the fields of biology and neuroscience into the domain of architecture, addressing our embodied and emotional responses to the built environment. His work urges architects to see the role of their profession not as the mere production of objects, but rather as the understanding and making of experiences.

Language, like architecture, is one of the key tools to do so: literary language is used to understand our relation to our environment, to describe and construct experiences in real and imagined worlds. The capacity to perceive the world is connected with the capacity to make stories: we tell stories to make sense of the world. Literary imagination is a key human skill to respond to our environment—to understand it, to interpret it, and to change it. What distinguishes stories from mere description, among other elements, is the presence of characters. Without character, a story can hardly develop; without characters, it becomes difficult for a reader (or listener) to develop empathy, and to mentally take part in the story. In this book, architecture and landscape are not described in neutral terms; instead, they are interwoven with social stories: these episodes of paradise are populated. We can meet nymphs in the gardens of Greek myth, dream with Poliphilo and Filarete about lush forests and voluptuous pleasures of architecture, mourn with Ruskin for the lost paradise of Venice when he returns to the then-rundown city; we can be astonished as Jung by the flower motifs in the mosaics of the Mausoleum of Galla Placidia in Ravenna; we can understand the American dream of Arcadia with Emerson and his fellows, who initiated their Brook Farm Commune. Times fuse, voices of the past speak to us through their stories; their desire can be ours, and we can empathize with them.

Each episode comes with new characters. The word *epeisodion* in ancient Greek referred to the moment in a tragedy when a new actor would arrive to the stage; the episode was the beginning of a new act within the larger whole of the play. Although the different episodes all have their own function in the play, and are organized in a certain order, they can also be seen as independent activities in themselves. The episodes in this book can be read separately, each as an intriguing description of the way in which paradise was dreamt, imagined, or even built in different times in history. These episodes, stories of different times and places, imaginative descriptions of paradise, take us through history: from the Persian gardens to Greek myth, from the Roman representations of paradise to Renaissance poems and dreams, from baroque to the American arcadia, and finally into the cities of the twentieth century and their counterparts in dystopia. The episodes in this book celebrate the human capacity to imagine places of delight, whether in dreams or as built realities. And, as this book makes clear, these imaginations are without exception architectural, full of spatial detail, describing the perfection of proportions, the wealth of architectural materials, the preciousness of each stone in the city, and the joining of the built and the natural: sublime nature meets architectural perfection. In these literary worlds we can inhabit paradise, for the time we spend in the story.

There is one particular kind of paradise, which is said to have existed, and that perhaps still exists, in multiple places in our contemporary world. In the episode about the ancient city of Alexandria, the library is described as "walled-off paradise, a garden complex with colonnades along which to walk, read or converse with others." Shouldn't we regard the library, in general, as a form of paradise: a place of tranquility, to read, study and meet, a safe, free space for study and exchange? This physical and mental space of reading and writing, of gathering knowledge, of thought and understanding, of connecting and exchanging with others, is a space where Harry Francis Mallgrave, given his impressive and vast scholarship, must have spent a lot of time. Perhaps, the space of scholarship can be seen as a timeless condition of paradise—and this book as an invitation to enjoy the delights of reading, and (re)discovering these essential stories of human experience and imagination.

Klaske Havik
Professor of Architecture
Delft University of Technology

Notes

1. Rob Aben and Saskia de Wit, *The Enclosed Garden: History and Development of the Hortus Conclusus and Its Reintroduction into the Present-day Urban Landscape* (Rotterdam: 0101 Publishers, 1999), 32.
2. Edward W. Soja, *Thirdspace: Journeys to Los Angeles and Other Real-and-Imagined Places* (Malden; Oxford; Carlton: Blackwell Publishing, 1996), referring to Henri Lefebvre, *The Production of Space* (London: Blackwell Publishing, 1991), originally published as *La production d'espace* (Paris: Editions Anthropos, 1974).

PREFACE

In his literary masterpiece *Invisible Cities*, Italo Calvino—through the voice of Marco Polo at the court of Kublai Khan—takes us on a tour of imaginary cities. He paints cities of wonder, cities of despair, cities of memory, and cities of desire. Among them are cities where buildings have spiral staircases encrusted with seashells and artisans make perfect violins, astronomical cities where every street follows a planet's orbit, and thin cities built on open latticework suspended between the steep faces of two mountains. In the last city, one must take extra care where one sets down one's foot. The city of Diomira has sixty silver domes. In the city of Anastasia, where one can purchase agate, onyx, chrysoprase, and other varieties of chalcedony, the women seen bathing in gardens have been known to invite strangers to disrobe and chase them in the pools. In the transparent city of Moriana, the alabaster gates are translucent in the sunlight, coral columns support serpentine pediments, and villas are entirely made of glass. Yet Moriana also has an obverse, where one stumbles upon "an expanse of rusting sheet metal, sackcloth, planks bristling with spikes, pipes black with soot, piles of tins, blind walls with fading signs, frames of staved-in straw chairs, ropes good only for hanging oneself from a rotten beam."[1]

Calvino's cities are intentionally surreal, chimerical, and allegorical in their composition; they were not intended to be utopian, or dystopian. Instead, they are fanciful, poetic, and sensuous acts of a creative imagination, specific in nuance and materiality, and enchanting in the light that filters through them. As with every artistic creation, they are manifestations of what Johan Huizinga once named the play instinct, or what can also be called the paradisiacal instinct. It is the urge to be poetic, to bring some beauty to this world, and, more directly to our theme, to build a paradise or garden in which to dwell.

The idea of paradise, rooted in most religions, has sometimes been interpreted as a "nostalgia for Eden," a projection of oneself beyond the present life into another, happier existence.[2] This is true for some religions, but the idea also has a similarly long line of non-theological development that can be found on the cave walls of Chavet and Lascaux, in the ancient libraries of Alexandria and Pergamon, in the troubadour songs and literature of the Middle Ages, in the teahouses of Kyoto, and in landscape theories of the eighteenth century; it even occasionally made a halting appearance in the hardened world of the twentieth century. The paradisiacal instinct, in its full range of configurations, spans from the garden in its most basic form to the making of houses, temples, and ultimately cities. Yet the paradisiacal instinct is at the same time small; it arises from within oneself and not from any ideological manifest. In this sense, it is quite a different impulse from the idea of utopia, which is often filled with legislative and moral mandates imposed on human behavior from above. The two pursuits, it is true, occasionally overlap, but utopians think on a grand scale and wants to remake the world in line with avowed behavioral or formal imperatives. They dream of "remodelling the 'whole of society' in accordance with a definite plan or blueprint," as Karl Popper once described the urge.[3] The bigger the scale and the grander the imposition, the better. Yet the paradisiacal instinct springs from within oneself as a vitality of self-expression. It is the human impulse to create or secure some measure of personal bliss, to build a place for one's imagination and pursuit of happiness to run, and to proffer or maintain some vision of beauty in the face of the often-ugly built world. If utopians seek power and control, paradisiacally minded people have no such penchant. Their efforts are generally limited and humble: the first leafage of a spring planting or a candlelit dinner for two will generally satisfy the instinct.

Yet it is somewhat interesting that the vast majority of utopian writers have rarely taken the designed environment into their calculations. It is as if the built world is immaterial or has no relation to the health and contentment of those who inhabit these artificial creations. Only in the dystopian literature of a few twentieth-century novels does the physical environment come into play—in a negative way, of course. Plato, for instance, lived within the artistic and architectural splendors of fifth-century Athens, yet he conceived the Callipolis of his republic in the abstract terms of moral regulations, preferably by standards he himself enacted. Although well-traveled and keenly interested in the world, he seems to have been oblivious to the artistry and refinement of his Athenian surroundings. Beauty he relegated to the ideal world, somewhere outside of the walls of the cave. The early church fathers of Christianity, like their Islamic successors, often did the same by pushing the idea of paradise into the afterlife and imagining instead a society to be governed by ecclesiastical decree, predicated on a liberal amount of personal sacrifice. Sixteenth-century utopians from Thomas More to Francis Bacon envisioned a better society in terms of some miraculous transformation of human mores yet set it within the existing streetscapes of their day. And Enlightenment thinkers also tended to focus on the ideal political structure that would lead to a more equitable world. Few took account of the influence the built environment can have on human happiness.

And then there was that great political and cultural experiment that began around the start of the twentieth century that went by the moniker of modernity. Although the voices of the era may have been well-intentioned, the next 100 years barely survived the political experiments, revolutions, pogroms, wars, and cultural upheavals; all were the result of utopian impulses seeking to reform society in radical ways. Even the once-grandiose vision of the teeming and fast-paced metropolis with its steel-and-glass towers, patched together in the second half of the century, no longer looks quite so appealing in light of our city's many social and cultural failings. Their shortcomings have become even more evident in our era of air travel, globalism, social media, and pandemics. Like every utopian impulse, the towers once symbolized a brave new world, yet today our ever-expanding urban hardscapes offer little solace to the millions who must labor within them. The instinct to flee to nature and repair one's spirit is but a dream many privately hold in order to make it through another day. The fortunes of the most well-intentioned foundations or philanthropists will do little to solve the problems that lack a technological solution. And the rude and censorious digital world has not brought us together but removed us further from an Edenic society.

The word "paradise" comes down to us from the Latin *paradisus*, Greek *paradeisos*, and old-Persian *pairidaēza*, which, in its earliest usage, referred to a walled garden. It also came to signify a cool, shaded place, hunting parks, and the gardens of temples and private residences, in which groves, vineyards, orchards, and flowers were cultivated for their beauty. From this usage, the Greeks adopted the word *paradeisos*, and in their early literature it also became synonymous with such fictive yet serene places as the Isles of the Blessed, the Garden of the Hesperides, and the Elysian Fields. As the Garden of Eden became a fixture in Judeo-Christian and Islamic cultures, it also came to be associated with the idea of a celestial paradise or heaven. Yet from a broader perspective, and notwithstanding the various colorations of the word, paradise has always been associated with the garden or with nature, with places of surpassing natural beauty, but also places, as we are now beginning to learn, more alive and intertwined with well-being than we ever imagined. The animate sense of relaxation in a garden has also always been multicultural and universal.

Metaphorically, the word "paradise" has been used in many other ways. Is not every artistic expression—from the poetry of Homer to the mosaic workers of byzantine Ravenna, from Gustav Klimt's *Tree of Life* to the water lilies of Monet—a manifestation of the paradisiacal instinct? The fragrance of paradise can be inhaled from a garden outside one's bedroom window, and its melodious vibration can be felt in a concert hall. Its emotional aura can also be gleaned in the peaceful contours of environments that offer seduction, surprise, solace, and shapeliness. Can we again imagine our homes or the cities in which we live in such Edenic terms?

Nevertheless, paradisiacal thinking in design seems to have fallen out of favor in recent years. Whereas we would be hard-pressed to find designers employing the word "paradise" today, it was scarcely more than a half century ago that the Finnish architect Alvar Aalto confessed that architecture always has "an ulterior motive always lurking behind the corner, the idea of creating paradise," and that without this motive our design efforts would become trivial.[4] Aalto's words, presented in a speech to builders in 1957, may seem quaint to some today, but might our perception be the result of the hardening of our culture and the lowering of our expectations over the past half century? I find his words particularly relevant because he was addressing the issue of human-centered design from the biological and anthropological perspective of his day, whereas we now have a much-expanded knowledge of ourselves. We have made major gains in understanding our evolutionary history, the workings of our genome, and the growth and development of the human nervous and emotional systems, in all of their complex interactions. Yet are we using this new knowledge to build a happier world? Or, are we simply following outdated aesthetic standards set down in the recent past—that is, architecture as the creation of aestheticized objects and cities as the random accumulation of these artifacts? Today we have an abundance of research on the apathetic if not fatalistic effects of environmental deprivation, yet have we ever seriously pondered what constitutes a healthy and emotionally gratifying built environment? Is it not time for planners and designers to redirect their focus back to what is important? Is it not time to raise the qualitative standard of how we live? Is it not time to situate human culture within the culture of nature?

Much of this book will focus on efforts to build paradise in some material way, to underline a motive that was not always acknowledged and that throughout much of its history has been confused with social and political agendas. The expressive range of this instinct is vast, and I will pursue it only through selected episodes taking place at particular moments of creative inspiration—some successful, some not. Anyone taking this approach would undoubtedly come up with a different set of examples of where and how the motive was given material form and where it has been thwarted.

Over a half century ago, the architect Christopher Alexander voiced the designer's alarm "that we may be turning the world into a place peopled only by little glass and concrete boxes."[5] We have sadly arrived at and gone well beyond this point, and we have replaced the little concrete-and-glass boxes with much bigger ones. Yet can we really claim that we have enhanced our culture? We continue to measure the success of our cities by the false drama of their skylines, while the individual search for paradise takes place in the streets, houses, shops, bars, and offices below. The growing angst of the metropolitan dweller pleads for a change of priorities, and yet we continue to accept far too uncritically the hardness of our built environments. Few will contest the fact that, from an ecological and social perspective (human ecology), we can build much more wisely and beautifully than we presently do. Our most severe limitation seems to be our low expectations.

Notes

1. Italo Calvino, *Invisible Cities*, trans. by William Weaver (Orlando, FL: Harcourt, 1974), 12.
2. The phrase "nostalgia for Eden" is a reference to Mircea Eliade, *The Sacred and the Profane: The Nature of Religion* (San Diego, CA: Harcourt Brace & Company, 1987), 207.
3. Karl R. Popper, *The Poverty of Historicism* (New York: Harper Torchbooks, 1964), 67.
4. *Alvar Aalto in His Own Words*, ed. by Göran Schildt (Helsinki: Otava Publishing Company, 1997), 215.
5. Christopher Alexander, "A City Is Not a Tree," *Architectural Forum* 122 (April–May 1965), 58.

ACKNOWLEDGMENTS

My special thanks to Klaske Havik, Bob Condia, Sarah Robinson, Mark Hewitt, Kim Coventry, Durganand Balsavar, Tatiana Berger, Tess van Eyck, Alia Fadel, and Allison Rose Olsen.

1

IMAGINING PARADISE

Sumer

One might seem to be on fragile ground in attempting to trace the paradisiacal instinct back to the beginning of *Homo sapiens*, but only because it is likely much older than that. In the 1960s, the remnants of the Paleolithic settlement of Terra Amata, dating to around 400,000 years ago, were found on a construction site in Nice, France. The archaeologist Henry de Lumley, over the few months during which construction was suspended, unearthed a series of what he deemed to be gabled huts with hearths, situated today on a bluff overlooking the Mediterranean Sea. The hearth in itself, with its offering of warmth and cooked food, seems like an important leap forward, but these settlers and builders were not modern humans. Most likely, they were members of either *Homo heidelbergensis* or Neanderthals.[1] Still, one must wonder if these early humans of no more than five feet in stature, when looking out over a sea eighty-five feet higher than it is today, did not view their southern horizon as a garden, one both captivating and transporting the spirit into a state of wonderment.

This finding calls to mind the distinction Mircea Eliade once made between the sacred and profane. He did so to define the "two existential situations assumed by man in the course of his history," but also to make the case that one cannot truly separate the "sacred" from "the ritualized building of the human habitation."[2] Both are aspects of the human impulse to survive by improving one's place in the world, and both are deeply rooted in our language. The English word for building, for instance, derives from the Proto-Indo-European *bhu*, "to dwell," and *bheue*, "to be, exist, grow." Throughout history, the building of the tomb, the house, the temple, or the city has been seen as the means through which human imagination, at many levels, redeems and reconstructs its vision of a lost or imagined paradise. One thinks in this regard of those southern European caves displaying palpable signs of human vitality and spiritualized thought, beginning close to 40,000 years ago. As Jean Clottes has suggested, people sketched their visions on cave walls for various reasons, one of which was to define a place for communal rituals, consisting no doubt of fire, dancing, and vocal chants or rhythms. The cave at Lascaux has a rotunda near its entrance called the Hall of Bulls, which displays a frieze of delineated masterpieces consisting of seventeen horses, eleven aurochs, six stags, one bear, and one unicorn—a hunter's paradise. The bodies of the animals were in some cases enhanced by surface moldings found on the cave walls. Also interesting is the instinct expressed in the narrow, dark, and arduous passages far into the womb of the cave, where, in the interpretation of Clottes, shamans crawled to explore the limits of sacralized consciousness and to mediate a communion

DOI: 10.4324/9781003178460-1

"between the world of the living and the world of the spirits."[3] The notion of an afterlife, a sense of a unified cosmos, is an early manifestation of the paradisiacal instinct.

Several writers have suggested that cities of the dead may have antedated cities of the living, and that the dead, in the view of Lewis Mumford, "were the first to have a permanent dwelling: a cavern, a mound marked by a cairn, or some other receptacle. These were landmarks to which the living probably returned at intervals to commune with or placate the ancestral spirits."[4] More recently, Robert Pogue Harrison has argued that "the ancient city was built on the foundations of the ancient house, and that the ancient house was built in turn upon the ancestor's grave."[5] The oldest known human habitats, the brushwood dwellings at Ohalo in Israel, date from 25,000 years ago, and the use of stone for housing could not have followed too many centuries thereafter. By the start of the first millennium, at sites such as Jefel Ahman and Dja'je in southern Turkey, we not only have evidence of monumental subterranean sanctuaries carved into the ground but also of the architectural transition from circular to rectangular housing forms.[6] Celestial thinking was similarly evident in the circular temples found at Göbekli Tepe, the oldest human-built sanctuaries. The complex was begun sometime after 9600 BC, atop a ridge overlooking a valley a thousand feet below. Its twenty excavated rings contain more than 200 steles with T-shaped profiles, many carved with insects, birds, bulls, and other animals. Circular rings were cut into the hillside, the largest 100 feet in diameter, inside of which circular stone walls formed a labyrinth. At the center of the pavement, standing alone, were two colossal T-shaped steles, likely representing deities. The landscape, located at the northern end of the fertile crescent and not too distant from the wellspring of the Euphrates River, was also attractive. "This area was like a paradise," says its lead archaeologist Klaus Schmidt, because the area would have had around it gently flowing rivers, herds of gazelles, geese and ducks, fruit and nut trees, and wild barley and wheat.[7] The sanctuary seemingly attracted clans of hunter-gatherers from great distances to participate in religious rites, and the building of the complex in itself involved hundreds of people simply to move and carve the works.

Stretching down into the Levant, a series of early towns were built around sacred springs. On the outskirts of Amman, the settlement of Ain Ghazal or "Spring of the Gazelle" attracted bands of hunter-gatherers at an early date and was regularly occupied from 7200 BC. At its height the village encompassed more than thirty acres and housed as many as 3,000 people. Square houses were permanently constructed, adults and children were buried under the floor, and numerous figurines and plaster statues have been unearthed. Its nearby sister town of Jericho was another primordial site formed next to an abundant spring, and was frequented by hunter-gatherers around the start of the tenth millennium. Five hundred years later, the first circular huts of sun-dried brick appeared and, by the start of the ninth millennium, the town was permanently settled with as many as seventy dwellings. Again, the dead were buried beneath the floors of the houses. The undressed stone walls of Jericho, some as tall as twenty feet, were started around 8,000 years ago, and outside the rampart was a moat. Inside the walls was a circular tower deemed to have been used for both ceremonial and cosmological purposes.[8]

One of the more interesting of the late Neolithic villages is Çatalhöyük in southern Anatolia, which dates to around the turn of the eighth millennium. At its height, it housed as many as 10,000 people. The town once again vividly portrays the paradisiacal undercurrent of domestic building. It was built on a high plateau, and the town's most arresting feature is that its rectangular houses have no streets. One gained access to them only through roofs that formed a second plateau, from which people descended directly into their homes with ladders. The significance of this higher plane has been likened to Jacob's dream at Bethel, in which angels ascended and descended to and from heaven by means of a ladder, although here the more practical reasons were defense as well as protection from the heat.[9] Çatalhöyük also had no collective places of worship. In fact, there seems to have been no distinction between domestic and ritualized space. As at Jericho, the bones of ancestors were buried in the floors, often with burial gifts, and their spirits continued to inhabit the dwelling along with the offspring. Other adornments included statues of fertility goddesses, rams, and bull heads in addition to painted columns and plastered walls. At an excavation level dating to 6200 BC, archaeologists found an image of an erupting volcano—the world's earliest known landscape painting.[10] Another curious feature of the site is that the connecting rooms within each house were not accessed by doors but by smaller openings, forcing one to bend down or even crawl from one room to another. Moreover, many of these rooms, with little or minimal natural light, may indeed have taken on the nocturnal atmosphere of a cave.[11] In addition to the cosmology, the main living areas, when lit from above or by a few courtyards, presented a rather cozy living abode of ancient sophistication.

It is also not too far-fetched to suggest that with the fixed habitation of the Neolithic era also came the garden, which was obviously first used for the production of food, but which, because of this urgency, soon acquired other consecrated values. Plants and trees, in mirroring the course of life, became emblems of fertility, and nature itself became sacrosanct. Socialization also came into play. When humans began to form towns and cities, the responsibility for the fertility of the fields—their periodic renewal—passed from the individual to anointed leaders who could divine the will of the gods. At this stage, certain plants acquired ineffable values unique to particular deities. From here, it would not take long for still another meaning to emerge, which is the joy of immersing oneself within one's own human creation—the cultivation of the garden for its sensorial beauty.

Within Judeo-Christian and Islamic accounts of creation, humanity begins with the Garden of Eden, but these accounts were based on older traditions of Mesopotamia and Egypt. Due to a condition of climate cooling in the seventh millennium, tribes migrated from the north into the river valleys of southern Mesopotamia and began the transition toward urban cultures. Here the human race also underwent further changes in lifestyles. The fertile plains, together with the regulation of waterways, yielded the possibility of a grain diet and the pasturing of animals. During this period, the gods of local shrines of smaller towns came to be replaced by the more powerful gods of the sun, moon, and sky, just as local leaders would come to be replaced by the unchallenged authority of kings and pharaohs. It was through their more direct connections to divinities, as religious practices prescribed, that these new leaders derived their moral and political authority.

The invention of writing in both Sumer and Egypt in the fourth millennium yielded the codification of trade and law, but also of scripture and the social organization needed for the complex functioning of the city. Together, they provided the planning and logistical tools for the deployment of thousands of laborers to build the temples, palaces, ramparts, and irrigation canals. Initially what emerged was a series of smaller city-states not unlike those of later Greece and Ionia, in which the majority of the population worked their own fields in addition to participating in civic tasks related to the economy and administration of the state. The temple became the centerpiece of these efforts because every member of the city followed its counsel.

What was gained with this new idea of a city was not a departure from earlier religious practices but, in the Mesopotamian valley at least, a magnification of a grander Edenic impulse. It was the passage, as Numa Denis Fustel de Coulanges has noted, from the family "to the phratry to the tribe to the city."[12] The city not only instituted a structure for collective efforts but also a cosmology of its own. It represented an ordered hierarchy of at least one deity, and by elevating the temple to a higher plane than that used for everyday commerce, it also enhanced the paradisiacal character of the city. The holy mountains of the Mesopotamian valley—the *axis mundi*, or earthly pillars connecting heaven and earth—were the means through which humans could commune with their gods, and they also elevated the stature of urban residents. They became "objects of civic pride," as Henri Frankfort once described them.[13]

The siting of the first Sumerian cities, together with their social structure, were divinely sanctified by the mythology of their creation. By all Sumerian accounts, Eridu was the first city. It was originally (with higher sea levels) a seaport on the Persian Gulf, and it is said to have been built on the actual site of paradise—that is, the garden "wherein grew a glorious tree" bearing fruit resembling "white lapis-lazuli."[14] The land for the temple and the city, however, did not belong to humans but to the gods, because in Sumerian scripture it was the gods who first occupied the Mesopotamian landscape and divided up the land, with each god selecting a place for his or her sanctuary. Initially, the gods built their own temples and entrusted lesser deities to maintain them. Only when these lesser deities revolted did the gods create humans from the fecund womb of the mother goddess. Effectively, humans were conceived as indentured servants, charged with the task of cultivating the holy lands and maintaining the temples so essential to the cosmic order.

Yet humans, as biblical scripture also later emphasized, were created imperfectly. We therefore have another special caste of men dispatched from the heavens to bridge this divide between the sacred and profane—the class of kings. They were human in part but also partly divine and made "in the image of" god. Mesopotamian annals endowed them with good looks and large statures, high intelligence and athletic skills, and unmatched supremacy in hunting and warfare. They were also the stewards of the land and its production. They were responsible for the cultivation of food stocks as well as maintaining the cultic tree within "the garden of paradise as symbolized by the temple grove." If these temples occupied the various sites of paradise, then one should not be surprised that kings actually assumed "the title of 'gardener,' Sumerian *nu-kiri*, Accadian *nukarribu*."[15] The horticultural knowledge of kings was therefore extensive, and they "were as proud of their horticultural expertise as they were of their prowess on the battlefield. They frequently transplanted the exotic botanical species of conquered territories, boasting they thrived better under their green thumb than in their natural habitats."[16]

Because agriculture and its fertility were generally the domain of goddesses, kings were also expected to consort with female deities or their hierodules to maintain the cosmic fertility cycle. This was the case with the kings of the early dynasties at Uruk, where the fertility goddess Inanna had her own precinct. The pattern continued into later times, and among the official titles of King Shulgi, who ruled the city of Ur around the turn of the third millennium, was that of "husband" to Inanna. And on New Years' day, kings in several Mesopotamian cities consummated a ritual union with the high priestess in service to her temple, in order to renew the temple and fertility of the land.[17] One Sumerian hymn, celebrating the abundance of yield brought by Inanna's intercession with her husband Dumuzi, speaks to this ritual:

> In your house on high, in your beloved house
> I will come to live,
> O Nanna, up above in your cedar perfumed mountain
> I will come to live,
> O lord Nanna, in your citadel
> I will come to live,
> O Nanna, in your mansion of Ur
> I will come to live
> O lord! In its bed I for my part
> will lie down too![18]

The fabled (and historical) King Gilgamesh, as portrayed in the Sumerian *Epic* bearing his name, seems to have been the one notable exception. He first ran into trouble on his heroic quest for paradise when he rejected the sexual overtures of Inanna, who subsequently devastated his home city of Uruk. Comparisons with later Judaic texts are interesting. Uruk, according to Sumerian mythology, was founded by Seven Sages who were sent down from heaven to civilize the notoriously errant human race, and Gilgamesh, although a demigod, personified many of these shortcomings. He was impulsive, violent, and abusive toward his people, and eventually he left his home city to seek eternal

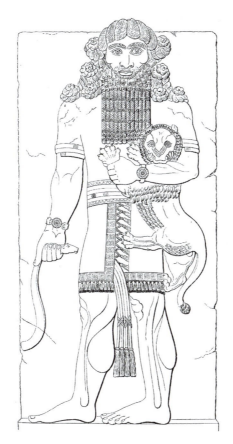

ILLUSTRATION 1.1   Gilgamesh Strangling a Lion, Khorsabad bas-relief found, c. 710 BC.

Source: From George Smith, *The Chaldean Account of Genesis* (New York: Scribner, Armstrong & Company, 1876).

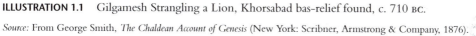

life. After various Herculean toils, he came to the cedar forest and twin peaks of Mount Mashu at the end of the earth, where he found a tunnel. He followed a path down to the garden of the gods, a Sumerian Eden marked by carnelian and lapis-lazuli trees. The clay tablet on which the narrative was written is unfortunately damaged, but we have a few scattered words—such as "coral," "sasu-stone," "abashmu-stone," "agate," and "haematite"—to suggest what he found in the garden.[19] Such a description precedes by 2,000 years Ezekiel's description of Eden, where "every precious stone adorned you: ruby, topaz and emerald, chrysolite, onyx and jasper, sapphire, turquoise and beryl."[20]

But Gilgamesh's tale does not end here. In the next tablet he takes a boat across the sea in search of another Eden, the island inhabited by the immortal seer Uta-napishti, who survived the Great Flood on an Ark that the god Enki had commanded him to build to preserve the human race. The flood was only the last and most severe of divine sanctions to punish human failings, and the wise man Uta-napishti attempted to tame and educate Gilgamesh by informing him of the extent of his royal duties, chief of which were to look after and protect the temples and properties of the gods (the earth) and to see that sacred rituals and the higher cosmic order were maintained. As a parting gift, Uta-napishti provided Gilgamesh with knowledge of an underwater plant that would restore his youth and bestow upon him immortality. The penitent king finds it, but shortly thereafter this treasure is stolen by a serpent—the saga of the gods once again denying humans entry into paradise.

In another Sumerian myth, "Enki and Ninhursag," the island on which Uta-napishti lived, was Dilmun, "the garden of the Great Gods and Earthly paradise, located eastward in Eden." Enki was the god of fresh water, knowledge, crafts, and creation, and Ninhursag was the earth mother and fertility goddess. Dilmun was "the land that knew neither sickness nor death or old age, where the raven uttered no cry, where lions and wolves killed not, and unknown were the sorrows of widowhood or the wailing of the sick."[21] It was also the island on which Enki and Ninhursag met and fell in love—with the latter, through the persuasion of her sexual favors, seducing Enki with his semen to bring waterways, rivers, and canals to her parched earth. Dilmun thus became Eden and her place of residence during the winter months, which she left each spring to roam and renew the earth.

Dilmun, incidentally, has its own archaeological history. Clay tablets confirming its existence, dating to the late third millennium, were deciphered by scholars in the nineteenth century, and William Albright, in drawing upon these efforts, has made the case that the paradise of Dilmun was none other than present-day Bahrain.[22] The island historically controlled trade routes between Mesopotamia and the Indus Valley as well as parts of what are now Kuwait, Qatar, and eastern Saudi Arabia. The debate over Bahrain led the archaeological team to make excavations on the island, and they soon found evidence of a thriving civilization going back to the early fourth millennium.[23] Subsequent excavations have found three superimposed temples dedicated to Enki, the oldest constructed around 3000 BC. The structure, as with many ancient temples, was built over a sacred spring, which was maintained in a basin of neatly cut limestone blocks—Enki's architectural gift to Ninhursag.

Tree of Life

Sumerian efforts to bring heaven down to earth was also manifested in the delineation of the holy citadel or walled precinct to house the main temples, palaces, and hallowed gardens. In the case of the divine city of Eridu, its architect was the god Enki, "the creator and the wise one" who, as one account relates, "placed the house upon you." One of his first acts was to plant the "tree of life" in the sacred grove adjacent to his sanctuary.[24] Eridu also acquired a somewhat unnatural appearance with the silting of the Euphrates River. The city was situated on a hillock within a larger geographic depression, some twenty feet below the surrounding landscape.[25] The land was quite arid, but the depression, in some months of the year, allowed subterranean waters to collect and form a lake encircling the "holy mountain" or shrine of Enki, where he dwelt with his wife in "his house of silver adorned with lapis lazuli."[26] As he was also the god of fresh water or "sweet water," Enki is said to have chosen this site specifically for its "muddy moisture"—that is, the soil that would give birth to the possibility of agriculture and eventually the human race.

The first written texts from the middle of the fourth millennium collectively speak to Eridu's foremost antiquity, and its urban settlements extended far into the sixth millennium. The earliest building unearthed, dating to around 5000 BC, is a small rectangular temple with a niche in one wall and a table for offerings. Modest as it was, it would soon be succeeded by a number of larger sanctuaries built on top of it, and toward the middle of the fourth millennium, or a thousand years before the first Egyptian pyramids, the city housed numerous limestone buildings and an estimated population of 10,000 people. Temples were generally part of a larger complex of buildings because, in addition to containing the deity's couch, living quarters, and altar, they were the administrative vehicles for managing the vast agricultural estates that surrounded them. Temple priests controlled not only tracts of groves, farming, and grazing lands, but they also oversaw the production of a number of other household and trade wares such as leather goods, jewelry, clothing, and other textiles. Temple communities, of which most cities had several precincts, therefore consisted of a cadre of priests, officials, gardeners, scribes, managers, potters, herdsmen, fishermen, tradesmen, and weavers. The king or governor coordinated the various temple activities into one self-sufficient municipal organization.

ILLUSTRATION 1.2   Assyrian relief panel depicting a winged supernatural figure tending to the Tree of Life, 883–859 BC.

Source: Metropolitan Museum of Art. OA public domain.

Another of Sumer's older cities was Uruk, which defines its own archaeological period comprising much of the fourth millennium. Here we find the birthplace of writing, the consolidation of urban institutions, and one of the earliest known celestial temples with a garden. Uruk traded with civilizations as far away as the Indus Valley, and at the start of the third millennium it had a population of 50,000 people. Its two major temple precincts were dedicated to the gods Anu and Inanna. The former sanctuary, which was built at the start of the Uruk period, was defined by a battered brick platform or early ziggurat, five acres in extent and lifted forty feet above the city. The Sumerian word for this sacred precinct or platform was *temen*, from which came the Greek word *temenos*, a holy grove or precinct dedicated to a deity. A single staircase, with one intermediate level, ascended to the top of the ziggurat. Here sat the temple, and after fourteen phases of reconstruction over many centuries it became known as the "White Temple." The tall temple structure with its tripartite plan and recessed brick walls was finished with a white plaster coating that could be seen from a great distance. Inside, the tall nave contained both a podium and stepped altar.

By contrast, the complex of sacred and governmental buildings in the lower Inanna district, the "House of Heaven," also rebuilt and modified over the course of a millennium, displays a great variety of structures and finishes. One of the earlier shrines to Inanna seems to have been approached through a courtyard, facing which were massive columns, nine feet in diameter, studded with terra-cotta cones set into plaster for weatherproofing. The use of different colored cones allowed artisans to form patterns of chevrons, zigzags, and triangles on the columns, emulating—in the opinion of one early archaeologist—the clay walls "lined with plaited mats, as they still are today in Southern Iraq."[27] There were also numerous terraces and courtyards surrounding the buildings in the Inanna district, which scholars have surmised were planted with gardens.[28] Uruk was also renowned for its walls, more than twenty feet in height and enclosing two square miles. Historically, they were attributed to Gilgamesh, as we see in the closing verse of one tablet of his *Epic*, when the hero, upon returning home, turns to his boatman and gestures with a proud display of his work:

> O Ur-shanabi, climb Uruk's wall and walk back and forth!
> Survey its foundations, examine the brickwork!
> Were its bricks not fired in an oven?
> Did the Seven Sages not lay its foundations?
>
> A square mile is city, a square mile date-grove, a square mile is
> clay-pit, half a square mile the temple of Ishtar [Inanna]:
> three square miles and a half is Uruk's expanse.[29]

The reference to a "square mile date-grove" documents that gardens of various kinds, with different species of plants, were incorporated into the city. Frankfort has reported that temple records frequently mention large tracts of "woods" under their dominion, which consisted of groves, orchards, vineyards, cultivated and fragrant plants, as well as trees used for lumber.[30] Depictions of sacred trees are everywhere in Mesopotamian iconography. One tree personified in the legend of the god Nim-Gishzida was called the "trusty tree" and guarded the gates of heaven.[31] Numerous temples related to the earth and fertility rites, such as the Temple of the New Year Festival at the court city of Assur, which was situated within a grove of designated sacred trees. At Enki's temple in Eridu, there was a Kiskanu tree, a "tree of life" whose "appearance is that of lapis-lazuli," and a sacred grove "casting its shadow, therein no man goeth to enter. In the midst are the Sun-god and the Sovereign of heaven, in between the river of two mouths."[32] Courtyard gardens were commonplace in palaces, and members of the royal family were often buried in courtyards within or adjacent to the palatial complex.

This was the case with the Sumerian city of Ur, which by the mid-third millennium enjoyed great prosperity and an allied network of cities spread across western Asia. When Leonard Woolley excavated the site in the 1920s and 1930s, he came upon a royal cemetery of more than 2,000 people within the city walls, adjacent to the sacred precinct. Inside were tombs of family members bringing their vast treasures with them into the afterlife. The tomb of one queen displayed prodigious wealth:

> On her head was an ornate headdress of gold, hammered to represent leaves and flowers and decorated with rosettes inlaid with lapis lazuli and carnelian. She wore massive golden earrings and a belt of gold, carnelian and lapis lazuli beads. Her body was wrapped in a cape on to which numerous beads of silver, gold and semiprecious stones were sewn, and she was adorned with gold pins, some of which were used to attach cylinder seals, including one inscribed with her name, "Queen Puabi."[33]

Inside her tomb were gold and silver jars overflowing with precious metals and semiprecious stones, a sledge, two oxen to pull it, a large wooden chest for her garments, a harp, and a gold-plated, bull-headed lyre. The wooden frame of the lyre was inlaid with pieces of shell, limestone, and lapis lazuli organized in geometric patterns. The bull's eye was formed of lapis lazuli and a shell. All of these materials had to be imported from other regions of Asia. On a less paradisiacal note, the queen was buried alongside five grooms, five guards, three personal attendants, and ten female attendants, the last of whom were dressed in fine gowns and jewelry.

Ur, with its somewhat orderly maze of urban housing, is perhaps best known for its great ziggurat. It was dedicated to the moon goddess Nanna in the twenty-first century by King Ur-Nammu, the founder of the Third Dynasty, and rebuilt in the sixth century by the Neo-Babylonian ruler Nabonidus. It was by any measure a colossal undertaking of labor and time, with a base of 190 feet by 130 feet and its sides oriented to the cardinal points. The main level consisted of a battered, two-tiered platform, ascended by three ceremonial staircases at right angles to each other. They met at a domed vestibule on the second level. The axial stair perpendicular to the complex likely continued up two or three tiers to the summit, on which sat the temple. Underscoring the design sophistication of the original work, the foundational lines of the walls forming the main platform were raised in the center of the sides to mitigate the optical illusion of sagging, and battered inward to strengthen it. Ur's holy mountain was an *axis mundus* connecting the population with the god on high. When Woolley excavated the ziggurat, he came upon a series of holes or vertical shafts in the terraced brickwork, which he believed were inserted to release moisture for gardens planted on the terraces. It seems more likely today that they were inserted to release moisture that built up in the brickwork, but this issue remains unsettled. Because these vast monuments were built with mud-bricks, none of the Mesopotamian ziggurats has survived the passing of time. One of the few descriptions we have is that of the fifth-century Greek traveler Herodotus, who scaled the rebuilt ziggurat in Babylon:

> The ascent to the top is on the outside, by a path which winds round all the towers. When one is about half-way up, one finds a resting-place and seats, where persons are wont to sit some time on their way to the summit. On the topmost tower there is a spacious temple, and inside the temple stands a couch of unusual size, richly adorned, with a golden table by its side. There is no statue of any kind set up in the place, nor is the chamber occupied at nights by anyone but a single native woman, who, as the Chaldeans, the priests of this god, affirm, is chosen for himself by the deity out of all the women of the land.[34]

The partially reconstructed ruins of the ziggurat remain today in the roiled landscape of the Iraqi desert, one of the last surviving artifacts of Sumerian civilization.

Gardens of Amun

Paralleling the growth and prosperity of Sumer in the third millennium was the rise of Egypt, a civilization indelibly impressed into human history with the great pyramids at Giza. Prior to this age, however, pre-dynastic and early dynastic rulers were buried in *mastabas*, or mound-like burial chambers built of mud-bricks, with an ever-expanding number of underground rooms. Pharaohs, together with their material trappings and numerous court attendants, made their temporal and spatial journeys into the paradise of the afterlife by passing through twelve regions of the underworld. When viewed in this light, the pyramids at Giza could be interpreted as little more than houses for the dead, were it not for an interesting transitional monument that preceded the pyramid proper. This is the stepped pyramid and unworldly city at Saqqara, built a short distance from Memphis for Pharaoh Djoser between 2680 and 2645 BC.

In Egyptian cosmology, the pharaoh was not just the instrument of God but also the true son of a god, who after death rejoins other deities in the underworld. With his passing, however, the pharaoh's *ka* or vital force remained behind, and the burial precinct at Saqqara was in effect a miniature city or paradise built for the pharaoh to continue his virtual rule of the empire. As Sigfried Giedion explained the theology, the "king's ka" dwelt within the reconstructed city. He issued orders in the government buildings and ran his ceremonial race in the Heb-Sed Court, and generally continued to inhabit the place in spirit.[35] In addition to the pyramid and its sub-terranean rooms, the royal city consisted of a series of courtyards, shrines, altars, sham gateways, storehouses, and two smaller replicas of government buildings—the first Egyptian monuments of hewn stone. The complex, almost forty acres in size, was guarded by a crenelated wall but also by a large, interior trench 130 feet wide, carved into rock and decorated with niches. The single entry consisted of a narrow passage through a grove of twenty pairs of limestone columns modeled on a bundle of plant stems, thought by some archaeologists to have been painted green. Several courtyards were within, some planted with gardens. One court in particular, known as the Heb-Sed Court, was a re-creation of a ritualized series of structures carved into stone to represent the temporary structures that were erected thirty years after the pharaoh's coronation as a way to renew his power. The rows of chapels along two sides of the narrow courtyard, each with a small forecourt, had doors, but behind them was only a shallow niche carved into the stonework. Like many buildings and temples within the complex, they were lithic recreations of timber structures. The extent of vegetation is unknown.

The paradise was designed by the pharaoh's architect, physician, and chancellor of affairs, Imhotep—the world's first architect to be identified by name, as well as by the ritualistic title "stretching of the cord." The main tomb started as a traditional yet much enlarged *mastaba* but then was transformed into a stepped pyramid. Originally it had four stepped layers, "like the hieroglyph for the mound of creation," but two more layers were added later.[36] The entire urban complex was built of a high-quality limestone from the nearby Tura quarries and aligned with the cardinal direc-tions. Imhotep, incidentally, would later be exalted as the divine son of Ptah, whereas the Greeks identified him as Asclepius, their god of medicine.[37]

All Egyptian houses, temples, and towns, like many of those throughout Asia, were "cosmologi-cally structured," in order to bring into balance the contrasting yet interactive powers of the heav-ens.[38] The royal and sacred city of Thebes became the capital of a unified Egypt at the start of the Middle Kingdom in 2050 BC, and serves as a prime example of this cosmological way of thinking. Homer described it as the affluent "city of a hundred gates," although some of the gates to which he refers were actually pylons to the various temples.[39] The city had four cardinal axes slightly tilted in a northeast direction with the river. Each has its own role in maintaining a balance of cosmic pow-ers. The north was associated with heaven and the south with earth; the east represented the daily rebirth of the cosmos, and the west the solar descent of death and regeneration. The pharaoh was charged with maintaining the forces, as it were. The west bank of the Nile at Thebes was largely given over to funerary monuments, temples, and tombs of the pharaohs. The Valley of the Kings lies just beyond.

The first of its mortuary temples, started in 1970 BC by Mentuhotep II, was carved into a spec-tacular hillside setting along the axis of the Karnak temple on the other side of the river. It was entered along the grand axis leading to a sequence of three terraced enclosures stepping upward, the first of which was a massive walled garden with rows of tamarisks and sycamore trees. Next to the temple today, grander in scale and better preserved, is the New Kingdom mortuary com-plex of Queen Hatshepsut, begun 500 years later. This "paradise of Amun," as it was known, was again an attempt to situate the burial chambers within the celestial garden and abode of the gods. Its processional entrance from the river, with double rows of sphinxes and acacia trees, led up to the pylon gate of the vast complex. One followed the processional path and stair-ramp up two additional terraces to the mortuary temple on the third level, whose courtyard was surrounded with double and triple colonnades. The garden terraces were planted with many species of trees, among them sycamores or incense trees imported from the "Land of Punt." As Edouard Naville has interpreted this act, Hatshepsut "by not confining her bounties to the temples, may claim to have diffused throughout her kingdom the culture of the incense-bearing sycamore, which prospered in Egyptian soil and was a notable addition to the material wealth of her subjects."[40] Water to feed these groves and flowers was brought to the complex by a canal. The location of the Land of Punt is still unknown, although it is believed to be on the Horn of Africa between Eritrea and Somalia.

Gardens, lakes, and fountains were also notable features of the temples on the eastern bank of Thebes. Its two great temple complexes, Al Karnak and Luxor, were dedicated to Amun-Ra—a kingdom now fortified with the merger of Amun, the god of Thebes, with Ra, the god of lower Egypt. The Al Karnak complex, started in the sixteenth century, had additions down through the first century BC, but its essential features were completed during the reign of Ramesses II in the thirteenth century. The complex, together with the nearby temple complex at Luxor, defined the acme of ancient Egyptian architecture.

The Karnak compound encompassed fifty-five acres within more than a half million acres of surrounding farmland. Its vast forecourt began at the river with a canal leading to a large pond, the avenue of the sphinxes, several pylons or gateways, and intermediate halls—all before arriving at the temple proper. The scale of the complex is colossal. The first hall (the last built) is the Great Hypostyle Hall with its 134 monumental columns, a symbolic forest with two styles of Campaniform columns representing the Papyrus plant of lower Egypt and the Lotus plant of Amun or upper Egypt. Both were etched and painted with symbolic emblems. The innermost sanctum is reached by ascending a few steps within each hall as the roof steps down. Several other temples of considerable stature are housed within or just outside the compound. A southern processional avenue, used by the pharaoh and high priest twice each year, passed by the sacred lake and other temples and led south a little over a mile to the temple complex at Luxor, the "southern harem" of Amun. The first temple was built by Queen Hatshepsut, but it was continually expanded with a series of colonnaded courtyards and hypostyle halls—added by Amenhotep III around 1400 BC. The first of these was a tight processional colonnade consisting of fourteen columns over fifty feet in height and capped with papyrus or "open-flower" capitals, leading into the great court.

Little remains of the city of Thebes itself, although with the arrival of the New Kingdom in the mid-sixteenth century it would become a thriving city known for its many gardens. The area between these two temple precincts at Karnak and Luxor likely presented a stupendous stage for ceremonial displays with its canals, basins, and fountains used for ceremonial purposes (birth, fertility, and the purification of the soul) as well as to support the gardens. The route was also lined with government buildings and the homes of the upper caste. Each pharaoh, following their successive conquests, attempted to outbid their predecessors with the importation of new and exotic species of trees and flowering plants. The compound for the Temple at Karnak, for instance, at one point had twenty-six gardens of various kinds, in addition to a botanical garden and a sacred pond.

The villas of high officials were similarly outfitted with gardens. The houses, located within walled compounds, were surrounded with trees, both ornamental and bearing fruit; several fish ponds with lotus blossoms; and arbors and vineyards. Ineni, the architect to Thutmose I, is reported to have had nineteen different species of trees in his house garden, and the palace of Amenhotep III at Malkata, on the west bank of the Nile, was renowned for its massive gardens. According to Marie Luise Gothein, the lush grounds had a pond of more than a mile in length on which Ineni would sail his pleasure bark with his wife, Tiye. In addition to exterior gardens, plant-forms were frequently a theme for interior murals.[41] When Amenhotep IV moved the capital city to Akhetaten in 1346 BC, he not only surrounded his palace with courtyards and ponds but also employed garden motifs

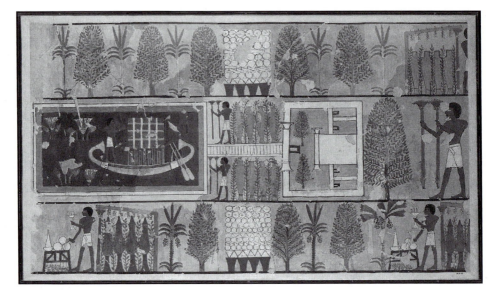

ILLUSTRATION 1.3   Facsimile painting by Charles K. Wilkinson (1921) of a garden in the Tomb of Minnakht, 1425 BC.

Source: Metropolitan Museum of Art. OA public domain.

on the walls, floors, and columns of the rooms. The portrayal of a garden in the Tomb of Minnakht (1479–1425 BC) reveals the botanic luxury of court officials. The house (center right) is accessed through a garden pathway, at the front of which is a pond (center left) large enough to support a bark. Orchards and vegetation of every kind surround the compound. Egypt's wealth continued to grow until the thirteenth-century reign of Ramesses II but then began a long period of decline until the country came under control of the Achaemenid Persians in 525 BC.

Nineveh and Persepolis

With the rise of Egypt as a cultural and military power in the second half of the third millennium, the Sumerian cities in southern Mesopotamia began to struggle for a variety of reasons, not the least of which was a decline in crop production. Sometime after 2340 BC, the Semitic-speaking Sargon I took control of most Sumerian cities, parts of Elam, and the Levant, and established a new capital at Akkad. His empire lasted only a little over a century, however, and we have to move forward another thousand years to find the garden elevated to its former idyllic scale. In the first quarter of the eleventh century, the Assyrian monarch Tiglath-Pileser began to knit the smaller states of the Mesopotamian valley into an empire that would stand for another 500 years. On one of his royal inscriptions, he documented his own garden:

> I took cedar, box-tree, and Kanish oak from the lands over which I had gained dominion—such trees as not among previous kings, my forefathers, had ever planted—and I planted [them] in the orchards of my land. I took rare orchard fruit which is not found in my land and filled the orchards of Assyria.[42]

This horticultural prowess would continue to grow with the increasing wealth of the Assyrian Empire. When the brutal monarch Ashurnasirpal II refurbished the court city of Nimrud in the ninth century, he began his building project by "cutting through a mountain peak" to bring water to his 900-acre city, which contained preserved open land for parks, gardens, farms, an arboretum, and zoological gardens. He also constructed numerous palaces and paradises in the sacred and royal citadels in the southwest quadrant of the city. As his court documents show, he purchased seedlings and seeds of pines, cypresses, junipers, almonds, dates, ebony, rosewood, olive, tamarisk, walnut, ash, fir, pomegranate, pear, quince, fig, and grapes, to name just a few. "Like a squirrel," he spoke of his private garden, "I pick fruit in the garden of delights."[43]

A century later, Sargon II, whose kingship, as legend has it, was owed to his success as a gardener, built the new capital city of Khorsabad. Here he created separate precincts for the palace, temples, and royal gardens. A letter by Sargon's governor indicates that among the orders placed for its gardens were 2,500 loads of apple trees, 450 loads of perfumed medlars, and saplings of almond, quince, and plum trees.[44] Not to be outdone, his successor Sennacherib relocated the Assyrian capital to Nineveh and set about rebuilding what can only be described as a paradise city, which included a palace "that knew no equal," temples, a library, and public and royal gardens. Throughout the city, he widened and straightened the streets and made them "as light as day." Yet in his gardens, as one fragmented royal description relates, he proudly displayed his grandest achievement:

> I made gardens in the upper and in the lower town, with the earth's produce from the mountains and the countries round about, all the spices from the land of the Hittites, myrrh (which grows better in my gardens than in its native land), vines from the hills, fruits from every country; spices and Sirdu-trees have I planted for my subjects. Moreover, I have cut down and levelled mountain and field from the land about the town of Kisiri unto the country near Nineveh, so that the plants may thrive there, and I have made a canal; one and a half hour's journey from the Chusur river have I brought water to flow in my canal, and between my plantations for their good watering. I have set a pond in the garden to keep water there, and in it I have planted reeds. . . . By the grace of the gods the gardens prospered, vines and fruit, Sirdu-wood and spices. They grew tall and flourished greatly, trees, and reeds also . . . palms, cypresses, and the fruits of trees.[45]

He was also able to feed his terraced gardens with one of his own inventions, a copper-and-bronze Archimedean screw—a discovery that preceded the reported invention of Archimedes by 350 years. The pump drew water from underground cisterns, and a bas-relief in the British museum depicts Sennacherib's son Ashurbanipal and his queen feasting in this Eden-like setting while being royally attended to by a troupe of musicians and courtiers. Who would deny such pleasure?

ILLUSTRATION 1.4   Ashurbanipal and his Queen Dining in an Arbor, c. 647 BC.

Source: From John Henry Wright, *A History of All Nations for the Earliest Times* (Philadelphia: Lea Brothers & Co., 1905).

Ashurbanipal died in 627 BC, and soon thereafter the Assyrian Empire collapsed into civil war, which ended when the combined forces of the Medes, Persians, Babylonians, Scythians, Chaldeans, and Cimmerians entered Nineveh fifteen years later and burned the city to the ground. For millennia, the Mesopotamian city-empires had controlled large areas of western and central Asia, and the culture became synonymous with its fabled ziggurats, palaces, and "hanging gardens," one mention of which has come down as one of the seven wonders of the ancient world. There is no doubt that the city of Babylon, with its population of 150,000 at its downfall, had a number of gardens of exceptional splendor and beauty, but an important historical correction has recently been made. Through the investigations of Stephanie Dalley, it is now conceded that Diodorus Siculus, in his mention of the "hanging gardens" in the first century BC, had confused Babylon with Nineveh. The famed gardens were none other than those terraced gardens adjacent to Sennacherib's palace in Nineveh.[46]

The Assyrian passion for large cultivated gardens—paradises—established a tradition throughout western Asia, and nowhere more so than in Persia. One of the military powers sacking Nineveh were the Medes, who, from their base in Iran, would build an empire as far as central Turkey, apart from the Neo-Babylonian empire forming to the south. In 559, Cyrus, the prince of Anshan in southwest Persia, assumed his father's crown in a province under Median control. Sensing a rival, the Median Emperor Astyages sent an army to subdue him, but Cyrus had meanwhile orchestrated a rebellion against the unpopular ruler. In 549, the victorious Cyrus melded the Medes and Persians into the Achaemenid dynasty, more generally known as the Persian Empire. Cyrus would go on to defeat the Lydian King Croesus in western Turkey, and he also later brought down the Neo-Babylon empire. In land area, the Persian Empire became one of the largest in ancient times, which extended from the Indus Valley in the east to Egypt, the Levant, Asia Minor, and Thrace in the west. A benevolent ruler, Cyrus spared the life of Croesus in defeat and allowed him to become his advisor. In Babylon, he did no harm to the population and even restored its aging temples and sanctuaries. In a passage from Isaiah whose translation some biblical scholars contest, Cyrus was anointed as the Lord's "messiah." Uncontested is the fact that he allowed the Jewish people to return to Palestine from Babylon, and he provided funds, as the Book of Ezra reports, to have the destroyed Temple of Jerusalem rebuilt.[47]

At the start of "The Magic Tale of the Ebony Horse" in *The Arabian Nights*, the Persian King Sābūr, the richest and wisest king of his time, "had three daughters, three fair moons in the night sky, and three wonderful flowers shining in a well-kept garden." Almost as an afterthought, the narrator lets us know that he also had a son, the "moon of moons."[48] That three wonderful flowers in a well-kept garden should be elevated alongside three daughters, three fair moons, and a son is perhaps fitting for an empire and a language that presented us with the word "paradise"—a culture that came to be associated with the name of Cyrus. In the mid-sixth century, he rebuilt his new capital at Pasargadae, located at the foot of a mountain in the fertile plain of the Pulvar River. The surviving parts of this "garden capital" consisted of two palaces, one private and the other an audience hall, along with two garden pavilions. The gardens were fed by narrow stone canals with basins at regular intervals, which brought water down the mountain and distributed it to the sizable landscape in two overlapping rectangular canals of more than 3,200 linear feet. Remnants of these main canals also indicate a ninety-degree extension in the direction of the audience hall, suggesting the fourfold cross-plan of the *chahar-bagh* that would become the model for Persian and Islamic gardens. The relationships of the gardens to the palaces and pavilions were exquisitely calculated. David Stronach, who led the British excavation of Pasargadae in the early 1960s, underscored this relationship when he noted that "each inner palace with its stately colonnades and deep, shadowed porticoes was first glimpsed amidst a profusion of trees, shrubs, and grasses."[49] Similarly, Cyrus seated on his throne would have had an uninterrupted view of his garden. Cyrus's tomb in the royal park at Pasargadae, as Arrian reported more than 200 years later, was also set within a grove where "all kinds of trees had been planted. It was also watered by a stream, and high grass grew in the meadow."[50]

Cyrus was succeeded by Cambyses II, who would lead a disastrous campaign against Egypt, and later by Darius I, who conquered Egypt but is better known for being repelled at a different front of Persian expansion—Marathon—in 490. Nevertheless, Darius was a prodigious builder. He rebuilt parts of Babylon, and in Egypt he completed a canal connecting the Red Sea to the Mediterranean. In Persia, Darius erected new palaces at Pasargadae and Susa, the last of which defined a new direction with its open, square Apadana or audience hall—a variation on the Egyptian hypostyle hall. The palace had a number of courtyards with gardens, the largest of which was given to the royal harem. An inscription provides many details of the palace's interiors. The Babylonians prepared the mud-brick, and the cedar came from Lebanon. The gold was brought from Lydia and Bactria, the lapis lazuli and carnelian from Sogdia, the turquoise from Chorasmia, the silver and ebony from Egypt, and the ivory from Nubia and Arachosia. Greeks and Lydians carved the stonework, and the men who adorned the walls were Medes and Egyptians. "By the grace of Ahura Mazda I constructed the magnificent palace in Susa," Darius records, "May Ahura Mazda protect me and my line and my country."[51]

Darius's greatest undertaking, however, was the new ceremonial capital of Persepolis, the partial ruins of which remain in place today. The site in the Fars region of southwest Iran was selected by Cyrus for its geographical remoteness, and its eastern flank was cut into the side of a mountain. The entire city is set on a platform, and its southern and western edges were raised as much as fifty feet above the valley floor. It was intended as a spring and summer complex because of the natural beauty of the area, and the groupings of rectangularly aligned buildings were accessible only by a single staircase at the northwest corner. Foreign dignitaries, after ascending a stair to the platform, passed through a propylaeum before entering another grand staircase to the Apadana of Darius. The ceiling once loomed sixty feet above

ILLUSTRATION 1.5   Cypress Tree with Immortal Guard, Apadana Staircase, Palace of Darius, 486 BC.

Source: Photo by Sarah Robinson.

the raised floor, and was supported on thirty-six interior columns, in a room accommodating 10,000 people. Another thirty-six columns formed a colonnade around three sides of the building's exterior. To the east of the building, Darius's son Xerxes would add a second throne room, known simply as the hall of one hundred columns. At the south end of the highly ordered complex were the palaces, the treasury and administrative rooms, gardens, and the quarters of the royal harem. The emperor and his family looked out over a landscape that was likely cultivated with groves and vineyards.

Aside from its scale and grandeur of these palaces, there was the novelty of the confluence of stylistic features. The raising of the royal city on a plateau had a lengthy tradition in western Asia, but the squared hypostyle halls appear almost Egyptian in character, along with traditional motifs of the architecture of Elam.[52] In the Apadana of Darius, for instance, the fluted columns were carved by Lydians and Greek Ionians, who were vassals under Persian rule. The column capitals of both audience halls employ a variation on the Egyptian lotus capital, on top of which were placed Ionic scrolls—again, as at Susa, flipped into a vertical position. Atop the scrolls were paired bull or griffin heads facing opposite directions, with the main roof beams resting on their backs between the two heads. It is a playful if not whimsical design, with the column capitals taking up as much as a third of the column's height.

Notwithstanding, one of the more noteworthy features of the reception hall of Darius are the bas-reliefs that still grace the staircase leading up to the Apadana. Panels are lined with a series of stylized cypress trees and lotus flowers, accompanied by an array of immortal guards and foreign dignitaries bearing presents. In Zoroastrianism, the cypress was the "tree of paradise." As the story goes, when Zoroaster found his first convert and patron in King Vishtaspa, Zoroaster himself went into paradise to prune a branch of a cypress, which he planted in the king's town of Kashmar. The tree grew up to become the largest and most noble tree in all of Persia, and the king built an impressive structure to complement its perfection. Some years later a caliph in Samarra, against the advice of augers, became so intrigued by the renown of the religious symbol that he ordered the tree to be cut down so that he could use the wood as roof beams for his new palace. Before the wood arrived on the backs of hundreds of camels, however, the caliph was killed by his own slaves.[53] The meaning of having someone pass through a forest of cypresses in order to enter Darius's reception hall seems clear. One was not just ascending to an audience hall but to paradise itself.

Notes

1. See Henry De Lumley (sous la direction de), *Terra Amata Nice: Alpes-Maritimes, France* (Paris: CNRS, 2009).
2. Mircea Eliade, *The Sacred and the Profane: The Nature of Religion* (San Diego, CA: Harcourt Brace & Company, 1987), 14.
3. See Jean Clottes, *Cave Art* (London: Phaidon Press, 2008), 25. See also David Lewis-Williams and David Pearce, *Inside the Neolithic Mind: Consciousness, Cosmos and the Realm of the Gods* (London: Thames & Hudson, 2005), 189–92.
4. Lewis Mumford, *The City in History: Its Origins, Its Transformations, and Its Prospects* (New York: Harcourt, Brace & World, 1961), 7.
5. Robert Pogue Harrison, *The Dominion of the Dead* (Chicago, IL: University of Chicago Press, 2003), 25.
6. See Trevor Watkins, "Pushing Back the Frontiers of Mesopotamian Prehistory," *The Biblical Archaeologist* 55:4 (December 1992); "New Light on Neolithic Revolution in South-West Asia," *Antiquity* 84 (2010), 621–34.
7. Klaus Schmidt, cited in an interview with Andrew Curry, *Smithsonian Magazine* (November 2008). www.smithsonianmag.com/history/gobekli-tepe-the-worlds-first-temple-83613665/. Accessed May 2018.
8. See R. Liran and R. Barkai, "Casting a Shadow on Neolithic Jericho," *Antiquity* 327:85 (March 2011). http://antiquity.ac.uk/projgall/barkai327/. Accessed August 2018.
9. Genesis 28:12.
10. Ekrem Akurgal, *Ancient Civilizations and Ruins of Turkey: From Prehistoric Times Until the End of the Roman Empire* (Istanbul: Haset Kitabevt, 1985), 3.
11. Lewis-Williams and Pearce, *Inside the Neolithic Mind* (note 3), 102–22.
12. Numa Denis Fustel de Coulanges, *The Ancient City: A Study of the Religion, Laws, and Institutions of Greece and Rome* (Mineola: Dover, 2006), 132.

13. Henri Frankfort, *The Birth of Civilization in the Near East* (Garden City, NY: Doubleday & Company, 1956), 57.
14. Theophilus G. Pinches, *The Old Testament: In Light of the Historical Records and Legends of Assyria and Babylonia* (London: Society for Promoting Christian Knowledge, 1902), 71–4.
15. Geo Widengren, *The King and the Tree of Life in Ancient Near Eastern Religion* (Uppsala: Lundeuistka Bokhandeln, 1951), 15–17.
16. William Brown, *The Seven Pillars of Creation: The Bible, Science, and the Ecology of Wonder* (Oxford: Oxford University Press, 2010), 91.
17. See Gwendolyn Leick, *Mesopotamia: The Invention of the City* (London: Penguin, 2002), 133.
18. Thorkild Jakobsen, *The Treasures of Darkness* (New Haven: Yale University Press, 1976), 126.
19. Tablet IX, *The Epic of Gilgamesh*, trans. by Andrew George (London: Penguin Books, 1999), 75.
20. Ezekiel 28:13.
21. Translation by Gateways to Babylon, www.gatewaystobabylon.com/myths/texts/retellings/enkininhur. htm. Accessed May 2018.
22. W. F. Albright, "The Location of the Garden of Eden," *American Journal of Semitic Languages and Literatures* 39:1 (October 1922), 15–31.
23. Geoffrey Bibby, *Looking for Dilum* (Ann Arbor: University of Michigan Press, 1969).
24. Ake Sjöberg and Eugen Bergmann, *Collection of the Sumerian Temple Hymns* (Locust Valley, NY: J. J. Augustin, 1969), 18.
25. See Leick, *Mesopotamia* (note 17), 2–3.
26. Cited from Sigfried Giedion, *The Beginnings of Architecture* (Princeton, NJ: Princeton University Press, 1964), 232.
27. William Andrae, "The Story of Uruk," *Antiquity* 10:38 (June 1936), 141. Joseph Rykwert has some interesting comments on Andrae's beliefs in *The Dancing Column: On Order in Architecture* (Cambridge, MA: Massachusetts Institute of Technology Press, 1996), 309–11.
28. Leick, *Mesopotamia* (note 17), 50. See also H. J. Lenzen, "Die Architektur in Eanna in der Uruk IV Period," *Iraq* 36 (1974), 111ff.
29. Tablet XI, *Epic of Gilgamesh* (note 19), 99.
30. Frankfort, *The Birth of Civilization* (note 13), 58–9.
31. Stephanie Dalley, "Ancient Mesopotamian Gardens and the Identification of the Hanging Gardens of Babylon Resolved," *Garden History* 21:1 (Summer 1993), 2.
32. Citied from Widengren, *The King and the Tree of Life* (note 15), 5–6. See also Arthur and Elena George, *The Mythology of Eden* (Lanham, MD: Hamilton Books, 2014), 153.
33. Marc Van de Mieroop, "Ur: Mesopotamian Centre of Power and Wealth," in John Julius Norwich (ed.), *Cities That Shaped the Ancient World* (London: Thames & Hudson, 2014), 21.
34. Herodotus, *The History of Herodotus*, trans. by George Rawlinson (New York: Tandy-Thomas Company, 1909), 1:177.
35. Giedion, *The Beginnings of Architecture* (note 26), 275.
36. Joseph Rykwert, "Holy Mountains," in Tony Atkin and Joseph Rykwert (eds.), *Structure and Meaning in Human Settlement* (Philadelphia, PA: University of Pennsylvania Museum of Archaeology and Anthropology, 2005), 89.
37. Jacquetta Hawkes, *The First Great Civilizations: Life in Mesopotamia, the Indus Valley and Egypt* (Harmondsworth: Penguin, 1977), 317.
38. David O'Conner, "Cosmological Structures of Ancient Egyptian City Planning," in *Structure and Meaning in Human Settlement* (note 36), 55.
39. Homer, *Iliad*, 9:383.
40. Edouard Naville, *The Temple of Deir El Bahari: Its Plan, Its Founders, and Its First Explorers* (London: Offices of the Egypt Exploration Fund, 1894), 24–5.
41. Marie Luise Gothein, *A History of Garden Art* (Cambridge: Cambridge University Press, 1928), I:14.
42. Dalley, "Ancient Mesopotamian Gardens" (note 31), 3.
43. Ibid., 4.
44. Ibid.
45. Gothein, *A History of Garden Art* (note 41), I:32.
46. Dalley, "Ancient Mesopotamian Gardens" (note 31), 7–10.
47. Erza 1:1–11.
48. *Arabian Nights: An Anthology* (New York: Everyman's Library, 2014), 861.
49. David Stronach, *Pasargadae: A Report on the Excavations Conducted by the British Institute of Persian Studies from 1961 to 1963* (Oxford: Clarendon Press, 1978), 109.
50. Arrian, *The Anabasis of Alexander*, trans. by E. J. Chinnock (London: Hodder and Stoughton, 1894), VI:34.
51. Cited from Christopher Tadgell, *Antiquity: Origins, Classicism and the New Rome* (Milton Park, Abingdon: Routledge, 2007), 216–17.

52. Seton Lloyd, "Architecture of Mesopotamia and the Ancient Near East," in *Ancient Architecture: Mesopotamia, Egypt, Crete, Greece* (New York: Harry Abrams, 1974), 65.

53. On the significance of the cypress tree in Zoroastrian theology, see Abraham Jackson, *Zoroastrian Studies: The Iranian Religion and Various Monographs* (New York: Columbia University Press, 1928). On Alexander the Great's destruction of the building, see Diodorus Siculus, *Library of History*, trans. by C. Bradford Welles, (Cambridge, MA: Harvard University Press, 1963), 17:69–72.

2

DIVINE CITIES

Mohenjo-Daro

In 1856 two British engineers were charged with building the first railway line from Karachi to Lahore within the Indus Valley. Toward the southern end of the line, one brother, in seeking local ballast for the rail bed, was told of the ruined town of Brahminabad, a short distance away. There he found a large quantity of "hard well-burnt bricks," which fitted his needs perfectly. A few months later his brother, working farther north, faced a similar problem and stumbled upon the ruined city of Harappa, whose bricks had already been partially recommissioned by local villagers. This brick bed for the new railway line—almost 100 miles of ballast by their account—was undoubtedly well suited to its purpose. What the two engineers did not know was that they were removing brick not from a recently abandoned town but from the ruins of an early human civilization that was as yet unknown. It was not until 1920 that an Indian and British team of archaeologists, under the direction of John Marshall, returned to Harappa and uncovered the foundations of a city that would give its name to this lost civilization. One year later, the Indian archaeologist R. D. Banerji unearthed the Indus Valley settlement of Mohenjo-Daro, 370 miles to the south. The two discoveries were certainly among the most important archaeological findings of the twentieth century.

The Harappan civilization reached its peak in the mid-third millennium, which makes it contemporary with Sumerian cities and Stonehenge. Yet in the early literature of these discoveries, we run into one of the great misdirections in archaeological history. For much of the twentieth century, it was assumed that Harappan civilization was a derivative one, the result of migrations or even conquests by more advanced agricultural cultures coming out of central Asia. Even the appellation "Indus Valley" given to this culture is somewhat incorrect, because a large number of these cities were located along a parallel river in northwestern India and eastern Pakistan—the Sarasvati, which has since dried into a riverbed. At its peak, between 2600 and 1900 BC, Harappan civilization extended from Pakistan and Afghanistan in the west to the Ganges and Yamuna River valleys in north-central India, as well as south along an 800-mile stretch of the western Indian coastline. Today over 2,000 sites are known, but only about a hundred have been excavated. At its height, Harappan civilization encompassed five million people and its geographical extent was twice the size of Mesopotamia or Egypt. Research today documents that Harappan culture was indeed indigenous in its genesis and emerged as a third wellspring of urban culture, alongside Mesopotamia and Egypt. Nevertheless, a number of interesting questions remain. How did such a civilization, known to

DOI: 10.4324/9781003178460-2

Babylonians by the name Meluhha, arise? And how could such an advanced civilization have been lost over so many millennia?

The town of Mehrgarh, situated on 500 acres of the Kachi plain of Pakistan, addresses the first question. The Neolithic site at the western edge of the Indus Valley was uncovered in 1974 by the French archaeologist Jean-François Jarrige. The town goes back to the eighth millennium and remained settled until the start of mature Harappan culture.[1] From the earliest documented period, 7000–5500 BC, there are remains of a farming village with quadrangular mud-brick houses oriented along the cardinal axes, whose seminomadic population lived on a diet of wheat and barley as well as the meat of sheep and cattle. The fact that they were already cultivating crops and livestock at the period dispelled earlier assumptions that farming was introduced into South Asia only at the start of the fourth millennium. Genomic evidence also suggests that the Indus Valley population was a mixture of "Iranian agriculturists" with "South Asian hunter-gatherers"—contacts that would have taken place well before the settlement at Mehrgarh.[2] Recent excavations also reveal other surprising things about Mehrgarhic culture. Graves from the earliest period show females buried with jewelry of lapis lazuli, turquoise, and seashells. Molar crowns found on the teeth of nine adults document that the town had the earliest known practice of dentistry.[3] Around the start of the sixth millennium, there is also evidence of cotton production, likely an invention of the Indus and Sarasvatian valleys. The city's second cultural phase, between 5500 and 3300 BC, saw the introduction of artistic pottery, glazed faience beads, and terra-cotta seals and figurines.

The city of Harappa began to develop toward the end of the second phase, or the start of the early Harappan period. The Indus and Sarasvatian valleys had good soil and grasses for grazing and herding cattle. The occupants grew crops of wheat, sesame, barley, and legumes, and invented new technologies for ceramics and jewelry. Also, in this period a system of weights was introduced for trading, and the first religious symbols appeared. When Harappa approached its mature period, beginning around 2600 BC, it was a prosperous economic and cultural center with a population of 40,000. The city imported goods from other parts of Asia and exported jewelry and cotton to Dilmun, Oman, and Mesopotamia. Harappan jewelry has been found in royal tombs of Babylon, testifying to its high value. Inside the city, oxcarts pulled merchandise along wide avenues and regular streets. Mud-brick houses by this date had given way to baked brick, and common deities were represented on seals and ceramic figurines. None of the images thus far unearthed depicts scenes of war, and there are also no indications of cities being purposely sacked or burned to the ground. All evidence points to a well-organized and affluent urban culture with few signs of discontent or warfare, a proverbial social garden within a world largely driven and shaped by military conquest and plunder. Yet there is one particular aspect of Harappan culture that supports a claim to being one of the earliest urban paradises: the innovation of a water-supply and drainage system for the city. This novelty is best seen in the city of Mohenjo-Daro, a preplanned community built around the time that Harappa was maturing as a city.[4]

The political structure of Mohenjo-Daro remains unknown, but everything indicates it was a major manufacturing center with a unified regional government that regulated trade with sister cities. The city eventually encompassed 740 acres, or twice the physical extent of Harappa. The city's geographic high point or citadel sits in the western portion of the settlement. Three other mounds or walled precincts, separated from the citadel by a few hundred yards, are closer to the Indus River along the east. These areas, like the western compound, contained a mixture of housing, public buildings, market areas, and workshops. Only four or five pockets of housing were excavated before Pakistan shut down diggings in 1964, evincing that they were built with great technical skill and planning. They were constructed of brick and placed on raised brick platforms. One large avenue, twenty-six feet wide, ran north and south, whereas smaller cross streets were ten feet wide. Both larger and smaller houses are interspersed throughout the city; all have complex floor plans and similarly high standards of workmanship, and some have interior courtyards.

Given the many difficulties of life in the third millennium, how paradisiacal it would have been for each house had to have had its own latrines and water for bathing and cooking. In Mohenjo-Daro virtually every house had a circular well, bathroom, and bathing area, the last with steps ascending to a platform for someone to shower the bather with water. The brickwork in the shower floors was tightly executed, and special curved bricks were used for the standard diameters of house wells. From the house, the wastewater was distributed by pipes to covered street drains and then recycled to the surrounding agricultural fields. The street drains were effulgent with running water, again underscoring the complexity of the engineering effort behind the idyllic intention. No comparable aquatic system existed anywhere else in the world, and in fact it would not be until much later times, and particularly in the Augustan period of Rome, that bathing and the systematic supply of water to the home would be afforded such a priority.

The culture of Mohenjo-Daro also had a number of unique aspects. It seems to have supported no standing army or warrior class, and its works of art do not depict rulers. Rather, it was a city financed by the production and exportation of crafts: jewelry, shells, chalcedony pearls, faience beads, and semiprecious stones such as carnelian, lapis lazuli, agate, and turquoise. In this regard, one has little difficulty in envisioning the glamor of its gaily dressed residents during city fairs or religious celebrations. The Indian star calendar, with its twenty-eight constellations, was invented in Harappan times, attesting to a knowledge of astronomy.[5] We know little of Indus Valley religious practices, but the carved image of the Pashupati Seal, dating from around 2300 bc, is quite revealing. It depicts a deity in a classic yoga position of meditation with three faces, wearing a headdress of water buffalo horns and a tuft of grass. Some have suggested that the figure, surrounded by wild animals, is an early representation of the god Shiva. Excavations have also uncovered statues and reliefs of dancing girls, unicorns, mother goddesses, horned deities, and the sacred Bodhi tree—themes of fertility and animism. The fact that the medicinal properties of the Bodhi or fig tree (*Ficus religiosa*) were already known is interesting, because this tree was similarly sacrosanct to the Hindus, Jains, and Buddhists.

12: M-304 A

ILLUSTRATION 2.1   Pashupati Seal found at Mohenjo-daro, c. 2350–2000 bc.

Source: Public domain. www.columbia.edu/itc/mealac/pritchett/00routesdata/bce_500back/indusvalley/protoshiva/protoshiva.jpg.

The state of architecture was also highly advanced. At the highest point of the western citadel are a number of large buildings, among them the ruins of a towering Buddhist stupa, which was built in the second century AD. Archaeologists have yet to discover what it was built over, but it likely would have been an earlier sacred site. Bordering it, along the west, is a surviving ancient building, a part of the town's original fabric, known figuratively as the College of Great Bath Priests. Its purpose remains unknown, but several archaeologists have speculated that it was a religious complex. Adjoining it is the "Great Bath," one of the more curious discoveries in all of archaeology. The bath, roughly twenty by forty feet in area and eight feet deep, was not especially large, but it was placed within a courtyard defined by rectangular brick pillars, vertically articulated, and with steps at each end for one to descend into the water. Another series of rooms surround it on all but the western side. Once again, the brick-work is exceptionally fine in its jointing, even though it is likely to have had a bituminous coating. To call the pool a bath is likely misleading. With its position on the citadel, it was almost certainly not a public bath, but more likely served a religious purpose of ritualized cleansing. One archaeologist has suggested that water, in a city that survived by its annual inundations, had to play a prominent role in the consciousness of its people, and that the people likely "attributed supernatural powers to the river and considered water to be sacred, much as the Ganges became a material manifestation of the goddess Ganga in later Hinduism."[6] It may even be speculated that water was the Harappan symbol for paradise, and certainly gardens were everywhere evident.

Harappan culture also found its way into later Hinduism. The Vedas are believed to have been put into written form in an early dialect of Sanskrit after 1700 BC, but many of the hymns, particularly the earlier ones of the Rigveda, are probably older. Suggestions of Hindu themes can be seen in a few images portrayed on Harappan seals and figurines. Loan words from the Dravidian language, an early variant of which was likely spoken in Harappan cities, are also found in the earliest hymns of the Rigveda. If meditation was practiced in Mohenjo-Daro, as the Pashupati Seal suggests, it forms another link with later Hindu culture.[7] All of this raises the question of why Harappan cities began to decline shortly into the second millennium.

Perhaps a better question may be to what extent did Vedic culture grow out of Harappan culture, or to what degree did migrations from outside the area influence the cultural changes that evolved in the second millennium. Supporting the claim of a smooth transition is the fact that many of these Harappan cities were not immediately abandoned but maintained their technological and trading networks for several centuries into the second millennium. There are signs, in fact, that Harappa was inhabited as late as 1300 BC. Nevertheless, a major genomic study published in 2009 documents migrations from the Eurasian steppes into northern India beginning around 2000 BC.[8] These were the people who, in settling in Pakistan and India, brought with them an early form of the Indo-European language and other significant cultural changes.

Climatic change also seems to have played an important role in this cultural transformation. Cores drilled in the Arabian Sea indicate that water discharged from the Indus and Sarasvati Rivers began to fall significantly after the twenty-second century, when the Sarasvati River began to shift its course and eventually dry up. The Great Bath at Mohenjo-Daro fell out of use a century or two before the city itself began to decline, suggesting that the Indus Valley was experiencing aridification. In addition to migrations into northern India, many urban dwellers from the Indus-Sarasvati areas may have migrated into the Ganga-Yumana valleys to the east, which picked up the Himalayan water that used to flow southwest. There was also a marked growth in the number of cities and populations on the Gangetic plains during the second millennium, and the Vedas speak as well of competing cultures. Thus, the traditional commentary on the "fall" of Harappan culture may not have simply collapsed into history but made substantial contributions to the development of Vedic culture, which became fully recognizable at the end of the second millennium with the primacy of the Sanskrit language, the codification of the Brahminic priesthood, and the hierarchical caste system. Yet what should be highlighted about Harappan culture—in distinction from the combative warrior gods of early Vedic culture—is the relative harmony of its societal norms, the mastery of artistic skills, and the religious emphasis on personal cleanliness, all lucid expressions of a paradisiacal instinct.

The Bodhi Tree

The historical Siddhartha Buddha, fittingly, was born in a sacred grove of the Nepalese town of Lumbini, sometime around the start of the fifth century BC. Although his parents, it is said, took great pains to shelter him from the three major miseries of the world—sickness, old age, and death—he, at the age of twenty-nine, eventually surrendered his material wealth for the life of a mendicant and wandered for six years contemplating the meaning of existence. His search took place during a period of change within Hindu practices, a movement away from the traditions of warrior gods and animal sacrifices and toward an individual emphasis on nonviolence, meditation, and asceticism. In the town of Bodh Gaya, after forty-nine days of meditation under a Bodhi tree, he found Enlightenment and began to preach as the Buddha, or the "awakened one." He set out the "Middle Way" between self-indulgence and self-mortification, and preached the "Noble Eightfold Path" of right view, aspiration, speech, conduct, means of livelihood, endeavor, mindfulness, and contemplation. The objective is for one to advance to the state of serene understanding and awakened perfection.

Buddhism was still a relatively minor sect in the fourth century BC when, in the winter of 326, Alexander the Great brought his army down the Himalayas and into the Swat Valley of Pakistan. He followed the headwaters of the Indus River and then turned east to confront the forces of Porus, the Hindu king of Punjab. At Hyaspes, an epic battle ensued when the Greeks confronted Porus's army, parts of which were mounted on war elephants. Alexander won the day with a brilliant tactical maneuver and celebrated his victory by founding two new cities. In proceeding eastward, however, his soldiers came upon another large army from the neighboring Nanda Empire, which controlled most of northeastern India. There Alexander's army mutinied and the Macedonian emperor was forced to retreat by dividing his forces into thirds for the journey home. Alexander died in Babylon three years later.

Alexander's first victory, however, inadvertently gave birth to another, equally expansive empire—not in the West but in the East. His victory over Porus and his installation of Greek governors had weakened the political structure of the Pakistani-Indian territories, and within two years after his departure, the son of one village chieftain, Chandragupta Maura, raised an army and, one by one, began to conquer the satraps of the region. He then turned his forces eastward and, after a series of battles, conquered the Nanda forces that had deterred Alexander. In 322, he established the Mauryan Empire. Chandragupta was still expanding his holdings when, in 305, Seleucus I marched into the region to reclaim Alexander's territories. The Greek general was unable to prevail, sued for peace, and took Chandragupta's daughter as a bride.

By the time Ashoka, the third ruler of the Mauryan Empire, had ascended to the throne in 268, the empire had swelled to encompass nearly all of India, Pakistan, and Afghanistan—a population of more than fifty million people. Ashoka, in fact, put the finishing touches on the empire during the first eight years of his reign, when he marched his armies into the eastern Indian state of Kalinga and crushed the last resistance, killing more than 100,000 combatants and civilians. Yet after surveying the carnage of corpses and maimed soldiers on the battlefield, Ashoka underwent a spiritual awakening, one of the more radical turns in the history of paradise. He converted on the spot to Buddhism and vowed to pursue the rule of peaceful nonviolence. As H. G. Wells described his historical legacy:

> Amidst the tens of thousands of names of monarchs that crowd the columns of history, their majesties and graciousnesses and serenities and royal highnesses and the like, the name of

Asoka shines, and shines almost alone, a star. From the Volga to Japan his name is still hon-
oured. China, Tibet, and even India, though it has left his doctrine, preserve the tradition of
his greatness. More living men cherish his memory to-day than have ever heard the names of
Constantine or Charlemagne.[9]

Until his death, in fact, Ashoka strictly followed and evangelized the rule of dharma, or the moral
teachings of Buddha, and energetically set about building an idyllic society predicated on truthful-
ness, concord, compassion, benevolence, tolerance for all religions, and a deep respect for nature.
His accomplishments, as Wells noted, were legendary. He is said to have privately supported 64,000
monks. The sacred text of the *Pali Canon* credits him with building 84,000 stupas and monasteries. Throughout India, he erected polished sandstone columns, thirty-two feet tall, on which he
engraved the teachings of Buddha for popular instruction. He sent his son and daughter to Sri
Lanka to spread the teachings, and he dispatched Buddhist missionaries to meet with Alexander II,
Antiochus II of Syria, Antigonus of Macedon, Magnas of Cyrene, and Ptolemy II at Alexandria—in
addition to the surrounding Asian countries. Politically, Ashoka instituted a grand program of social
welfare that included appointing "dharma ministers" who were charged with relieving suffering by
subsidizing large families and widows and improving the lives of citizens. Throughout the empire
he founded hospitals and veterinary care. He planted specific medicinal herbs, and he installed shade
trees and wells at regular points along roadways. He became a vegetarian and issued edicts against
cruelty to animals and the despoliation of the forest.

One of his more Edenic accomplishments was his transformation of capital city of Pataliputra
(present-day Patna) in northeast India, a city once known by the perfumed epithet "city of flowers."[10] Pataliputra was the linear city situated between the Ganges and Son Rivers, a city of 400,000
people. Its palisades, with its 64 gates and 570 towers, impressed the Greek historian Megastenes,
who ascribed the city's founding to Hercules. The later Roman traveler and rhetorician Aelian was
no less dazzled, reporting that "there are so many objects for admiration that neither Memnon's city
of Susa, with all its extravagance, nor the magnificence of Ecbatana is to be compared with them."
He went on to speak of public parks with tame peacocks and pheasants, the cultivated shrubs of
the royal gardens, and the "shady groves and herbage" around the city, their boughs "interwoven
by the workman's art."[11] In the fourth century AD, the Chinese monk Fa Hian described the royal
palace and halls as seemingly built by "spirits"—that is, the carving and inlaid sculptural works were
executed "in a way which no human hands of this world could accomplish."[12]

The site of this garden city fell into ruin by the sixth century, and it was only rediscovered in the
1890s by L. A. Waddell. For a number of reasons—the ruined state of the city, the exploitation of its
building materials, the annual flooding of the area with monsoon rains, and the fact that the present
city of Patna was built over parts of the city—very little of Ashoka's city has today been excavated.
Waddell, digging down twenty feet, found parts of the city's walls, the scattered remains of what he
believed to be the palace, and a system of underground wooden drainage. He also uncovered the
ruins of the Great Stupa at Pataliputra, and a column capital that, with its upright Ionic scrolls and
honeysuckle facing, he believed emulated those at Persepolis.[13] The Persian theme was picked up
and developed in a serious way by David Spooner in 1912, when, just south of the city, he uncovered one column of a hypostyle hall of eighty columns, which he argued was based on the design
of the hall of 100 columns at Persepolis.[14] There may have been some connection. Ashoka's family
(the generation of his grandfather Chandragupta) was from Taxila, Pakistan, along a trade route
into Afghanistan and by extension Persia. Pataliputra, some have speculated, may in fact have been
envisioned as the Persepolis on the Ganges.

Ashoka has another claim to paradise that few others in antiquity can match. It was his decision,
shortly after his conversion, to forgo the traditional royal hunting parties of his forefathers in lieu
of state pilgrimages to the holy sites of Buddha. To launch the first of these imperial spectacles, he

summoned his spiritual teacher Upagupta from his forest retreat, who then traveled on a river boat to Pataliputra accompanied by 18,000 monks. Upon meeting the emperor's retinue at the city, they first proceeded to Lumbini Garden, where Queen Maya gave birth to the Buddha after taking her ritual bath. Ashoka set up a column to mark the site, distributed gold to the residents, and rendered the village forever free of taxes. The holy procession then proceeded to Buddha's hometown of Kapilavastu, where Siddhartha, at the age of twenty-nine, renounced his royalty and became a mendicant. The retinue visited other sites as well: the sacred grove at Sarnath where Buddha first preached the dharma, Buddha's monastery at Sravasti, and the Stupa of Ananda where Ashoka handed out one million gold pieces. Yet the most important of his stops was at Bodh Gaya, the site where Buddha achieved Nirvana. There Ashoka commissioned and dedicated the grand Mahabodhi Temple (temple of the "great awakening") to enshrine the ideals of his master.

The colossal pyramidal tower temple, which is found in Bodh Gaya today, dates from the seventh century AD and its stupendous architectural aspect is from another era—a period in which a large number of Hindu and Buddhist tower-temples were built across South Asia. Yet the temple itself is not the centerpiece or sanctum of the sacred site, nor is the *vajrasana* or diamond throne that Ashoka is said to have erected at the spot where Buddha attained Enlightenment. Rather, what epitomizes this particular garden of paradise is the Bodhi tree, today said to be an actual descendant of the

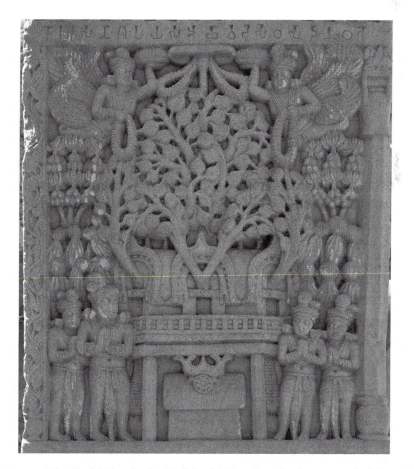

ILLUSTRATION 2.2   The Bodhi Tree in the Mohabodhi Temple at Bodh Gaya. Relief from the eastern gateway of the Great Stupa at Sanchi, third century BC.

Source: Photo by Biswarup Ganguly. Wikimedia CC BY 3.0.

original tree. The meaning of the tree is clear from the iconography of several sculptures found at the site and housed in a nearby museum, but perhaps its esoteric significance is most vividly portrayed by a bas-relief on the gateway to the Great Stupa at Sanchi, which depicts the original temple built by Ashoka at Bodh Gaya. The temple, as this image makes clear, is not the object or place of veneration; it is merely the house, the hothouse as it were, for the garden in which grows the sacred Bodhi tree. The tree itself is the alpha and omega of Enlightenment.

Sons of Heaven

In the Chinese fable *Peach Blossom Spring*, Tao Yuanming spins the yarn of a poor fisherman who one day rows up an unfamiliar river. Along the way he comes upon a garden of blossoming peach trees, which entices him to explore the bank and partake of their fragrance. At the end of the grove, he discovers a spring, and behind it a cave into the mountain. Exploring it, he eventually finds the entrance to a prosperous valley of colorful vegetation and exotic birds whose wings produce a delicate music. The people of the valley, attired in silk robes and possessing over 100 varieties of tea, dwell in perfect peace and happiness. Their ancestors may have known the ills of the world on the other side of the mountain, but this generation, in their innocence, listen to the fisherman's stories with both curiosity and understanding of the malleable nature of human behavior. The visitor is invited to remain in the valley and he accepts, once he returns to his village to pick up his belongings. Yet he is made to promise not to tell a soul about the location of paradise or he will never find his way back. The fisherman breaks his promise and tells the magistrate in the village, who soon tells others, and everyone in the village clamors to join the fisherman on his return journey. The rush turns into a stampede of boats along the river, as people, including the fisherman, become frantic to find the entrance to paradise, but all efforts are in vain.[15]

Some might interpret this story, written around the turn of the fourth century AD, in light of Adam and Eve's expulsion from paradise, but such a reading seems foreign to the Confucian culture out of which the tale arose. The idea of human sin and divine redemption does not seem to appear in Chinese literature. There is also no preordained fall of the human race, but only a continual failing of ethical behavior. Thus, a return to paradise, at least in Confucian culture, was predicated not on the guidance of some outside power but rather on the virtue of one's self-discipline and attention to social rituals. In one passage of the ancient *Book of Rites*, for example, the author speaks of the time when "a common spirit ruled all under the sky," a time when people of talent and virtue prospered, when kindness and compassion were shown to all, when selfishness did not exist, and when "the outer doors of homes remained open." It was the period of the "Great Union."[16]

Taoism is similarly steeped in the spirit of a virtuous commonweal, as when Chuang-Tzu, writing in the fourth century BC, spoke of the age of "perfect virtue," when

> men lived in common with birds and beasts, and were on terms of equality with all creatures, as forming one family—how could they know among themselves the distinctions of superior men and small men? Equally without knowledge, they did not leave (the path of) their natural virtue; equally free from desires, they were in the state of pure simplicity. In that state of pure simplicity, the nature of the people was what it ought to be.[17]

This age disappeared, curiously, "when the sagely men appeared," and their wheeling and tiptoeing on the themes of righteousness brought the human condition into a state of perplexity.

Confucius might have objected to this implied criticism of his ethic, but he too believed in a golden age. He lived the life of a government official, teacher, and wanderer, much as did Socrates, who was born (by one account of Confucius's life) one year after the death of Confucius. Yet the worldview of the Chinese philosopher might be closer to the Ephesian Heraclitus, whose notion of nature's continuous change underlaid with a universal *logos* is not too distant from Confucius's animistic belief in the cosmic forces of the heavens and their intersection with human fortunes—in essence, the belief that the actions of humans and nature are forever implicated. Neither philosopher left much room for religion as a response to this higher cosmic order. For Confucius, the elevation of society would come through the self-regulation and the cultivation of the virtues of responsibility, righteousness, courage, loyalty, erudition, benevolence, and ultimately the idea of *wu-wei*, or "effortless action." As the philosopher Mencius characterized this perspective one century after Confucius:

> What belongs by his nature to the superior man are benevolence, righteousness, propriety, and knowledge. These are rooted in his heart; their growth and manifestation are a mild harmony appearing in the countenance, a rich fullness in the back, and the character imparted to the four limbs. Those limbs understand to arrange themselves, without being told.[18]

The "golden age" for Confucius began with the Zhou dynasty and was personified, in particular, in the ethical greatness and scholarly demeanor of two men, King Wen and the Duke of Zhou. The former, also known as the sage-king, was the founder of the dynasty, although his military victories were not complete at the time of his death in 1056 BC. The Duke of Zhou was his son and younger brother to Wu, who was entitled to be Wen's successor. Yet with Wu's early death, the Duke then served as the administrative regent of the kingdom until the coming of age of Wu's son Cheng. The Duke, in his interim capacity, not only eliminated the militant factions opposing the new dynasty, but he also ruled the empire in a highly efficient and righteous manner. Like his father, he was seen as a paragon of benevolence in his personal conduct. Such virtue was enormously appealing to Confucius and Mencius in their own age of warring factions and political turmoil, but the Duke of Zhou had another accomplishment that would mark his name in Chinese history. In 1038, he laid out the new city of Chengzhou according to the principles of geomancy; seventeen years later he planned the new imperial city of Wangcheng, following an ideal plan that would later be recorded in the *Rites of Zhou*. He has also been credited with writing parts of the *I Ching* or *Book of Changes*, perhaps the most influential book in all of Chinese history.

The origin of the latter text has been lost in its own mythology. Its legendary founder was the god Fuxi, who, with the goddess Nüwa, created the first humans and is credited, among other things, with inventing hunting, fishing, and cooking. In observing the world in all of its complexity, he perceived there was a ruling cosmic order, which he captured with the eight trigrams; these are the mathematical variations of three superimposed lines, broken or unbroken. These trigrams or patterns, according to the *Book of Changes*, at any moment allow us to divine the changes taking place throughout the cosmos. King Wen is traditionally credited with superimposing two sets of trigrams above each other, forming a hexagram, which expands the eight possibilities to sixty-four. The hexagram is composed by the ancient method of casting yarrow stalks. The Duke of Zhou also attached meanings and an explanatory statement to each of the possible hexagrams, and Confucius and his later students wrote further detailed commentaries, known as the "Ten Wings." By the time of Confucius, the *Book of Changes* had acquired the hermeneutic patina of a classic, one widely in use and one involving divination, ethics, metaphysics, and cosmology. Continuing commentaries and refinements over the many centuries have added further luster to this finish, and the book continues to have philosophical interest today.

When Karl Jung wrote the introduction to the English translation of *I Ching* in 1949, he defined its central principle as "synchronicity," the coincidence of events in space and time, "a peculiar interdependence of objective events among themselves as well as with the subjective (psychic) states of the observer or observers."[19] Underlying this synchronicity is the metaphysical belief that there is a cosmic order whereby everything on the earth and in the heavens has its harmonious patterns within the scheme of things—an idea that has also on occasion been widespread in the West. When things are moving in systematic order, there is an equilibrium that leads to a positive outcome; conversely, when things are disordered and confused, bad results will ensue. The hexagrams portray qualities such as firmness and yielding as well as actions such as advance or retreat, but these yin/ yang conditions are in constant flux and do not represent a true duality of forces. Rather, they are relational elements engaging each other, forces from which a number of possible variations will unfold depending on the timing of one's actions. If one correctly discerns these ordered cycles of movements, one can achieve correct conduct and plan one's actions accordingly. In this way, individuals affect the outcomes of what is often ascribed to fate.

If the *Book of Changes* concerns itself with the cosmic order of the heavens, geomancy or *feng shui* takes into account the terrestrial forces of the earth in the optimal siting of houses, temples, and cities. An essential tenet of both philosophies is the idea of *chi*, which has the connotation of "life force" or "atmosphere" that infuses and animates a landscape. As Joseph Needham once described the concept:

> Every place had its special topographical features which modified the local influence of the various *ch'i* of Nature. The forms of hills and the directions of watercourses, being the outcome of the moulding influences of winds and waters, were the most important, but, in addition, the heights and forms of buildings, and the directions of roads and bridges, were potent factors.[20]

The objective of geomancy, then, is to design buildings and cities in line with the essential nature of the landscape and climate, to maximize the flow of *chi* and in this way approach the condition of paradise. This is particularly the case with the "form school" of geomancy, which emphasizes land formations and climatic features of the terrain in the planning, orientation, and design of buildings. Generally speaking, a work of architecture should not seek to dominate the landscape but adapt itself to what is given by nature, and the ideal landscape is one in which these forces are brought into balance. Ideal sites should have sloping rather than flat terrains; they should be shielded from the northerly winds by mountains, gentle ridges, or trees, and should have their entrances and orientation open to the south. Because the idea of *chi* connotes a gentle curve, such as one generally finds in nature, geomancy shies away from the use of straight lines—both in natural formations as well as in the layout of gardens.

The principles of the *Book of Changes* and *feng shui* provide a cosmological model for understanding the planning of feudal and imperial Chinese cities. At heart is the imperative of a concordance between the macrocosmic laws of heaven and their harmonic or microcosmic expression in human productions. The first step is to select the site, which can be done—as with Roman cities—only after an extensive process of divination. The next step is to make hallow the ground through sacrifices and then determine the "center of the land" with a gnomon. This sets out both the orientation along cardinal points and the fixing of the divisions within the walled town. The principle of centering or establishing the *axis mundi* is crucial because the emperor is deemed to be the son of heaven, and the emperor's palace should have its center directly on the polar star. We can see this principle illustrated in the seventeenth-century AD representation of Wangcheng. The city's axial streets (three and nine being auspicious numbers) should extend along the cardinal directions to maximize the flow of *chi*. A passage from the *Rites of Zhou* explains the start of this process after one has established the preliminary orientation: "He makes a square nine *li* on each side; each side has three gates. Within the capital are nine north-south and nine east-west streets. The north-south streets are nine carriage tracks in width."[21] The emperor's palace is in the middle, and temples and altars lend balance to its position.

Even though no Chinese city followed this diagram literally, the underlying symbolism or meaning is explicit—the imperial city, as in other cultures, was not seen as a commercial or trading center but as the cosmic center of the earth, the *axis mundi* through which the state draws its moral

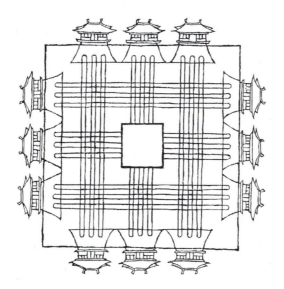

ILLUSTRATION 2.3   Ideal Royal Seat at Wangcheng, from the *Rites of Zhou*, second century BC.

authority from the heavens. This symbolism remained in place through the planning of all imperial cities. At the start of the Sui dynasty (AD 582), for instance, Emperor Wen relocated the imperial city back to the vicinity of the Han capital at Chang'an. The site selected for the city of one million people was situated at the foot of Longshou Mountain, which, according to geomancy, protected it from the climatic forces of the north and required the building of a lake at the south end of the city to balance the yin and yang forces. The walls defined a near perfectly square scheme and the palatial compound was situated at the north end and symmetrically placed with respect to the central axis. Below it, to the south, was the imperial or administrative city. A large north-south artery, 600 yards in width, divided the city down the center and two markets, east and west, were provided for residents. The imperial park and gardens were moved outside the north wall in this instance to maintain the perfection of the grid, and the patterns of some streets even incorporated hexagrams from the *Book of Changes.*[22] This ordering of the city, scripturally based on the movements of the heavens, was believed to ensure both the success of the emperor's reign and the long-term stability of the dynasty. It was the ideal city or paradise—in theory, at least. And it would become a model for many later Asian cities, including, as we shall see, the imperial Japanese capital of Kyoto.

City of Heaven

Chang'an would reach its peak during the Tang dynasty (618–906), in what is regarded as the golden age of Chinese literature and the arts. It was also during this period that China extended both its geographic reach and cultural influence. Yet early in the tenth century the great empire began to unravel because of internal strife, and eventually collapsed under the assault of Turco-Mongolic tribes from the north. Emperor Taizu's organization of the Northern Song dynasty in 960, with its capital in Kaifeng, offered a brief respite, yet within much-constricted borders. It was also around this time that we have one of the most sublime creations found in Chinese art, one imbued with a Confucian and Taoist understanding of nature. Titled *A Solitary Temple amid Clearing Peaks*, it is a scroll rendering of ink and light color on silk, executed by the hand of Li Cheng. He was a Confucian scholar, a Taoist, and a distant descendent of the ruling house of the former Tang dynasty. Yet he found no official appointment within the confused politics of his day and painted, as would a monk, "as an outlet for his emotions, with no interest in selling his paintings."[23] The painting depicts

ILLUSTRATION 2.4   Li Cheng, *A Solitary Temple amid Clearing Peaks*. Hanging scroll, ink on silk, c. 960. Nelson–Atkins Museum of Art, Kansas City.

Source: Wikimedia CC BY-SA 3.0.

a temple complex at the base of a dramatic precipice, below which, along the bank of the river, are a few buildings. Across from them on a path is a rider on a donkey, possibly Li Cheng himself, about to cross the bridge. What makes this scroll so powerful is its dimension and spatial depth, the scale or juxtaposition of the dwarfed donkey-rider and his servant within the vast majesty or supremacy of nature herself. The mammoth yet foggy peaks that rise in the background take up half of the image, and even the strong horizontal lines of the temple below are mitigated by the oscillating and prickly shapes of the trees. The path up to the temple would be torturous were it not for the sound of the nearby waterfall, but the path of Taoism was not expected to be easy to navigate.

The artwork represents the calm before the storm, because peace or stability continued to be elusive. Already nomadic tribes were pressing at the northern border, and their strength continued to grow. Kaifeng was sacked in 1127 and its leaders fled and reestablished the Southern Song dynasty in the city of Hangzhou. In 1206 the Mongolian Genghis Khan began assembling what would become the largest empire the world has ever seen, extending from Korea across Asia as far as Poland and the Levant, from Siberia to parts of India. The one exception was the Southern Song dynasty, but it too fell in 1271 to his grandson Kublai, the fourth of the Great Khans. Kublai then began construction of another grand Chinese city: Dadu, or present-day Beijing.

Numerous volumes have been devoted to Kublai Khan, and historians almost universally view him as the complex man. As a grandson of Genghis, he was a warrior and a product of the fierce Mongol military culture. Yet like Alexander, Kublai often accepted submission without violence. He was well versed in Confucian rites, manners, and customs, and, although his mother was a Christian, he was raised by a Buddhist nurse. Kublai was also interested in the major religions and in fact, after his conquest of Tibet, in negotiations with the "scholarly sage" Lama Sakya Pandita, he converted to his teacher's sect of Buddhism. From this diverse background he nurtured a sincere curiosity about the world and surrounded himself with Chinese scholars and welcomed visitors from the four corners of the world to his court—one of whom was Marco Polo.

The city of Dadu, based on the model of Chang'an, was built adjacent to the ancient city of Zhongdu. Dadu's walls have moved over centuries, but the imperial quarter, the so-called Forbidden City, today remains in the same location. It was originally a square city with its eleven gates laid out according to the *Rituals of Zhou*. The western part of the imperial quarter was designed as a vast picturesque park with lakes, which were viewed and accessible from the splendid palaces of the royal family. Khan was fond of natural settings, and his imperial gardens—with their several lakes and islands, artificial mountains, grottos, temples, pavilions, and exotic plantings—emulated the grandest paradises of Assyria and other parts of Asia and vastly outstripped them in scale. He even constructed a private nature preserve nearby, in which he would regularly hunt wild game with his tamed leopard in pursuit. One Franciscan friar visiting the gardens of Dadu around 1325 described the picturesque park next to the main palace in bedazzling terms:

> And within the enclosure of the great palace there hath been a hill thrown up on which another palace is built, the most beautiful in the whole world. And this whole hill is planted over with trees, wherefrom it hath the name of the *Green Mount*. And at the side of this hill hath been formed a lake [more than a mile round], and a most beautiful bridge built across it. And on this lake there be such multitudes of wild-geese and ducks and swans, that it is something to wonder at, so that there is no need for that lord to go from home when he wisheth for sport. Also within the walls are thickets full of sundry sorts of wild animals; so that he can follow the chase when he chooses without ever quitting the domain.[24]

Marco Polo's observations are no less animated. After describing Khan's palace, "the largest that was ever seen," he expounds upon the features of the park filled with stately trees, grasses, the presence of white harts, musk-deer, roebuck, stags, and the great variety of fish within its ponds. Its principal feature, however, is the Green Mount, 300 feet tall, over a mile in circumference, and planted with a dense growth of trees:

> And I assure you that whenever the Great Khan hears tell of a particularly fine tree he has it pulled up, roots and all and with a quantity of earth, and transported to this mound by elephants. No matter how big the tree may be, he is not deterred from transplanting it. In this way he assembled here the finest trees in the world.[25]

Khan even blanketed the soil with lapis lazuli so that his view of the hill would be intensely green, at the top of which he built a "large and handsome" palace, which was also entirely green.

One would think that the architecture and gardens of Khan's city would have been the high point of Polo's travels, but he lavishes even higher praise on the city of Quinsai, or present-day Hangzhou—the city that found its way into Italo Calvino's *Invisible Cities* as a surreptitious Venice. Even after this erstwhile capital of the Song dynasty was incorporated into Khan's empire, it remained Asia's largest and wealthiest city. Polo was not hesitant to describe it as "without doubt the finest and most splendid city in the world," and in enumerating its many attractions he more than doubles the amount of prose he expends on Dadu.[26] Quinsai, according to Polo, was known as the "city of heaven," but what made it so special?

The city, as Polo reports, had a circumference of 100 miles and housed a population of more than a million people. The coastal city was bordered on the east by a major river and on the west by a large and scenic lake, which still exists. It was China's major trading center, with wide streets paved with stone and brick, and, as Polo would write, 12,000 arched bridges (by one almost contemporary count, the actual number was 347).[27] These stone and wooden bridges allowed goods to be transported through the city via a system of canals, and the main north–south street, 120 feet wide, was a visual spectacle in itself:

> Along this street you may see passing to and fro the continuous procession of long carriages, decked with awnings and cushions of silk, which seat six persons. These are hired by the day by gentlemen and ladies bent on taking pleasure-trips. Countless numbers of these carriages are to be seen at all hours of the day passing along the middle of this street on their way to the gardens, where they are welcomed by the garden-keepers under arbours specially designed for the purpose. Here they stay all day long enjoying a good time with their womenfolk; and then in the evening they return home in these carriages.[28]

Polo was similarly impressed by the ten principal markets of the city, each a half square mile, in which 50,000 people gathered three days a week to buy or sell "everything that could be desired to sustain life."[29] But above all, Polo admired the imperial palace built by the deposed King Facfur, "the most beautiful and splendid palace in the world," in which on "every wall and every ceiling nothing met the eye but a blaze of gold and brilliant colour."[30] The quarters for the royal concubine alone contained ten courtyards, each with "fifty chambers with their gardens," housing a thousand ladies. The majority of the imperial precinct was devoted to the royal paradise—that is,

> [to] lakes filled with fish and groves and exquisite gardens, planted with every conceivable variety of fruit-tree and stocked with all sorts of animals such as roebuck, harts, stages, hares, and rabbits. Here the king would roam at pleasure with his damsels, partly in carriages, partly on horseback, and no man ever intruded.[31]

The Venetian merchant was only slightly less impressed with the massive distribution system for goods, the city's 3,000 public baths (some with hot water for foreign visitors), the professional firefighting force, and the beauty of the city's lake, thirty miles in circumference and surrounded with palaces, mansions, abbeys, monasteries, and greenery. The lake, however, was a place for people of all classes to gather at the end of the working day, and thus toward evening it was filled with an endless procession of recreational boats and barges. Situated on the lake were two islands, each of which sported a large palace that could be rented for special events, such as weddings.

It was this combination of the city's gaiety, civility, and "garden of earthly delights," to borrow a title from Hieronymus Bosch, that seemed to impress Polo most of all. The men did not carry arms and the city showed no signs of strife or crime. Not only did the men dress well, but their "refined and angelic" wives adorned themselves with silks and jewelry. Adultery did not exist, and the city in fact had a moral code by which it was a major offense to insult a lady. The famed courtesans of Quinsai, "highly proficient and accomplished in the uses of endearments and caresses," were luxuriously dressed and attended to by maids in richly decorated apartments.[32] All residents, even visitors, were treated with dignity, which was possible, as Polo psychoanalyzed the situation, because "their minds and thoughts are intent upon nothing but bodily pleasure and the delights of society."[33]

Polo's encomiums have long been recognized for their hyperbole, but Quinsai, through the well-traveled byzantine eyes of Polo, seems to have been a genuinely Edenic place. Its colorful building materials, baths, canals, gardens, and lakes, its sheen of luxury, and the city's highly efficient markets with access to the Pacific Ocean—all no doubt reminded him of his native Venice, only larger and more exotic. Yet there might also be another explanation for the many superlatives lavished on the idyllic city in his panegyric. Perhaps this thirteenth-century garden city, where a significant portion of the population spent their days socializing in gardens or on the lake, at this particular moment in human history really was the "city of heaven."

Notes

1. See Jean-François Jarrige et al., "Mehrgarth, Neolithic Period: Seasons 1997–2000," *Mémoires de la missions Archaeologiques Francaises en Asie Centrale et en Asie Moyenne. Tome XV. Serie Indus-Balochistan* (Paris: De Boccard, 2013), 490.
2. Priya Moorjani et al., "Genetic Evidence for Recent Population Mixture in India," *The American Journal of Human Genetics* 93 (September 5, 2013), 422–38.
3. A. Coppa et al., "Early Neolithic Tradition of Dentistry," *Nature: International Journal of Science* 440 (April 6, 2006), 755–6.
4. See Michaël Jansen, "Mohenjo-Daro, City of the Indus Valley," *Endeavour* 9:4 (1985), 161–9; "Water and Sewage Disposal at Mohenjo-Daro," *World Archaeology* 21:2 (October 1989), 177–92.
5. See Jane R. McIntosh, *A Peaceful Realm: The Rise and Fall of the Indus Civilization* (Boulder: Westview Press, 2002), 199.
6. Jansen, "Water and Sewage Disposal at Mohenjo-Daro" (note 4), 182.
7. See Andrew Lawler, "Indus Collapse: The End or the Beginning of an Asian Culture?" *Science* 320 (June 6, 2008), 1281–3.
8. David Reich, "Reconstruction Indian Population History," *Nature* 461 (7263) (September 24, 2009), 489–94; Moorjani et al., "Genetic Evidence for Recent Population Mixture in India" (note 2), 422–38.
9. H. G. Wells, *The Outline of History: Being a Plain History of Life and Mankind* (New York: Macmillan Company, 1920), I:432–3.
10. Prakash Prasad, "Glimpses of Town Planning in Pataliputra," *Proceedings of the Indian History Congress* 44 (1984), 111–12.
11. Aelian, *On the Characteristics of Animals*, trans. by A. F. Scholfield (London: William Heinemann, 1959), 33.18.
12. James Legge, *Records of Buddhistic Kingdoms* (Oxford: Clarendon, 1886), 77.
13. Laurence Waddell, *Report on the Excavations at Pataliputra* (Calcutta: Bengal Secretariat Press, 1903).
14. On Spooner's work see Mary Stewart, "D. B. Spooner at Kumrahar: The Persepolitan Legacy," *Bulletin of the Asia Institute New Series* 7 (1993), 193–201.
15. Fergus M. Bordewich, *Peach Blossom Spring: Adapted from a Chinese Tale* (New York: Simon & Schuster, Green Tiger Press, 1994). For the different meanings of the peach tree in Chinese mythology, see Edward Werner, *Myths and Legends of China* (New York: Dover, 1994).
16. *The Lî Kî (The Book of Rites)*, trans. by James Legge (1885), Bk. 7 (LîYun), 1–2. www.sacred-texts.com/cfu/liki. Accessed May 2021.

17. *The Writings of Chuang Tzu*, 9.2, trans. by Stephen McIntyre. http://nothingistic.org/library/chuangtzu. Accessed May 2021.
18. *The Works of Mencius*, 7.1.21, trans. by Stephen McIntyre. http://nothingistic.org/library/mencius. Accessed May 2021.
19. Karl Jung, Foreword to *The I Ching or Book of Changes* (Princeton, NJ: Princeton University Press, 1950).
20. Joseph Needham, *History of Scientific Thought* (Cambridge: Cambridge University Press, 2005), II:359.
21. Nancy Shatzman Steinhardt, *Chinese Imperial Planning* (Honolulu: University of Hawai'i Press, 1990), 33.
22. Ibid., 95–6.
23. Charles Lachman, "On the Artist's Biography in Sung China: The Case of Li Ch'eng," *Biography* 9:3 (Summer 1986), 58.
24. *Cathay and the Way Thither; Being a Collection of Medieval Notices of China*, trans. and ed. by Colonel Henry Yule (London: Hakluyt Society, 1866), I:128–9.
25. Marco Polo, *The Travels*, trans. by Ronald Latham (London: Penguin, 1958), 125–7.
26. Ibid., 213.
27. See A. C. Moule, "Marco Polo's Description of Quinsai," *T'oung Pao*, 2nd series 33:2 (1937), 118.
28. Polo, *The Travels* (note 25), 221–2.
29. Ibid., 214.
30. Ibid., 225.
31. Ibid., 226.
32. Ibid., 216.
33. Ibid., 219.

3

ORACLES AND AUGURY

Arcadia

In Hesiod's famous poem on the genesis of the human race, he reports that the first race of mortal men in the golden age enjoyed a life without sorrow, toil, grief, and "with legs and arms never failing they made merry with feasting beyond the reach of all evils."[1] The earth and its fruits were bountiful, and when they died, they did so as if falling asleep. After death, their kindly spirits still roam the earth, "clothed in mist," and keep watch on successive human generations. The golden age, however, was followed by generations of the silver, bronze, and heroic ages, each of which was flawed. Yet Zeus, upon overthrowing Cronos, allowed the warriors of the heroic age to live at the end of the earth on the "isles of the blessed," situated somewhere within the swirling ocean. It is not quite the paradise of Sumerian imagination, but the problem for Hesiod is that he and his generation were living in the succeeding "iron age," in which "men never rest from labour and sorrow by day, and from perishing by night."[2] The garden, in his era, has become the farmhouse and life is one of toil, disease, and anxiety. There is no return to the past, at least not until the present human race is extinguished by the gods, allowing them to take another stab at human creation.

Homer was little more forthcoming about paradise, scenes of which he describes on several occasions. The cave of the "fair-tressed nymph" Calypso is surrounded by a "luxuriant wood, alder and poplar and sweet-smelling cypress, wherein birds long of wing were wont to nest." At the entrance of the cave was a "garden vine, in pride of its prime, richly laden with clusters." There were also "fountains four in a row," and nearby "soft meadows of violets and parsley were blooming," of such beauty that "even an immortal, who chanced to come, might gaze and marvel, and delight his soul."[3] The isle of Syria is a place of "good land, rich in herds, rich in flocks, full of wine, abounding in wheat." Neither famine nor sickness comes to the land, and when men grow old, "Apollo, of silver bow, comes with Artemis, and assails them with his gentle shafts."[4] In the wrestling match with Proteus, Menelaus is told by this servant of Poseidon that he would return home and someday enter Elysium. In the stately translation of Alexander Pope:

> Elysium shall be thine; the blissful plains
> Of utmost earth, where Rhadamanthus reigns,
> Joys ever young, unmix'd with pain or fear,
> Fill the wide circle of th' eternal year:
> Stern winter smiles on that auspicious clime:

DOI: 10.4324/9781003178460-3

> The fields are florid with unfading prime;
> From the bleak pole no winds inclement blow,
> Mould the round hail, or flake of fleecy snow;
> But from the breezy deep the blest inhale
> The fragrant murmurs of the western gale.[5]

Nowhere, however, is the idea of paradise more vividly portrayed by Homer than when Odysseus, naked after a shipwreck, passes out on a beach at Scheria, where Athena sees to it that he is awakened by "a cry as of maidens, of nymphs who haunt the towering peaks of the mountains, the springs that feed the rivers, and the grassy meadows!"[6] Nausicaa, the island's princess, revives him with water, food, and clothing, and upon entering paradise city, Odysseus marvels at the harbor and elegant ships, the tall city walls crowned with ingeniously crafted palisades. The ships are engineered to move without pilots and steering oars; they

> understand the thoughts and minds of men, and they know the cities and rich fields of all peoples, and most swiftly do they cross over the gulf of the sea, hidden in mist and cloud, nor ever have they fear of harm or ruin.[7]

At the "high-roofed" palace of King Alcinous, Odysseus also finds an architecture seemingly of another world. The walls are wrought of solid bronze, the door frames are silver, and the doors themselves are made of gold. The soft textile fabrics on the benches are "cunningly" woven by women instructed at the loom by Athena. The candelabra, drinking vessels, and dinnerware are

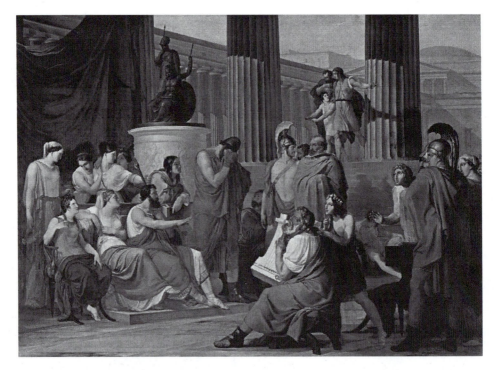

ILLUSTRATION 3.1   Francisco Hayez, *Ulysses at the Court of Alcinous*, 1814–15. Odysseus is weeping as the blind minstrel Demodocus sings about Odysseus and Achilles at Troy while playing the harp.

Source: Courtesy of the Yorck Project.

exquisitely crafted. A genial spirit, represented in the king's love for festive celebrations, the lyre, and dance, pervades the palace. Perhaps more splendidly, adjacent to the entrance is a great garden of tall and luxuriant pear trees, pomegranates, olive trees, fig trees, and apple trees, which bloom throughout the year. Beyond them are the king's vineyards, and farther on are the trim garden beds of every species of flower, in which "are two springs, one of which sends its water throughout all the garden, while the other, over against it, flows beneath the threshold of the court toward the high house; from this the townsfolk drew their water."[8] All is meticulously crafted.

Poetry aside, lush natural terrains in Greek mythology were the domains not of heroes but the nymphs and satyrs who frequented the sacred groves, rivers, grottos, and springs. Dodona, Delphi, and Epidaurus were paradises known for their supernatural powers, and all were located, initially at least, outside of cities. Dodona was dedicated to the mother goddess Rhea or Gaia before it became the oracle of Zeus. Priests and priestesses made their prophecies by going into the sacred grove and interpreting the rustling of oak leaves. Burials and sacred rituals at Delphi, situated on a spectacular southern slope of Mount Parnassus, date back well into the second millennium, may date back to Neolithic times, and it became a famed oracular site toward the close of the Mycenean era. Its presiding earth-spirit was the fertility goddess Gaia, who was guarded by the dragon Python. Apollo, with his slaughter of the Chthonian monster and installation of the virgin priestess Pythia, came late to the tradition. Epidaurus was different, in that its paradisiacal springs were salubrious. It became a sacred precinct in the Mycenean era and was dedicated to the god Asclepius, the god of healing. Asclepius married Epitone, the goddess of soothing pain, and their offspring included Hygieia, the goddess of health, and Panacea, the goddess of medicine. The healing sanctuary, with its hot and cold springs flourished in the seventh century and three centuries later its waters still attracted visitors from around the Mediterranean for their therapeutic powers.

Because of the rural setting, political structure, and organic development of the relatively small Greek city-states, there were few gardens within cities. Residences often had walled-in gardens, cultivated for both vegetables and flowers, but large gardens were rare. By the fifth century, however, travelers were bringing back reports of the paradises of western Asia. In a dialogue of Xenophon, for instance, Socrates and others discuss the visit of the Spartan admiral Lysander to the paradise of Cyrus the Younger at Sardis, where

> Lysander was astonished at the beauty of the trees within, all planted at equal intervals, the long straight rows of waving branches, the perfect regularity, the rectangular symmetry of the whole, and the many sweet scents which hung about them as they paced in the park.[9]

Lysander was similarly amazed to learn that Cyrus himself had designed it. Xenophon used this tale to convey the moral that it is a leader's duty to instill a horticultural ethic by inspecting his governors' land on a regular basis, for if he sees "the soil in a state of active cultivation, full of trees and fruits," he should distinguish the governors with gifts and seats of honor.[10] Even Plutarch, in writing about the Athenian general Alcibiades in the first century AD, could still impress his readers by commenting on the extravagant garden of Tissaphernes in Sardis, known "for its refreshing waters and grateful lawns" and named after Alcibiades: "everyone always called it by that name."[11]

If large gardens were difficult to plan within the crowded confines of Greek cities, we hear of them outside the walls and usually associated with sacred sites. The Academy, which became synonymous with the teachings of Plato, was a shrine to Akademos or Hekademos, and it had altars dedicated to Athena, Zeus, Prometheus, Hephaestus, Hermes, Hercules, and Eros.[12] It was also the site of the gymnasium where Athenian boys took their physical and educational training. In the sixth century the Athenian tyrant Hipparchus enclosed the park within a wall, and later Cimon, the hero at Marathon, transformed "the Academy from a waterless and arid spot into a well-watered grove, which he provided with clear running-tracks and shady walks."[13] Plato likely set up his Academy in the existing gymnasium but within a defined museum or shrine dedicated to the "Muses," which he decorated with statues of the Graces.[14] Not only were mathematics and dialectics taught, but there was likely a physical regimen of gymnastics as well. Archaeologists have now uncovered the site of the gymnasium and its peristyles. Plato, reportedly, also had his own private garden as well.

The Lyceum associated with Aristotle likely operated in a similar way. The site was originally a spring with a sanctuary to Apollo and the Muses, situated in a wooded area near the River Ilissus. Either Pisistratus or Pericles built the first gymnasium with a peristyle, which Lycurgus repaired and expanded in the fourth century. It is often said that Aristotle had rooms for study, lecturing, and library at the Lyceum, but it is now generally conceded that—given his status as a Macedonian or non-citizen—he gave his public lectures at the Lyceum but lived and taught from a nearby house.[15] His school was nevertheless referred to by the Greek word *kipos* or "garden," and the same term was also applied to the school of his younger contemporary Epicurus, the founder of Epicureanism. Although the latter's house was inside the walls of Athens, Epicurus's community of disciples, known as the "little garden," acquired its name because discussions took place just outside the Dipylon gate of Athens in a private garden, which his pupils maintained. Here Epicurus preached his philosophy of "happiness," predicated on a peace of mind found in fraternity, conversation, and

ILLUSTRATION 3.2 Plato Academy Mosaic, first century BC. From the House of T. Siminius Stephanus, Pompeii. Naples National Archaeological Museum.

Source: Photo by Jebulon. Public domain.

a moral generosity of spirit. Echoes of a garden as a place for social and learned tranquility would later resonate with Cicero, and once again in the Italian Renaissance.

In fourth-century Athens we find a split between the Homeric tradition of Elysium, as interpreted in Athenian drama and poetry, and the rationalist teachings of Plato and Aristotle, which were contemplating the fabric of an ideal society on earth. At least this is the theme poignantly conveyed by the Greek writer Lucian in *A True Story*, a satire composed in the second century AD. In Homeric fashion, Lucian sets off on a sea voyage with fifty acquaintances, which takes him, among other places, to the moon and inside the belly of a whale. Eventually his ship stumbles upon the "Isle of the Blest" under the rule of Rhadamanthus, the fabled son of Zeus and wise king of Crete. After witnessing two trials, one involving the sanity of Ajax and the other the true husband of Helen, Lucian is granted permission to remain in paradise, but only for six months. The city is "all of gold" and its ramparts are emerald. It has seven gates, all of single planks of cinnamon. The foundations of the city are ivory and the temples are built of beryl with altars of amethyst. Circumventing the city is a river of the "finest Myrrh," and one-month seasons produce twelve vintages of grapes each year. The blossoms of one tree take the shape of a unique type of stemware, for which one only has to put down the glass and—to the delight of the oenophile—it is immediately refilled with wine.[16]

All of the major players of Greek literature, save one, are present in this paradise: Homer, Odysseus, Achilles, and Socrates, although the last is repeatedly threatened with banishment for his lack of good cheer. Homer confesses to Lucian that he is actually Babylonian by birth, and Pythagoras, we are told, has undergone seven transformations and lived in seven different bodies. Hesiod beats Homer in a footrace, and Socrates, in a battle with invaders on the beach, is cited for bravery and awarded a "park" in the suburbs, in which he sets up an Academy of the Dead. When Lucian is forced to leave the island, he is handed a letter from Odysseus for Calypso, which, as he later reads, says that the Greek hero was sorry that the Phaeacians had

> sent me home, and there I found that my wife had a number of suitors who were living on the fat of the land at our house. I killed them all, and was afterwards slain by Telegonus, my son by Circe. Now I am on the Isle of the Blest, thoroughly sorry to have given up my life with you and the immortality which you offered me.[17]

Plato was the only Greek celebrity not residing on the Isle of the Blest, because "he was living in his imaginary city under the constitution and the laws that he himself wrote."[18]

Atlantis

In the two dialogues *The Republic* and *Laws*, Plato presents the constitution of his "imaginary city," a description that has long served as the core text of Western utopian literature. *The Republic* was written sometime after 388 BC, the year in which he, in Syracuse, met Dion, the brother-in-law to the tyrant Dionysius I. Dion introduced the philosopher to Dionysius, who in short order rejected his teachings. After Dion was subsequently banished from the city for threatening the tyrant's rule, Plato's life was also in jeopardy—a situation that was resolved by Plato being sold on the slave market in Aegina. A second trip to Sicily two decades later resulted in similar misfortunes, reinforcing the cruel lesson about the divide between philosophy and real politics.

Plato's ideal society spelled out in the *Republic*, which consisted of artisan, warrior, and guardian classes, has long been a fascination of academicians. Somewhat oddly, for those interested in architecture, the text contains not a single line concerning the material aspects of the ideal environment. Architecture, which Plato once likened to weaving and embroidery, seems to have figured little into his thinking. The philosopher was no less scornful of artisans, which betrays a no small measure of haughtiness. In his alchemical hierarchy, craftsmen are made of brass and iron, whereas those philosophers who command political power are mingled with gold.[19] He was similarly forthcoming as to which arts he would ban from his city: the poetry of Homer and Hesiod, most dramatists and actors, almost all music (save the Dorian and Phrygian modes), and the imitative arts of sculpture and painting.

Yet he was at least insistent on excluding all ugliness from his fair city, which raises a few questions. He was born sometime around 427, or just a few years after the completion of the Parthenon and the death of Pericles. As an Athenian, he witnessed the building of the Temple of Hephaestus and the Erechtheum. Historians have long proclaimed Athens, its buildings, and its agora to be quintessential models of artistic sophistication and the democratic polis, respectively. One must wonder, what did Plato think of the layout of buildings on the acropolis or the agora? What did he think about the bas-reliefs from the workshop of Phidias, or the gold-and-ivory statue of Athena placed inside the Parthenon, a work that was later recorded as one of the seven wonders of the world?[20] More importantly, did Plato believe that a well-crafted urban environment could have any moral or behavioral influence on the individual? With regard to the last question, he seems to indicate that it does, although seemingly as an afterthought. In his last dialogue, *Laws*, written thirty years after the *Republic*, he returns to his ideal city and provides a few additional details. The size of a city is to be limited to 5,040 households, and citizens are now divided into four classes. The city, like the countryside, is to have twelve sectors, each with its own agora and temple, and the latter is to exercise moral control over the population. For the siting of cities, he advises the rather obvious precautions of choosing locations free from damaging winds and excessive heat, areas not prone to flooding and with good soil. To these, he adds one qualification related to the spirit of the place: "And in all such qualities those spots excel in which there is a divine inspiration, and in which the demigods have their appointed lots, and are propitious, not adverse, to the settlers in them."[21]

To this suggestion of divination there is also a somewhat unexpected concern for the appearance of the city. He prefers cities that do not have defensive walls, yet if walls are needed, he goes on to elaborate, "the private houses ought to be so arranged from the first that the whole city may be one wall, having all of the houses capable of defence by reason of their uniformity and equality towards the streets."[22] In other words, the view of the wall is to be shielded behind the houses along domestic streets. Another sensitivity toward a city's appearance is found in his advice to bring irrigation and gardens to the city, for reasons that seem to transcend human health and cleanliness:

> The fountains of water, whether of rivers or of springs, shall be ornamented with plantations and buildings for beauty; and let them bring together the streams in subterraneous channels, and make all things plenteous; and if there be a sacred grove or dedicated precinct in the neighbourhood, they shall conduct the water to the actual temples of the Gods, and so beautify them at all seasons of the year.[23]

What he is suggesting is a softening of architectural forms with vegetation, to which he adds one other feature, which is that the ideal city should be circular, "for the sake of defence and for the sake of purity."[24]

Plato probably placed more importance on purity than defense, but why should a city be circular? In his fragmented dialogue *Critias*, he describes the lost city of Atlantis as circular, a description he ascribes to Solon in conversations with Egyptian archivists. In a cosmology similar to Sumerian accounts, the gods had originally divided up the earth and created humans to maintain their parcels. Athena claimed Athens and Poseidon chose Atlantis. The latter city was said to lie beyond the pillars of Hercules and in area it was larger than Africa and Asia.[25] Not long after the creation of humans, some 9,000 years before Plato's day, Athens and Atlantis had fought a war in which the Athenians were victorious. Athens was originally built on extremely rich and fertile land with abundant springs, and the acropolis at one time encompassed a much larger footprint until numerous floods washed soil away and left behind a "mere skeleton." The Atlanteans, who were descendants of Poseidon and his mortal lover Cleito, were similarly devout in the beginning, yet with its Edenic landscape of fragrant flowers and abundant natural resources, the city grew wealthy and its people began to cultivate luxurious habits. As the divine line of their ancestry gradually faded over generations, their behavior also began to change: "human nature got the upper hand, they then, being unable to bear their fortune, behaved unseemly, and to him who had an eye to see, grew visibly debased, for they were losing the fairest of their precious gifts."[26] The unmistakable moral is that an abundant landscape and luxurious buildings corrupt human behavior.

Atlantis also had a mythological origin. The city was carved out of the landscape by Poseidon, who formed a series of concentric circles of land separated by rings of canals and joined by bridges. The innermost ring or center island contained the royal palace, royal statues, and the temples of Poseidon and Cleito. The walls of Poseidon's temple were plated with silver, its pinnacles were gold, and its roof was ivory. The ceiling was "curiously wrought" with gold and silver and orichalcum, a reddish metal unique to this island. A colossal golden statue of Poseidon showed him standing in a chariot drawn by six horses, surrounded by a sea of Nereids atop dolphins. Other rings featured housing, gardens, a grove sacred to Poseidon, other temples, springs, baths, gymnasia, a hippodrome, and military barracks. The entire island was surrounded by a wall, and the interior rings were successively made of orichalcum, tin, and silver. It is at this point that the manuscript breaks off, and we do not have the explanation of how the Athenians defeated the Atlanteans. Yet it is probably safe to assume that the Athenians, disdainful of luxury and adhering to tenets of the *Republic*, were less ostentatious, which gave them an advantage. Yet, aside from geometric purity, why must an ideal city be circular? Surely Plato was aware of the ridicule that Aristophanes, a few years earlier in his comedy *The Birds*, had heaped upon the Athenian astronomer Meton of Colonus for proposing a circular city:

> With the straight ruler I set to work to inscribe a square within this circle; in its centre will be the market-place, into which all the straight streets will lead, converging to this centre like a star, which, although only orbicular, sends forth its rays in a straight line from all sides.[27]

Aristophanes had Meton and his "tools for measuring the air" unceremoniously booted out of the unbuilt avian city of Nephelococcygia. Plato's suggestion for a circular city also comes at an interesting time, in that it was a period in which a body of planning theory was forming, one born not out of a fascination with geometry but with an emerging view of the city as an integrated social and physical environment.

Athens itself was in the midst of a major building campaign. Like many Greek cities, it began as a defensive settlement late in the fourth millennium atop the rocky outcrop or acropolis (literally, "high city"). Later it was a Mycenaean settlement with a palace—Homer noted its "well-built citadel"—and by the ninth century the city began to exert influence over Attica. The Temple of Athena Polias was built on the acropolis in the sixth century, and only then did the city begin to take shape on lower ground north and west of the acropolis. Still, it was relatively small: by the start of the fifth century its walls were roughly one mile in diameter. When the Persian monarch Xerxes broke through the pass of Thermopylae in 480, before his defeat at Salamis, he sacked a depopulated Athens twice and destroyed all temples and public buildings. The city thereafter pursued a defense by founding the Delian League of Aegean and Adriatic city-states, and in short order became a major sea power. By mid-century, the city had acquired a level of affluence to allow Pericles to embark on a major building campaign, and the city blossomed artistically.

The first major project was the reconstruction of the port town of Piraeus, but more on this shortly. The rebuilding of the temples on the acropolis was the next order of business. Much was changed. A large Doric gateway, the Propylaea, was constructed at the west end of the acropolis,

ILLUSTRATION 3.3   Leo von Klenze, Idealized view of the Acropolis and the Areopagus in Athens, 1846. Neue Pinakothek, Munich.

Source: Wikimedia CC BY-SA 4.0.

gathering together an asymmetrical grouping of buildings that included a painting gallery and the Temple of Nike. Its axis, the arrival point of the annual Panathenaea festival, was changed, seemingly to center on the island of Salamis where the Greeks destroyed the Persian navy. The destroyed Temple of Athena Polias, which had originally occupied a central position, was not rebuilt. It was replaced with the Erechtheum to its north, the smaller temple complex housing the sacred precincts and altars of ten gods and heroes. It was named for Erechtheus, the son of Athena and mythical founder of the city. The complex is known for the perfection of its Ionic order and for its six caryatids draped in luxurious chitons, supporting a porch. They were not, as the Roman architect Vitruvius once explained, the enslaved wives from the Peloponnesian town of Carya, complicit in the Persian invasion of Greece.[28] The town of Carya was known for its cult of Artemis Caryatis, a ritual in which maidens, with baskets on their heads, performed a dance around her sacred tree. The Erechtheum was also the site of Athena's walled garden and sacred olive tree.

The Temple of Athena Parthenos (the virgin), better known as the Parthenon, was the largest and most complex of the temples dedicated to Athena. Many architectural scholars, notably William Bell Dinsmoor, have referred to it as "the most remarkable building in the world."[29] This point is debatable, but what makes this celestial temple stand out from others were its numerous "visual refinements," or gentle curves, which the architects built into the design to give its massive forms the appearance of elastic strength and visual vitality. These effects might be described as un-Platonic, in the sense that the curves both mitigated and visually enhanced its geometry with optical illusions. Each side of the stylobate or stepped platform on which the temple sits has a slight upward arching toward the center to counteract the visual distortion of sagging when a large building is seen at a distance. Because the columns are the same height, the lines of the entablature above the columns also curve. The columns also have a slight inward tilt of their axes to add visual strength, and the corner columns, which can be seen against the open air, are slightly thicker to bring their visual perception in line with adjacent ones. The width of the triglyph sculptures, running around the outside of the building, are adjusted to be wider toward the middle and narrower at the corners. The columns also have a swelling curve or entasis in their vertical direction, lending strength to them. Because the temple's curves are very subtle, they are almost invisible and seem to allow the building to breathe. To these visual refinements must be added the richly polychromatic detailing of the entablature, including the pedimental figures, the metope and frieze panels, the gilded acroteria of stems and tendrils topping the building—all designed in the workshop of Phidias. And then there was the colossal gold-and-ivory statue of Athena inside, forty feet tall, with a shallow pool placed in front to enhance her divine aura. None of the other new buildings on the acropolis was situated in ways to suggest a regular order. Their angles were seemingly calculated for the annual Panathenaic processions, in which parts of temples only gradually reveal the full epiphany of their perspectives. All was theatrically composed as to allow a wondrous perceptual feast.

The rebuilding of the thirty-seven-acre agora or city square was also ongoing in Plato's time. The key to the rebuilding efforts was a Temple of Hephaestus, which, with many of the same optical refinements as the Parthenon, was set back on an elevated plateau on the west side of the agora, setting up a visual axis into the square. Its monumental staircase was pushed forward to the western edge of the agora, where it could be used for seating during special events. Along the west side was the new colonnaded shrine, the Stoa of Zeus, the Royal Stoa, the old and new city council houses, and a circular building or *tholos*. The south end of the agora was defined by a new colonnaded structure housing the judiciary. Another new Stoa was angled along the northern end of the agora, at the corner where the Panathenaic way diagonally entered the square. Known as the *poikile* or "painted" Stoa, its porch was famed for its public murals, among them one by Polygnotus depicting the Greeks storming the walls of Troy. None of these buildings defined a rectangular edge to the agora, whose dimension, with its interior grove of plane trees, was in any case sufficiently large to defy a sense of enclosure. The geometric mind of Plato must have been mystified at what was taking place.

Hippodamian Way

Athens's organic and artistic approach to town planning stood apart from another line of planning theory that was developing within the network of new cities being founded around the Mediterranean at this time. One feature of the movement was the regular alignment of streets and buildings, although this was scarcely a novelty in itself. Many Egyptian, Etruscan, and Mesopotamian cities had created orthogonal street alignments. The use of the grid was less common in cities around the Mediterranean basin due to its rugged or mountainous terrain. It was on this issue that Aristotle, following Plato, would weigh in on the matter, although his remarks were also largely relegated to political concerns. He did make known his preference for the "antiquated mode" of crowded and irregular streets" over the regular grid, because it "made it difficult for strangers to get out of a town and for assailants to find their way in."[30] In his *Politics*, Aristotle at least credits Hippodamus of Miletus for introducing the "modern fashion" of regularly laid-out streets, and thereby anoints him as the inventor of "the art of planning cities."[31] Yet Aristotle, two generations younger than Hippodamus, was not particularly enamored with the Milesian's ideas. He raises his name in a disparaging way by commenting on his personal eccentricities: his flowing hair and odd manner of dress, which included wearing "expensive ornaments" on "cheap" garments. Aristotle also casts him as "aspiring to being adept in the knowledge of nature" and as someone who made "inquiries about the best form of government."[32] Aristotle also matter-of-factly reports that Hippodamus had designed the new Athenian port city of Piraeus, but he gives no details.

The scholar Jean-Pierre Vernant has discussed the ideas of Hippodamus within the context of Greek democracy and the role that the Greek *polis* and agora had played. The process began in the late seventh century with the Athenian rationalization of social life, buoyed by the philosophical and cosmological traditions of the Milesian philosophers Thales and Anaximander. Within this framework, Vernant describes Hippodamus as a political theorist, cosmologist, and democratic planner whose urban designs featured the agora as the lynchpin of the city, around which all other parts are organized. He viewed the city as a combination of sacred, public, and private spaces giving life to a larger social order. In Vernant's words:

> Hippodamos conceives of the physical universe and the human world as entities whose constituent elements, being not entirely homologous, are not organized according to equivalence, but determine one another according to proportions, in such a way that their very divergence produces the unity of a *harmonia*.[33]

Gerard Naddaf has also stressed the similarity of Hippodamus's views with Anaximander's cosmology, in particular, the "reciprocal relation between the microcosm of the city and the macrocosm of the universe."[34] Just as a planetary system operates within a balanced "law of measure" to sustain its cosmic harmony, so does a city need a balance of political forces to maintain its social harmony.

Hippodamus has been variously credited with the planning of Miletus, Piraeus, Thurii, and Rhodes. The disputed date of his birth (ranging from 498 to around 480) has cast doubt on the first or last of the four, but there are other variables at play. The Persians sacked Miletus in 480 and used it as a base to launch their invasion of Greece. The city, as Herodotus reports, had been made "bereft of its inhabitants" after the occupiers killed "most of the men and made the women and children slaves."[35] The rebuilding of the city would have taken place later, because the Persians, after losing their naval battle at Salamis, remained in control of Ionia until Cimon defeated them at Eurymedon in 466. The rebuilding of Miletus was likely undertaken sometime after this date. The city had been founded on a rocky promontory along the Aegean coastline of

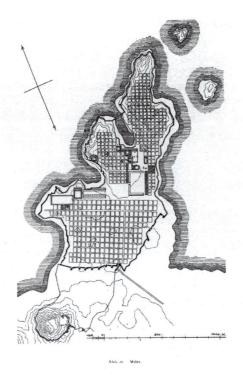

ILLUSTRATION 3.4   Plan of Miletus, c. 400 BC.

Source: From Armin von Gerkan, *Griechischen Städtanlagen: Untersuchungen zur entwicklung des Städtebaues im Altertum* (1924). File from Wellcome Images CC BY-SA 4.0.

Turkey, and in the fifth century excelled as Ionia's major cultural center, known in particular for its school of philosophy. This reputation was reinforced by the Milesian Aspasia, the mistress to Pericles. After moving from Miletus to Athens in 450, Aspasia became a close friend with Socrates and was highly regarded within Athenian philosophy circles. Her relationship with Pericles could not be legalized due to a "citizen" law in effect, but she has also been credited with ghostwriting Pericles's funeral oration, as recorded by Thucydides. Armand D'Angour has characterized her as "perhaps the most extraordinary woman in all of classical antiquity."[36] It was the simplicity of the rebuilding of Miletus, however, that made it so influential for later city planning. Prior to its sacking, the city had a small agora at the base of its northern harbor. The new plan enlarged it with a new marketplace, government buildings, and eventually the Temple of Apollo. Around this extended civic center, three modular areas of gridded streets were staked out—two to the north and eventually a third to the south.

The plan for Piraeus was similar. It was Pericles's ambition to create a new world-class port three miles south of the city center, whose access to and from the city he protected with two city walls running down to the coastline. Hippodamus laid out a gridded town on the east of the much-expanded and well-defended harbor, which also featured a major agora, the Hippodameia. With the founding of the Delian League, Piraeus soon became the busiest port in the Mediterranean, and goods from around the world flowed into Athens. The idea of the grid was considered not just for its geometry. Uniform blocks regulated sea breezes into the city and controlled urban densities, and were therefore hygienic. Property lines could also be precisely defined and deflect future property disputes.

The city of Rhodes, founded in 408, was the most intriguing and paradisiacal of the new towns that epitomized the ideas of Hippodamus. It was founded by colonists from three nearby towns and as the city matured, the geographer Strabo, writing four centuries later, praised it for its wise government, planning, and architecture: "With regard to harbours, roads, walls, and other buildings, it so much surpasses other cities, that we know of none equal, much less superior to it."[37] Parts of the city's plan, which has come to light in recent years with the aid of aerial photography, has also disclosed a near north-south street layout of seeming simplicity yet with a skillful flexibility of parts.[38] The city sits at a northeastern promontory of the island, on a site that gently terraces down from the high ground at the west end toward the three harbors along the east. The original extent of the plan was much grander than the small medieval city later defined by walls. The area adjacent to the two open harbors on the northeast contained the large agora with its emporium, and a grouping of sanctuaries occupied the higher ground along the western promontory of the peninsula. The grid, in the east/west direction, was subdivided into long parallel blocks and major avenues, into which were inserted temples, gymnasia, and governmental buildings. In effect, the avenues defined a necklace of sacred, public, and private zones at a scale nowhere found in any other Greek city at this time.

The orator Aelius Aristides, in his commemorative Rhodian oration to the city's survivors following a devastating earthquake in AD 142, exalted the city's former greatness and beauty with its "many great harbors" and "handsome docks," and goes on to note that the city possessed "temples and statues, of such number, size and beauty, that they were worthy thank offerings for all the rest of the world, and that it was impossible to decide which of them one would admire more." He then describes the city's walls, its large central park, temples, paintings, statues, and bronzes, and the garden-like acropolis on the western edge of the city, "full of fields and groves." Its houses below were so ordered, he noted, that "nothing is higher than anything else, but the construction ample and equal, so that it would seem to belong not to a city, but to a single house."[39] In excavating the site of the gymnasium, archaeologists have since found inscriptions documenting the presence of a library, one of the earliest of its kind.[40]

The natural bowl of the terraced city allowed many residents to have a three-directional panorama of the city and surrounding sea, which was certainly idyllic. Yet it also had, as Diodorus

ILLUSTRATION 3.5 Placido Costanzi, *Alexander the Great Founding Alexandria*, 1736.

Source: Courtesy of Walters Art Museum. Wikimedia CC BY-SA 3.0.

reports, a downside. When Antigonus, one of Alexander's *diodochi* or generals competing for his succession, sent his son Demetrius to capture the city in 305 BC,

> the old men and women were looking on from their homes, since the city is shaped like a theatre, and all, being terror-stricken at the magnitude of the fleet and the gleam of the shining armour, were not a little anxious about the final outcome.[41]

The siege of the city nevertheless failed, in part for what came down to a battle of wits between two architects. Demetrius brought with him the famed Athenian architect Epimachus, who had designed the largest and most sophisticated siege machine ever constructed. The Rhodians countered by imploring their retired city architect Diognetus to return to office. He responded in the night by having small channels dug outside the walls and diverting the city's water into them. When the siege engine approached the wall the next day, it became mired in mud before reaching the wall and could not be extricated. Demetrius realized he had been outwitted and was forced to end the siege and leave behind his huge store of military equipment.[42] The Rhodians pounced on the equipment, not for its military value but to sell it and finance a statue to the sun god Helios—the famous Colossus of Rhodes, another of the ancient world's seven wonders. There was, however, one serious flaw in the planning of this paradisiacal city. It remains situated on a branch of the fault line separating the African and Anatolian tectonic plates. The major earthquake of AD 227 brought down both the Colossus and indeed much of the glorious Hellenic city.

Cities of Muses

Alexander the Great was not your typical warlord, as one might expect of someone tutored at the knee of Aristotle. Plutarch informs us that Alexander carried a copy of the *Iliad* with him on his travels and regularly beseeched his friend Harpalus to send him works by philosophers, playwrights, and poets. "Aristotle he admired at the first," Plutarch goes on to say, "more than he did his father, for that the one had given him life, but the other had taught him a noble life."[43] This education led to the second aspect of his character, which is that he often spared the cities he conquered and, with a few exceptions, did not murder or enslave their inhabitants. After taking control of Greece, Alexander crossed over into Anatolia to push the Persians back further, where he also saw firsthand some of the famed palaces and paradises. When he routed the Persian forces at Issus in 333 BC, he did not bother at first to pursue the fleeing Darius, who in his haste had abandoned his mother, wife, children, and other ladies at the court. Alexander treated them with respect and married one of them, as we will see.

A third quality of Alexander that distinguishes him from other conquerors—and one that has been generally underestimated by historians—is that he viewed himself as a builder, a great founder of cities. Over a single decade, in fact, he founded seventy new cities. He was likely accompanied on his travels by several architects, the most prominent of which was Dinocrates of Rhodes, who was obviously well schooled in the Hippodamian tradition. In a later professional fable, the Roman architect Vitruvius recounts how Dinocrates, in seeking an audience with Alexander, was first blocked by court officials:

> Therefore Dinocrates, thinking he was mocked by them, sought a remedy from himself. Now he was of ample stature, pleasing countenance, and the highest grace and dignity. Trusting then in these gifts of nature, he left his clothes in the inn, and anointed himself with oil; he wreathed his head with poplar leaves, covered his left shoulder with a lion's skin, and holding a club in his right hand, he walked opposite the tribunal where the king was giving judgment.[44]

After sparking Alexander's interest, Dinocrates promised to bring forth ideas and designs worthy of renown, one of which was to shape Mount Athos into a figure of a man, in whose left hand were the ramparts of a very extensive city. After the king pointed out the limitation of not having enough agricultural land to sustain the population, he invited Dinocrates to become one of his personal architects and, as Vitruvius notes, commissioned him to lay out Alexandria.

Yet the first city associated with Alexander was Priene, a small Ionian town situated sixteen miles north of Miletus. Its high promontory faced south and overlooked the Maeander River valley and the Aegean. Above it was another acropolis, which was virtually inaccessible. The city, known for its magnificence in antiquity, was started by the Persian satrap Mausolus, but Alexander took over the project and completed the Temple of Athena. The temple's architect was "celebrated builder" Pythius, who would later join Satyros in co-designing the great Mausoleum at Halicarnassus—another of the seven wonders of the ancient world. Pythius also wrote a book on architectural proportions that has been lost to time. The plan of Priene rivaled the plan of Miletus. The east-west streets were paved, and the main one leading from the western gate ran through the town center. The rectangular agora, conceived as a civic rather than trading center, was placed in the center of the city, with civic buildings enclosing the north side. The three other sides of the agora had colonnaded buildings and colonnades, but an area was left open along the south to allow a panoramic view of the sea. The Temple of Athena, theater, and a gymnasium were situated on higher ground, and the lowest part of the city, below the agora, had a stadium and another gymnasium enclosed within the city walls. A spring from behind the acropolis brought an abundance of water to the city, which was distributed by pipes to every part of town. The city thrived into Roman and Byzantine times, but it suffered a somewhat cruel geological fate—the aggradation or silting of the Maeander River combined with the marine regression of the Aegean. Today the ruins of the ancient town, like those of Miletus and Ephesus, are more than five miles inland.

After Darius's defeat at Issus in southern Anatolia, Alexander marched his army south through Syria and Palestine and crossed into Egypt, where he was greeted as a liberator. Almost two centuries earlier the country had become a satrapy of the Achaemenid Empire, but fought (with some Greek assistance) to win its independence at the start of the fourth century. Persia nevertheless persisted, and in 343 a belligerent Artaxerxes III again took control of Egypt and ended the pharaonic line. Alexander promised to reverse Egypt's fortunes by offering a co-federation or merger with his expanding empire, an offer that gained legitimacy after the general crossed nearly 500 miles into the western desert to consult the famed oracle of Amun at Siwa, where he was proclaimed to be the son of a god and a pharaoh. Alexander's next step, as Plutarch relates, was "to found a large and populous Greek city which should bear his name." With the divine intervention of a dream that had recalled Homer's mention of the island of Pharos, Alexander's next course of action was set:

> Accordingly, he rose up at once and went to Pharos, which at that time was still an island, a little above the Canobic mouth of the Nile, but now it has been joined to the mainland by a causeway. And when he saw a site of surpassing natural advantages . . . he said he saw now that Homer was not only admirable in other ways, but also a very wise architect, and ordered the plan of the city to be drawn in conformity with this site.[45]

The site, a thin strip of coastline wedged between the sea and Lake Mareotis, was eminently defensible. A canal was constructed to bring fresh water from the Nile, and another canal fed the lake, creating a major inland harbor for transporting goods. A second harbor was created when the island of Pharos was connected to the city with a causeway. The famed lighthouse, another of the world's seven wonders, would be located at its northern tip. At the eastern end of the city's coastline was a promontory jutting into the sea, which became the site of Alexander's palace, with the museum or library nearby.

The first task of Dinocrates was to lay out a street system with the infrastructure of water channels, cisterns, and drainage. The sites of the major sanctuaries, palaces, and agora were selected early, and Dinocrates set down a grid but at a slight angle from the shoreline to allow the sea winds to moderate the climate and promote good health. Two major avenues formed the spine of the city. Diodorus describes the east-west avenue with its colonnade as "remarkable for its size and beauty."[46] Strabo, who visited the city around 25 BC, noted that all of the streets of the town allowed for the passage of horsemen and chariots, which in itself would have made the city unique.[47] Richard Tomlinson has noted that the generous scale of Alexandria's plan compares favorably with the Macedonian royal town of Pella, another Hippodamian plan and, in fact, the birthplace of both Alexander and his father Philip.[48]

The Mediterranean city was not only liberally planned but also ideally situated for the trade with Europe, Africa, Arabia, and the Middle East, and political fortunes played into its success. After founding the city, Alexander left to chase down Darius—a trip that, due to his curiosity, would eventually take him to India. On his return, he fell ill in Babylon and died, leading to the dissolution of the empire and the so-called *diodochi* wars, when several of his generals fought for parts of his empire. Ptolemy, in fact, had left Babylon shortly after Alexander's death to claim Egypt. It was a bold move, yet one in which stakes were raised when he hijacked the corpse of Alexander en route from Babylon to Macedonia. With the now-divine body in custody, Ptolemy was anointed the first pharaoh of the Ptolemaic dynasty with its capital at Alexandria.

Ptolemy was a brilliant military strategist, but he was also a scholar. As a close friend of Alexander since childhood, he too had received his education under Aristotle, and his foremost desire was to have Alexandria surpass Athens and become the preeminent cultural center of the ancient world. His ambition would prove successful in the end, particularly through the efforts of his two immediate successors, Ptolemy II and Ptolemy III. By the start of the first century BC, Alexandria was the largest and most prosperous city in the world with its magnificent library and large ethnic communities of Greeks, Egyptians, and Jews. The architecture of Alexandria played a prominent role in sculpting the city's image. Strabo notes that the areas set aside for public facilities and palaces occupied as much as a third of the city's land area, because "each of the kings was desirous of adding some embellishment to the places dedicated to the public use, so, besides the buildings already existing, each of them erected a building at his own expense."[49] Ptolemy commissioned the first sanctuaries, including the shrine to entomb Alexander's body. He began work on the city walls, harbor, agora, and his palatial complex on the Promontory of Lochias. This last area, it was said, entranced sailors on incoming ships because of their "groves and numerous lodges painted in various colours."[50] Ptolemy II completed the causeway to Pharos and its lighthouse, which approached 400 feet in height. It quickly became a tourist attraction because it had multiple terraces several hundred feet in the air for people to enjoy refreshments as they imbibed the spectacular seaside vistas. At the southwest quadrant of the city, Ptolemy II also built a racecourse and athletic stadium where regular athletic and artistic festivals were held, similar to the Greek Olympics. Adjacent to them was the first temple with a vast portico—the Serapaeum—dedicated to the Egyptian sun god Serapis. The complex, placed on a terrace, would eventually house its own public library. Ptolemy III continued to extend the palace district in the northeast quadrant of the city by adding new gardens and groves, a theater, law courts, and gymnasium. The gymnasium and the court of justice had a portico exceeding 600 feet in length, and it was the site on which Octavian mounted a podium in 30 bc to declare his victory over Mark Antony and Cleopatra. He also pleased the crowd by announcing that he would not destroy the city because of its great size and beauty.[51]

Yet the pride of the city, and the reason why all the major scholars of the Hellenistic world converged on Alexandria, was the Museum, or "shrine of the Muses," the world's first research library. Both Egypt and Mesopotamia were noted for their archival documentation, but their works were mainly related to matters of state and their inventories were generally not accessible to the public. The invention of the Phoenician alphabet in the eleventh century offered a more precise way of representing ideas, but the written language was slow to advance. Homer seems to have been the first poet whose writings were written down around 550 bc, but it was only in the second half of the fifth century, and particularly in Athens, that writing began to be widely taught and a book industry began to flourish. The sculptor Polycleitus prepared a discourse on his *kanon* or proportional system around this time, as did the architect Ictinus in explaining his design for the Parthenon—both works now lost. The first significant library across disciplines was the private library of Aristotle, which he used for his teachings. When he died, this collection was passed on to his successor Theophrastus.

Shortly after his succession to pharaoh, Ptolemy, himself the author of a lost history, invited Theophrastus to Alexandria to tutor his son. His intention may well have been to purchase Aristotle's library, but Theophrastus declined the invitation and sent his son Strato instead. Soon thereafter, Demetrius of Phalerum, a student of Theophrastus, arrived in Alexandria. He had been deposed as ruler of the city in 307 by Cassander, a *diodochi* who had gained control of Macedonia. Both Strato and Demetrius were eager to assist Ptolemy in creating a library, and the monarch sent out numerous buyers across the Mediterranean with large purses at their disposal. By the start of the third century the palace was overflowing with books or scrolls, and Ptolemy began the construction of the library to house the collection. Among the early works commissioned for the library was the Greek Septuagint translation of the Hebrew Bible, which Demetrius orchestrated by bringing seventy-two Hebrew scholars to Alexandria where, in isolated cells, each prepared an independent translation. All were identical, it was said, thereby proving the authenticity of the translation. In another notable event—a swindle, in fact—Ptolemy III asked the city of Athens for the certified or official versions of the plays of Aeschylus, Sophocles, and Euripides in order to copy them, and he was willing to post a bond of fifteen gold talents for their safe return. Ptolemy made the copies but sent only the copies back to Athens and forfeited the bond.

The Museum, when completed by Ptolemy II, was a large walled-off paradise or garden complex, into which was inserted residence halls, storage areas, lecture halls, meeting rooms, exedras, and colonnades along which to walk, read, or converse with others. It was located near Ptolemy's palace and the shrine that housed the remains of Alexander, and it was administered by a scholar and priest appointed by the king. Euclid and Archimedes were two of the more illustrious names to find residence at what became, in effect, an institute for advanced study. It was a residency very much sought after because invited scholars and scientists were paid large salaries, given free lodging and food, and were exempted from all taxes. Toward the end of the first century, in a city of a half million people, the collection had grown to around 500,000 scrolls, some of which contained multiple books. Hundreds of thousands of books were also held at a public library set up in the Serapeum.

The famed library, although surviving into the first few centuries of the common era, was nevertheless battered by political and natural forces. Pompey Magnus, after his defeat at the hand of Julius Caesar, made his escape to Alexandria, hoping to rebuild his army. There he was murdered by the child-pharaoh Ptolemy XIII. Caesar, with only a small portion of his army, proceeded to Alexandria in part to avenge Pompey's death, but he had walked into a tense situation because Ptolemy's rule was being challenged by his older sister and wife, Cleopatra. Caesar, after reportedly spending one night with Cleopatra, jumped to her side in the civil war. With his small force, he managed to survive by seeking refuge in the lighthouse until his reinforcements arrived. In the end he claimed victory, but not before a fire had broken out in the city and destroyed a part of the library's collection. It was perhaps in response to this damage that Mark Antony, another lover of Cleopatra, later bestowed on her the gift of 200,000 volumes from the rival library at Pergamon.[52] It is unknown if the volumes were actually transferred, but Alexandria was fated to undergo still other calamities. Octavian put down another rebellion in 30 BC, as did Emperor Aurelian 300 years later; both conflicts resulted in significant damage to the city. A tsunami flooded the city in AD 365, and violent conflicts between rival Christian factions were quite destructive to the city's institutions. Hypatia, the Neoplatonic female head of the Museum, was brutally murdered by a mob of Christian monks in 415. Muslim forces captured the city in 642, but the library was likely long destroyed.

The Anatolian city of Antioch, with its great temple of the Pythian Apollo situated in a wooded glen, is said to have rivaled the beauty of Alexandria, but another Anatolian city did as well: Pergamon. Of course, the city could not claim the divine pharaonic sanction of Alexandria; in fact, one early report suggests just the opposite. John of Revelation, in mourning the martyrdom of Antipas in the first century AD, wrote a threatening letter to the "angel" of the church in Pergamon urging its people to renounce their unholy behavior: "These are the words of him who has the sharp, double-edged sword. I know where you live—where Satan has his throne." John goes on to warn the Pergamonians to repent their immoral ways, "Otherwise, I will soon come to you and will fight against them with the sword of my mouth."[53] Satan's throne is presumed to refer to the great altar dedicated to Zeus in Pergamon, parts of which can now be admired in the Pergamon Museum in Berlin.

Pergamon was another town liberated by Alexander and is only slightly older than Alexandria. It has another interesting connection with the emperor, which is that the city's two oldest temples, dedicated to Athena and Asclepius, were founded by Barsine, a Persian noblewoman who was culturally a Greek. She was the daughter of the Satrap of Phrygia, who opposed the Persian king Artaxerxes. In 354 BC, the Persian army put down the rebellion and the king fled with his daughter to the Macedonian capital of Pella—that is, to the safety of its ruler Philip, father of Alexander. The young crown prince likely first met Barsine there. Her family was later pardoned and returned home, and Barsine eventually married Memnon of Rhodes, who was an army commander under Darius. Because Memnon was not Persian, Darius insisted that Barsine stay at his court to secure Memnon's loyalty. She was therefore with Darius when Alexander defeated his army at Issus, and she was captured when Darius ingloriously fled. Alexander, Plutarch informs us, generally sought no intimacy with any captured woman, but he made an exception for Barsine because of "her high birth and beauty."[54] Their marriage resulted in a son named Hercules, but before his birth Alexander, about to move his army eastward, sent Barsine to live in Pergamon for her safety. The lineage of the son posed a problem during the later *diodochi* wars, when Cassander had both mother and son killed.

Pergamon scarcely existed when Xenophon visited the fortress in 399 BC, after leading the famous "March of the Ten Thousand" mercenaries out of Persian-held territories following the death of their employer, Cyrus the Younger. Xenophon provides us with no description of the town, which suggests that it was then little more than a military outpost.[55] With the death of Alexander, the growing town reverted to the *diodochi* Lysimachus, upon whose death the Greek city in Anatolia became a rump state. Power therefore shifted to the local ruler Philetaerus, who just happened to have the war chest of Lysimachus in his arsenal. Philetaerus used the 9,000 talents of silver to launch his own Attalid dynasty and build another great cultural center. His son Eumenes took down the Seleucid king Antiochus, and Eumenes' son Attalus, assuming the throne in 241, pushed back the Celtic incursion of the Galatians, along with other victories. Attalus added to the city's monuments and his money attracted the best artists of the day. His building of the library, as Pliny the Elder reports, set off a fierce competition with the Ptolemies for the purchase of books, so much so that Ptolemy V stopped the exportation of papyrus to Pergamon to slow its expansion. Eumenes II reciprocated by inventing a special parchment from animal skins, which the Romans called *pergamena*.[56] Attalus II, the last of the city's great leaders, continued the expansion of the library and added further embellishments to the city.

Pergamon also had one other distinction beyond its library, which was its spectacular setting.[57] The perspective of Friedrich Thiersch's nineteenth-century reconstruction of the acropolis, looking north, even omits one of the city's most scenographic features—the steeply raked amphitheater, seating 10,000 people, which slides down the hillside along the western side of the acropolis. The stage, situated 120 feet below, sat atop a two-story portico leading to the Temple of Dionysius. The city's plan consisted of a series of walled terraces, steeply stepping down with the topography and connected with a single road—a one-street town on the acropolis. The oldest part of the city with the fortress held the high ground, although its largest temple, the Temple of Trajan, is of later

ILLUSTRATION 3.6   Fredrich Thiersch, Reconstructed view of Pergamon, 1882.

Source: Wikimedia CC-PD-Mark/Pd-Art (PD-old)/PD US expired.

Roman vintage. Below this level sat the sanctuary of the Temple of Apollo, which, though started by Barsine, was likely completed in the first part of the third century. It was framed on two sides by a two-story colonnade. The library, which sat behind the north wing of the Stoa on higher ground, likely predated the colonnade because it was entered through the colonnade's second story. It had a large room for reading and meetings and had three partitioned areas for scrolls. Below the sanctuary, in the Thiersch drawing, sits the large precinct of the Great Altar of Zeus, the scourge of John of Revelation. Its frieze depicts the Olympian gods and the mythological pursuits of Telephos, the founder of Pergamon and son of Heracles. Below it, not seen in the rendering, was the upper agora. From there, the road leads down to another complex of civic buildings of the middle city, including the temples of Demeter, Hera, and Asclepius, three gymnasia, the lower agora, and residential areas.

In the river valley below the middle city was Pergamon's famous Asclepeion or healing center, which—with its temple, system of pools, and staff of physicians—rivaled the sanctuaries at Kos and Epidaurus. In Roman times the spa and religious center underwent a major expansion, which included a colonnaded sacred road of access of more than a half mile in length. The popularity of the healing center can be measured by the Roman amphitheater attached to it, which seated 3,500 people. As a footnote to what has been said, we should report that during the *diodochi* wars, Aristotle's private library, coveted by Ptolemy, was brought to a cave for hiding near Pergamon. When the scrolls were later found, they were partially restored but then confiscated by the Roman general Sulla. In Rome they were copied and critically transcribed by the Aristotelian scholar Andronicus of Rhodes, thus bringing together the cultural pendant of Athens, Rhodes, Alexandria, and Pergamon.[58] If the last three cities fashioned themselves as intellectual rivals to Athens, the idyllic Pergamon at least boasted the distinction of being the seat of Clio, Asclepius, and the devil.

Campus Agrippa

Few major cities in antiquity were founded without divine sanction. In Greece, the process was generally initiated by consulting the oracle at Delphi, whereas in Rome the starting point was augury. The founding of a new city always entailed soliciting good omens, followed by elaborate preparation and a series of religious rites. When the Theban general Epaminondas defeated the Spartans at Leuctra in 371 BC, he decided to found the three cities of Megalopolis, Mantineia, and Messene. Pausanias gives us details of the founding of Messene, whose population had been driven out of the area three centuries earlier. The command to build came to Epaminondas in a dream, in which "an ancient man, closely resembling a priest of Demeter," promised victory over Sparta but on the condition that he "restore to the Messenians their fathers' land and cities." Another allied general experienced a similar vision and was told to dig in Messenia, where "yew and myrtle" were growing on Mount Ithome. There he found a brass urn in which "were inscribed the mysteries of the Great Goddesses."[59] This document provided the site for the city, and Epaminondas next consulted the oracles of Bacis and other seers. At an auspicious time, Epaminondas ordered stone to be brought to the site and had plans drawn up for streets, temples, and ramparts. On the first day of the foundation, the Thebans, Argives, and Messenians made sacrifices to their respective gods, and the new residents of the city also summoned their deceased heroes of the past to return and dwell with them. Only on the following day did workers begin the construction of the temples, houses, and city walls—all to the sound of music from Boeotian and Argive flutes.[60]

The Romans were no less ritualistic in founding their cities, so much so that Virgil, in the *Aeneid*, felt compelled to provide a retrospective mythical backdrop for the founding of Rome. It begins when the ghost of Hector appears to Aeneas, the son of Venus and Anchises, as the walls of Troy were being breached. Hector urges him to flee the city at once, taking with him the household gods and the sacred flame of Vesta, which can never be extinguished. Aeneas, with his father and a small fleet, first sail to Thrace and attempt to found a city, but a spirit cautions them away. Next, they consult the Delian Oracle, where they misinterpret the reading and sail to Crete on another false start. Next, they venture to Greece, where a son of Priam foretells their future in Italy, but only if they sail around Sicily and consult the Sibyl at Cumae. Aeneas reaches Sicily, where his father dies, but when the hero attempts to proceed, Juno unleashes a terrible storm that drives the Trojan fleet to Carthage, along the African coast. There, Aeneas has his doomed love affair with Queen Dido. Aeneas eventually reaches Cumae, where the Sibyl escorts him into the underworld and Elysium. He greets his dead father and has his future foretold. He then makes it to the site of Rome on the Palatine Hill but is met with a war incited by deities opposing his fate. It is only when Aeneas slays his antagonist in combat that the future of Rome, now protected by the Trojan gods and the sacred flame of Vesta, becomes assured. One of the more interesting aspects of Virgil's poem are the number of ritual burials that take place along the journey, which, as Robert Pogue Harrison indicates, seem to be sacrifices to mark out retrospectively "the ground for Rome's future political claims on those territories."[61]

Virgil's hardships take place fifteen generations before Romulus who, in the eighth century, establishes the city of Rome. The original site on the Palatine Hill was chosen by Romulus, who bested his brother Remus in an augury by claiming to have seen more birds of omen (vultures) than his brother.[62] The Roman ritual of augury, as it evolved, was quite elaborate. An augur would first select a high site with a view of the horizon. Animals had to be sacrificed to examine their livers and determine the salubrity of the region. The augur would then quarter the site into sections and draw a diagram on the ground with his staff to determine, through observation, which regions were divinely favored. Once the perimeter of the city was chosen, the ground had to be purified by additional rites. One stage of this process was to dig a hole near the center, into which the future inhabitants would throw special offerings; in the case of Rome, it was the soil from each resident's hometown. Another step was the cutting of a furrow around the city with a bronze plowshare. There were other ceremonial and judicial aspects to the foundation, such as setting up a "stele" to record the founders and dates, drafting records to document the legal and constitutional rights of citizens, and drawing of lots for the distribution of land.[63] All of these rituals were remembered in annual celebrations of a city's founding. In 28 BC, following his victory over Antony at Actium, Augustus dedicated a Temple to Apollo on the Palatine Hill, on the presumed spot where the initial augury took place.

This is scarcely the place to dissect the Roman worldview, but if there is something curious about Roman architecture and the ideal city, it is the fact that with all of Rome's organizational genius, as seen in the scale and complexity of its military and engineering feats, the Romans were always quite willing to assimilate the cultural accomplishments of others. Few other cultures of this period did so. The Persian satraps in control of its conquered territories generally mocked local deities, and although the Hellenistic Greeks appreciated a few aspects of Egyptian culture, they appropriated little from it. Yet if the Roman Republic lacked a tutor of rhetorical or moral theory, Cicero simply translated Greek concepts and introduced the Neo-Attic style to educate Roman orators and philosophers. Similarly, the only book on architecture to survive from classical antiquity, written by the Roman architect Vitruvius, was largely a compendium of Greek and Hellenistic writers.

This is not to say that Vitruvius did not also bring something to the table. In fact, what he brought was a celestial description of design that could be reduced to a single sketch—a sketch not his own but one drawn by Leonardo da Vinci 1,500 years later, the Vitruvian Man.[64] It depicts a male figure with legs closed and open, with arms out to the sides and uplifted, set within a circle and a square. The radius of the circle begins at the navel, as Vitruvius describes it, yet Leonardo was unable to center the square from this location and therefore moved the center point down to the man's genitalia. The idea nevertheless remains. It suggests that the human body is not just the center of architectural practice but of the cosmos more generally, and that every part of the human body—being divinely wrought—is mathematically proportioned. The human face from the chin

ILLUSTRATION 3.7   Leonardo da Vinci, *Vitruvian Man*, c. 1492. Gallerie dell'Accademia, Venice.
Source: Wikimedia CC-PD-Mark.

to the top of the forehead is one-tenth of the body's height, as is the hand from the wrist to the tip of the middle finger. The distance of the chin to the crown of the head is one-eighth. The foot is one-sixth of the body's height; the width of the breast is one-fourth. These proportions or mathematical relationships are brought together under the concept that Vitruvius refers to as "symmetry" (*symmetria*), which is somewhat different from our understanding of the word:

> Architects must grasp this principle thoroughly. It is produced from proportion, which is called *analogia* in Greek. Proportion is the correspondence of members to one another and to the whole, within each work, measured by means of a fixed part. That is how symmetries are calculated. No temple can be put together coherently without symmetry and proportion; unless it conforms exactly to the principle relating the members of a well-shaped man.[65]

This design relationship between the sacred temple and the human body becomes more interesting when Vitruvius adds still another Greek term to the mix—that of *eurythmia*—or eurythmy. Indra Kagin McEwen equates it with the "*ratio*" and "visual coherence and proportion that borders on the divine."[66] Everyone, Vitruvius argues, can see this eurythmy and feel our inner accord with the building's appearance, but only the architect knows how to attain it:

> Proportion (*eurythmia*) implies a graceful semblance; the suitable display of details in their context. This is attained when the details of the work are of a height suitable to their breadth, of a breadth suitable to their length; in a word, when everything has a symmetrical correspondence.[67]

This combination of *symmetria* and *eurythmia* defines for Vitruvius both harmony and beauty, and here the image of the well-shaped man is impressed with a female alter ego. For the Latin word Vitruvius chose for beauty was not the graceful Latin word *pulchritudo*, which Cicero would have chosen, but *venustas*, which connotes "sexual attraction."[68] Linguistically and sensuously, it derives from the goddess Venus. Again, the precedents are interesting. As Varro interprets the word, Venus is the force of love that binds the hot semen of the male with the cool water of the female. She was born, as Botticelli edifyingly portrayed her, from the "foam masses" once the fiery seed fell from heaven into the sea, and from this conjunction of fire and water came not only the force called "life" but also a seductive or voluptuous charm, which, like our hormonal responses, is internally compelling.[69] Beauty for Vitruvius is not a pretty facade, it seems, but a visceral or corporeal response when form is divinely inspired and therefore harmonious.

The text of Vitruvius was formatted in ten books, but nowhere else does he attain such heights of theory. Only in Renaissance Europe, in fact, was he first seriously read; he was little known in Rome in his day. An older contemporary of Augustus, Vitruvius first worked for Julius Caesar as a military architect, a tenure that ended abruptly with the Ides of March. Within a few years he allied himself with Octavian and was one of the engineers involved with Rome's water systems, likely under the initiative of Agrippa—and here, as we shall see, arises another alignment of the empyreal stars.

Rome, when it entered the Augustan Age, was anything but a great city. It was overcrowded, crime-ridden, prone to frequent fires, and had foul water and unsanitary conditions. Over the previous two centuries Roman armies had taken down every major military power in its path: Macedonia, Carthage, Corinth, Athens, Pergamon, Syria, Palestine, and Alexandria—the last in 30 BC. Political figures accumulated great wealth during this expansion, with perhaps the most infamous example being Marcus Scaurus, who once imported 360 marble columns from abroad for a one-month theatrical run. "But then, why such indulgence?" asks an angry Pliny the Elder, "or how do vices more insidiously steal upon us than under the plea of serving the public?[70] Pompey, who viewed his lengthy and successful defeat of Mithridates in the East within the divine tradition of Alexander, at least projected a more modest front. In returning to Rome, he viewed a dramatic performance in Lesbos and vowed to build for Rome its first marble theater, to which he attached a small temple. He even stopped in Rhodes and Athens to raise money. He constructed the lavish work (approaching the later Colosseum in its seating and scale) on the Campus Martius and nearby erected his own residence, replete with porticoes and extensive pleasure gardens. Rome in the mid-first century, as Augustus would later famously record, was still a city of brick.[71]

Mark Antony, Julius Caesar, and Octavian also felt Rome's cultural inferiority, when each in turn viewed Alexandria and saw firsthand the world's most attractive city with its wide boulevards and verdant gardens. Antony, notably, refused to leave the city and Cleopatra, while Julius Caesar at one point contemplated moving Rome's imperial capital to Alexandria.[72] At the time of his assassination, he also had massive plans on the drawing boards for rebuilding Rome. This sight of Alexandria similarly seized the young Octavian, who would become Emperor Augustus. After taking down Antony in Alexandria, he embarked on one of the grandest building campaigns ever undertaken. He founded hundreds of cities across Europe and the Mediterranean, and financed major temples and urban renovations in Rome. He also responded to Rome's lack of sanitary infrastructure, whose importance cannot be understated. Strabo, writing during the reign of Augustus, noted that whereas the Greeks "had the repute of aiming most happily in the founding of cities, in that they aimed at beauty," the Romans had more pressing matters at hand; namely, "the construction of roads and aqueducts, and of sewers that could wash out the filth of the city into the Tiber." To some, such concerns may sound mundane, but water also allows the urban garden. As Strabo reports on Agrippa's early success:

> And water is brought into the city through the aqueducts in such quantities that veritable rivers flow through the city and the sewers; and almost every house has cisterns, and service-pipes, and copious fountains—with which Marcus Agrippa concerns himself most, though he also adorned the city with many other structures.[73]

The reference to "many other structures" is something of an understatement, because Agrippa's vision for Rome was nothing short of magnanimous. A man of humble birth, he met Octavian in the year when both turned eighteen and studied rhetoric. Caesar was already looking kindly on Octavian as a potential heir, and Agrippa's fortunes rose along with those of his friend. Both accompanied Caesar on his campaign in Spain in 45 BC, and the following March, both were training with his Macedonian legion in Apollonia, when Caesar was murdered at the Senate. They were united in their struggles with Brutus and Antony over the next thirteen years, when Agrippa displayed himself as an outstanding military leader. The decisive victory against Antony at Actium in 31 BC was owed to his strategy, but Agrippa had already distinguished himself in Rome with his rebuilding of the water system. He first improved the water output of the Aqua Tepula, and then—displaying his larger vision for Rome—built the Aqueduct Virgo, which brought water to a previously undeveloped part of the city.

For several centuries the Campus Martius or "Field of Mars" was a low-lying, grassy area north of the Forum along the Tiber, serving as a camp or training ground for the Roman military. Because the area was swampy and prone to flooding, few permanent structures were built there. With better flood-control measures, the land close to the Capitol began to be settled with a few villas and showpieces, as we have seen with Pompey. Julius Caesar also had his plans to develop the area with a new theater and voting hall, to which Agrippa added a large portico and numerous works of art. It was at the time the largest building in Rome, yet it was only the start of a massive building campaign, one upon which Agrippa, who owned considerable land in the area, aggrandized into a larger vision—something of a cross between Alexandria's palace district and the paradise of Daphne outside of Antioch. He knew both cities well, and he began with three self-financed projects, the Pantheon, the Basilica of Neptune, and the Baths of Agrippa.[74]

The Pantheon, which occupies the same site as Hadrian's Pantheon today, was erected in the mid-20s BC. The temple was destroyed by fire in AD 80, and it was restored by Domitian. This version also went up in flames and was again rebuilt by Hadrian. Historians have traditionally treated the work as entirely Hadrian's, but new studies reveal that Agrippa's original building likely had a circular colonnaded court, which later dictated the form of the Pantheon. The lone historical description of it before the first fire suggests it was a work of high artistic ambition. "The Pantheon of Agrippa," Pliny the Elder noted, "has been decorated by Diogenes of Athens, and the Caryatides, by him, which form the columns of that temple, are looked upon as master-pieces of excellence."[75] The interior column capitals were covered with a brass coating of "Syracusan metal." Attached to the rear of the Pantheon was the Basilica of Neptune, which Agrippa dedicated to the sea god in celebration of his naval victories. It was thematically outfitted with naval motifs (as a few surviving remnants demonstrate) and surrounded by the Portico of the Argonauts, which contained paintings of mythical Greek heroes. The largest and most important part of this complex, however, were the Baths of Agrippa, which were conceived in a manner similar to Hellenistic gymnasia—again, only a fragment remains. The complex began as a small hot-air bath, but with the completion of the Aqua Virgo, it grew into the size of a soccer field in both directions. It was situated south of the Pantheon along the same north-south axis, and, according to several accounts, it was as much an art gallery as a bath. Among its many works was a statue of Apoxyomenos by Lysippus and two paintings of Ajax and Aphrodite that Agrippa had purchased from the city of Cyzicus for a princely sum. Yet the baths were only part of a much more extensive garden that likely extended all the way to the Tiber, with fields for exercising, a canal for swimming, a colossal reflecting pool or ornamental pond that could entertain small boats, and a series of porticos with pleasure gardens, shade trees, fountains, paved promenades, and covered areas for conversations and poetry recitals. Pliny the Elder marveled at Agrippa's energy and accomplishments, noting that in his aedileship he had erected 170 public baths, 300 statues and 400 columns—all in a single year.[76] In speaking of the "Campus Agrippa," Strabo records that the number of porticoes, theaters, garden precincts, and costly temples in close

ILLUSTRATION 3.8   Fragments of the Basilica of Neptune, attached to the rear of the Pantheon, Rome, 33–25 BC.

Source: Photo by Lalupa. Wikimedia CC BY-SA 3.0.

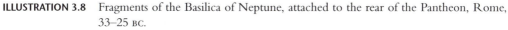

succession to one another give one the impression "that they are trying, as it were, to declare the rest of the city a mere accessory."[77]

Today, almost nothing remains of this Roman paradise, which he willed to the people of Rome upon his death in 12 BC. The pond and green spaces are now densely packed with buildings (a few exceptional ones by Michelangelo and Francesco Borromini), and the racecourse that Domitian attached to the campus is now the Piazza Navona. The Pantheon with its concrete roof survives in its third-generational form. Agrippa also built the first bridge across the Tiber, where he owned land as well, and within sight of his campus is a small villa uncovered in 1879 in the garden of the Renaissance Villa Farnesina. It has been partially excavated, and some of its frescoes have since been restored in a style that Vitruvius once lamented as decadent. Yet its most interesting feature is that it contained, among other areas, rooms for bathing, exercising, dining, and theatrical performances.[78] The villa is now believed to have been built by Agrippa as a wedding present for the bride of his third marriage—Julia, the daughter of Augustus. The two sons produced by this marriage, Gaius and Lucius Caesar, were adopted by Augustus to secure his line of succession, yet here another dimension of the story unfolds.

The French city of Nimes was founded in 28 BC to house war veterans who had participated in Julius Caesar's Nile campaigns. The site itself seems haunted by paradisiacal spirits. By one early twentieth-century account, the city "was a sacred spot in the centre of a druidical forest," where megalithic monuments and dolmens are still "found in the depths of woods of white and evergreen oak."[79] The city's Roman name of *Nemausus* derives from the local Celtic god, *Volcae Arecomici*, and Augustus and Agrippa were sensitive to the spirit of the place. They updated the city baths and added other ornaments to the town, and near the sacred spring they constructed a nymphaeum

ILLUSTRATION 3.9 Maison Carrée, Nîmes, France, AD 4–7.

Source: Photo by Krzysztof Golik. Wikimedia CC BY-SA 4.0.

dedicated to the goddess Diana. Today the ruins stand adjacent to thirty-seven acres of Mediterranean gardens—*Les Jardins de la Fontaine*—an eighteenth-century complex that has few rivals in France. Agrippa also built another temple within footsteps of the nymphaeum, the Maison Carrée, dedicated to his sons Gaius and Lucius Caesar. They did not outlive Augustus, but the temple did, aided by a later renovation of Hadrian. One eighteenth-century writer, Arthur Young, described the Maison Carrée as "the most elegant, and the most agreeable building I have ever seen." Another lauded it for its beautiful simplicity and nobility, "which strikes everybody."[80] Still, a third eighteenth-century visitor apparently unnerved the local townspeople with his odd behavior:

> Here I am, Madam, gazing whole hours at the Maison quarrée, like a lover at his mistress. The stocking weavers and silk spinners around it, consider me as a hypochondriac Englishman, about to write with a pistol, the last chapter of his history.[81]

The visitor, writing to Madame de Tessé, was Thomas Jefferson, and he later hired a French architect to use the temple as the basis for the design of the Virginia State Capitol. One wonders if the local druids, the ancient and highly educated physicians of woodland culture, who understood the restorative benefits of the forest, were not in part responsible for his infatuation?

The Maritime Theater

The Roman historian William MacDonald once made the observation that if someone wanted to understand Roman urbanism, one should do so not by focusing on its streets or grid systems but rather on its urban furniture—that is, its arches, temples, fountains, gardens, and baths.[82] If we accept his advice, then one place to start is not with a city at all, but with the thirty-odd buildings of Hadrian's

Villa, built during AD 117–134. The valley complex, for a resident of one, is about twice the size of the city of Pompeii, and it was the creation of a well-traveled and learned man with absolute power, unlimited resources, and a prodigious ambition for leaving behind an architectural legacy. Conceived during the *Pax Romana* or peace throughout much of the empire, it dwarfed all such paradises before its time, even today. In its present ruined state, pillaged of its art works and precious materials over centuries, it nevertheless remains one of the great monuments of European history.

Villas were not uncommon in Roman times. Cicero is said to have had at least eight of them. Augustus gave the Neopolitans the island of Ischia in exchange for his favorite resort on the island of Capri, whereas the hated Tiberius actually retired from Rome to the same island for his own safety. Nero's Golden House may have occupied large parts of the Palatine, Esquiline, and Caelian Hills in Rome, but his Mediterranean villa at Capo d'Azio embellished two scenic miles of coastline along the Tyrrhenian Sea. His advisor, the Stoic philosopher Seneca, was no less outfitted with estates and properties. The palace of the Emperor Domitian occupied a large part of the Palatine, but his villa at Castel Gandolfo with its gardens, nymphaea, theater, and hippodrome formed a credible practice run for Hadrian's later efforts. Yet what distinguishes Hadrian's city was not the scale of his work as much as its exquisite execution. He sought to create an urban museum reflecting the world's artistic and intellectual accomplishments. Much was garnered on his travels to Athens, Rhodes, Pergamon, Antioch, and Alexandria.

If the son of the wealthy proconsul Celsus had endowed the city of Ephesus with its famed library in AD 117, Hadrian invested his own villa with two large libraries, one for Latin and one for his Greek holdings (he preferred to speak Greek over Latin). Views from the libraries looked out upon the nearby nymphaeum of the Temple of Venus, and the distant view from the elevated temple supposedly evoked for Hadrian the "thick wooded slopes" of the Thessalian "Vale of Tempe," where Apollo pursued Daphne until her father transformed her into the laurel tree.[83] Similarly, if Athens had its Painted Stoa and Academy, Hadrian's Villa would have the same—not as a replica but rather as a magnified mnemonic variation on the theme. His version of the stoa—a four-sided peristyle with rounded ends, more than 700 feet in length and housing a large pool and gardens—dwarfed his Athenian counterpart. One can only imagine the colorful artistic works and precious materials with which Hadrian decorated its walls, all for his physician-recommended midday stroll of two miles, or seven circuits around the enclosure. After the walk, he likely retired to his Heliocaminus for a refreshing bath, only one of four bath complexes on the estate. Hadrian's other option upon leaving the Stoa was to enter Philosophers' Hall, a large apsidal structure with a vaulted ceiling, whose seven niches were populated with statues—a pantheon not to divinities but to philosophers.

The Academy or Academia, inspired by Plato, is situated on what might be viewed as the acropolis, or the highest terrace at the southwest end of the estate. It consisted of a complex of rooms, including a smaller, domed version of the Roman pantheon, the so-called Temple of Apollo. These rooms enclosed an extensive peristyle courtyard and garden space on three sides. Its entrance belvedere is an architectural masterpiece of positive and negative curvilinear spaces, whose governing circle, from which all half-circle variations emerge, is ninety feet in diameter.[84] For years scholars have debated the purpose of the complex, but researchers have now noted that the entire set of rooms is oriented according to the summer and winter solstices, and the Temple of Apollo may in fact have functioned as a large sundial coordinating the times of the winter rituals and festivities associated with the Saturnalia of Dionysus, and the summer festivities connected with Fors Fortuna. Similarly, the circular drum of the Roccabruna, another temple aligned along the same axes but located a distance away, was a celestial observatory.[85]

Not unrelated in spirit are the so-called Canopus and Maritime theater—both of which seem to cater to contrary poles of emotional contentment. The Canopus, perhaps the most photogenic part of what survives of the estate, is a long narrow pool of almost 400 feet in length, surrounded with an open colonnade. The pool, with its statuary, is seemingly a place of seclusion and reflection, but at the south end extends a massive half-domed sanctuary carved into the hillside—the Serapeum—which suggests its purpose was one of entertainment. Hadrian had of course visited the shrine of the Serapeum in Alexandria, but he certainly knew as well the Serapeum at Canopus, a town along the branch of the Nile fifteen miles south of Alexandria. It was a town known less for its piety than for its revelry. A few pious people during the day did visit the sanctuary and seek cures, Strabo records, but every night the town became crowded with boats from Alexandria,

> with people on the boats who play the flute and dance without restraint and with extreme licentiousness, both men and women, and also with people of Canopus itself, who have resorts situated close to the canal and adapted to relaxation and merry-making of this kind.[86]

The Maritime Theater or island villa, with its geometric nuances, is an architect's delight, and seems by contrast to be a place of serious conversation. Effectively, the circular platform, which is sunk eight feet below the landscape around it, is an island surrounded by a pool, which is surrounded by an Ionic colonnade, and the whole sealed off from the world by a perimeter circular wall. The wall's circumference is the same as that of the Roman Pantheon—certainly not by accident. The island in plan—defined by its colonnade, fountain, gardens, library, places for dining, and heated baths—is also an ingenious exercise of curvilinear and square geometries playing off one

ILLUSTRATION 3.10 Maritime Theater, Hadrian's Villa, Tivoli, c. AD 120.

Source: Photo courtesy of Sarah Robinson.

another. Historians have sought its inspiration in everything from Plato's Atlantis to the Herodium built by King Herod, which Hadrian is known to have visited. In any case, the theater likely served as a place for evening dining and entertainment of a purely intellectual kind. Given the theater's extraordinarily impressionistic qualities, one wonders how Hadrian, when the building was in full costume, survived each experience without succumbing to his own apotheosis.

The Tivoli estate had much more, including summer and winter palaces, various nymphaea, and a sumptuous reception hall, the Golden Court, with its expansive colonnade. It was likely used only a few times a year, yet its precious materials are said to have put every Seleucid or Persian monarch before Hadrian's time to shame. Perhaps a more appropriate metaphor for the entire complex might be Elysium—the great Western canon of architecture and ideas intentionally recreated in Hadrian's inflated self-image. The estate of seven square miles was not only vast in size but also resplendent with vineyards, groves of olive, cypress, oak, and bay trees, and a multitude of small and large private gardens within courtyards. One can lay awake at full night simply imagining the exotic botanical species that were imported from around the world to impress its lone resident. Eleanor Clark, in her now classic description of the estate, noted that at Hadrian's Villa "the garden is the house," in the sense that the buildings, however magnificent in their precious materials, are grand follies within the landscape for the demigod to sit back and enjoy the limited terms of his divine office. Hadrian appeared at the apogee of the Roman Empire, but it was an empire, as Edward Gibbon famously chronicled, fated to fall. A few Eastern conquerors, to be sure, would in future centuries attempt to recreate their visions of paradise on such a grand scale, but the audacity of this paradise would never again be matched in the West.

Notes

1. Hesiod, "Works and Days," in Hugh G. Evelyn-White (trans.), *Hesiod: The Homeric Hymns and Homerica* (Cambridge, MA: Harvard University Press, 1973), 11.
2. Ibid., 15.
3. *The Odyssey*, trans. by A. T. Murray (Cambridge MA: Harvard University Press, 1976), V:62–75.
4. Ibid., XV:406–11.
5. *The Odyssey of Homer* (London: G. B. Whittaker, 1827), IV:565–70.
6. *The Odyssey* (note 3), VI:122–4.
7. Ibid., VII:558–63.
8. Ibid., VII:127–31.
9. Xenophon, *The Economist*, trans. by H. G. Dakyns, IV:15–23.
10. Ibid., IV:7.
11. Plutarch, "Alciabades," in Bernadotte Perrin (trans.), *Plutarch's Lives*, (London: William Heinemann, 1916), XI:24.
12. See R. E. Wycherley, "Peripatos: The Athenian Philosophical Scene-II," *Greece & Rome* 9:1 (March 1952).
13. Plutarch, "Cimon," in Bernadotte Perrin (trans.), *Plutarch's Lives*, II:14.
14. Diogenes Laertius, *Lives of the Eminent Philosophers*, trans. by Robert Drew, 4.1–2.
15. A.-H. Chroust, "Did Aristotle Own a School in Athens Between 335/34 and 323 B.C.?" *Rheinisches Museum für Philogie* 115:4 (1972), 310–18.
16. "A True Story," in A. M. Harmon (English trans.), *Lucian* (London: William Heinemann, 1913), II:313–15.
17. Ibid., 341.
18. Ibid., 321.
19. Plato, *The Republic*, 4.401, 4.415.
20. In his early dialogue *Greater Hippias*, he noted that Phidias was a "good craftsman," 289e-90a-b.
21. *Laws*, V:747.
22. Ibid., VI:779.
23. Ibid., VI:761.
24. Ibid., VI:778.
25. *Critias*, 108.
26. Ibid., 121.
27. Aristophanes, *The Birds*, 992–1017.
28. Vitruvius, *On Architecture*, trans. by Frank Granger (Cambridge, MA: Harvard University Press, 1970), I:1.5.

29. William Bell Dinsmoor, *The Architecture of Ancient Greece* (New York: W. W. Norton & Company, 1975), 164.
30. Aristotle, *Politics*, 1330b:26–31.
31. Ibid., 1267b:22.
32. Ibid., 1267b:27–8.
33. Jean-Pierre Vernant, *Myth and Thought Among the Greeks*, trans. by Janet Lloyd (New York: Zone Books, 2006), 250.
34. Gerard Naddaf, "On the Origin of Anaximander's Cosmological Model," *Journal of the History of Ideas* 59:1 (January 1998), 28.
35. Herodotus, *The History of Herodotus*, trans. by George Rawlinson (New York: Tandy-Thomas Company, 1909), 6:22.
36. Armand D'Angour, *Socrates in Love* (London: Bloomsbury Press, 2019), 191.
37. Strabo, *The Geography of Strabo, trans. H. C. Hamilton (London: Henry G. Bohn, 1857),* 14:2.
38. See John Bradford, "Fieldwork on Aerial Discoveries in Attica and Rhodes," *The Antiquaries Journal* 36:1–2 (April 1956), 57–69.
39. Cited from Carlo Franco, "Aelius Aristides and Rhodes: Concord and Consolation," in *Aelius Aristides: Between Greece, Rome, and the Gods* (Brill Online), 225–7.
40. See Lionel Casson, *Libraries in the Ancient World* (New Haven: Yale University Press, 2001), 355.
41. Diodorus Siculus, *Library of History*, 20:83.
42. Vitruvius, *On Architecture* (note 28), 10:16, 6–8.
43. Plutarch, "Life of Alexander," (note 11), *Plutarch's Lives*, VIII.
44. Vitruvius, *On Architecture* (note 28), I.2:Preface.
45. Plutarch, "Life of Alexander" (note 11), 26. On the architecture and the founding of Alexandria, see Judith McKenzie, *The Architecture of Alexandria and Egypt: 300 BC–AD 700* (New Haven: Yale University Press, 2007).
46. Siculus, *Library of History* (note 41), 17:52.
47. Strabo, *Geography* (note 38), 17:8.
48. Richard Tomlinson, *From Mycenae to Constantinople: The Evolution of the Ancient City* (London: Routledge, 1992), 99–100.
49. Strabo, *Geography*, 17:8.
50. Ibid., 17:9.
51. Plutarch, "Life of Antony," (note 11), 80.
52. Ibid., LVIII.
53. Revelation 2:12–16.
54. Plutarch, "Life of Alexander," (note 11), 21.
55. Xenophon, *Anabasis*, 7:8.
56. Pliny the Elder, *Natural History*, 14:11.
57. On the archaeology of the city, see Ekrem Akurgal, *Ancient Civilizations and Ruins of Turkey* (Istanbul: Haset Kitabevt, 1985), 69–111.
58. See Theodore Vrettos, *Alexandria: City of the Western Mind* (New York: The Free Press, 2001), 38.
59. Pausanias, *Guide to Greece*, 4:26.
60. Ibid., 4:27.
61. Robert Pogue Harrison, *The Dominion of the Dead* (Chicago, IL: University of Chicago Press, 2003), 27.
62. Plutarch, "Life of Romulus," (note 11), 9–10.
63. For aspects and interpretations of the rituals, which this text draws upon, see Joseph Rykwert, *The Idea of a Town: The Anthropology of Urban Form in Rome, Italy and the Ancient World* (Cambridge, MA: Massachusetts Institute of Technology Press, 1995), 41–71 and 97–162; Indra Kagin McEwen, *Vitruvius* (Cambridge, MA: Massachusetts Institute of Technology Press, 2003), 162–7.
64. Vitruvius, *On Architecture* (note 28), 3:1.2–4.
65. Ibid., 3:1.1. I have used the translation of Indra Kagin McEwen.
66. Kagin McEwen, *Vitruvius* (note 63), 196.
67. Vitruvius, *On Architecture* (note 28), I:2.3.
68. A point also made in Alberto Pérez-Gómez, *Attunement: Architectural Meaning After the Crisis of Modern Science* (Cambridge, MA: Massachusetts Institute of Technology Press, 2016), 43.
69. The analysis of Kagin McEwen, *Vitruvius* (note 63), 200–1. See Varro, *On the Latin Language*, 5:61–3.
70. Pliny the Elder, *Natural History*, 36:2.
71. Plutarch, "Life of Pompey" (note 11), 42.
72. Suetonius, "Caius Julius Caesar," 79.
73. Strabo, *Geography*, 5:3.8.
74. The classic study of the buildings of this period is Thomas H. Dyer, *A History of the City of Rome: Its Structures and Monuments* (London: Longmans, Green & Co., 1865).

75. Pliny the Elder, *Natural History*, 36:4.
76. Ibid., 36:24.
77. Strabo, *Geography*, 5:3.
78. See Diane Favro, *The Urban Image of Augustine Rome* (Cambridge: Cambridge University Press, 1996), 166.
79. J. Charles-Roux, *Nimes*, trans. by Henry Varley (Paris: Louis Robin, 1913; Forgotten Books reprint), 9.
80. Ibid., 52.
81. "Thomas Jefferson to Madame de Tessé," *Founders Online* (March 20, 1787). https://founders.archives.gov. Accessed May 2020.
82. William L. MacDonald, "Roman Urbanism," *Journal of Architectural Education* 41:3 (Spring 1988), 30.
83. Ovid, *Metamorphoses*, I:568.
84. For an analysis, see William L. MacDonald and John A. Pinto, *Hadrian's Villa and Its Legacy* (New Haven: Yale University Press, 1995), 94–5.
85. Marina De Franceschini and Giuseppe Veneziano, "Architecture and Archaeoastronomy in Hadrian's Villa Near Tivoli, Rome," *Nexus News Journal* 15:3 (November 2013).
86. Strabo, *Geography*, 17:17.10.

4

PARADISES OF FAITH

City of David

Although the arid and rocky landscape of much of Palestine, together with the smaller populations of tribal peoples, allowed none of the ostentatious palaces and cultivated landscapes we find elsewhere in western Asia, the garden nevertheless figures prominently in Judaic traditions. The Book of Genesis opens with the Garden of Eden, and the Temple of Solomon came to be seen as a symbol for the lost terrestrial garden. The scholarship and archaeological discoveries of recent years have very much reinforced the symbolism of the garden within Hebrew culture.[1]

Human settlements in Palestine, as we have seen, may go back to Jericho and beyond, but the first historical documentation relating to its cities appears in the fourteenth century. Egypt controlled Palestine for much of the second millennium, and archival documents there suggest that Jerusalem toward the end of this period was little more than a highland stronghold along the eastern ridge of the eventual city, with little distinction and no monuments. Palestine was initially inhabited by pastoral nomads and later by settlers from the East, the Semitic-speaking Canaanites. With the collapse of both the Hittite and Mycenaean civilizations around 1200 BC, bands of migrants found their way into the area, most prominently the Philistines, who set up coastal towns along the coast of Gaza. It was in this period that the Israelites first began to distinguish themselves culturally from their Canaanite neighbors, and their strength grew as Canaanite cities fell into the disorder of the day. By the middle of the eleventh century the Israelites began to take the upper hand in northern Palestine, in part due to their larger populations and more fertile lands. By the start of the tenth century, the ten Israelite tribes in the north numbered around 40,000 people, whereas the population of the two Judean tribes in the more rural south, in which Jerusalem was located, has been estimated at around 5,000. The population of Jerusalem during the reigns of David and Solomon, early in the first millennium, is believed to have been around 2,000.[2]

David, a native of Bethlehem, was a chieftain and is acclaimed to have united all twelve Jewish tribes, although this achievement too has been disputed. After taking Jerusalem from the Jebusites in 1003, he renamed it the "City of David" and from there laid out a royal line, the "House of David," which would have longevity. The choice of Jerusalem as David's capital is interesting, because the landscape is rocky and borders on a desert. The main source of water for the town was the productive Gihon Spring, not far from the later Temple Mount. As the Book of Ecclesiastes records David's words: "I undertook great projects: I built houses for myself and planted vineyards. I made gardens and parks and planted all kinds of fruit trees in them. I made reservoirs to water groves of flourishing trees."[3] The sentiment and the

DOI: 10.4324/9781003178460-4

phrasing is quite similar to the boasting of other monarchs, albeit on a smaller scale. David built a palace for himself and he also transferred the Ark of the Covenant to Jerusalem, which scriptures say contained the stone tablets of the ten commandments dictated to Moses on Mount Sinai. The Book of Exodus records the words of Yahweh to Moses: "Then have them make a sanctuary for me, and I will dwell among them. Make this tabernacle and all its furnishings exactly like the pattern I will show you."[4] The dimensions of the temple and its parts were thus deemed to be a celestial, and there should be only one temple in the city of Jerusalem. As the first-century AD historian Flavius Josephus wrote:

> Let there be then one city of the land of Canaan, and this situate in the most agreeable place for its goodness, and very eminent in itself, and let it be that which God shall choose for himself by prophetic revelation. Let there also be one temple therein, and one altar, not reared of hewn stones but of such as you gather together at random; which stones, when they are whited over with mortar, will have a handsome appearance, and be beautiful to the sight.[5]

David, for a while at least, ignored the vision and continued his warring ways, but Yahweh, the monotheistic Jewish God, brought down a plague upon the city and David purchased a "threshing floor" atop Mount Moriah from the Jebusite Araunah to serve as the location for the altar. He then made preparations for building the temple, although its construction fell to his son-in-law and successor Solomon.

ILLUSTRATION 4.1   Temple of Solomon, Latin Estienne Bible, 1540.

Similar to what had transpired earlier with Moses, the Book of Chronicles (likely written in the fifth or fourth century) relates that David handed over the plans for the temple to Solomon: "All this, David said, I have in writing from the hand of the Lord, and he gave me understanding in all the details of the plan."[6] The command for one temple for one city was thus fulfilled, although polytheism was still prevalent during the reigns of David and Solomon. For the construction of the temple, Solomon consulted King Hiram of Tyre, who reportedly sent his chief craftsman Huram-Abi to overview construction. He was a man "trained to work in gold, silver, bronze and iron, stone and wood, and with purple and blue and crimson yarn and fine linen," moreover, he could "execute any design given to him."[7] Set on a platform, the temple took a rectangular form with a porch in front, accentuated by two freestanding hollow brass columns. The capitals in the "shape of lilies" were festooned with chains of pomegranates in two encircling rows. A stepped altar was also placed in front of the temple for offerings, together with a colossal cast-metal water basin known as the "Sea," which was used for ablutions. The exterior of the temple was finished in a brilliant white stone dressed at the quarry, and in the temple precinct there were likely different trees.[8]

The interior of the temple also had a pronounced Edenic theme. It consisted of two main rooms: the sanctum and an inner sanctum, or "Holy of Holies." Inside the latter was the Foundation Stone or threshing floor on which Abraham had placed Isaac for sacrifice. It was also the stone on which Jacob had his dream of angels descending and ascending from and to heaven with a staircase. The Ark, placed behind the Foundation Stone, was guarded by two winged, gilded cherubim fifteen feet tall. The sanctum, as Josephus later reported, had pine doors carved with cherubim, palm trees, and open flowers overlaid with hammered gold. The room was paneled with cedar and carved with cherubim, palm trees, and open flowers. Entry to the Holy of Holies—a thirty-foot cube— was gained through paneled doors of olivewood also carved with cherubim, palm trees, and open flowers, and also overlaid with gold. The walls, floor, and ceiling were outfitted with gold panels, including the platform on which the Ark was placed. The temple in Hebrew accounts is generally referred to as the "palace of God." Psalms describes it as "his holy mountain" placed "in the city of our God. It is beautiful in its loftiness, the joy of the whole earth."[9] Solomon concluded his dedication by noting that he had built the temple in the name of the Lord: "I have a place there for the Ark, in which is the Covenant of the Lord that he made with our fathers when he brought them out of Egypt."[10] The dedication ceremony is scripturally portrayed as a ritualized event with much pomp and grandeur, and its intention was to declare Jerusalem as the new Eden—the radiant sun of the Hebrew people.

This religious calm, however, would not last for long. The ten northern tribes of Israel soon broke away from Judea and pursued their own political and economic relations with Egypt and the Phoenician states. They also reinstated the worship of Baal and his consort, the fertility goddess Asherah. Jerusalem, by virtue of its temple, continued to have some standing, although to a lesser extent. Problems for both kingdoms arrived when Assyria began to expand its vassal states in the eighth century. The ten northern tribes were conquered, rebelled, and its capital city Samaria was destroyed in 722. Judea, under the rule of Hezekiah, pledged allegiance to Sargon II, but some years later, as his successor Sennacherib was occupied elsewhere with wars, they too rebelled. In retaliation, Assyrian armies marched west in 701 and, as Assyrian documents report, sacked forty-six Palestinian cities, including the major Judean city of Lachish. Hezekiah thwarted the destruction of Jerusalem by returning Judea to the status of a vassal state, but his religious reforms were less successful. It was not long thereafter that the worship of Baal and Asherah resumed in Jerusalem.

With Ashurbanipal's death late in the seventh century, the Assyrian Empire began to crumble, and Nineveh itself was sacked. In 605, the Babylonian king Nebuchadnezzar II succeeded his father and began to reconstitute the Old Babylonian Empire, whereby Jerusalem, for the next two decades, became a pawn between the two competing powers of Egypt and Babylonia. In the end, Nebuchadnezzar would prevail, destroy a rebellious Jerusalem, burn its temple to the ground, and take the city's population into exile. For many Jewish people, the event was equated with Adam and Eve's expulsion from paradise. The opening verse of the book Jeremiah likens the terrible moment of despair to the violation of a woman: "How doth the city sit solitary, *that* was full of people! *how* is she become as a widow! she *that was* great among the nations, *and* princess among the provinces, *how* is she become tributary!"[11] It was only with the destruction of the Neo-Babylonian Empire by Cyrus the Great in 538 that the Israelites in Babylonia were offered the opportunity to return to their homeland—at the time when the main books of the Torah were being put into final form.

Yet little progress on repairing the city was made. Almost a century later, Nehemiah, the Jewish scribe and cupbearer to the Persian Emperor Artaxerxes, sat down and wept when he heard that the walls and gates of Jerusalem had not been restored.[12] Nehemiah was later sent by Artaxerxes to be the governor of Judah with the mandate to rebuild the city and its ramparts, just as Ezra had a few years earlier been sent to reintroduce the teachings of the Torah. The rebuilding of the temple and the city was now likened to a return to Eden, and Ezekiel, writing in exile prior to Cyrus's decree of return, makes explicit:

> This is what the Sovereign LORD says: On the day I cleanse you from all your sins, I will resettle your towns and the ruins will be rebuilt. The desolate land will be cultivated instead of lying desolate in the sight of all who pass through it. They will say, "This land that was laid waste has become like the garden of Eden; the cities that were lying in ruins, desolate and destroyed, are now fortified and inhabited."[13]

Ezekiel, in his vision, famously goes on to speak of being placed on top of a high mountain overlooking the new Jerusalem and the new temple. The latter sits on a spring and has water flowing from under its threshold on each side and the waters collect into one large river with the power to renew the earth:

> Fruit trees of all kinds will grow on both banks of the river. Their leaves will not wither, nor will their fruit fail. Every month they will bear, because the water from the sanctuary flows to them. Their fruit will serve for food and their leaves for healing.[14]

The second temple was started around 520 with limited resources and to decidedly mixed reviews. One of the leaders of the rebuilding effort, Haggai, who admitted that it was less imposing than the first temple, said, "How does it look to you now? Does it not seem to you like nothing?"[15] Josephus, writing more than 500 years later, noted that the priests, Levites, and those of older families, upon viewing the result, "were disconsolate, and not able to contain their grief, and proceeded so far as to lament and shed tears on those accounts."[16] Persian rule was nevertheless lenient and brought some prosperity and stability to the city, and when Alexander and his army approached the city almost two centuries later, after the siege of Tyre, he saluted the apprehensive scarlet-clad high priest and went up into the temple to offer sacrifice. He then promised that Jews everywhere in his empire would have the right to practice their religion.[17]

Alexander's death in 323 would also result in instability. The Ptolemies from Egypt first ruled Jerusalem with leniency, and the city of Alexander's founding in fact became a haven for many educated Jews. Yet near the start of the second century, the Seleucid king Antiochus III took forcible control of the city and began a process of Hellenizing it, which resulted in suppressing Jewish culture and banning Torah law. His son, in fact, rededicated the Temple of Jerusalem to Zeus. These events led to the Maccabean Revolt, beginning in 160 BC, and to conflicts between orthodox and reformist Jewish camps. Moreover, it was scarcely coincidental that around this time that the Book of Daniel—written by an exiled Jew living at Babylon—introduced the eschatological theme of the coming end of the world. A century later, Pompey's conquest of Judea brought the city under

Roman control, and Jerusalem, now made a regional center, flourished for a while. Herod, who was appointed king of Judea by the Romans, even undertook a massive rebuilding campaign that would entail not only Jerusalem and its monuments but also numerous large-scale projects within the expanded Judean kingdom. His reign, however, is better known for his tyrannical rule, famine, taxation, and political unrest.

Nevertheless, Herod would play a key role in Jewish architectural history. He was born in Judea and was a convert to the Jewish faith. His father Antipater pledged allegiance to Pompey, but Herod later formed a close relationship with Mark Antony and Augustus, the last of whom enhanced Herod's personal wealth with a share in a copper mine. He lived a life of luxury, much to the disdain of the poor population, but he was at the same time an energetic builder in service to Rome's interests and his own. Among his many projects were the new harbor town of Caesarea Maritima, a temple to Augustus at Samaria, the fortress at Masada, a winter palace at Jericho, and the idealized palatial/urban complex known as the Herodium—or more appropriately in Arabic, *Jabal-al-Fureidis*, or "Mountain of the Little Paradise." The design of the Herodium was an act of sheer bravado harking back to earlier eras. Situated in the Judean desert a few miles southeast of Bethlehem, the five-story palace was built inside a volcanic-like mound with central courtyards and a tall northern tower. The upper two stories of the palace, with all the royal trappings, looked inward over a swimming pool and gardens, and the tower provided a privileged view of the desert landscape. Along the norther rim of the volcanic form, Herod added a royal theater seating 400 people, a racecourse, and a lower palace with a large hall, possibly a nymphaeum, embellished with pools, courtyards, and gardens. Below it stood nothing less than a small town with a vast pool, in whose center was a tholos or circular structure that could only be reached by boat. The pool was surrounded by an equally grand garden, enclosed by a portico. The effort almost seems more manic in its building instinct than paradisiacal.

Herod's megalomania was scarcely less contained when he decided, around 25 BC, to replace the 500-year-old Temple of Jerusalem. His plan initially met with local opposition, but he softened dissent by employing tens of thousands of workers on the project, even training priests to be masons to avoid profanation. The first stage was erecting a monumental platform of the Temple Mount, more than a thousand feet along three sides. Altogether, it encompassed thirty-six acres, or one-sixth of Jerusalem's land area. Some of the limestone blocks for the wall weighed as much as fifty tons, and the south wall loomed more than 100 feet above the street. A fragment of the western wall, known as the Wailing Wall, remains in place today. On the terrace, a portico ran around three sides of the platform, but the southern enclosure took the form of a two-story classical Greek Stoa. Its 162 Corinthian columns were arranged in four rows and overlooked a vast courtyard that accommodated 20,000 people for events such as Passover. The vertical reach of the new temple, much expanding in dimension, towered above all else. Josephus, who viewed the building firsthand, commented on one aspect of the main facade that was particularly striking:

> Now the outward face of the temple in its front wanted nothing that was likely to surprise either men's minds or their eyes; for it was covered all over with plates of gold of great weight, and, at the first rising of the sun, reflected back a very fiery splendour, and made those who forced themselves to look upon it to turn their eyes away, just as they would have done at the sun's own rays. But this temple appeared to strangers, when they were coming to it at a distance, like a mountain covered with snow; for as to those parts of it that were not gilt, they were exceedingly white.[18]

The temple's ornamental theme was once again the Garden of Eden. The gate into the temple, seventy feet tall, was not only covered in gold panels but also had "golden vines above it, from which clusters of grapes hung as tall as a man's height." In front of the inner doorway to the Holy of Holies

ILLUSTRATION 4.2   Herod's Temple, c. 20–10 BC. Model of Jerusalem by Berthold Werner.

Source: Wikimedia CC BY 3.0.

was a "Babylonian curtain, embroidered with blue, and fine linen, and scarlet, and purple," signifying for Josephus "all that was mystical in the heavens."[19] Josephus similarly described the curtain to shield the Ark as "very ornamental, and embroidered with all sorts of flowers which the earth produces."[20]

The rebuilding of the new temple would be completed by the end of the century, but of course the ending to the story would not be a happy one. For more than a century the Jewish community had been resisting both the Hellenization and Romanization of the city, and with Herod's death in 4 BC the political situation deteriorated. Later Roman governors and emperors continued to misread the local situation and to handle any opposition with brutality. When Herod's son Archelaus placed a Roman golden eagle over the temple's entrance, his act was greeted with angry demonstrations, leading to the deaths of 3,000 Jewish protesters. The rebellion rapidly intensified, and Varus, the Roman governor of Syria, brought 20,000 soldiers into Palestine, where he razed dozens of towns, crucified thousands, and by some accounts sold 30,000 Jews into slavery. Augustus replaced Archelaus in AD 6, but Jewish resistance remained strong. The crucifixion of Jesus was in part due to the tensions between the Roman and Jewish communities. The emperor Caligula inflamed the city a decade later when, after declaring himself a deity, he attempted to place his statue in the Temple of Jerusalem. Tensions only eased when he was assassinated the following year. Splinter sects within Judaism also inflamed divisions. The inevitable conflict came to a head with the Jewish revolt in the years 66–70. The eruption began when the Roman procurator Florus removed a large quantity of silver from the temple to build an aqueduct, and a band of Zealots responded by overpowering the Roman garrison in Jerusalem. The revolt spread across Palestine, and in response Nero dispatched the Roman general Vespasian with 60,000 troops to put down the insurrection. The Herodium itself was one early casualty, as it was used as a base by the rebels. The Jewish forces eventually assembled in Jerusalem and instigated what became a civil war among themselves by killing their own moderate leaders. The endgame of the suicidal strategy was now evident. After Vespasian was proclaimed emperor and returned to Rome, his son Titus took over the assault on Jerusalem, which by this time had now narrowed down to a few dozen insurgents holed up inside the Temple. He employed various measures to dislodge them and eventually retook the temple. Although he ordered the damaged building to be preserved, the anger of the Roman soldiers led to looting and the burning of the temple. Titus then erased all physical traces of the temple's existence. Despite this lack of evidence, or more likely because of it, there have been endless attempts to reconstruct the temple, one of the grandest architectural monuments of its era.

The temple would never be rebuilt, but what is striking about its destruction is that this templar symbol of one religion passed into another religion as the paradisiacal city of "New Jerusalem," given voice in the New Testament by John of Revelation:

> I saw the Holy City, the new Jerusalem, coming down out of heaven from God, prepared as a bride beautifully dressed for her husband. And I heard a loud voice from the throne saying, "Now the dwelling of God is with men and he will live with them. They will be his people, and God himself will be one with them, and be their God. He will wipe every tear from their eyes. There will be no more death or mourning or crying or pain, for the old order of things has passed away.

Like Ezekiel before him, John in his vision—one that marries Jewish and nascent Christian traditions—not only describes the Day of Judgment but also Eden's

> river of the water of life, as clear as crystal, flowing from the throne of God and of the Lamb down the middle of the great street of the city. On each side of the river stood the tree of life, bearing twelve crops of fruit, yielding its fruit every month.[21]

Today the site of the Temple of Jerusalem is occupied by the Dome of the Rock, an early Islamic architectural jewel completed in 692. On display inside is the rock of Abraham and Isaac—in Islamic scripture, the rock from which Mohammed ascended to heaven to join Abraham, Moses, and Jesus in paradise.

New Jerusalem

The idea of paradise within Judeo-Christian culture carried with it a great deal of ambiguity. If Adam and Eve first lived in the Garden of Eden before their expulsion, then paradise was logically someplace on earth, or as scripture indicated, somewhere east of Eden. The Jewish historian Josephus referred to the garden as somewhere "in the east," and its garden "was watered by one river, which ran round about the whole earth." This river, in his interpretation, became the wellspring for the four major rivers known to the ancient world: the Euphrates, Tigris, Nile, and Ganges.[22] In other scriptural references, paradise was a place to which the good would one day return, either before or after the final day of judgment. In the apocryphal Book of Enoch, for instance, the prophet, on his tour of the earth, describes "four beautiful places" within a great mountain chain in which, as his guide the angel Rafael relates, were intended as assembly places for the dead awaiting the final day of reckoning. Only one, however, was paradisiacal—that prepared for the souls of the just.[23] Other interpretations of Eden were allegorical. Philo Judaeus, a Hellenized Jew living in Alexandria during the time of Jesus, dismissed the Genesis account of God creating a paradise as "mere incurable folly." Why would He need such a pleasant abode for himself, or for his creations? Why would he fill it with unfamiliar plants such as the tree of life, tree of knowledge, or tree of immortality? "Now these cannot have been trees of the land, but must indisputably have been plants of a rational soil," he goes on to say, "which as a road to travel along leading to virtue, and having for its end life and immortality."[24]

The word "paradise" appears only three times in the New Testament. The first, in the Gospel of Luke, is when the repentant thief crucified alongside Jesus asks to be remembered, and Jesus responds that "today you will be with me in paradise." The second is in the book of Revelation, when John threatens the wayward church leaders of Ephesus but then promises that "to him who overcomes, I will give the right to eat from the tree of life, which is in the paradise of God." Revelation ends with the "holy Jerusalem, coming down out of heaven from God," whose "brilliance was like that of a very precious jewel, like a jasper, clear as crystal," and whose river of life flowed "from the throne of God and of the Lamb down the middle of the great street of the city."[25] It is a four-square city with twelve gates, inscribed with the twelve tribes of Israel, and constructed of pure gold.

The third appearance of "paradise" in the New Testament is problematic. In Corinthians, Paul relates his own apocalyptic vision, whether

> it was in the body or out of the body I do not know—God knows. And I know that this man—whether in the body or apart from the body I do not know, but God knows—was caught up to paradise. He heard inexpressible things; things that man is not permitted to tell.[26]

Paul does not expand upon his experience, but an apocryphal writing from the third century (once attributed to Paul) expands upon his vision. Paul is led by an angel to the golden gates of the third heaven, a realm of paradise that he does not describe in detail, but which he uses as a lament of those who do not see the many good things that the Lord has prepared for them. From there, he descends into the second heaven, supported by the river Oceanus that surrounds the earth. Here the light is "seven times brighter than silver," and it is here that the good reside until the Last Judgment. In it flows a river with milk and honey, tall trees laden with fruit, and every vine had "ten thousand branches and each branch had upon it ten thousand bunches of grapes and in each of these a thousand single grapes."[27] Paul next enters the City of Christ, a city built entirely of gold with twelve walls, each of which has twelve towers and through which flows the four rivers of Eden—the rivers of honey, milk, wine, and oil. It is here that he meets up with a number of Old Testament figures and, after a lengthy descent into Hell and observing its tortures, Paul returns with the angel to paradise. It is now the actual paradise from which Adam and Eve were evicted, and Paul describes a few of its delights, including the tree of life. Although scant in its description, the work presented the young church with the problem of defining the idea of paradise.

Ambrose, the bishop of Milan, was one of the first to take up the challenge in the late fourth century. He opens his dissertation, "On Paradise," first by shying away from the "danger" of trying to understand its meaning. Yet after accepting Eden's authenticity as an earthly garden, he goes on to offer his own allegorical interpretation of paradise as given in Genesis. In citing Philo Judaeus, Ambrose draws upon the duality of *nous* (mind, man) and *aisthesis* (emotion, woman) to argue that the story of Eden was an allegory on the rational mind being deceived by the emotion of the senses. In this interpretation, paradise becomes "a land of fertility—that is to say, a soul which is fertile-planted in Eden, that is, in a certain delightful or well-tilled land in which the soul finds pleasure." The source from which the four rivers flowed and irrigated paradise is none other than the Lord Jesus Christ, "the Fount as well as the Father of Eternal life." The garden's four rivers, in turn, represent the Ciceronian virtues of prudence, temperance, fortitude, and justice.[28]

In another writing, "Death as a Good," Ambrose goes on to ponder the issue of whether paradise is a temporary place to house the good until the Last Judgment, or heaven itself. Here he again takes an allegorical tack by conceiving paradise as a short-term station after death. He draws upon Plato, the Fourth Book of Ezra, and passages from Song of Songs to argue that death is not something to be feared for the pure of heart at least, but something to be embraced because it releases the soul from the fetters of the body. After leaving the body, the soul—metaphorically a "sister spouse" united in matrimony with the body—does not immediately descend into heaven but is suspended for a while in a garden of righteousness, an interpretation that he gleans from the Song of Songs:

> I have come into my garden, my sister, my bride; I have gathered my myrrh with my spice, I have eaten my honeycomb and my honey, I have drunk my wine and my milk. Eat, O friends, and drink, drink your fill, O lovers.[29]

Paradise for the pious Christian is the place where one awaits the reckoning of the Last Judgment—one of the "many rooms" of "my Father's house" to which Jesus alluded in the Gospel of John.[30]

Augustine, a student of Ambrose, was next to consider the issue. During his stay in Milan, Augustine converted to Christianity and wrote a treatise on music—the first of the seven liberal arts that he intended to situate within a Christian framework. In drawing upon the Pythagorean and Platonic traditions, he argued that music could very much affect the soul, and that these changes were physiologically induced by certain numerical ratios.[31] Shortly after completing the treatise, he had his own Pauline calling to ministry at his mother's deathbed, wherein the two collectively had a vision of paradise. In 391, he returned to Africa, sold his inheritance. and founded a monastery—reportedly "in a garden that Valerius [the bishop of Hippo] had given me"—to which he later added a church, cloister, exedra, and portico.[32]

No problem perplexed Augustine's theological mind more than the meaning of paradise. He wrote no fewer than three books on Genesis, in addition to other extended commentaries. And although he consistently defended a literal interpretation of the garden, he clearly preferred an allegorical one. In *Confessions*, for instance, he interpreted each act of creation (the sky, the plants, the water, and creatures) symbolically. Light, for instance, becomes the enlightenment that the human soul receives, the sky becomes a skin that unfurls as a scroll with God's message, and the newly created birds are the messengers that spread the word of God.[33] In his most focused writing on this subject, *The Literal Meaning of Genesis*, he points out that there are two interpretations, literal and figurative, but that he prefers a third—which is to allow both. In this way the tree of life can be read symbolically and literally, and the river that flowed out from Eden actually "watered paradise, that is, all the beautiful and fruit-bearing trees which shaded all the land of that region."[34]

Augustine's view of Genesis generally held sway down to Aquinas, but equally important is the view of paradise he expounded on in his *City of God*—twenty-two books that dominated Christian theology well into the Middle Ages. The impulse for the book was Alaric's sack of Rome in 410 and the collapse of the Western Roman Empire. It was only a century earlier—with Constantine's Edict of Milan in 313—that Christianity had been legalized as a religion, but the general antipathy of early Christian sects toward Greco-Roman culture had hindered its advance within literate circles. Augustine was the exception in that he was a great admirer of Plato, and he believed that the Greek philosopher, on a trip to Egypt, had listened to the prophet Jeremiah, or at least had been enlightened by reading the Judaic prophetical scriptures.[35] In *City of God*, Augustine sought to situate the church within the West's philosophical tradition, while at the same time to contest the belief of many Roman exiles that Christianity had contributed to the fall of the empire. His approach was to construct two cities: the human city and the city of God. One is the city of the body with its mortality and passions; the other is the chaste city of the eternal soul. One is the city of litigation, wars, suffering, and physical pain; the other is the city of love and obedience, serene enjoyment and bliss, whose only treasury will be that of truth. The earthly city is built for the glory of men, whereas the heavenly city is built for the human soul to prove its worthiness to reside with God for eternity. Augustine does not say anything about the physical fabric of the city of men, except to say that it will always be characterized by human limitations. In this way, "true happiness" is unattainable in our present life, although a lesser form of felicity can indeed be gained with spiritual effort. If a transcendent paradise in either its natural or built form were to be found on earth, then it must be sought within a designed community of like-minded people (as Plato had legislated) articulated through its Christian monuments of celebration. Augustine, in these early and less affluent days of the church's formation, did not address the nature of these buildings.

The Monastic Way

Although Augustine upon his return to Hippo had founded a monastery, he was by no means the first to seek a divinely sanctioned paradise in this way. Hinduists, Buddhists, and Taoists had sought a physical and social separation from worldly affairs. The eremitic tradition of Judaic culture goes back to the ninth century BC, when the prophet Elijah visited the desert to hear the voice of God. The cenobitic or monastic line of Judaism was represented by the sect of Essenes, the self-exiled authors or collectors of the Dead Sea Scrolls who founded the community of Qumran. The first of the Christian "Desert Fathers" was Paul of Thebes who, in the third century, fled to a cave in the desert of the upper Nile, where he lived his ascetic life to the ripe age of 113 years. His appearance in a dream to St. Anthony, as the latter's biographer Athanasius reports, led the future father of Christian monasticism to seek out his counsel in the desert, after which he too sold his worldly goods and apportioned his money among the poor. He then retired to the desert west of Alexandria, where, with his later follower Amun, he founded the three famed monasteries of Nitria, Kellia, and Scetis. Eventually, Anthony sought a quieter existence on a mountain near the Nile, and later still along the Gulf of Suez, where he practiced his philosophy of manual labor by weaving rush mats and attending to his garden.

All of these early efforts were largely outside of clerical overview, but by the mid-fourth century, the coordination of monastic life became inevitable with the creation of theological councils and an ecclesiastical hierarchy. The writings of Basil the Great, himself a long-practicing ascetic and founder of a monastic settlement as well as the archbishop of Caesarea, argued for the need to balance the ministry of the church's teachings with the desire of some for a life apart from worldly affairs. One of the church fathers with whom Augustine was in early contact was the scholar Jerome, the translator of the vulgate and Hebrew bibles. Jerome was born along the eastern Adriatic coast and studied in Rome, Constantinople, and Jerusalem. He was ordained a priest in 365, but with the stipulation he maintain his separation from worldly affairs. Yet five years later he was appointed the bishop of Antioch and undertook the ministries of attending to the poor. After another stay in Rome, Jerome returned to Antioch and later went to Alexandria, where he became aware of the monastic efforts of St. Anthony. After a visit to the monastery at Nitria, he settled in Palestine in 388, where he lived the rest of his life in seclusion in a cave outside of Bethlehem. There he worked on his writings and translations, and it was there that Augustine, through correspondence, sought his advice on his own exegesis of scriptural issues.

The monastic movement came into regular organization in the fifth century, with the first issue being the determination of its organizational framework and specific mission. Two distinct models had shown themselves. One was the creation of a secluded or walled-off existence, expressly a "paradise" on earth, from which one could achieve personal salvation alone or in communion with others. These monasteries and nunneries were seen as anointed places situated between heaven and earth, not only cut off from the outside world but tightly regulated with a strict regimen of prayer, fasting, sexual abstinence, and labor. Early monks and nuns of these orders generally modeled themselves on the eremitic example of St. Anthony, Jesus, and John the Baptist. The fourth-century ascetic John Chrysostom praised those who have fled to the wilderness from urban marketplaces and the tumults of men, who "know no worldly sorrows, no grief, no care so great, no dangers, no plots, no envy, no jealousy, no lawless lusts, nor any other thing of this kind." They now converse with groves, mountains, and springs in solitude, much as Adam did before his fall, when he tended the paradise of Eden:

> Had he no worldly care? But neither have these. Did he talk to God with a pure conscience? This also do these; or rather they have a greater confidence than he, inasmuch as they enjoy ever greater grace by the supply of the Spirit.[36]

The second monastic model, the predominant one in later medieval times, was to remain in relative proximity to towns and cities and engage in church functions, such as administering to social and spiritual needs. Two of the later monastic orders—the Dominicans and Franciscans—sought these goals in different ways. In 1216, Dominic de Guzman received the papal bull for the Dominicans, who initially concentrated their efforts in university towns such as Segovia, Paris, and Bologna. During these same years, Francis of Assisi left his hermitic life to found one of the largest and most successful of the mendicant orders in caring for the sick and indigent. The Franciscans expanded rapidly and extended their reach to the steppes of Genghis Khan.

The guiding "rule" initially directing the majority of monastic orders was set down 500 years earlier by Benedict of Nursia. Born in 480, he lived his early years as a hermit in a cave outside of Sabiaco, Italy, where he also founded several monasteries. Later, he shifted his base to Monte Cassino in southern Italy. The Benedictine rule, as later written down by Pope Gregory, consisted of seventy-three chapters, which covered every aspect of monastic life—from enclosed enclaves to the renunciation of property, strict obedience to the abbot, near silence of the monks, regular fasting, manual labor, and extreme humility. The articles also prescribed the Christian virtues of prayer, practicing charity, loving one's enemies, and accommodating the sick, indigent, pilgrims, and guests. It regulated the monk's daily routine of prayer, manual or intellectual labor, and sleeping. The supreme abbot was elected to specified requirements:

> An abbot who is worthy to preside over a monastery ought always to remember what he is called and to justify his title by his deeds. For he is deemed in the monastery the representative of Christ . . . and so an abbot ought not to teach, establish, or order anything contrary to the spirit of the Lord's revealed will, but let his commandments and teaching, as being the leaven of divine justice, sprinkle the minds of the disciples.[37]

When Charlemagne assumed the crown of the Holy Roman Empire in 800, the Benedictine Order was preeminent. The emperor himself created over 200 new monasteries, which, because monks were also coming from noble families, were increasingly incorporated into the political structure. The ideal of an isolated monastic paradise has passed this order, as their properties and edifices grew in size and in many cases sustained nearby villages. The largest complex in France was Cluny in southern Burgundy, founded in 910 by Berno on land granted to him by the Duke of Aquitaine, William I. The initial plan was loosely based on the plan of the Swiss monastery of St. Gall, which dates from around 830 and has one of the few surviving artifacts documenting monastery design. Cluny's architecture was initially modest, consisting of a simple church, attached cloister, chapter house, dormitories, refectory, and abbot's house. Following the destruction of the monastery by Hungarian raiding parties in the mid-tenth century, Cluny enlarged its church with a choir and two towers. Beginning in 1088, however, Hugh of Semur started a third phase of construction that would last forty-two years. The size of the monastery expanded both its wealth and its population to over 1,000 members—a vast commercial enterprise by medieval standards.

Spiritual pushback became inevitable. In 1098, Robert of Molesme led a group of twenty-one monks out of a Benedictine monastery to found a new abbey at Cîteaux. The goal of the Cistercians was to return to the rule of Benedict with a renewed focus on spirituality. Bernard of Clairvaux became the face of the new movement when he joined Cîteaux in 1113 with thirty of his followers. Two years later the charismatic leader founded another new abbey at Clairvaux, and shortly thereafter another at Fontenay—the last an architectural masterpiece of understatement. The contrast between the churches at Cluny III (one of the largest churches in Europe) and Fontenay could not be more vivid, and the difference goes well beyond the scale of the buildings. In an *Apologia* penned to William, Abbot of St. Thierry, Bernard railed against the opulent lifestyles and laxity of the Benedictines, their lack of concern for the poor, and the extravagant height, width, and length of their churches. Above all, he lamented the secular and "deformed beauty" of their cloister decorations: carved figures of lions, centaurs, apes, serpents, and other figurative beasts of the high Romanesque style. "Good God!" he says in conclusion. "If one is not ashamed of the absurdity, why is one not at least troubled at the expense?"[38]

The architecture of the church, cloister, and few ancillary buildings at Fontenay, built under Bernard's direction, shun any form of ornament. It is through their spartan simplicity—the cloister embellished only with a garden and well in the center, the bare refectory in which the monks took their meals, the stone floors on which they slept—that these reformed monasteries aspired to be spiritual paradises. Bernard, in fact, referred to his monasteries as a *paradisus claustralis* (cloister of paradise), the sanctified and physically isolated world of the spirit as it prepares for the journey to heavenly Jerusalem. His success as a reformer can be measured by the fact that 280 Cistercian monasteries were constructed in his lifetime.

One means to enact this desired spiritual awakening, Bernard believed, was through music and architecture. The Cistercian leader was convinced, like Augustine before him, that the power of music with its simple musical harmonies could be translated into beautiful visual forms. The ratios that he used in the layout of his vaulted churches were 1:2, 2:3, and 3:4, or the musical intervals of

ILLUSTRATION 4.3   Abbey of Fontenay, 1118, Marmagne, Burgundy, France.

Source: Photo by Myrabella. Wikimedia CC BY-SA 4.0.

the octave, fifth, and fourth. At Fontenay, for example, the length of the church is twice the width of the transepts, and the width of the nave is twice that of the side aisles. The chapter house, great hall, and refectory were laid out in square modules. Bernard also restricted the use of natural light to the area around the altar and indirect nave lighting from one side. His plain interiors, even in the daytime, have the quality of quasi–darkness, a darkness dramatized by evening candlelit rituals. Acoustic qualities were of paramount importance to Cistercian monks with their Gregorian chants, the monophonic interweaving of modes and cadences to achieve special acoustical effects. Many larger churches at this period had reverberation times of around ten seconds, which demanded a slow and layered phrasing of tones. Bernard or his architects sought the same effect with relatively small churches, seemingly through their proportions, surfaces, and barrel vaults. The one design flaw at Fontenay—the straight wall behind the altar—was corrected in later churches with a curved apse. The monastery church at Thoronet in Provence, started in the last quarter of the twelfth century, achieved a remarkable reverberation time of fourteen seconds in the low and middle frequencies.[39] It later became the model for Le Corbusier's monastery at La Tourette.

   With the churches at Clairvaux, Fontenay, and Thoronet, we are looking at a time when the purpose of architecture was not to contain space but to modulate or exaggerate the auditory and celestial experience of the divine within carefully designed atmospheric conditions. The monks participating in these spiritual chants during their evening or nighttime prayers most likely experienced their songs not as emanating from an earthly place but as dramatic overtures issuing from the celestial garden of paradise itself. And perhaps this was not an accidental discovery. The first abbot of Thoronet was a certain Folquet de Marseille, whose musical fame Dante knew well enough to place this once celebrated troubadour in the third heaven, the sphere of Venus.[40] Dante himself must have suspected his divine powers.

Eyes of Ravenna

From its inauguration by Constantine in 330 to its sacking by Islamic armies in 1453, Constantinople (present-day Istanbul), straddling the continents of Europe and Asia, shone as the cultural capital of the classical world. It was on the Asia side that Constantine defeated his imperial rival and united the Eastern and Western Roman Empires, and his new capital would soon become a place of drama, intrigue, theology, scholarship, and architectural showpieces. Before his death in 337, he enticed many Roman patricians to move to the new city. A builder, like Hadrian before him, he endowed the city with a great hippodrome, numerous baths, churches, temples, and an enchanting sprinkling of gardens. When still seated in Rome, the Roman protector of Christianity had commissioned the Basilica of St. Peter's over the site of the saint's burial place. From Constantinople, he commissioned the Church of the Holy Sepulcher around the presumed tomb of Christ in Jerusalem. In Bethlehem, he anointed Christ's birthplace with the Church of the Nativity. In his own namesake city, he began work on the Church of the Holy Apostles, to which he attached his own tomb. He believed himself to be the thirteenth apostle of Christ—an odd inflation of self-esteem for someone who, among other things, executed his eldest son, drowned his wife, and did not commit to baptism until his deathbed. Yet the city prospered during his reign, struggled for a while afterwards, and then—over the reign of 90 emperors and 123 patriarchs—rose to become the West's largest and wealthiest city.

It was during the reign of Justinian, who assumed the crown in 527, that the magnificence of the empire truly began to unfold. Prior to his ascension, this adopted heir of the previous emperor had caused quite a stir by being granted a special dispensation to marry Theodora, a stage performer of popular renown. It seems to have been a genuine love affair that rarely comes along with a crown, and she too would prove to be an able and much-accomplished empress. Over his thirty-eight-year reign, Justinian defeated the Vandals and Ostrogoths, restored Dalmatia, Sicily, parts of Spain and Italy to imperial holdings, and twice fended off the Persians to the south. His most notable architectural achievement was the Church of the Hagia Sophia, or "Holy Wisdom." No church of its size had ever been attempted before: a central dome 164 feet tall and of over 100 feet in diameter, joined at two ends by similarly dimensioned half domes, and the latter in turn supported at their sides by four apses and rectangular walled areas. The boldness of the design, however, aimed a little too high, at least for this particular earthquake zone, as parts of it soon collapsed and it has been repaired on three other occasions. None of this detracts from the grandeur of its inspiration—the refined detailing of its filigree Corinthian capitals or its walls and ceilings originally incrusted with gold mosaics and colorful marbles.

Yet the extraordinarily high artistic standards of the Justinian era can be better studied in another fabled byzantine city, Ravenna, Italy. Beginning in 402, Ravenna served as the regal capital of the Western Roman Empire for much of two centuries. It claimed this distinction because fifth-century Rome had been detached from its eastern defender by invasions. The Visigoths came in 410 and plundered the city. The Huns visited Italy forty-two years later, and the Vandals from the African coastline again sacked Rome in 455. The Ostrogoth and Arian Christian warlord Theodoric, with a wink and a nod from Constantinople, took possession of Ravenna in 489 and sagely ruled a large part of Italy until his death in 526. Arianism was a sect of the Christian church stemming from a theological dispute going back to the third-century priest in Alexandria, who had argued that Christ, as the son of God, was not one and the same but subordinate to his father. The belief was condemned by the First Council of Nicaea in 325, convened by Constantine, but it continued as a prominent sect of early Christianity. Theodoric, in any case, gave nominal allegiance to the Eastern Empire, but more to our purposes, he built lavishly. He drained the marshes around the city, improved the port, repaired aqueducts, and built an Arian Cathedral, Arian Baptistery, his own palace, and his mausoleum. His most important work was the church of Sant' Apollinare Nuovo with its many beautiful mosaics still in place. Ravenna, then a city of a mere 10,000 people, would within a few decades became a veritable museum of art.

Yet Ravenna has other historical charms. Dante lies buried in the graveyard beside the Basilica of San Francesco. Lord Byron made the city his home in the early nineteenth century, and Oscar Wilde, in a poetic recital given at Oxford's Sheldonian Theatre in 1878, lamented the city's fallen splendor:

> But thou, Ravenna, better loved than all
> Thy ruined palaces are but a pall
> That hides thy fallen greatness![41]

Wilde was also a great admirer of Sarah Bernhardt, who visited Ravenna in 1884. She did so to view the mosaics of the Empress Theodora and thereby design the costumes for her rendition of Theodora in Victorien Sardou's highly successful production of the play of the same title. Wilde had seen Bernhardt's earlier performance as Lady Macbeth, which inspired him to write *Salomé* in French, which he dedicated to the actress. Yet certainly one of the more curious travelers to Ravenna was Carl Jung, the Swiss psychologist. In one of his first bouts with his own unconscious, he came to the city in 1913, where he "fell into a strange mood" and was "deeply stirred" by the Mausoleum of Galla Placidia.[42] One of Jung's interpreters, Jay Sherry, associates Jung's experience with Bernhardt, Salomé, Hypatia, Elijah, and the New Testament figure of Philemon, who once received a letter from the apostle Paul.[43] In an image painted by Jung in his *Red Book*, he portrays Philemon perched atop a small model of the Mausoleum of Theodoric, behind which are rondels in the deep blue sky—similar to those found in the Mausoleum of Galla Placidia.[44]

The so-called Mausoleum of Galla Placidia is also a more-than-respectable gateway into the beatific world of Ravenna. Galla herself was a historical figure cut from gilded cloth. She was the daughter of the last emperor of the united Roman Empire, Theodosius the Great, who died in 395. She was also the half-sister and wife to two other emperors, and later, upon her return to Ravenna in 425, she became the imperial *Augusta* and regent to her son and future emperor Valentinian III. There, Galla commissioned the church of Santa Croce, and she later added to it a cruciform chapel or oratory, which is known as her mausoleum. It contains the oldest and some of the best mosaics in Ravenna, which collectively create, as Jung discovered, a quasi-mystical atmosphere of blue light that resonates from the garden mosaics and figures of various apostles. As Gillian Mackie has observed, the fifth-century Christians appropriated the Persian word "paradise" to refer to a mausoleum attached to a church, because the chamber was presumed to be a garden of water, trees, and flowers, where the souls of the dead await the Second Coming.[45]

The ultramarine vaulted ceiling of the central dome is resplendent with gilded, eight-petaled flowers, and the figural lunettes depicting apostles within the supporting drums are similarly cast against a deep blue background. What is most striking, however, are the barrel-vaulted ceilings of the four arms of the plan, three of which are outfitted with sarcophagi. The two vaulted ceilings of the east and west arms are articulated with conventional floral vignettes, but the other two—one now generally referred to as the "Garden of Eden"—are more abstract and tapestry-like, yet until recently they have received little commentary. Their patterns consist of stylized floral motifs: two variations on rosettes and a third a daisy-like flower, the motif that Jung found so appealing. One historian has gone so far as to interpret the motifs as "a microcosm of the Earthly Paradise."[46]

Theodoric's death in 526 preceded by a year Justinian's ascendency to the throne. Although the new emperor was initially occupied with wars elsewhere, the Arian sect in Ravenna remained a problem to resolve. Justinian did so by having his general Belisarius take the city from the Goth Vitiges in 540. Two major churches were then under construction. One was the Basilica of Sant'Apollinare in Classe, the largest of the early Christian basilicas. Its wide nave is notable for the sage-green veining

ILLUSTRATION 4.4   Empress Theodora and Attendants, Basilica of San Vitale, Ravenna, AD 547.

Source: Photo by Petar Milošević. Wikimedia CC BY-SA.

of its marble columns and for its spectacular apsidal vault featuring the transfiguration of Christ. The other church is arguably the greatest artistic production of the entire Byzantine era: the Basilica of San Vitale. Justinian assumed control of the city just in time to be incorporated into its brilliant mosaic fabric.

San Vitale had been started by Bishop Ecclesius in 526 and was in its final stages of completion. The tall octagonal structure with a ground-story ambulatory and second-story gallery—the subsequent model for Charlemagne's palatine chapel at Aachen—at first seems to dwarf the visitor because of its tall and relatively modest central space. And the blue haze that "deeply stirred" Jung in the Placidia Mausoleum here assumes a distinct Edenic aura due to the green-and-golden shroud of its mosaics. The brilliance of mosaics and marbles is everywhere to behold, transporting one seemingly to another and more perfect world. In moving toward the altar, one's gaze is first directed to the hemispheric mosaic in the chancel apse, in which a beardless Christ, accompanied by angels and saints, sits on a globe in the Garden of Eden with its four stylized rivers. It is only when one steps into the ambulatory behind the altar that the two upper side panels accompanying the main mosaic become fully visible. They depict on one side Emperor Justinian and on the other Empress Theodora. Both bring offerings to the church and both are accompanied by their imperial retinues.

Their mesmerizing power comes from their purposely large eyes, evincing power, and a tinge of anxiety as well as distant serenity. The beautiful Theodora in her embroidered royal robes and heavily pearled diadem and collar (silhouetted with a halo) poses not deific. She is human—all too human, sufficiently so to transport us into another more sensual yet no less divine world of Byzantium. Naturally, she stands in a tastefully outfitted garden pavilion with two priestly officials and her ladies-in-waiting, the latter dressed in brilliant dresses with red slippers. Her penetrating and centrally focused eyes do not so much stare down upon us they allow us to read another human soul with all of our terrestrial hopes, fears, and pleasures. The artists of these San Vitale mosaic panels have presented us a moment of profound inspiration, one that is rare even in the world of high art. When one gazes into the eyes of these persons depicted almost 1,500 years ago, one is enchanted with a delight similar to what must have visited Oscar Wilde in the 1880s, when, from his Parisian theater box, he viewed the posed and similarly adored Sarah Bernhardt in her production of *Theo-dora*. Eyes can be paradisiacal when they lure us into another world whose only limits are human imagination.

City of Light

Mont-Saint-Michel, with the ruins of its once-proud abbey church, is one of France's most recognizable landmarks, one to which tourists throng every year. The first church on the rocky outcrop preceded Charlemagne and was constructed in the early eighth century. Monks inhabited the site in the following century, at least until the Vikings captured the mount in 847. The monks eventually returned, but by the next century they had succumbed to a less-than-pious life of comfortable affluence. Toward the end of the tenth century, Richard I, the Duke of Normandy, evicted the monks and handed the abbey over to the Benedictine Order. Around 1020, his son Richard II commissioned work on a new abbey church, and its four central piers, supporting the massive tower that today still dominates the island's silhouette, were started around 1060. This was just a few years before Richard's grandson, William I, led his Norman army across the English Channel to conquer England.

Mont-Saint-Michel occupies a similarly elevated position in the account of Henry Adams, the nineteenth-century polymath who chose both the abbey and the contemporary composition of the *Song of Roland* as the opening themes for his *Mont-Saint-Michel and Chartres*. Although not all architectural historians have followed Adams in the high esteem that he held for this particular abbey, there are insights in his literary and historical tract that have eluded others. In suggesting a tourist route for his American readers, Adams casts Mont-Saint-Michel and Chartres as two poles along an evolutionary line that he—in a disinterested, nineteenth-century manner—traces through the Romanesque churches at Coutances, Bayeux, Caen, Rouen, and Nantes. One should, he believed, view and study all before setting one foot in the Gothic masterpiece of Notre-Dame de Chartres.

If the French architect and historian Eugène-Emmanuel Viollet-le-Duc (Adams's factual guide) had argued that Norman churches lacked the grace of proportions, Adams excuses this shortcoming because Norman architecture was honest, bold, large in spirit and scale, and unapologetically masculine, like the Conqueror William himself. Yet the cathedral at Chartres, in the judgment of Adams, offers a different sentiment, a softer but no less ardent expression of scholastic humanism. The abbey church on the mount was dedicated to Michael the Archangel, who mercilessly dispatches evildoers to the brimstone of hell. The delicately feminine features of Mary's visage in the sculpture and glass work at Chartres, as personified in her magnificent twelfth-century chancel window "La Belle Verrière," projects not fear but the hope of a personal mediator, someone approachable and able to hear our supplications. Through this cult of Marianism, which pervaded both the Cistercian abbeys and urban cathedrals of the twelfth and thirteenth centuries, many believed that they would find salvation and gain entry to paradise. The Cistercian connection with Mary was still strong almost three centuries later when Dante, after entering the Empyrean of paradise's tenth heaven, drafted Bernard of Clairvaux to serve as his personal intercessor to the Virgin Mary so that he too might view the Eternal Light.[47]

The beginning of Gothic architecture is typically defined by the engineering innovations of the cross-ribbed vault used in conjunction with the pointed arch and flying buttress, which all but obviates the style's deeper cultural or emotional impact.[48] Others have attempted to define Gothic architecture through its iconography or didactic exposition of biblical parables. The thirteenth-century Bishop of Mende, William Durandus, by contrast, saw the design of churches more generally as the ordering of symbolic elements. He compared the layout of a church to the human body, in which the chancel is the head, the transepts the arms, and the nave the trunk of the body. The four walls represent the doctrines of the four evangelists, the foundational floor signifies the church's faith, and the roof signifies its charity. The glass windows are the Holy Scriptures, the piers are bishops and doctors, and the entrance door symbolizes Christ. Durandus was not entirely pedantic. He repeatedly refers to the church as the "Temple of Jerusalem," and on one occasion even equates the church's cloister with "the porch of Solomon's Temple" and the "celestial Paradise."[49]

It is with this last association that we have our first insight into Gothic theology, and the inspirational prophet in this regard is once again John of the Book of Revelation. Consider this passage describing New Jerusalem:

> The wall [of the city] was made of jasper, and the city of pure gold, as pure as glass. The foundations of the city walls were decorated with every kind of precious stone. The first foundation was jasper, the second sapphire, the third calcedony, the fourth emerald, the fifth sardonyx, the sixth carnelian, the seventh chrysolite, the eight beryl, the ninth topaz, the tenth chrysoprase, the eleventh jacinth, and the twelfth amethyst. The twelve gates were twelve pearls, each made of a single pearl. The great street of the city was of pure gold, like transparent glass.[50]

Abbot Suger was the organizational spirit behind the Abbey Church of St. Denis, the first Gothic church begun in 1135. In chronicling his efforts, he clearly draws on this passage. Describing the golden altar panel in the upper choir, for instance, he reports matter-of-factly that he ornamented this panel with "a multifarious wealth of precious gems, hyacinths, rubies, sapphires, emeralds and topazes, and also an array of different large pearls—[a wealth] as great as we had never anticipated to find."[51] Consider also his description of the cross of St. Eloy placed on the altar:

> *Every precious stone was thy covering, the sardius, the topaz, and the jasper, the chrysolite, and the onyx,*
> *and the beryl, the sapphire, and the carbuncle, and the emerald.* . . . Thus when—out of my delight
> in the beauty of the house of God—the loveliness of the many-colored gems had called me
> away from external cares, and worthy meditation has induced me to reflect, transferring that
> which is material to that which is immaterial, on the diversity of the sacred virtues; then it
> seems to me that I see myself dwelling, as it were, in some strange region of the universe
> which neither exists entirely in the slime of the earth nor entirely in the purity of Heaven,
> and that, by the grace of God, I can be transported from the inferior to the higher world in
> an anagogical manner.[52]

Erwin Panofsky, the first modern art historian to translate and comment on these passages of Suger, attributed his fondness for gems (in the age of St. Bernard's condemnation of all church ornaments) to Suger's reading of Pseudo-Dionysius the Areopagite, a fifth- or sixth-century Syrian writer of mystical and Neoplatonic persuasion. In medieval times, he was identified as Dionysius the Areopagite, a first-century convert of the apostle Paul and presumed to be the first bishop of Athens. To make matters worse, through what seems to what seems to have been an erroneous coding of his manuscript, Pseudo-Dionysius also came to be conflated with St. Denis, the third-century martyr and bishop of Paris and the namesake of Suger's Abbey.[53] Thus, through a series of circumstances, the theology of Gothic architecture—its sensuous and mystical play with color and light—may have arisen in part through the conflation of three individuals from three different centuries!

It is with the Cathedral of Chartres that this consummation emerges in its full force of attraction. The town's first church of the fourth century was burned to the ground by the Duke of Aquitaine in 743, and the second church suffered a similar fate at the hands of piratical Danes in 858. A third church also fell victim to fire in 1020, by which date the cathedral school, under the leadership of Bishop Fulbert, had emerged as one of the leading intellectual centers of Europe. Its humanist focus centered on the seven liberal arts overlaid with a prominent Platonic outlook. After the fire, Fulbert led the construction of a much grander cathedral, although still Romanesque in style. Another fire damaged the western end of the building in 1134, leading to a rebuilding—coinciding with the building of St. Denis—the latter now evolving into the mature Gothic style. At Chartres, however, this march was delayed by the fire of 1194, which destroyed most of the town along with the cathedral. Only parts of the crypt and the western wall survived. It was then that a rapid (and what contemporaries called a miraculous) building campaign ensued, funded by European monarchs and the labors of many masons and peasants, who erected and roofed the present building fabric over the next twenty-five years. The beatific finishing touches were applied soon thereafter.

What many visitors to the cathedral first admire are the sculptures of the three portals, the royal portal at the western end and the much-expanded portals of the southern and northern transepts. Those of the royal portal, thematically dedicated to Christ, are the oldest and date from the mid-twelfth century, or around the time that Suger was dedicating the Abbey of St. Denis. They are notable for having an unnatural or unearthly thinness in the way their stretched bodies, garments,

ILLUSTRATION 4.5   Central Bay of the Royal Portal, Cathedral Notre-Dame des Chartres, 1145–55.

Source: Photo by Andreas F. Borchert. CC BY-SA 4.0.

and unstable feet are worked into the vertical lines of the Gothic fabric, a fault that not a few historians have censured. Others dispute such a reading. In a talk given to the South Kensington Museum in 1858, John Ruskin faulted the statues' "exaggerated thinness of body and stiffness of attitude," but he then goes on to offer an interpretation that perhaps draws close to the Pseudo-Dionysian mysticism of the twelfth century:

> but they are noble faults, and give the statues a strange look of forming part of the very building itself, and sustaining it—not like the Greek caryatid, without effort—but as if all that was silent, and stern and withdrawn apart, and stiffened in chill of heart against the terror of earth, had passed into a shape of eternal marble; and thus the Ghost had given, to bear up the pillars of the church on earth, all the patient and expectant nature that it needed nor more in heaven. This is the transcendental view of the meaning of these sculptures.[54]

The works of the expanded north and south porches, each with vast populations of sculptures situated within three portals, were chiseled some seventy-five years later and are far more naturalistic in appearance. Some, in fact, are among the greatest artistic productions of the Middle Ages. Henry Adams was particularly attracted to the north porch, which "belonged to the Virgin" and whose attributes of femininity, grace, and beauty he went to great lengths to exalt. "The glory of Mary was not one of terror," he notes at one point, "and her Porch contains no appeal to any emotion but those of her perfect grace. If we were to stay here for weeks, we should find only this idea worked into every detail."[55]

Yet the exterior of Chartres, with its 2,000 pieces of sculpture, is only the sanctuary's lithic wrapping to a Christmas present, as it were, because it is when one enters what was then called the "door of paradise" that one experiences the full transplantation to the immaterial or "higher world" that earlier transfixed Suger. If churches in early Christian as well as in Gothic times were often referred to as "New Jerusalem" or "City of God," the Cathedral of Notre-Dame de Chartres may have been one of the few exceptions. At least one French king referred to it as the "celestial court of the Mother of God," the heavenly place in France where she resided on earth.[56] The ethereal medium to achieve this aim was the color of light. The bold decision of the architect of Chartres—allowed by the structural artifice of doubled flying buttresses—was to do away with the interior second-story gallery and open the entire upper half of the nave to glass: two tall lancet windows and a rose in each structural bay. This artifice thereby doubled the amount of light introduced into the church, both through the first-story aisle walls and the enclosing nave wall above. And this innovation does not take into account Chartres's three blissful and grand rose windows, one in its western entrance wall and the other two at the facing of its transepts.

The glass, of course, was stained glass, that which Suger elevated to a high art at St. Denis, but which the glass masters at Chartres (the only French cathedral today with original glass intact) seem to have been taken to the pitch of perfection. The glass was first tinted in its cooking pot with the addition of metallic oxides, then later painted with a vitreous pigment to add nuance or detail to the composition, which even a black-and-white photograph captures.[57] Yet it is through the atmospheric effects of color that the cathedral comes to life. The art historian Hans Jantzen has described the interior of Chartres as imbued with a "reddish, violet light." When combined with the intensity of tones and the audacious spatial dimension of the now-softened architecture, it becomes a "supernatural" light, invoking "a feeling of having 'overcome the world' of material things."[58] In a similar way, Otto von Simson has argued that the guiding inspiration behind Gothic architecture was nothing less than to represent a "supernatural reality," to have its sanctuary serve as the "threshold to heaven."[59]

Viollet-le-Duc, who in the 1830s made annual visits to Chartres to record its every detail, in part ascribes the secret of the cathedral's glass work to the "limpid blue" that is often used as

ILLUSTRATION 4.6   Notre-Dame de la Belle Verrière, c. 1180.

Source: Photo by MOSSOT. Wikimedia CC BY-SA 3.0.

a background, which, he argued, sets off or endows all of the other colors—the reds, yellows, greens, and whites—with a "luminous quality" through their harmonious proportional composition.[60] His example is the famous "Tree of Jesse," a twelfth-century glass composition in one of the western lancet windows below the rose. The central panels, ascending up to Mary and Christ at the top, are all treated with this blue background, and the other colors play against it. Yet every rule has its exceptions. In "La Belle-Verrière," the twelfth-century window to which we referred earlier, this same blue is used for Mary's halo and gown, the last of which frames the child Jesus in his brownish, deep-red clothing. Here, however, the very successful background to these figures is brilliantly rendered in a luminescent scarlet that seems to emanate from another world. It is a fool's task to attempt to do justice to the polychromatic splendor of Chartres, which can only be experienced in person. Perhaps Adams best summed up this heavenly city's atmosphere by noting that this court of Mary contains "all the hues of Paradise."[61] It is difficult to dispute this assessment.

Notes

1. Among many other studies, see Arthur and Elena George, *The Mythology of Eden* (Lanham, MD: Hamilton Books, 2014); Margaret Barker, *The Gate of Heaven: The History and Symbolism of the Temple of Jerusalem* (Sheffield: Sheffield Phoenix Press, 2008); Israel Finkelstein and Neil Asher Silberman, *The Bible Unearthed: Archaeology's New Vision of Ancient Israel and the Origin of Its Sacred Texts* (New York: Simon & Schuster, 2001); and Dinah Dye, *The Temple Revealed in the Garden: Priests and Kings* (n.p.: Foundations in Torah Publishers, 2015).
2. Wayne T. Pitard, "Before Israel: Syria-Palestine in the Bronze Age," in Michael Coogan (ed.), *The Oxford History of the Biblical World* (Oxford: Oxford University Press, 1998), 33–77.
3. Ecclesiastes 2:4–6.
4. Exodus 25:8–9.
5. Flavius Josephus, *Antiquities of the Jews*, 4, VIII:5. Cited from *The Works of Flavius Josephus*, trans. by William Whiston (Philadelphia, PA: John C. Winston Co., n.d.).
6. 1 Chronicles 28:19.
7. 2 Chronicles 2:13–14.
8. 1 Kings 6:1–35. Psalms 92:12 makes reference to a palm and cedar tree planted in the house of the Lord.
9. Psalms 48:1–2.
10. 1 Kings 8:21.
11. Jeremiah 1:1. See also 2 Kings 24:13–14 and 2 Baruch 3:4.2–7.
12. Nehemiah 1:1–4.
13. Ezekiel 36:33–35.
14. Ibid., 47:12.
15. Haggai 2:3.
16. Josephus, *Antiquities of the Jews* (note 5), 11:4.2.
17. Ibid., 11:8.5.
18. Josephus, *Antiquities of the Jews* (note 5), 5:5.6.
19. Ibid., 5:5.4.
20. Josephus, *Antiquities of the Jews* (note 5), 3:6.4.
21. Revelation 21:1–4.
22. Josephus, *Antiquities of the Jews* (note 5), 1.3.
23. *The Book of Enoch*, 5:22.1–13. Cited from the translation of George H. Schodde (Andover: Warren F. Draper, 1882).
24. Philo Judaeus, "About the Planting of Noah," in C.D. Yonge (trans.), *Works of Philo Judaeus* (London: Henry G. Bohn, 1854), 1:422–4.
25. Revelation 2:7, 21:11, and 22:2.
26. Paul, 2 Corinthians 12:3–4.
27. "The Vision of Paul the Apostle 22." www.gnosis.org/library/visionpaul.htm. Accessed February 2021.
28. *The Father of the Church: Saint Ambrose, Hexameron, Paradise, and Cain and Abel*, trans. by John J. Savage (Washington, DC: Catholic University, 2003), 294.
29. "Death as a Good," in Michael P. McHugh (trans.), *The Fathers of the Church: Saint Ambrose, Seven Exegetical Works* (Washington, DC: Catholic University, 2003), 85–6. The citation is from *Song of Songs* is 5:1.
30. Gospel of John 14:2–4.
31. Brian Brennan, "Augustine's De Musica," *Vigiliae Christianae* 42:3 (September 1988), 267–81.
32. Marie Luise Gothein, *A History of Garden Art: From the Earliest Times to the Present Day*, trans. by Laura Archer-Hind (Cambridge: Cambridge University Press, 2014), 1:171.
33. Augustine, *Confessions*, 13:15, 15–16, 13:21–9.
34. Saint Augustine, *St. Augustine: The Literal Meaning of Genesis*, trans. by J.H. Taylor (New York: Newman Press, 1982), 2:44.
35. *Saint Augustine: Concerning the City of God Against the Pagans*, trans. by Henry Bettenson (New York: Penguin, 2003), 314.
36. John Chrysostom, *A Commentary on the Gospel of St. Matthew*, 68:3. e-Catholic 2000. www.ecatholic2000.com/fathers/untitled-711.shtml#_Toc390303853. Accessed December 2018. For an excellent history of monasticism, see Gert Melville, *The World of Medieval Monasticism: Its History and Forms of Life*, trans. by James D. Mixson (Collegeville, MN: Liturgical Press, 2016).
37. "Chapter 2," in *The Rule of Saint Benedict* (London: S.P.C.K., 1931). https://oll.libertyfund.org/titles/2202. Accessed December 2018.
38. Bernard of Clairvaux, "The Apologia to Abbott William of St.-Thierry," 29. Cited from Conrad Rudolph, "Bernard of Clairvaux's Apologia as a Description of Cluny, and the Controversy Over Monastic Art," *Gesta: Current Studies on Cluny* 27:1–2 (Chicago, IL: University of Chicago Press, 1988), 127.
39. Ugo Magrini and Anna Magrini, "Measurements of Acoustical Properties in Cistercian Abbeys," *Building Acoustics* 12:4 (2005). See also Marilyn Stokstad, *Medieval Art* (New York: Routledge, 2018), 216–18.

40. Dante Alighieri, *The Divine Comedy*, Paradiso, Canto 9.

41. Oscar Wilde, *Complete Works of Oscar Wilde*, ed. by Robert Ross (New York: Bigelow, Brown & Co., 1909), Vol. 1, 12.

42. C. G. Jung, *Memories, Dreams, Reflections*, recorded and edited by Aniela Faffé (New York: Vintage Books, 1965), 284.

43. See Jay Sherry, "A Pictorial Guide to *The Red Book*." https://aras.org/documents/pictorial-guide-red-book. Accessed January 2019.

44. C. G. Jung, *The Red Book (Philemon)*, ed. by Sonu Shamdasani (New York: W. W. Norton & Company, 2009), 154.

45. Gillian Mackie, "Abstract and Vegetal Design in the San Zeno Chapel, Rome: The Ornamental Setting of an Early Medieval Funerary Programme," *Papers of the British School at Rome* 63 (November 1995), 180.

46. Lisa Onontiyoh West, "Re-evaluating the Mausoleum of Galle Placidia" (Master's thesis, Louisiana State University, 2004), 52–4. https://digitalcommons.lsu.edu/gradschool_theses/1328. Accessed January 2019.

47. Alighieri, *The Divine Comedy* (note 40), Canto 33.

48. See, for instance, John Onians's contrasting view on Abbot Suger and St. Denis in *European Art: A Neuroarthistory* (New Haven: Yale University Press, 2016), 177–80.

49. William Durandus, *The Symbolism of Churches and Church Ornaments*, trans. by John Mason Neale and Benjamin Webb (Leeds: T. W. Green, 1843), 24–9, 34–5.

50. Revelation 18:21.

51. Abbot Suger, "The Book of Suger, Abbot of St.-Denis: On What Was Done Under His Administration," in Erwin Panofsky (trans.), *Abbot Suger: On the Abbey Church of St.-Denis and Is Art Treasures* (Princeton, NJ: Princeton University Press, 1979), 55.

52. Ibid., 63–5. See also "The Crafted Bodies of Suger: Reconsidering the Matter of St-Denis," in Kim Sexton (ed.), *Architecture and Body, Science and Culture* (London: Routledge, 2018), 45–67.

53. Otto von Simson, *The Gothic Cathedral: Origins of Gothic Architecture and the Medieval Concept of Order* (Princeton, NJ: Princeton University Press, 1974), 104–6.

54. John Ruskin, "The Deteriorative Power of Conventional Art Over Nations," in *The Two Paths: Being Lectures on Art* (London: Smith, Elder and Co, 1859), 34–5.

55. Henry Adams, *Mont-Saint-Michel and Chartres* (New York: The Heritage Press, 1905/1957), 76.

56. An epithet employed by Charles V, in a letter of 1367, see Simson, *The Gothic Cathedral* (note 53), 164 n. 17.

57. Elizabeth Carson Pastan, "Glazing Medieval Buildings," in Conrad Rudolph (ed.), *A Companion to Medieval Art: Romanesque and Gothic in Northern Europe* (Malden, MA: Blackwell Publishing, 2006), 443.

58. Hans Jantzen, *High Gothic: The Classic Cathedrals of Chartres, Reims, and Amiens* (Princeton, NJ: Princeton University Press, 1984), 60–9.

59. Simson, *The Gothic Cathedral* (note 53), XIV-XV.

60. Eugène-Emmanuel Viollet-le-Duc, *Dictionnaire raisonné de l'architecture français du XIe au XVIe siècle* (Paris: Libraires-Imprimeries Réunies, n.d.), 390ff.

61. Adams, *Mont-Saint-Michel and Chartres* (note 55), 133.

5
RENAISSANCES

Poetry

Between Dante's vision of the celestial paradise (1320) and Thomas More's Utopia (1516), there falls an interesting divide. Dante, when escorted around the spheres of heaven by Beatrice, had the opportunity to view or converse with the spirits of a score of interesting people, among them Justinian, Folquet de Marseille, Thomas Aquinas, King Solomon, Dionysius the Areopagite, Boethius, Isidore of Seville, the Venerable Bede, Joshua, Roland, Charlemagne, Trajan, St. Peter, John the Evangelist, Adam of Eden, and St. Bernard, who interceded on his behalf for the Virgin Mary. In More's *Utopia*—satire or not—there are no compelling personalities. Although people are encouraged to be kind and generous and allowed a modicum of social and intellectual intercourse, there is no personal or private property, no freedom to travel to another town without permission, no individual expression with apparel or jewelry, no desire to improve one's lot, in fact seemingly no inclination to dream outside of the present, presumably palmy state of affairs. What a dreary place utopias tend to be! The town's three-story houses, each occupied by ten to sixteen adults, are served by collective dining areas. They are "good," yet "so uniform that a whole side of a street looks like one house." In any case, people rotate between houses every ten years, presumably to offset the tedium of the built environment. Each of the fifty-four cities in Utopia, "all large and well built," are identical in their plan, with only modest variations due to the topography. If there is a hint of pleasant imagery in More's fairyland, it is found only in the gardens behind the lengthy blocks of housing, in which are cultivated vines—not for wine, certainly, but for fruits, herbs, and flowers. Inhabitants of different streets vie with each other in demonstrating their horticultural skills, so much so that, as More's doughty traveler Raphael Hythloday relates, "there is indeed nothing belonging to the whole town that is both more useful and more pleasant."[1]

This divide between Dante and More has been described as the literary passage from the religious concept of paradise to the secular one of utopia, or what Frank and Fritzie Manuel have referred to as the "Promethean act of defiance."[2] Utopias signal the advent of human initiative to set about improving living and social conditions, or so the utopian argument runs. Certainly, the secular nature of the new utopian ideal represented in More's seminal work is distinct in its absence of a transcendental or outside hand, yet the same can also be said for the Platonic ideal of making the world a better place through the expedient of political and moral impositions. In this regard, the presumed rationalist tenor of the humanist movement toward the end of fifteenth-century Italy had only one foot on the Neoplatonic side of this divide, while one foot remained on the

DOI: 10.4324/9781003178460-5

other side—that is, within the bawdy and poetic medieval traditions of minstrels, troubadours, and balladeers. These traditions, moreover, continued to prosper and even strengthen well into the Renaissance.

The sensuously amorous, allegorical, and generally bucolic character of this tradition can be found in the early thirteenth-century poem *Le Roman de la Rose*, a work initiated by Guillaume de Lorris. This romantic seduction within a dream takes place in an enchanting walled garden, unmatched by any on earth and into which the poet gains access with the assistance of a beautiful maiden. There the dreamer comes across a number of deities, among them Beauty, Wealth, Largesse, Generosity of Spirit, and Youth. Later, followed by Love, he finds the fountain at which Narcissus met his fate, which directs him to a part of the garden laden with rose bushes, and one exceptional rose in particular. He is unable to pick it, however, because he is met with the garden's defenders, among them Rebuff, Reason, Shame, and Chastity—effectively forcing him to learn the etiquette of seduction. Lorris did not complete his poem, but, as Jean de Meun picks up the theme later in the century, the suitor is eventually successful in plucking the rose. It is done only with the intervention of Venus herself, who seems to have been far more accessible in medieval times than she is today.

We can also find the same free spirit in the fourteenth-century romances of the two patriarchs of Italian humanism, Petrarch and Boccaccio, whose writings shaped Italian literature for several centuries to come. Dante had died in 1321, three years before Marco Polo was buried in the church of San Lorenzo in Venice, and during these three years Petrarch, whose father was a friend of Dante, was studying law in Bologna. The legal background allowed him to hold various clerical offices during the Avignon Papacy of John XXII, where he reportedly also took the "minor orders." Petrarch has been called the father of humanism for his extraordinary classical library, as well as for his discovery of Cicero's *Letters to Atticus* in the library of Verona Cathedral, fragments that he painstakingly pieced together and copied. This manuscript allowed a more intimate perspective of Roman society than what was commonly known.

Petrarch was a prodigious writer, but his fame largely rests on two major poetic collections: *Il Canzoniere* (Song Book) and *Trionfi* (Triumphs), both written in the Tuscan language. The former, a collection of 366 poems, is generally provincial and passionate in tone, and the first poem is the key to their inspiration. For it was in the Avignon church of St. Clare in 1327 that he first laid eyes on his beloved Laura de Noves, a married woman for whom his unrequited love would remain the theme of much of his verse. Even after her death in 1348, he did not cease his expressions of love, because a few years thereafter he started work on *Triumphs*—a descriptive series of classicized Roman-inspired pageants moralizing the themes of faith, love, and the fleeting nature of life. Love conquers youth, chastity conquers love, death conquers all but fame, but even fame has its temporal limits. The only consolation is the eternity of paradise, where Petrarch hopes at last to be reunited with Laura.

Petrarch's younger contemporary and friend Boccaccio followed a similar track. An illegitimate son of a wealthy Florentine banker, he studied law and the classics in Naples, but with his first exposure to the poetry of Petrarch in 1334 he rapidly penned a series of allegorical romances and the nature of love, either gained or lost through a struggle. His *Commedia delle Ninfe Fiorentine* (Comedy of the Florentine Nymphs, 1343) and *Ninfale fiesolano* (Tale of the Fiesole Nymph, 1345), written upon his return to Florence, have a decidedly bucolic tone. The former, although allegorical, is also paradisiacal in that it tells the story of the simple hunter Ameto, who, when relaxing in the Tuscan countryside, hears the song of a goddess. Entranced by its beauty, he tracks the voice to a stream within a lush landscape, whereupon he meets a band of nymphs, their gowns loosened, refreshing themselves from the heat of the day. The nymph who is singing is Lia, and naturally Ameto falls in love with her. He meets the same nymph a second time, but then a long winter ensues and he pines to see her again. At last spring arrives, and on the feast day of Venus he again chances upon Lia, who takes him to a secluded part of the forest, where they are joined by other exquisitely attired

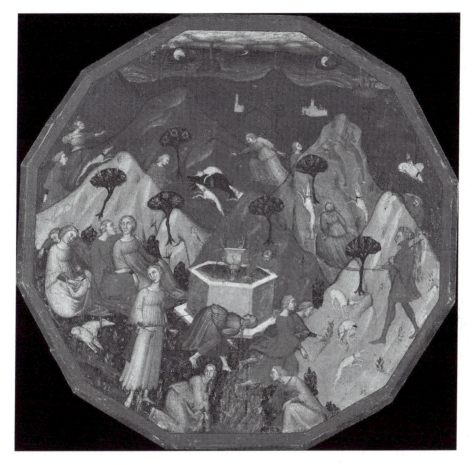

ILLUSTRATION 5.1   Ameto's Discovery of the Nymphs, 1410, Metropolitan Museum of Art.

Source: CC0 1.0 Universal Public Domain Dedication.

nymphs. The celebratory day, which includes a song contest among two shepherds, culminates in the evening when Ameto, now sitting in a meadow beneath a laurel tree, gathers with the seven nymphs beside a clear fountain. Here he listens to their stories of amorous affairs, at the conclusion of which Venus herself descends upon the gathering. The nymphs remove Ameto's tattered clothing and give him a ceremonial baptism in the fountain, from which he emerges transformed from a brute into an enlightened man. He now comes to see that the seven nymphs, in their enticing carnal forms, actually represent the seven divine virtues of wisdom, justice, temperance, fortitude, charity, hope, and faith.

The amatory nature of Boccaccio's writings is given even greater license in his *Decameron*, a work that Robert Pogue Harrison has characterized as personifying the Epicurean delight in pleasurable conversation, or the "aesthetics of storytelling."[3] The setting for the book was the plague that ravaged Florence in 1348, in which thousands died and all social life came to an abrupt halt. Boccaccio saw firsthand the changes in human morality or ethical standards that accompanied the black death, and he composed the story in which ten wealthy Florentines, seven women and three men, quarantine themselves in a palace in Fiesole, with a garden so sublime that all conceded that "if there was a paradise on earth, it could be in no other form, nor was it possible to add any thing to it."[4] Over the course of two weeks, each of the ten relate an evening story on the themes of love, greed, the corruption of the church, and the fickle nature of fortune—stories from the sensual and the bawdy to the morally refined. Boccaccio was clearly challenging the line of Florentine decorum, yet there was an important underlying issue here, which is how does one preserve the idea of beauty or maintain an earthly paradise within a world of insufferable disease and death. The sensualist or humanist legacy of Petrarch and Boccaccio would pass down to Chaucer and Shakespeare, but the afterlife of their ideas remained strong in Italy as well. In 1483, 133 years after the appearance of *Decameron*, Lorenzo de Medici commissioned four paintings from Sandro Botticelli to depict its story of Nastagio degli Onesti. And Boccaccio was likely an inspiration for the most curious fifteenth-century book related to architecture, the *Hypnerotomachia Poliphili*. It is a tale of beauty, love, lust, and buildings, situated where else but in the dreamscape of paradise.

Erotica

Generally known in English under the title *The Strife of Love in a Dream*, the *Hypnerotomachia Poliphili* seems to have been completed in 1467, and the book, with its exquisite woodcuts, was printed by the prestigious Venetian house of Aldus Manutius only in 1499. Over the years it has engendered considerable critical scrutiny within literary circles, but uncertainty still surrounds its author. Its inscribed name is Francesco Colonna and there are two fifteenth-century candidates with this name, yet neither has an especially strong case for being the author. Liane Lefaivre, a historian who has examined the book from an architectural perspective, has argued—compellingly—that Colonna was a pseudonym for Leon Battista Alberti, one of the leading polymaths and preeminent architectural writers of the time.[5] Another historian, Alberto Pérez-Gómez, has characterized *The Strife of Love* as "the first narrative articulation of architectural practice" in the modern age, one expounding "a poetic vision that sets a temporal boundary to the experience of architecture, showing that architecture is not only about form and space but about time and experience."[6] The historian Anthony Blunt has written that the book's great popularity in the following centuries was due to its conflation of oneiric descriptions of buildings with love stories infused with unsubdued eroticism.[7] It seems to be the perfect book to consider from the perspective of building paradise.

The plot of the love story, although convoluted in two books, is relatively simple. The love-smitten but scorned Poliphilo falls into a sequence of dreams within a dream, which begins in an idyllic landscape and his search for his beloved Polia. After overcoming the perils of a deep and dark forest, he hears the song of a nymph and—like Boccaccio's Ameto—sets out to find its source. He first stumbles upon the ruins of a huge and fantastic temple, presumably dedicated to the goddess of love, to which he gives an exhaustive description. When he eventually enters the complex, he is chased by a dragon, from which he barely escapes through a tunnel. He emerges into another bucolic countryside where he is found by five flirtatious nymphs, who were on their way to the bathhouse. They invite him along, tease him for his unease with their nudity, and even provide him with a potion that gives him an embarrassing erection—all for their amusement. Eventually, they lead him to their queen, where he enjoys a sumptuous feast and proclaims his love for Polia. Once again, his description of the palace and gardens is lengthy.

Eventually, the queen appoints two nymphs to guide him to a mountain at the foot of which are three doors: those of spiritual abstinence, worldly power, and love. He naturally chooses the last and behind it finds a now-enamored Polia, although he does not at first recognize her. She leads him on another tour, on which they encounter an idyllic landscape of nymphs with their lovers and several triumphal processions before arriving at a temple where a priestess proclaims Polia's betrothal to Poliphilo. Cupid next transports the two lovers on a boat with singing nymphs to the island of Cytherea, the birthplace of Venus. After another quite lengthy description of the circular gardens

ILLUSTRATION 5.2   Poliphilo in the Garden with Polia. *Hypnerotomachia Poliphili* (Venice: Aldus Manutius, 1499).

Source: Wikimedia.

of Venus—with its groves, meadows, rivers, colonnades, hedges, and flowers—Poliphilo and Polia arrive at the fountain of Venus in the center, where the goddess herself unites them in marriage. In the much shorter second book of the volume, Polia recounts her side of the story, her pledge of chastity to the goddess Diana, her confusion about Poliphilo's pursuit of her, and her own sexual awakening. The saga concludes with the two lovers in a tight embrace, at which point Poliphilo awakens from his dream and regrets that it was not longer.

The story is obviously an allegory, and here is where it becomes interesting. Poliphilo describes in some detail the beauty and sensuous charm of the many nymphs that he encounters, and of course that of his dear Polia, but lengthier sections of the book are given to his descriptions of gardens, and still lengthier ones to his disquisitions on paradisiacal buildings, which are often depicted with the same superlatives that he attaches to his lover. On first coming to the ruined temple of Venus at the start of his saga, for instance, he notes:

> As I hurried up to this deserted place, I was seized with an unexpected joy, and stopped to admire at leisure the immensity and stupendous height of the structure, which was such a bold example of the architectural art, considering with astonishment the weight and density of this fragmented and half-ruined building. It was of white Parian marble, with its square and rectangular stones fitted without cement, placed equally and level, smoothed and painted with red along their edges as exquisitely as could be, so that the thinnest needle could not have penetrated into the borders or cracks between one edge or another.[8]

This passage and the details of this particular description continues for another fifty pages. At coming upon the bathhouse and fountain in which he was entertained by the nymphs, he reports his thrill and excitement, not so much with their beauty as with the lines of the building:

> Two fluted pilasters were carefully carved in this noble stone, resting with their bases above a straight cyma with a gullet, dentils and cordings. Its capitals supported a small beam, zophorus and cornice, above which another quarter of a square was assigned for the frontispiece. All its lineaments were carved in the same single block and unadorned, except that I saw in the angular concavity or place of the frontispiece a wreath containing two doves drinking from a little vase. The entire space bounded by the colonnettes, gullets and beam was cut back and hollowed out, and contained an elegant carving of a nymph.[9]

The bas-relief was of such exquisite beauty, Poliphilo goes on to say, that he doubted that Praxiteles' carving of Venus—that "which was of such beauty than men burned with sacrilegious lust for it and ravished the statue by masturbating"—had equaled it. Similar passion erupts when Poliphilo arrives at the "superb, sumptuous and magnificent" palace of Queen Eleuterylida, whose "ideal situation and marvellous symmetrical design" induces "such joy and gratitude" in Poliphilo that he ranks its architect as "preeminent over all who had ever built."[10] There is in his descriptions, as Lefaivre has noted, the frequent use of the adjective "voluptuous" (*voluptas*), an adjective that Poliphilo attributes to Polia as well as to the buildings. The two loves of Poliphilo—Polia and the fantastical buildings of which he dreams—seem to be interchangeable in their effect on him. Even the sight of Venus standing "naked in the middle of the transparent and limpid waters of the basin" does not bring to his mind such rapture.

Another question that has been raised about the *Hypnerotomachia Poliphili* is in what direction does the allegory flow? Does Poliphilo's love for the voluptuous Polia become a metaphor for the desire inherent in the architectural body, or is the voluptuous architectural body in fact a means, as Lefaivre has suggested, "to recategorize architecture through its aestheticization, which was part of a greater movement toward the aestheticization of life"?[11] Botticelli's two paintings, *Primavera* and *The Birth of Venus*, which follow only a decade or so after the completed manuscript of *Hypnerotomachia Poliphili*, argue on behalf of the latter reading.

In any case, the metaphor or conflation of the human body with building was not an isolated feature of the early Renaissance. Antonio di Pietro Averlino, more commonly known as Filarete, remarks in his near-contemporary treatise that

> building is nothing more than a voluptuous pleasure, like that of a man in love. Anyone who has experienced it knows that there is so much pleasure and desire in building that however much man does, he wants to do more.[12]

This erotic summation follows a pregnant passage in which Filarete compares the design of a building with the process of childbirth:

> The building is conceived in this manner. Since no one can conceive by himself without a woman, by another simile, the building cannot be conceived by one man alone. As it cannot be done without a woman, so he who wishes to build needs an architect. He conceives it with him and then the architect carries it. When the architect has given birth, he becomes the mother of the building. Before the architect gives birth, he should dream about his conception, think about it, and turn it over in his mind in many ways for seven to nine months, just as a woman carries her child in her body for seven to nine months.[13]

Filarete was a curious figure, yet not lacking in imagination. The birth recorded in his architectural treatise, *Book of Architecture* (c. 1464), is not of a building but of a city, delivered at a banquet to

Milanese aristocrats. They had dismissed the practice of architecture as a trade, and Filarete counters with the many areas of knowledge that an architect must possess, to which he gives sustenance by outlining the ideal city of Sforzinda. It is a lengthy and convoluted tale, not unlike the labyrinth that makes its appearance in several forms. The castle and lighthouse at the port city, for example, is a square labyrinth, in which each interior wall rises a story or two higher, mimicking the form of a wedding cake fifteen stories in height. Another, the "garden" labyrinth, is a square system of canals of more than a mile on each side, at the center of which is the square garden laid out like a map of the earth with the ocean in the center. In a biblical sense, all of the canals flowed in and out of the center.[14] Filarete's Sforzinda is also polychromatic in a playful way. Just as people dress and adorn themselves with beautiful vestments and jewelry according to their social rank, architecture should reflect this passion. For this reason, each building "should be clothed and adorned with beautiful stones. In addition to the beautiful stones, it should be decorated with beautiful and noble carvings, with gold and colors. Paint them and make them as beautiful as possible."[15]

In addition to the enormous scale of the urban elements he depicts, another prominent feature of his descriptions is the highly didactic nature of the buildings, whose murals and reliefs exhort virtues and relate historical episodes. The large and elaborately outfitted House of the Architect, for instance, had allegorical images on its exterior of Virtue, Vice, Will, Talent, Reason, Fame, and Memory, in addition to a portrait of the architect himself. The house is also a school in which students learn not only knowledge of the building trades but also geometry, measures, proportion, astrology, arithmetic, philosophy, music, rhetoric, and medicine. Two-thirds of the land for the house is given over to its garden. Filarete's often-cited House of Virtue and Vice, is a large square building, on top of which is a circular tower. The youths who enter the building have a choice between two doors. One door of vice descends downward to brothels, pubs, and gambling dens, from which there seems to be no return. The other door leads into a passage of thirty-one rooms, in which, one by one, the students must master the various sciences. Upon completing this phase of their education, they progress upward into the circular tower one level at a time, learning the seven liberal arts and seven virtues. Upon reaching the pergola at the top of the complex, they are rewarded with a doctorate, overseen by the colossal statue of Virtue in the center, represented as a man wearing armor and holding a date palm in one hand and a laurel in the other. A flame flutters above his head.

Filarete's city has several other unusual features, articulated with delightful ink drawings made on the pages. He seems to have a fascination with Egyptian obelisks and other decorative motives, and one image even depicts pagoda-like towers surrounding a Brunelleschian dome. The city is situated in the magical and mysterious paradise of the "Inda valley." It is not a classical rebirth that Filarete is seeking in his architecture, but, as Berthold Hub has argued, a "*prisca architectura,*" or the original "truth" of the building instinct. Hub compares Filarete's efforts with Marsilio Ficino's contemporaneous search for a "*prisca theologia*"—that is, the original Judeo-Christian truth that is rooted in Egyptian and Asian cultures. It even seems that in 1466 Filarete intended to travel to Constantinople and India, although his death intervened.[16] We will never know these plans with any certainty, but such an intention is not far-fetched in light of his treatise. There is a theatrical aspect to Filarete's imagination, but a serious side as well, one infused with the early Renaissance ideal of paradise.

The depth of his fancy might be also compared with Leonardo da Vinci's ideal city, which he sketched after the plague of 1484 had seized the city of Milan.[17] Leonardo's focus was decentralization, hygiene, straight and broad streets, and a canal system that could be used both for transportation and hygiene. Yet there was a political dimension as well. His city was a two-tiered city: an upper level consisting of gardens and pedestrian bridges to which only the nobles or the upper class would have access, and a non-articulated lower level for commoners, with fields only partially open to light. Although commoners did enjoy a number of hygienic improvements with the city's hydraulics, sluices, locks, and paddle wheels, what Leonardo's seemingly treeless city lacks—especially evident in a notable artist with commanding genius—is any sense of poetry or creative playfulness.

Leonardo, in the midst of a pandemic, had donned the utopian hat of a Silicon Valley technocrat. Filarete, with all of his eccentricity, gave free rein to the paradisiacal instinct.

Concinnity

If indeed Leon Battista Alberti was the author of the *Hypnerotomachia Poliphili*, then we have still another dimension revealed of this *uomo universale*, whose broader contribution to fifteenth-century Italian theory remains too little appreciated. Like Boccaccio, he was an illegitimate son born to a wealthy Florentine family, and by early accounts he was an exceptional athlete, conversationalist, classicist, writer, mathematician, geometer, architect, and advisor to princes and popes. Deprived of inheritance, he took his doctorate in canon law in Bologna and first found employment as the secretary to Cardinal Albergati, the bishop of Bologna. He eventually worked his way into the papal chancery in Rome, where he took the Holy Orders. At the chancery he formed friendships with like-minded scholars such as Poggio Bracciolini, who had a few decades earlier stumbled upon the manuscript of Vitruvius that would lead Italian architecture into the Renaissance.

When Pope Eugenius IV was driven out of Rome in 1434 by demonstrations, Alberti accompanied him to Florence, where, as the dome of the cathedral was being completed, he fell in with the circle of artists that included Filippo Brunelleschi and Donatello, the first to whom he dedicated the Tuscan translation of his text *On Painting*, a book discussing the new technique of perspective. Between 1436 and 1443, Alberti followed the papal court to Bologna, Ferrara, back to Florence, and then to Rome. In the last city, he, alongside Flavio Biondo, measured and studied the ruins of ancient Roman monuments. Biondo, between 1444 and 1448, would publish his three volumes of *Rome Restored*, the first archaeological mapping of the city's lost classical past. At the encouragement of the humanist Leonello d'Este, the Marquis of Ferrara, Alberti began his own treatise on architecture, in which he attempted to interpret the ten books of Vitruvius in light of new archaeological evidence. The book, *On the Art of Building in Ten Books*, appeared in 1452 and would become the second foundational text for the Italian Renaissance. Alberti had by this date already tried his hand at practice. In 1446 he was commissioned by Giovanni Rucellai to design the facade of his palace in Florence. The wealthy wool merchant, since the mid-1440s, had been buying adjoining properties surrounding his ancestral home on the Via della Vigna Nuova, and he wanted to unite them behind a single facade. Alberti designed the template, which, with its arches, pilasters, and horizontal layering of floors, was one of the first mature expressions of the Florentine Renaissance. A few blocks away, Alberti designed the glorious facade for the existing Gothic church Santa Maria Novella, which remains today a gem within the Florentine cityscape.

In addition to his friendship with Leonello d'Este, the "gentle prince" of Ferrara, Alberti was friends with several other humanist scholars, among them Tommaso Parentucelli, who was elected Pope Nicholas V in 1447. Alberti was his architectural advisor and consulted on several projects at the Vatican. The architect also had a friendship with Cardinal Prospero Colonna, who was narrowly defeated by Nicholas for the tiara and crossed keys. When Prospero, with his baronial Roman lineage, began renovating the Quirinal Palace in Rome in the 1440s, he commissioned Alberti to restore the gardens that he believed once belonged to Gaius Maecenas, a patron of Emperor Augustus. Alberti was similarly close to Prospero's brother Stefano, with whom he likely advised on the renovation of the recently reclaimed family holdings at Palestrina, northeast of Rome. Alberti certainly knew Stefano's son Francesco Colonna, who has been viewed by some as the author of the *Hypnerotomachia Poliphili*. Additionally, Alberti was a confidant to Gianfrancesco Gonzaga, the Marquis of Mantua, as well as to Federico da Montefeltro, the humanist *condottieri* and later Duke of Urbino. In the 1460s, Leon Battista also made regular trips to Urbino to escape the summer heat of Rome. There he conferred with Federico on the design and expansion of the new palace, a commission that was eventually given to Francesco di Giorgio Martini. The ducal palace was noted

ILLUSTRATION 5.3   Leon Battista Alberti, Facade for Santa Maria Novella, Florence, Italy, 1465–70.

Source: Photo by author.

for its thermal baths, the enclosed hanging gardens separating the duke and duchess's apartments, the private loggias on the southwest side, which provided commanding views of the rolling countryside. Yet the palace is perhaps most famed for its artistic conversations. The ideal city was certainly a subject of discussion, because surviving from this period are three wooden panels of cities, installed in a piece or pieces of ducal furniture. Each contains a painted perspective of an ideal city, classical and symmetrical in its forms. For many years Alberti was assumed to be the author of these panels, although it is now believed that they were painted a few years after his death in 1472. In any case, they present a vivid demonstration of the humanist mind pondering not a political utopia but an urban vision more angelic and aesthetic in its outlines.

Alberti's close relationship with the papacy continued with the election of Pius II in 1458. In the following year the pontiff was traveling to Mantua with Alberti, and the entourage stopped in Pius's native town of Corsignano. Many of the buildings were dilapidated, and Pius decided to rebuild them and re-christen the town as Pienza, the seat of his summer residence. On a high ridge overlooking a broad Tuscan valley, the setting itself is idyllic, and Alberti was likely an early consultant on a project carried out by others. The patterns of some roads were altered, and forty buildings were refurbished or constructed altogether, including the papal palace, bishop's palace, town hall with a loggia, and the new cathedral of Santa Maria Assunta. The larger buildings were centered in the town and loosely organized around a trapezoidal piazza perfectly scaled to the town's size. Local stone and travertine were used throughout, and the detailing of the new buildings was both individually varied and well crafted. The facade of the pontiff's palace, built by Bernardo Rossellino, was a near replica of Florence's Rucellai Palace, in which he too was involved. The church was set off by the diverging walls of two palaces, and stunning views of the Tuscan countryside extend along the south. The pope's palace contained a cortile or center court, enclosed on the southern hillside by a three-story loggia stepping down into a large garden, seemingly floating above the picturesque landscape. This attempt at an ideal city was a great success.

Alberti's ties to Florence, to which he returned in the 1460s, were also strong. The Medici and Alberti families were of the same political party, and Alberti had known Cosimo since the latter had returned from his Venetian exile in 1434. Alberti became a part of the Medici orbit, but there is also a more interesting connection. Rucellai, Alberti's patron in the 1440s, was the original owner of Poggio a Caiano, a farming estate near Prato. At one point, Rucellai asked Alberti to design a new villa for it, but this project stalled and later Lorenzo de Medici, the grandson of Cosimo, fell in love with the property and bartered an exchange of properties with Rucellai, for which Cosimo would hire Giuliano da Sangallo to design his villa.[18] Nevertheless, the idea of a Ciceronian *hortus* or garden villa had long been brewing in Alberti's mind. In two early writings of the 1430s, *On the Family* and *The Villa*, he exalted the ideal of the suburban villa in idyllic terms and spoke of its trees, orchards, gardens, places for walks, conversation, and meditation.[19] He also discussed the villa in his architectural treatise:

> I would therefore make it slightly elevated; and I would make the road leading up to it rise so gently that visitors do not realize how high they have climbed until they have a view over the countryside. Meadows full of flowers, sunny lawns, cool and shady groves, limpid springs, streams, and pools, and whatever else we have described as being essential to a villa—none of these should be missing, for their delight as much as for their utility.[20]

What makes this particularly interesting is that a decade after Alberti wrote these lines, Cosimo de Medici would establish his academy at his Careggi villa outside of Florence, where he employed Marsilio Ficino to translate the writings of Plato. Alberti attended at least some lectures of Ficino, and the city was in any case lively with intellectual discussions about the ideal of beauty and classical learning.[21]

And here Alberti made perhaps his most significant contribution to the fledgling Renaissance. Many writers have characterized Alberti's notion of beauty as idealized or even Platonic in its essentials—pointing to a passage in his tract on painting in which he praises the Greek painter Zeuxis, who chose not one model but the best features of five beautiful maidens to represent Venus. Such an explanation may be taken as idealization, but the passage can also be interpreted in another manner, which is Alberti giving license to painters to improve upon nature in order to express as "much loveliness" as possible.[22] In fact, Alberti's views of painting scarcely differ from his view of building design. The architect has the professional obligation to invest designs with beauty because comeliness, as he variously stated, projects power, displays social status, elevates the reputation of the city, and pleases the owner. "Who would not claim to dwell more comfortably between walls that are ornate rather than neglected?" he says in one passage.[23]

There is also a rather well-pronounced physical or corporeal vein in Alberti's conception of beauty, which we have seen in other fifteenth-century writings. In the prologue to his architectural treatise, for instance, he notes that a building is a "form of body," one that is composed of both "lineaments" (design) and "matter" (materiality), "one the product of thought, the other of Nature."[24] And this corporeality is more than casual in this passage on the building fabric:

> The physicians have noticed that Nature was so thorough in forming the bodies of animals, that she left no bone separate or disjointed from the rest. Likewise, we should link the bones and bind them fast with muscles and ligaments, so that their frame and structure is complete and rigid enough to ensure that its fabric will stand on its own, even if all else is removed.[25]

Similar metaphors run throughout his text. Columns and engaged columns are the bones of the building, the infill walls and paneling are the muscles and ligaments, the finish of the building is the skin.[26] The roof also has its "bones, muscles, infill paneling, skin, and crust," and the walls should not be too thick, "for who would not criticize a body for having excessively swollen limbs?"[27] Perhaps the most sensual of his metaphors is when he describes the most important part of the house—the bosom—"although you might refer to it as the 'court' or 'atrium.'"[28]

Alberti's corporeal metaphors are also apparent in his discussion of beauty and ornament. He famously defines beauty as "that reasoned harmony of all the parts within a body, so that nothing may be added, taken away, or altered, but for the worse," and beauty is a "great and holy" matter because it is rarely found in nature.[29] He supports such a proposition with a passage from Cicero, in which the protagonist recounts that he once watched a parade of youths in Athens and observed that "there was scarcely one [handsome youth] to be found in each platoon of the training-corps."[30] This might seem a curious way to elevate the idea of beauty to Platonic proportions, but this was not his intention. Yet it did allow the humanist to introduce the idea of "ornament," which becomes a way of making what is displeasing "less offensive" and what is pleasing "more delightful."[31] For him, the chief ornament of architecture is the column, because it confers grace and dignity to a building.[32] The chief ornament of a library is its collection of rare and classical manuscripts because of the wisdom they convey.[33] The chief ornaments of a city are its "open spaces set aside as ornament and for recreation," such as race courses, gardens, ambulatories, and pools.[34] The streets should even "meander gently like a river flowing now here," not for any logistical reason but because "it is no trifle that visitors at every step meet yet another facade."[35] It is not surprising that the chief ornaments of the country villa are the "gardens full of delightful plants, and a garden portico, where you can enjoy both sun and shade."[36]

In addition to the corporeal and experiential nature of beauty, there is for Alberti one fitting keystone to his celebration of beauty, one that elevates it to one of Dante's celestial spheres. This is the notion of *concinnitas*. The rarely used English word "concinnity" adequately conveys its meaning of a skillful and harmonious fitting together of parts of an ensemble, but Alberti, as we might expect, drafts the term from Cicero's rhetorical theory. As Cicero had noted in the *Orator*, "Words when connected together embellish a style [*habent ornatum*] if they produce a certain symmetry [*aliquid concinnitatis*] which disappears when the words are changed, although the thought remains the same."[37] This "certain symmetry" is not a trivial thing upon which anyone can stumble; it is a "fundamental rule of Nature" by which one measures a building's rhetorical and sensory eloquence.[38] Following Augustine, it allows such things as harmonic proportions to be a part of good design, and it also counters the most grievous sin of poor design, which is "deformity." Most importantly, it grounds the intuitive recognition of beauty not only in one's conceptual understanding of beauty but also in the pre-reflective or emotional appeal of human desire:

> For about the appearance and configuration of a building there is a natural excellence and perfection that stimulates the mind; it is immediately recognized if present, but if absent is even more desired. The eyes are by their nature greedy for beauty and *concinnitas*, and are particularly fastidious and critical in this manner.[39]

Albertian concinnity, in the end, seems to be nothing less than another oneiric rendition of "Polia." Although this cleric never married and is said to have lived a life of abstinence, Alberti seems to imagine beauty as a decorous, virtuous, yet voluptuous maiden with facial and bodily features of perfect concinnity, strolling with him hand in hand through the ornamental garden of paradise.

Gardens of Delight

Alberti died in 1472, squarely between two years that would also have compelling significance in the course of the young Renaissance—1453 and 1492. The first is the year in which Constantinople fell to Ottoman forces, now posing a spiritual and military threat to the Vatican and Europe;

the second is the year that Christopher Columbus made his first voyage to America, which saliently affected European thinking in many ways. We will pursue the latter event in a later chapter, but the effects of the former can be seen in the architectural competition between the theological citadels of Christianity and Islam—in their respective designs for the Basilica of St. Peter's in Rome and the Süleymaniye Mosque in Istanbul.

Following his capture of Constantinople, Sultan Mehmed II (the Conqueror) turned his attention to the Balkans and surrounding islands, forcing a confrontation with Venice over its Aegean holdings. The so-called Venetian War, which lasted fifteen years, proved to be a catastrophe for Venice, which surrendered to Mehmed with Ottoman troops on the outskirts of the city in 1479. Nearly all of the Balkan Peninsula was ceded to the Ottomans, including the Dalmatian coastline. In the following year Mehmed, eying Rome, took the port city of Oranto on Italy's boot. Pope Sixtus IV called a Crusade in 1481, which did retake the city, but things remained tense until Mehmed's death later in that year. A second wave of European campaigns was set in motion by Sultan Süleyman the Magnificent, who ruled from 1520 to 1566. He not only used the Balkans as a springboard to Italy but also marched his armies into Hungary and parts of Germany with the intention of taking Vienna and Rome simultaneously. He did make it to the gates of Vienna in 1529, but due to poor weather and difficulties with supplies, he was forced to retreat to Buda. He pondered another assault in 1532, but threats along his eastern flank from the Persian Safavid dynasty eventually forced him to redeploy his military forces.

Accompanying Süleyman on many of his military ventures was his architect Sinan, who, by his own account, was certainly the most productive architect of the sixteenth century, with a portfolio of over 300 built projects. Sinan followed architectural developments in the West, knew the history of the Byzantine Empire, and had the inspiration of the Hagia Sophia before him as well. In the 1550s he began the vast complex of the Süleymaniye Mosque, now adopting the structural system used at the Hagia Sophia, yet he added better illumination to it. The dome was actually smaller than its predecessor, but in the 1570s Sinan tried again with a larger mosque in Edirne and succeeded in surpassing the dome of the Hagia Sophia.

The papacy in Rome followed these developments closely. The rebuilding of St. Peter's began in 1506 when Julius II charged Bramante with the monumental task of building a new basilica around the existing church. Bramante began work with the south choir ambulatory, but then both Julius and Bramante died a few months apart. Julius's successor, the Medici Leo X, embraced the ambition and elevated Bramante's assistant Raphael to lead the project, but the artist's death in 1520 again halted work. Peruzzi and Sangallo the Younger were the next two architects to take charge, but their work ceased with the sack of Rome in 1527 by mutinous troops of Charles V. After several years of inactivity, Sangallo resumed the project in the 1540s, but with his death the project passed into the hands of Michelangelo, who both increased the scale of the project and designed the spectacular crowning dome, one of the great engineering feats of the sixteenth century.

The building competition between Sinan and Michelangelo defined one dimension of this religious rivalry, but there was also another, far more pleasing one taking place on the horticultural field—the competition of building paradises. The Islamic garden, as we will see in the next chapter, achieved its height in southern Spain and in South Asia, and we have already noted the opening salvo in the West, Cosimo de Medici's estate at Careggi, which became a setting for the academy. As Cosimo related later in life, the garden was where he would invite Ficino to bring his Orphean lyre and his latest translation of Plato for a stroll of the landscape in order to "feed his soul."[40] Lorenzo de Medici expanded upon the idea in the 1480s with his villa Poggio a Caiano, the land that he bartered from Rucellai. The large estate contained expansive orchards and vineyards, but it was principally known for its formalized walled garden, shielded from the world yet viewed from the villa's major rooms. The papacy, which for several decades had been at war with Medici Florence, soon came around to see the enchantment of gardens. Prior to starting the rebuilding of St. Peter's,

ILLUSTRATION 5.4 The Dome of the Basilica of St. Peter's, Vatican City, Rome. Designed in 1547, completed 1690.

Source: Photo by author.

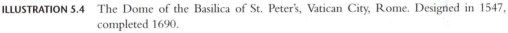

Bramante designed a three-tiered garden, extending from the pontiff's living quarters to the Belvedere Palace several hundred yards away. Eventually a cortile was formed with buildings, but originally it was an open garden with promenades, arbors, and fountains. At the lowest level, adjacent to the papal residence, pageants and spectacles were performed for the pontiff's entertainment.

With the design of the Villa Madama in 1517, a short distance north of the Vatican, we have a grander vision of an idyllic garden. It was commissioned by Lorenzo's son, Cardinal Giulio de Medici, also the brother to Pope Leo X and himself a later pontiff. Giulio employed Raphael to design the extravagant villa. Its inspiration was Pliny the Younger's Laurentian Villa, which in Roman times overlooked the sea at Ostia and offered arbors for reflective walks. Here the elevated landscape provided a majestic view of Rome's skyline and surrounding countryside. At the center of the villa was an open circular courtyard with wings axially extending along two sides. Only one of the wings was built, and it is difficult to piece together the full design, but the intention was to surround it with a Roman theater, a fish pond, gardens, and promenades. At one end, off the loggia, was a formal garden, and on the opposite side, beneath the unbuilt wing, a series of three hanging gardens were planned—the third and lowest in the shape of a hippodrome—cascading down the hillside. Leo died in 1521 and Giulio ascended to the papacy two years later, slowing construction, which halted entirely with the burgeoning Protestant Reformation in 1524. Nevertheless, a stay at the partially completed villa was a frequent request of dignitaries visiting the city in later years.

The Sack of Rome in 1527 also sent artists fleeing the city, and this disruption would last several decades. Giulio Romano, who had worked on the Villa Madama, had earlier moved to Mantua, where Federigo Gonzaga invited him to transform his hunting lodge into a grandiose suburban palace, the Palazzo del Te. The lodge originally stood on an island surrounded by lakes and canals, and offered shaded promenades and a large garden. Today the palace is best known for Romano's playful architectural effects as well as his stunning interior murals. Its mannerist style was rivaled only by Michelangelo's design for the vestibule of the Laurentian Library in Florence.

ILLUSTRATION 5.5 Hubert Robert, The Oval Fountain in the Gardens of the Villa d'Este, Tivoli, 1760, National Gallery of Art, Washington, DC.

Source: Open Access Image. CC0 1.0.

The Renaissance garden came to fruition by mid-century. Every duke, pope, cardinal, and member of a wealthy family in Italy competed to outdo each other in their playful use of vegetation, mythology, labyrinths, terraces, porticoes, pools, and fountains. In an age when travel was measured in days by horseback or coach, the vast gardens and water spectacles of Piero Ligorio at Villa d'Este, a garden cascading down the hillside at Tivoli, must have seemed like a recreated Elysium with its flooding grottoes and scattered nymphaea. Parts of the garden ornaments were pilfered from the ruins of Hadrian's Villa below it. Goethe, in his visit of 1787, reported in his diary that Tivoli was "one of those experiences which permanently enrich one's life."[41] It became a frequent haunt of artists, such as Giovanni Battista Piranesi, Hubert Robert, and J. M. Turner, who would visit the paradise to record its scenic effects.

No less idyllic was the former hunting lodge in Bagnaia, transformed by four cardinals into the Villa Lante. The complex and gardens served as a summer retreat for the upper echelon of the clergy. In 1556 Cardinal Gianfrancesco Gambra brought in Vignola to design the villa, but it was the fanciful allegory on which the design was based that defined its prestige: the evolutionary tale of the history of the earth. The experience begins deep in the forest, where one finds fountains with prehistoric and early historic animals. The main water axis begins with a nymphaeum at the tree line, where waterfalls splash out of caves into a mossy fountain known as the "Deluge." Framing the event are two small loggias designed by Vignola, referred to as the Houses of the Muses, which served as places for rest and pleasant conversation. From there, the water cascades axially down a series of terraces and basins, passing through fountains featuring lobsters (the first cardinal's heraldic emblem), cascades (a water chain), giants (allegories of the rivers Tiber and Arno), and lights (reason). At this point, the stream arrives at two casinos framing the axis (the second built later), bespeaking architecture's secondary role within the larger Renaissance version of the Garden of Eden. The casinos, wonderfully endowed with murals, overlook a vast parterre on the lowest level, with a sizable square basin in the center representing the calm sea of civilization. High culture is also portrayed with another feature of the Villa Lante. Between the fountains of the giants and that of lights is a massive stone table with a runnel of cool water running down the center, the "Table of the Cardinal." When the prelate hosted banquets, he would place wine bottles in the runnel so that they would have the proper temperature for his guests. Eden has rarely been imagined in such scrupulous detail.

Yet the culmination of the paradisiacal instinct in sixteenth-century Italy would be found not in a cardinal's table but in the achievements of Andrea di Pietro della Gondola, better known as the Palladio. He was born in Padua in 1508, the son of an artisan and apprenticed to a stonemason. In another mason's workshop in Vicenza in the 1530s, he met his humanist tutor Gian Giorgio Trissino—a refugee of the Sack of Rome. Trissino was in fact the attendant to Clement VII, the Medici pope who had commissioned the Villa Madama, and it was in Trissino's private library in Vincenza that Palladio studied philosophy, astronomy, music, Greek, and Latin, and was introduced to the ten books of Vitruvius. It was also through Trissino's academic programs that Palladio met a number of leading humanists and architects, among them Alvise Cornaro, Daniele Barbaro, Sebastiano Serlio, and Jacopo Sansovino, the last of whom would design the library in Venice opposite the Basilica of St. Mark's. Having made the transition from mason to architect, Palladio completed his education in the early 1540s, when Trissino took him on extended trips to Rome to measure and record the ancient monuments, a century after Alberti's efforts. All the buildings were classical, but Palladio did not fail to study the Villa Madama. By decade's end, the young architect had established his presence, having completed various commissions, among them the Palazzo Thiene in Vicenza and the remodeling of the city hall, now known as the Basilica Palladiana. Here he wrapped the irregular medieval fabric with a classical shell of two-story colonnades with arched openings. Until his death in 1580, he would complete dozens of other villas, as well as two major churches in Venice, San Giorgio Maggiore and the Redentore. The view of the former, across the lagoon from St. Mark's, remains today one of the best-known visual icons of Venice.

The Villa Barbaro does not stand atop everyone's list of Palladio's best designs, but it epitomizes the paradisiacal splendor of the humanist mind. The relatively low-key rural villa does not, for instance, match the geometrical perfection of the Villa Rotunda outside of Vincenza, a circular hall set within a nine-square floor plan with four identical porches looking out over the landscape in four directions—a fitting setting for Joseph Losey's filmed production of Mozart's *Don Giovanni*. Rather, the Villa Barbaro is a private affair, almost idiosyncratic with its somewhat hidden main entrance within a loggia, yet when one climbs to the main floor, one has no doubt that one has arrived at a very special paradise—the collaborative efforts of Palladio, the Barbaro brothers, the sculptor Alessandro Vittoria, and the gifted hand and imagination of Paolo Veronese.

The Barbaro brothers had studied at the University of Padua and both were eminent figures within the Venetian Republic. Daniele pursued the path of a classical scholar and writer. He also wrote voluminously on various other subjects, and between 1549 and 1551 he served as the Venetian ambassador to England. He was the official historian of the Venetian Republic, and in 1552 he represented Venice at the Council of Trent, the starting point of the Catholic Counter-Reformation. He had met Palladio at one of Trissino's gatherings and later invited the architect to prepare the drawings for his annotated Italian translation of Vitruvius, which appeared in 1556. To complete this work, both Daniele and Palladio traveled to Rome once again to survey classical sites. Stopping at the Villa d'Este along the way, the garden's designer, a friend of Palladio, gave the visitors a tour of the elaborate water system feeding the gardens. Daniele, in fact, dedicated his translation of Vitruvius to Cardinal Ippolito d'Este. Marc'Antonio Barbaro was no less involved with the arts, although he achieved his fame principally as a statesman while serving as the Venetian ambassador

ILLUSTRATION 5.6 Palladio, Villa Barbaro at Maser, Italy. 1560–70.

Source: Photo by Hans A. Rosbach. Wikimedia CC BY-SA 3.0.

to Istanbul. He was there on the eve of the naval Battle of Lepanto, when Venetian and Spanish navies confronted the Ottoman fleet in the Gulf of Patras. The Christian forces won the battle, but it was a hollow victory because they were unable to free the Venetians held prisoners on the island of Cyprus. Barbaro, who was imprisoned by the Sultan, negotiated their release in Istanbul, but at the cost of surrendering more Venetian territory to the Ottomans. The Barbaro brothers, although notable, were not noblemen, even though the family name predates the founding of the Venetian Republic. Nor were they particularly wealthy, which delayed the completion of the villa. They were, like Palladio himself, self-made individuals who rose to the top of the social hierarchy through talent and effort.

Beauty is a word that is often associated with the architecture of Palladio, and it is a word that he defined with great specificity on the first page of his treatise, *Four Books of Architecture*:

> Beauty will result from the form and correspondence of the whole, with respect to the several parts, of the parts with regard to each other, and of these again to the whole; that the structure may appear an entire and compleat body, wherein each member agrees with the other, and all necessary to compose what you intend to form.[42]

What he is articulating is the Albertian notion of concinnity, a point that he emphasizes in his book by supplying the dimensions of all of his rooms. This principle of numerical proportionality has sometimes been lauded as the key to his universal approbation, but there is more to Palladio than what simply meets the eye. One aspect, certainly, is the overall corporeal presence or spatial feeling one experiences in a Palladian room, what Witold Rybczynski has described as scaling—that is to say, the relationship of parts (say, the size of a window in relation to the wall) and how it enhances both the sense of self within and the view without.[43] Another feature of Palladio's designs is the siting of his buildings. The Villa Rotunda, which functioned as a casino or place of entertainment, was placed atop the crest of a hill. The Villa Barbaro, by contrast, is subdued and bucolic. It is nestled into the edge of a tree line in the foothills of the Dolomite Alps, a geological force serving as a counterpoint to the horizontal and tripartite division of the building itself. The Barbaro brothers inherited an older farmhouse and vinicultural estate at the death of their father in 1549, and they decided to share and expand it. Many Venetian families who owned country villas were at the time directing them to agricultural purposes because the Ottomans were shutting off the importation of food from the East. Palladio viewed the country villa from a different perspective. He suggests that the rural life, with its proximity to nature, not only invigorate one's "strength and health" but also improves the mind, which "fatigued by the agitations of the city, will be greatly restor'd and comforted, and be able quietly to attend the studies of letters, and contemplation."[44]

The primary axis leading through the vineyards toward the villa has a gatekeeper at the fountain of Neptune, the ceremonial husband of Venice. The god, however, looks not outward to the countryside but back toward the villa in what has been interpreted as a nod of aesthetic appreciation. At the fountain, the villa, with its ochre cast, asserts itself from its wooded backdrop, and originally one approached its Ionic temple facade through its "beautiful gardens" populated with statuary.[45] The ground floor of the central pavilion is utilitarian in its functions, thus the stage production begins on the main level. Here the central axis outside cuts all the way through the house and culminates at a large rear courtyard enclosed by a semicircular nymphaeum with a grotto cut into the hillside. The nymphaeum houses various deities, and it surrounds "a small lake," as Palladio himself described it, "which serves for a fish-pond."[46] Gods are everywhere to be found in this romp through the garden, watered by a complex hydraulic system from a spring. The tall rooms on the main level of the central pavilion are entirely Palladian in scale and spatial character, yet what elevates the villa to sublimity are the detailing of the rooms boldly accentuated by the masterful frescoes of Veronese.[47] The latter illustrate the relatively new technique of *quadratura*, or the use of perspectival, exaggerated foreshortening on ceilings and walls to create three-dimensional effects—an art earlier practiced by Giulio Romano at Mantua. Combined with this technique is the use of *trompe l'oeil*, or visual deceptions introduced to blur the line between reality and illusion, or between the actual three-dimensional architectural forms and the appearance of similar forms created by the murals. The painter plays off the talents of the architect.

The overall theme of Daniele's iconographic scheme is cosmic harmony or the divine laws that govern all, including the arts. Olympian scenes occupy the ceilings, whereas the wall panels below are largely fictive landscapes of the countryside with villas and ruins. Sophisticated humor—puns and interjections—is everywhere on display. A ceiling panel of the Hall of Bacchus presents the deity in the clouds offering grape juice to two shepherds, accompanied by a muse playing a violin. To the left and right of this panel are two foreshortened panels with arbors and vines, seemingly extending the ceiling into the sky. Musical themes are also prevalent throughout. In the Hall of the Cross, pairs of nymphs play a number of instruments—tambour, flute, violin, lute—and in one instance a three-dimensional door molding frames a trompe l'oeil mural of a small girl stepping out between two doors. The main room of the Hall of Olympia stands at the end of the main enfilade and opens to the rear courtyard. The seven major deities of the zodiac, allegories of the four terrestrial elements and the four seasons, all participate in the gathering, but below them the wife and children of Marc'Antonio look down upon the guests looking upward. Even Veronese makes an appearance in an enfilade panel as a rural hunter in Palladio's theater. Such playfulness would be replicated in nearly all of the grand baroque palaces that would crop up across Europe over the next two centuries, but here they are realized in a relatively small and inexpensively fabricated stucco-and-brick villa. Two brothers with a dream of paradise—a belief that presentiments of the divine could be experienced in the earthly world—found an architect and a painter to make it real.

Utopias

Palladio was eight years old when Thomas More's *Utopia* appeared in 1516, and with the publication we have a new term that will compete with the notion of paradise. Yet the twin ideas of paradise and utopia, as we suggested earlier, are not as close in their meaning as it might seem, although it is possible for both ideas to be pursued simultaneously. Paradises generally spring from a person's inner yearning for happiness in life, and they can be manifested in the garden or in the joy of creative expression. It has no political underpinning. Utopia, by contrast, is often founded on a moral imperative to alter human nature and its social structure. Hence, utopian writers are inherently exacting or importunate, and all political revolutions are born from this impulse. Utopians deal with promulgating cold, hard (self-presumed) facts; paradisiacally minded people are concerned with cultivating gardens and mending the soul. Utopians tend to focus their attention on cities, which today are often the scene of anger, debilitation, and apathy. Paradisiacally minded people cultivate gardens, figuratively speaking, because they repair the ailing urban landscapes of humanity's narcissistic and utilitarian making.

We can also see these distinctions in the utopian literature of the sixteenth and seventeenth centuries, even in what is arguably the first such effort—Niccolò Machiavelli's *The Prince* (1513). It was written as a political guide but it was also, as the final chapter makes clear, an effort to preserve the humanity of Machiavelli's beloved Florentine culture. By contrast, Thomas More's *Utopia*, written three years later, dispenses with everything past and imagines an entirely new political structure. The people of More's novel, as we noted earlier, have moved beyond personal property and individual expression. They are quite content in their collective mannerisms and have become, by More's ethical decree, an ideal society. Each city in utopia's cities is divided into four equal quarters, each with a market, hospital, communal dining halls, and other necessary entities. If one has seen one city, one has seen them all. People wear the same style of clothing, have the same social values, and the garden is seemingly the only outlet left for creative expression. More's cities may be "large and well-built," but they also come at a significant human sacrifice—a planned environment lacking individual expression. "One might withdraw in horror from this calculated elimination of variety," as Colin

ILLUSTRATION 5.7 Title Page to Thomas More's *Utopia*, 1615.

Rowe once noted, "and quite rightly so, for the ideal city, though an entertaining type to inspect, is often a somewhat monotonous environment."[48] More's utopia, like Plato's republic before him, is one impressed with the thumbprint of a grand social planner, an impulse that inevitably demands the moral conformity of the masses and their habits of thought.

It was perhaps not coincidental that this appeal to morality was voiced at a time when European countries were eradicating the indigenous populations in the New World and facilitating global networks of slavery. The line between utopia and vassalage, to use a better word, is rarely drawn with exactitude. Francesco Patrizi's *The Happy City*, which appeared in Venice in 1553, seems to be the exception. Its focus is on happiness, which derives from the pursuit of three things: longevity of life, the pursuit of virtue, and comfort. Longevity demands a particular care of the body, and in this regard the climate and location of the city are important, although he offers no advice for the architectural environment. Pursuit of virtue is self-evident, but the desire for comfort is where his model breaks down. To provide this comfort, he is forced to insert into his city an inferior (and unhappy) class of people, consisting of peasants, artisans, and merchants. They attend to the city's food production, manufacturing, and the running of the infrastructure. Above this inferior class is an oligarchic and Platonic class of warriors, magistrates, and priests who can dedicate their lives to the pursuit of virtue and happiness. Rules have to be in place. The gentry are indoctrinated as to their self-importance through communal education. In short, they are bred to live as families and work together as clans in a brotherhood of ruling elites. To preclude the lower classes from thoughts of rebellion, their family members are not allowed to dwell under the same roof. Overseeing this oligarchy is someone akin to a sage who, with his vast knowledge of astrology and other domains, selects the ages and people allowed for procreation and the timing of their acts.

Tomasso Campanella's *The City of the Sun* is not very different in spirit from that of Patrizi, although here utopia more easily crosses over into dystopia. The personal life of Campanella certainly contributed to his displeasure with humanity. He joined a Dominican monastery in his native Calabria, but he left without permission to pursue his interest in philosophy and astrology. In 1594, during the Inquisition, he was arrested in Padua on the charge of heresy and imprisoned in Rome for three years. After returning to Calabria, he soon found trouble by participating in a rebellion against the Spanish authorities, who at the time controlled southern Italy. He was tortured, confessed, and likely would have been executed if he had not feigned madness. For the next twenty-seven years he remained in a dungeon, where he wrote his short utopian novel around 1602, only a small part of his vast literary output.

The novel, a conversation between a grandmaster of the Knights Hospitaller and a Genoese sea captain, describes a land "below the equator" known as Taprobane, on which the captain had shipwrecked. Here he was treated as a guest in the most advanced social system on the earth. All property and pleasures were shared in common, there was little or no crime or social strife, education was universal, wonder drugs had been perfected, and manual labor had been reduced to four hours a day. People lived between 100 and 200 years. The society was ruled by a high priest called Metaphysic, under whom three princes commanded the forces of power (military), wisdom, and love. Below them was another bureaucratic layer of magistrates. All residents wore the same toga—the men's falling above the knees, the women (for whom cosmetics were forbidden) below. Sleeping quarters and meals were shared in common, often with music, and children were reared by a collective. Again, only a few individuals, the most handsome and beautiful, were selected for procreation, with the timing of intercourse again prescribed by the magistrate of eugenics.

The circular form of the city proposed by Campanella was based on Atlantis, only here were seven circuits of three-story row housing, each on more elevated ground. At the center was a circular temple decorated with astrological motifs. The architecture possesses little interest, but what makes his city unique is that on the first floor and frieze of each of the seven circuits, exterior and interior, are paintings or reliefs depicting the sum of human knowledge. Youths receive their education not through reading books but by studying these panels. Maxim Gorky, who was familiar with Campanella, seized upon the political possibilities of this stratagem and brought it to the attention of Vladimir Lenin during the Russian Revolution, and it became the inspiration for the poster art of Soviet Realism.[49] Campanella, however, was deeply religious, and he viewed his utopian cosmogony as a reformed Catholicism—a "natural" Christianity—which would emerge with the elimination of personal property and the denial of personal ambition. It is nevertheless difficult to square his system with his vision.

It was only a few years later that another cleric, this time a Lutheran pastor, would put forth his utopian vision born out of the Reformation. Lewis Mumford, for one, much admired Johannes Andreae, "his fine intelligence and his candor," and characterized him as someone who stood apart from the crowd of utopian thinkers of the early seventeenth century.[50] The German Andreae was a reformed Rosicrucian who knew the works of Campanella, and in fact once visited him in prison. His book *Christianopolis* appeared in 1619, or one year after the start of the Thirty Years' War—the religious war between Catholics and Protestants that devastated central Europe. Within the context of this period, the ideal of a Christian society taking its roots back to the humble beginnings of Christ himself was therefore quite appealing.

After a shipwreck at sea, the protagonist finds himself stranded on an island, and after some preliminary interrogations he is led into the town of Christianopolis, an educated commune of 400 pious members. The city's plan and the dull building blocks of the residential quarters are again unnoteworthy, and near the center is a four-story college that dispenses education. At the advanced level, the college has a massive library and eight theaters for teaching such things as the ancient languages, grammar, rhetoric, metaphysics and ethics, mathematics, and astrology. The social structure is largely egalitarian, with a minimal ruling class, and children leave home at an early age for their collective education. Chastity is paramount, and sex is allowed only for procreation. People are skilled in trades and work only four hours a day, because one is encouraged to have time for spiritual contemplation. At the very center of the town is a large circular temple seventy feet tall, which accommodates the entire population for church services.

There is, however, one paradisiacal feature of the town that is nearly unique to utopias of this period, which is the attribute of gardens. The moat around the town is stocked with fish, and the areas beyond produce crops. Row houses have vegetable gardens in the rear, and the area around the college has two gardens, one for vegetables and medicinal herbs and the other a pleasure garden, inside of which are caged birds (for their songs) and beehives (for their fragrance). It is a garden envisioned for contemplation, paradisaical yet also didactic. People "learn here to judge the value of human beauty," says Andreae, but also to plot the course to the afterlife—the fact that "we are born, we grow up, we are in our prime, we droop, and pine away."[51] Yet this enigma possesses as well a greater meaning for paradise:

> Rather let us wonder at those who, though they love the earth most of all, neglect entirely that which is the best of the earth, its use and beautiful decoration. Yet they are not willing to seem to burden the earth, though they tread it with crude feet. Let us lament the lost paradise and long for its restoration. For though we look upon natural objects now with faulty vision, when our sight has been restored through the cross, we will behold all things not on the surface, but in their inmost depths.[52]

Notes

1. Thomas More, "Utopia," in *Ideal Commonwealths* (New York: The Colonial Press, 1901), 35–6.
2. E. Frank and Fritzie P. Manuel, *Utopian Thought in the Western World* (Cambridge, MA: Belknap Press, 1979), 112–13.

3. Robert Pogue Harrison, *Gardens: An Essay on the Human Condition* (Chicago, IL: University of Chicago Press, 2008), 92.

4. "Third Day," in John Payne (trans.), *Stories of Boccaccio (The Decameron)* (The Bibliophilist Library, 1903), 132.

5. See Liane Lefaivre, *Leon Battista Alberti's Hypnerotomachia Poliphili: Re-Cognizing the Architectural Body in the Early Italian Renaissance* (Cambridge, MA: Massachusetts Institute of Technology Press, 2005). Lefaivre considers Alberti within the context of his entire literary output, in particular those works dealing with the allegorical themes of love, dreams, and mythological archetypes.

6. Alberto Pérez-Gómez, *Polyphilo or the Dark Forest Revisited: An Erotic Epiphany of Architecture* (Cambridge, MA: Massachusetts Institute of Technology Press, 1992), XIV.

7. Anthony Blunt, "The Hypnerotomachia Poliphili in 17th Century France," *Journal of the Warburg Institute* 1:2 (October 1937), 117–37.

8. *Hypnerotomachia Poliphili: The Strife of Love in a Dream*, trans. by Joscelyn Godwin (New York: Thames & Hudson, 1999), 22.

9. Ibid., 70–1.

10. Ibid., 92.

11. Ibid., 192. For a different reading of the *Hypnerotomachia Poliphili*—architecture as a metaphor grounded in the erotic impulse—see Pérez-Gómez, *Polyphilo or the Dark Forest Revisited* (note 6).

12. *Filarete's Treatise on Architecture: Being the Treatise by Antonio di Piero Averlino, Known as Filarete*, trans. by John R. Spencer (New Haven: Yale University Press, 1965), II:8r, 16.

13. 2:7v, 15.

14. For an interpretation of his labyrinths, see S. Land, "Sforzinda, Filarete and Filelfo," *Journal of the Warburg and Courtauld Institutes* 35 (1972), 391–7.

15. *Filarete's Treatise on Architecture* (note 12), 7:48v, 84.

16. Berthold Hub, "Filarete and the East: The Renaissance of a *Prisca Architectura*," *Journal of the Society of Architectural Historians* 70:1 (March 2011), 18–37.

17. For Leonardo's sketches, see I. A. Richter, ed., *Selections from the Notebooks of Leonardo da Vinci* (London: Oxford University Press, 1952), 213–14.

18. Frank Borsi, *Leon Battista Alberti* (New York: Harper & Rowe, 1977), 60.

19. See Anthony Grafton, *Leon Battista Alberti: Master Builder of the Italian Renaissance* (New York: Hill and Wang, 2000), 186–7.

20. Leon Battista Alberti, *On the Art of Building in Ten Books*, trans. by Joseph Rykwert, Neil Leach, and Robert Tavernor (Cambridge, MA: Massachusetts Institute of Technology Press, 1988), 4:2, 295.

21. On Alberti and Ficino, see Joan Gadol, *Leon Battista Alberti: Universal Man of the Early Renaissance* (Chicago, IL: University of Chicago Press, 1969), 10.

22. Leon Battista Alberti, *On Painting*, trans. by John R. Spencer (New Haven: Yale University Press, 1966), 92–3.

23. Alberti, *On the Art of Building* (note 20), 9:2, 156.

24. Ibid., Prologue, 5.

25. Ibid., 3:12, 81.

26. Ibid., 6:12, 180; 3:7–8, 70–73; 3:12, 81.

27. Ibid., 3:12, 79; 7:10, 219.

28. Ibid., 5:17, 146.

29. Ibid., 6:2, 156.

30. Cicero, *De natura deorum*, trans. by H. Rackham (Cambridge, MA: Harvard University Press, 1979), I:79, 77.

31. Alberti, *On the Art of Building* (note 20), 6:2, 156.

32. Ibid., VI:13, 183.

33. Ibid., 8:9, 287; 7:1, 191.

34. Ibid., 9:4, 300.

35. Ibid., 4:3, 101.

36. Ibid., 4:5, 106.

37. Cicero, *Orator*, trans. by H. M. Hubbel (Cambridge, MA: Harvard University Press, 1971), 24:81.

38. Alberti, *On the Art of Building* (note 20), 9:5, 303.

39. Ibid., 9:8, 312.

40. On the academy, see James Hankins, "Cosimo de'Medici and the 'Platonic Academy,'" *Journal of the Warburg and Courtauld Institutes* 53 (1990), 144–62.

41. Johann Wolfgang von Goethe, *Italy Journey: 1786–1788*, trans. by W. H. Auden and Elizabeth Mayer (San Francisco, CA: North Point Press, 1982), 341.

42. Andrea Palladio, *The Four Books of Architecture*, trans. by Isaac Ware (New York: Dover, 1965), 1:1, 1.

43. Witold Rybczynski, *The Perfect House: A Journey with the Renaissance Master Andrea Palladio* (New York: Scribner, 2002), 244–7.

44. Palladio, *The Four Books* (note 42), I2:12, 46.
45. Cited from Paul Holberton, *Palladio's Villas: Life in the Renaissance Countryside* (London: John Murray, 1990), 97.
46. Palladio, *The Four Books* (note 42), 2:14, 49.
47. On the murals of Veronese, see Anne-Sophie Molinie, *Les Fresques de la Villa Barbaro* (Mayenne: Canopé, 2015).
48. Colin Rowe, "The Architecture of Utopia," in *The Mathematics of the Ideal Villa and Other Essays* (Cambridge, MA: Massachusetts Institute of Technology Press, 1976), 206.
49. Manuel and Manuel, *Utopian Thought in the Western World* (note 2), 272.
50. Lewis Mumford, *The Story of Utopia* (New York: Boni and Liveright, 1928), 81.
51. Johann Valentin Andreae, *Christianopolos: An Ideal State of the Seventeenth Century*, trans. by Felix Emil Held (New York: Oxford University Press, 1916), 268.
52. Ibid., 269.

6

PARADISE GARDENS

Tea House in the Garden

The particularities of Japan's terrain have in many ways shaped its culture. In contrast to the rolling plains of eastern China, the islands of Japan were a creation of long-standing tectonic and volcanic forces, the so-called Rim of Fire, which geologically produced a multitude of finely textured mountains (in ancient times viewed as deities) separated by narrow river valleys. In AD 794, the Japanese emperor Kamnu founded the new imperial capital of Kyoto (Heian-kyo) in one of these valleys. The plan of the city—which would remain the imperial seat for the country until 1868—was based on the Tang dynasty capital of Chang'an, and from the perspective of geomancy the city was ideally situated. It was protected along the north, west, and east by a chain of hills, and it was framed within the valley by two rivers and an abundance of brooks and springs. Moreover, the moisture in the valley's air often produces an atmospheric haze or dew that promotes lush floral growth. With the founding of the city began the Heian period in Japanese history, one generally seen as a prosperous and peaceful one: the golden age of feudal Japan.

The rectangular plan of the new capital aspired to perfection. The city's main north-south axis or grand avenue, 280 feet wide and a little under three miles in length, led from the ceremonial Shinto Gate at the south end to the imperial precinct at the north, in which were housed the Great Hall of the Imperial Court, the Court of Abundant Pleasures, the Imperial Palace, and some fifty other buildings or ministries. It was enclosed by a wall with fourteen gates. South of the complex was the Shinsen'en Garden, originally the emperor's pleasure garden and nature reserve. Its lake served the nobility as a place for divination but also for moon-viewing by boating parties. The remainder of the city was parceled into square blocks divided by streets and alleys. Two symmetrical markets were planned in the southern part of the city, and the main gate on each side was graced with a temple complex. In addition to serving as imposing imperial symbols, their pagodas were intended to contain the *chi* or celestial energies that might otherwise flow out of the city toward the south.

The housing of the upper classes during the Heian period was defined by the Shinden style, or curved-roofed architecture. The residences were structured around a main hall with a broad, deep canopy, at the center of which were the living and sleeping areas sealed off by a movable system of screens. Surrounding these areas was a belt of open rooms whose size and use could be adjusted by partitions. Verandahs extended the low-hanging eaves out further, which created the cavernous darkness of classical Japanese interiors; conversely the gardens outside became the main source of light. As the nineteenth-century poet Jun'ichirō Tanizaki, in his book *In Praise of Shadows*, speaks

DOI: 10.4324/9781003178460-6

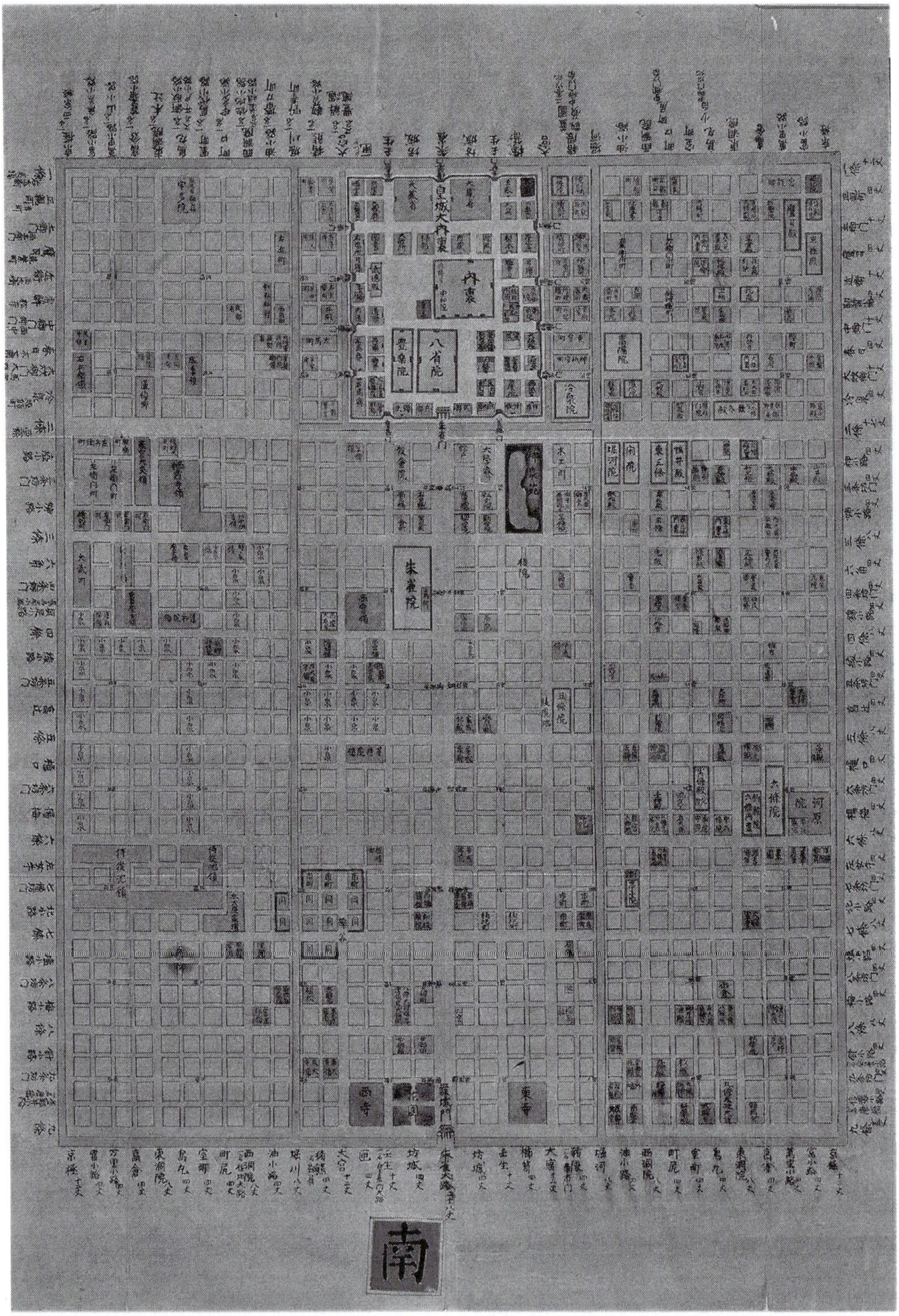

ILLUSTRATION 6.1 Plan of Kyoto (Heian-kyo), transcribed by Mori Koan (1750).

Source: Public domain.

to the aesthetics: "The light from the garden steals in but dimly through paper-paneled doors, and it is precisely this indirect light that makes for us the charm of a room."[1] Attached to the main hall, in a rectilinear network, were a series of smaller pavilions joined by sheltered breezeways, generally forming a U-shaped ensemble of buildings sharing the garden on the south. The house and the garden were inseparable. The main hall looked over a narrow court into the garden, which would generally feature one large pond or series of ponds with islands, bridges, and vegetation.

In almost every regard, Kyoto was conceived as an ideal city in an ideal location. Yet the city in its development, as it proceeded into the Middle Ages, did not follow its plan. As Matthew Stavros has noted, the western half of the city, which suffered from a surfeit of groundwater, never entirely filled out its gridded allotments, and later development tended to concentrate itself in the eastern half of the rectangle.[2] Soon thereafter the western market disappeared, and eventually the western temple and the ceremonial main gate. The eastern half of the city also underwent changes. As political power in the coming centuries devolved from the emperor to a cadre of aristocratic families, the northeastern quadrant with its abundance of palaces became known as the "upper city," a precinct onto itself. The southeastern quadrant or "lower city" became occupied by tradesmen and other classes. Another factor contributing to the transformation of the city was that, beginning in the ninth century, a number of Buddhist temples, communities formerly barred from building within the city limits, were constructed in the adjacent hills east of the city. These complexes composed, in effect, small cities unto themselves and shifted the population center of the city toward the east. Today, Kyoto's roughly 2,000 temples and gardens associated with these complexes, together with a few of the surviving aristocratic palaces, define the city as a UNESCO World Heritage Site. It is indisputably one of the most beautiful cities in the world.

Notwithstanding the failure of Kyoto's ideal plan, the new imperial city and Heian culture in general came to be shaped by two other factors that would influence the development of the garden. One was a body of garden theory passed down from China, which would evolve into a specifically Japanese approach to gardening. The second, in two waves, was the introduction into Japan of Pure Land Buddhism and Zen Buddhism. They brought with them a philosophical temper to be explored through the cultivation of the garden.

The *Sakuteiki*, the world's oldest manual of garden design, was written in the late eleventh century by Tachibano no Toshitsuna, although it was based on already well-established standards. A literal translation of its opening words regarding the making of a garden defines its essential attribute—the "act of setting up stones upright." The stones were already understood as the central elements of the garden, and they were not just any stones.[3] They had to be carefully selected specifically for the mood and symbolism to be conveyed. The treatise lays out all of the details of planning a garden, including the education of the gardener. The novice should travel widely and view firsthand the most scenic landscapes of Japan, which, at a miniaturized scale, can serve as inspirations for design. The first stage of design entails selecting the appropriate style or styles of the garden—the ocean style, broad river style, mountain torrent style, wetland style, and reed style, for example. When the plan is ready to be executed, the next step is to dig out the pond and determine the direction that the water will flow into and away from it. It is only at this stage that one shapes the landscape with rocks, islands, vegetation, and bridges. These islands also have their styles: mountain, meadow, forest, rock shore, cloud, mist type, cove beach type, slender stream, tide land, and pine bark. Details are vital to a culture fastidious with design. The ideal waterfall should be between three and four feet in height, because when it is lower it reveals "the source of the water flowing behind and the composition consequently lacks depth and appears insignificant." Conversely,

> waterfalls appear graceful when they flow out unexpectedly from narrow crevices between stones half-hidden in shadows. At the source of the waterfall, just above the Waterfall Stone, some well-chosen stones should be placed so that, when seen from afar, the water will appear to be flowing from the crevices of those boulders, creating a splendid effect.[4]

Other stones, either bottom stones or larger ones, can be placed in the water to modulate the sound and visual effects.

"Pure Land" Buddhism brought still another dimension to garden design. Its aim was to employ the garden as a means to enlightenment, a vision of paradise. Classic images of the Amida Buddha—literally the "boundless light"—depict him in a lotus garden surrounded by the celestial lake, centered within the cosmos. This branch of Buddhism accepts the fact that the world will always be corrupt, and thus aspirants should seek out the "pure land" or peaceful bliss of nature, also known as the "western paradise." Earthly beauty or a landscape that surpasses all others in its majesty is equated with a state of spiritual deliverance. Pure Land gardens are those described in the *Sakuteiki* and are built around a large pond or water systems with islands, bridges, and prominent rocks. One can view the garden from within the Amida room of a hall, but one can also experience it kinesthetically by strolling through the garden and imbibing the multisensory experience. The pond may become the ocean, and rocks islands, within which are miniaturized places that evoke the Western Paradise. The Pure Land garden is thus rich in sensory appeal. In 1929, when the young architect Richard Neutra visited the imperial gardens of Katsura, in Kyoto, he was simply overwhelmed by the "humanized naturalism of the Japanese landscape," by the "multisensorial appeal of the sounds, odors, and colors of nature, the thermal variations of shade, sunlight, and air movements." He recorded as well the vestibular effects of walking through the gardens,

> how the inner ear busily records for us our turns, accelerations, and retardations when, following a magical paving pattern, we haltingly walk the irregular windings of a carefully planned, non-repetitious path or tread the willful zigzag of simple planks bridging a lotus pool.

It was, for him, the closest thing on earth to "a lost paradise to man"; that is, "nature pure and simple, untouched nature."[5]

ILLUSTRATION 6.2   Tea House at Katsura Imperial Villa, Kyoto, early seventeenth century.

Source: Photo by KimonBerlin. Wikimedia CC BY-SA 2.0.

The later introduction of Zen Buddhism brought an even more intense focus on the garden, which now became a dry garden of raked gravel with miniaturized vegetation, stones, and moss. It was designed to create the proper mood for meditation, and these gardens tend to be smaller, more intimate or miniature in their detailing, and more austere in their features. They, like a landscape painting, were also intended to be viewed from a single location, although they remain highly tactile in their details. They may pose an enigma to the aspiring monk by stressing abstract qualities such as irregularity, impermanence, or intricacy, or they may also intensify the latent forces of nature. The monk Yousai, who introduced the Rinzai school of Zen Buddhism into Japan in the twelfth century, also designed the dry garden at Kenninji in Kyoto. It had no pond but simply a canvas of gravel and moss, on which are placed a few selected features of rock formations and colorful vegetation. The famed dry garden of the Ryōanji, or "temple of the peaceful dragon," is roughly thirty by eighty feet, walled on three sides, and visually accessible from a platform area. The ground is raked gravel and within it are fifteen large and small stones arranged in island groupings for the visitor to ponder. Some visitors have interpreted it as the voice of silence; John Cage, after making 170 sketches, composed a minimalist score of music that he titled *Ryōanji*. The film director Takahiko Iimura has characterized the garden as the concretization of the Japanese idea of "*ma*-space"—vaguely, the idea of a void, intervals, or the consciousness of the duration of space and time.[6]

Yousai also introduced the tea ceremony into Japan. In the opening pages of his classic *Book of Tea*, Okakura Kakuzo joins the Sung poet Lichihlai in lamenting the three most deplorable things in the world: the ruin of a young mind through bad education, the degradation of fine paintings through vulgar admiration, and the waste of fine tea through incompetent manipulation. The last calamity refers not only to the preparation of tea but also to its decorous presentation. Teaism, in Kakuzo's view, is synonymous with both Zen and Taoism, and these three manners of observing and understanding ritual collectively compose "a religion in the art of life."[7]

ILLUSTRATION 6.3   Dry Zen Garden at Ryōan-ji, Kyoto, before 1680.

Source: Photo by DXR. Wikimedia CC BY-SA 4.0.

Tea was first appreciated for its medicinal value, but within a few centuries it would evolve into a ceremonial act of aesthetic self-realization. Exalted in this regard was the sixteenth-century tea master Sen no Rikyu, who is also known for the high standards of his designs for flower containers, tea pots, and scoops. He was an avid gardener. One story that has followed him down through centuries was his famed garden of morning glories, which were then quite rare in Japan. The imperial regent, having been told of the beauty of the garden, asked to see it. Rikyu invited him to a morning tea at his house, and when the ruler arrived, he found no garden but only a ground of gravel and sand. Frustrated, he entered the tea house with anger but it was quickly appeased because, as Kakuzo relates: "On the tokonoma, in a rare bronze of Sung workmanship, lay a single morning-glory—the queen of the whole garden!"

In contrast to the majestic architecture of villas and monasteries, the *chashitsu* or tea house stands out for its supreme modesty. It originated as a room within a larger pavilion, but by the fifteenth century it took the form of an isolated cottage or straw-roofed hut with a sitting room open on one side to a verandah and small courtyard. The alcove housed a simple altar for the requisite flowers and incense. The customary tea house, approximately ten feet square, was outfitted with tatami mats and served a maximum of five guests. Although feigning modesty, if not poverty, the tea house was both a highly refined and costly pavilion due to the selection of high-quality materials and their work-manship. A low door required a bow or gesture of humility on the part of the entering guests, and the remote locations of the tea house allowed no sound to intrude except that of nature. The dress, movements, and gestures of the tea host were ceremonial but also attended to a natural simplicity.

Yet the garden was once again essential to the entire tea experience. For it was in passing from the domestic house through the garden to the tea house that one removes, as it were, the concerns of the outside world and attains the proper frame of mind for the ceremony. The *roji* or path to the tea house is generally neither linear nor well demarcated. It meanders through vegetation and the irregularities of stepping stones, forcing the guest to lower their gaze and enjoy the pebbles, pine needles, mossy surfaces, lanterns, and other details along the way. For Christopher Tadgell, "the Zen garden was ideally—but by no means invariably—organized so that the path serving the blind tea-room symbolized passage between engaging artifice and the primitive purity of undefined wilder-ness."[8],[9] If every tea master was also a garden designer, however, it symbolized something more—the path through the garden became the rites for the passage to paradise.

Court of Lions

In one of the tales of *The Arabian Nights*, a shepherd in search of his missing she-camel went into the desert and stumbled upon a vast city filled with palaces and pavilions yet no one was living there. The city gates were inlaid with jewels and jacinth, the buildings were built of gold and silver, pillars were made of chrysolite and rubies, rivers ran underneath the pavilions, the streets were flanked with fruit trees and palms, and the gardens were planted with ambergris and saffron. He loaded him-self up with as many jewels as he could carry and returned home, whereupon he was summoned by authorities to explain his discovery. It became apparent to one of the ruler's advisors that the shep-herd had found the "city of many-columned Iram," and the advisor related the story of its founding. The most powerful ruler on earth, Shaddad, had read a description of paradise and decided to rep-licate it on earth. He summoned the 100,000 kings over which he ruled (each with 100,000 chiefs, and each chief with 100,000 warriors) and demanded that they begin mining operations for the precious materials for his city. After twenty years, Shaddad ordered his kings to bring him their best architects, engineers, artisans, and laborers and commenced building the city, which was to contain a towering castle, 1,000 pavilions, each with 1,000 columns of chrysolite and ruby. The construc-tion took another 300 years but, when finished, Shaddad prepared his vast retinue to move to his paradisiacal capital. When they were within one day of arriving at the new city, however, Allah sent down a "mighty rushing sound" that killed everyone—an auricular warning about human vanity.[10]

ILLUSTRATION 6.4   Courtyard of the Great Mosque of Damascus, also known as the Umayyad Mosque.

Source: Photo by Vyacheslav Argenberg. Wikimedia CC BY 4.0.

The Quran makes only a passing reference to Iram, but its verses overflow with more than a hundred descriptions of paradise. Islam drew upon the Old Testament and the fall of Adam and Eve in the Garden of Eden. The Quran differs from the New Testament, however, in that its vision of heaven is the garden of paradise. It is a lush and fragrant garden with shady vales, fountains, and rivers of pure water, milk, wine, and strained honey. The righteous live in an ideal climate, sit on golden couches shaded by fruit-laden branches, and are dressed in fine silk with elaborate brocade. They wear bracelets of gold and drink from silver vessels and crystal goblets. They are attended to by youths who do not age. The appeal of abundant water and lush gardens was apparently strong for Mohammed, who was born into the Quraysh desert tribe on the Arabian Peninsula, an area in which vegetation was scarce.

From its humble beginnings, Mohammed's religion with its armies spread outward in every direction. Warriors conquered Persia in the mid-seventh century and continued eastward into Afghanistan and Pakistan. Forces moved northwest into the Levant and took Damascus in AD 634. Armies also moved westward across Egypt and North Africa and into the Iberian Peninsula, where in the eighth century and beyond it would achieve its artistic flowering. The change in religious culture also carried with it a stylistic change in building. The Dome of the Rock, the Islamic shrine atop the Temple Mount in Jerusalem started by Umayyad Caliph Abd al-Malik in 687, is an octagonal form with an interior circular drum and dome supported on columns and piers. Its double ambulatories are outfitted with brilliant inscriptions and foliated patterns, and its use of slightly pointed arches formed of alternating bands of differently colored marbles would become a standard motif of later mosques.

Al-Malik's son, Caliph al-Walid I, built the Great Mosque of Damascus in the first two decades of the eighth century on the site of a Christian church dedicated to John the Baptist (itself built on the site of a Roman temple). Much of the interior of the church was removed and reused, as the hall of worship was extended laterally in both directions, forming a south wing (170 yards in length) of what would become a double-story rectangular plaza—one of the great urban squares in the world. The square itself features three architectural gems: an ablution fountain near the entrance to the mosque, the Dome of the Clock, and the octagonal Dome of the Treasury, outfitted with exquisite mosaics resting on eight Corinthian columns. The walls of the mosque interior were originally carpeted with mosaics depicting the Garden of Eden, created by thousands of Byzantine craftsmen, imported from Egypt, Persia, Greece, and Morocco. Damascus at this time was also famed for its vast number of private palaces.

Islam also created several new cities, among them Kufah, a new capital started in 638 and originally based on a four-square plan with the mosque and palace at the center. Each of the squares, in turn, has a *maydan* or urban plaza at its center. It too has a Great Mosque, one that has recently undergone renovation. In its geometric conception, however, Kufah would be rivaled by the "Round City of Baghdad," started by the Abbasid Caliph al-Mansur in 762 and completed four years later. The Abbasid Uprising destroyed the Umayyad dynasty, and al-Mansur murdered every member of the family line—save one, who we will return to shortly. Situated along the west bank of the Tigris and fed by a system of canals, Baghdad's three circular walls were over a mile in diameter and were pierced by four vaulted gates, each topped with a gilded dome. Inside, its four grand avenues intersected at the domed Palace of the Golden Gate and the main hypostyle mosque. The four axes were not oriented to cardinal points but were rotated at forty-five-degree angles to them. Surrounding the palace and mosque were government buildings, among them a library, the "House of Wisdom." Some housing was concentrated between the palace and middle walls of the city, whereas outside the city were four residential and commercial districts, a reviewing ground, gardens, hippodromes, bathhouses, and palaces.

In Islam's spread west across northern Africa, with a semitropical climate, the garden became more developed. The paradise garden was a good fit with the atrial type of housing of native Berber populations, in which the main rooms were oriented inward around a central court. Palaces with their gardens were renowned in such cities as Fez and Marrakesh, but none of sufficient scale to match the Great Eastern and Western Palaces in Cairo. The city along the Nile was founded in 970 by the Fatimid Caliphate, which had previously been based in Tunisia. The two grand palaces were centered within an enclave large enough to house the 30,000 members of the ruling class apart from others in the city. The Western Palace was actually built over an existing garden known as the *Bustan Al-Kafur*, or "Garden of Camphor Trees," yet the entire palatial complex was known for its many majestic gardens and courtyards with outdoor pavilions, fountains, and even tunnels large enough to allow members of the royal family to travel by horseback between the gardens and parts of the palaces.

The best-preserved examples of the Islamic gardens are today to be found in Al-Andalus on the southern Iberian Peninsula, and in particular in the prosperous cities of Cordova, Seville, and Granada. Their story begins with the Umayyad prince Abd al-Rahman I escaping persecution in Damascus and fleeing along the coastline of northern Africa. In 755, he crossed over to Spain, where he gained local support, overthrew the regional governor, and proclaimed himself the ruler of a new and independent caliphate. After numerous wars and rebellions, he and his successors transformed the former Roman colony of Cordova, with its excellent climate and abundant springs, into one of the largest and wealthiest cities in the world, rivaling Constantinople with an estimated tenth-century population of a half million people. The city's residents, as contemporary texts report, were courteous, polished, endowed with exquisite taste, and donned a richness of dress. The city was also the preeminent cultural center within a more rural western Europe, which at the time had no city that could match Cordova for its many libraries, teachers, poetry recitals, and public baths.

At its height, Cordova is said to have 60,000 palaces and at least as many gardens—the latter built by extending the aqueducts constructed by the Romans.

Al-Rahman, upon his arrival, embarked upon two major tasks. One was to construct a palace and gardens of suitable grandeur for a caliph; the second was to build his own "Great Mosque" to contend in grandeur with the Mosque of Damascus. The Cordova Mosque, which partly survives today as one of Europe's finest architectural treasures, was started in 784 as a relatively modest ten-aisle, twelve-bay meeting hall with a vast courtyard or enclosed orchard along the north. The characteristic motif of the design was the superimposed or double-story open arches, dressed with alternating red-and-white voissoirs, supported on columns of porphyry, jasper, onyx, and marble. The materials for the interior forest of columns were largely taken from nearby Roman temples and monuments. In the ninth century, the mosque was enlarged by twenty bays, and between 950 and 980 al-Rahman III and his son al-Hakam II added the interlacing arches and Edenic *mihrabs* or prayer niches along the south wall, executed in gold, silver, and brass. Around the turn of the millennium, al-Mansur increased the mosque by half again, expanding it with another eight aisles. When completed, the mosque consisted of a vast rectangular system of 544 bays supported on 856 columns, making it one of the most sublime, if not surreal, architectural creations ever built. Unfortunately, a religious war intervened. In 1523, Charles V ended Islamic rule and rudely inserted a large Gothic-and-Renaissance church into the middle of the complex. The stylistic personalities of the two competing architectures scarcely survive one another.

Remnants of the original palace of al-Rahman do not survive, but there are a few descriptions of his paradise garden, a project that reportedly took forty years to complete and involved 10,000 workmen. According to one account:

> His passion for flowers and plants went even so far as to induce him to send agents to Syria and other countries, with a commission to procure him all sorts of seeds and plants; and, when brought to Andalus, these productions of distant regions and various climates failed not to take root, blossom, and bear fruit in the royal gardens, when they afterwards spread all over the country. From this garden originates the pomegranate, called *Safari*, which in point of flavour, smallness of seed, and abundance of juice, has not its equal in the world.[11]

Although this particular paradise is lost to time, the ruins of the palace of al-Rahman III, the *Madinat al-Zaha* or "shining city," remain today and excavation continues. This extraordinary complex, conceived as a new town to honor his wife, has a commanding site in the foothills of the Sierra Morena outside Cordova, terraced on three levels. The upper level housed the caliph's palace, halls, mosques, residences for high officials, the mint, baths, and gardens. The Prince's Garden was accessible only to a few of the caliph's entourage. The middle terrace, roughly 500 feet by 400 feet in dimension, was a four-square garden with a single pavilion or reception hall near the center, surrounded by four pools. On the lowest level was still another garden of similar dimensions, only a small part of which has been excavated. One can only imagine the Moorish splendor of the site a little more than a millennium ago, although the city itself survived less than a century.

We learn something more of the character of this paradise by turning to another of the Andalusian gems, the city of Granada, whose Spanish name means "pomegranate." The city and the palaces of the Alhambra, set on a ridge that once housed a Roman camp, has long been loved by painters, poets, and artists of every persuasion, but one can scarcely mention the city without noting the nineteenth-century writer Washington Irving who, in 1829, lived for three months in the palace's nearly abandoned halls, and it was there he wrote his famous book *The Alhambra*. In one of his tales, he relates the story of a young prince Ahmed, whose horoscope at birth noted that he would achieve greatness, if he were protected from a minor personality flaw—his amorous temperament.[12] His father built a palace to isolate him from the world and hired an Egyptian scholar to teach him every field of knowledge, everything except the notion of love. The plan worked for a few years, but the more the young prince wandered in the palace's enchanting gardens, the more he was prone to plunge into "delicious reverie" and pursue his interest in music and poetry. The shocked father decided to remove him from contact with the garden and placed him in the palace's tower, where the prince eventually learned the language of the birds. Neither the hawk, owl, bat, or swallow ever discussed with him the idea of love, but then one day a dove, chased by a hawk, flew into his cell and spoke of his love for his mate, and the fact that every creature has an ideal mate. The prince was at first mystified with the idea of "love" and the dove, to educate him, later dropped off a picture of a princess, similarly kept in waiting. The prince plotted his escape to find the princess and searched Granada, Seville, and Cordova with no success. Eventually he found her in Seville, but because he was a Muslim in a Catholic city, he was not allowed to compete for her honor. Yet with the aid of a magic carpet handed down by Solomon, he makes an escape with her back to his palace and the story has a happy ending.

The moral of the story is the power of a garden to restore one's human nature, and the gardens of the prince's palace were those of the Generalife, one of the great surviving gardens of the Islamic world. The word Generalife comes down from the Arabic words *jannet* (paradise) and *al-arif* (architect), or "Paradise of the Architect." The palace was built by Sultan Muhammad III in the early fourteenth century on an adjacent spur of land, separated from the Alhambra ridge by a narrow ravine now joined with a bridge. Water and gardens flow through every part of the palace, whose main garden is the Courtyard of the Aqueduct, a long, narrow walled-in garden with a channel of water running down the middle, fed by the arching sprays of water from marble basins on each side, crisscrossing each other. The vegetation between the walls and pathways was originally sunken in beds so that the flower and fruit would float above the pathways. Other gardens abound in the Generalife, and west of the Aqueduct court facing the Alhambra, are gardens cascading down the ridgeline, also abundant with cypress trees.

The Alhambra too has its gardens, courtyards, and fountains, and in fact it has been heralded by poets as an "emerald necklace" of palaces and gardens. One of the first courtyards the visitor meets upon climbing the hill is the Cuarto Dorado, or "golden chamber," with its filigree loggia at one end and a scalloped circular fountain set within an octagonal opening of the marble floor—a masterpiece of understatement. Adjacent to it is the Court of the Myrtles, the largest of the enclosed courts with a pond in the middle, flanked by marble walkways and rows of myrtles. At one end of the pond is the Comares Tower with the imposing, richly decorated Hall of Ambassadors or throne room. The room's power is derived from its walls, seven feet thick, into which glazed niches are seemingly carved. Its major feature, above the highly ornamented walls, is the pyramidal ceiling seventy-five feet above the floor, carved with 8,000 interlocking cedar pieces representing the seven heavens of the Islamic paradise.

The Alhambra also has its myriad legends, ballads, and folk tales. When Irving first arrived there, he tells us that his cicerone Mateo, upon first leading him into the Court of Lions, showed him traces of blood in the pavement and warned him that at night one could still hear the "the murmurings of a multitude; with now and then a faint tinkling like the distinct clank of chains." These were the sounds made by the wraiths of thirty-six Abencerrajes who, as legend would have it, were invited there for dinner only to be beheaded by the cruel Sultan Muley Hacén. Yet the story did not dissuade Irving from taking up residence in various apartments and exploring every inch within the palatial complex, so that he might experience firsthand the aura of the place. He later discerned that the specters of the Abencerrajes were none other than the "bubbling currents and tinkling falls of water, conducted under the pavement through pipes and channels to supply the fountains."[13] The remote bedroom that Irving eventually settled in, much to the worry of the chatelaine Dame Antonia, had been the boudoir of Elizabetta of Farnese, daughter of the Duke of Parma and second wife to Philip V. Yet originally it had belonged to Lindaraxa, a Moorish beauty and favorite of Muhammed VIII, whom she had sheltered after he had temporarily lost his throne. Upon his return, he rewarded her with a room overlooking a beautiful garden, which today is known as the Garden of Lindaraxa. Irving had chosen the room for the delectable fragrance emanating from the vegetation:

> Four centuries had elapsed since the fair Lindaraxa passed away, yet how much of the fragile beauty of the scenes she inhabited remained! The garden still bloomed in which she delighted; the fountain still presented the crystal mirror in which her charms may once have been reflected; the alabaster, it is true, had lost its whiteness; the basin beneath, overrun with weeds, had become the lurking-place of the lizard; but there was something in the very decay that enhanced the interest of the scene, speaking as it did of that mutability, the irrevocable lot of man and all his works.[14]

Guidebooks report that Lindaraxa's garden, with its cypresses, acacias, orange trees, and box bushes, is much photographed by visitors today.

Yet the greatest paradise of the Alhambra is just a few steps away from Lindaraxa's bedroom: the Court of the Lions. It is arguably the greatest surviving work of Islamic architecture. It is part of the third palatial complex started by Muhammad V in 1370, and its courtyard is a masterpiece of decorum: 115 feet by 65 feet in dimension, with the four water channels of a *chahar-bagh* alluding to the four rivers of paradise. From off-court basins, they feed water to the center of the courtyard, where there is a pool in which stands a large basin on the backs of twelve sculpted lions. The four quadrants articulated by the water channels were also originally sunken gardens almost three feet below the paths and planted with groves of orange trees, the blossoms of which were likely at eye level.

ILLUSTRATION 6.5   The Court of the Lions, Alhambra.

Source: Photo by Armandoreques. Wikimedia CC BY-SA 2.0.

What makes this courtyard so special—one inspired by the celestial "Courtyard of the Maidens" within the Alcázar Palace at Seville—is its detailing. The delicately fashioned arcade is constructed of filigree plaster supported on single and double marble columns. They are modulated in their spacing to create a subtle rhythmic effect. The axis on the north side of the court leads to the Hall of Two Sisters, a part of the sultana's residence noted for its stalactite dome with a star in the center. Complementing it on the south is the Hall of Abencerrajes, with a similar domed ceiling and an eight-pointed drum springing from stalactite pendentives. From every perspective the courtyard presents a subtle and mesmerizing spirit. If its model in Seville is palatial in exhausting every last ounce of its human energy, the Court of the Lions with its gurgling fountain is an understatement, a highly sensualized yet nevertheless modest pantheon dedicated to the architectural deities of scale, proportion, detail, sound, light, and shadow. Perhaps the murmuring sounds that Mateo heard in the Court of Lions were not the watery sounds of underground pipes, as Irving had deduced, but the spectral stirrings within a human heart at this glimpse of paradise—presented not as an idea but as a refined yet profoundly sensory experience that today seems unworldly in our pale and ruder age. The often-cited remark of the baroque poet and writer Lope de Vega perhaps best summed up the Alhambra's presence: "I do not know what to call this land upon which I stand. If what is beneath my feet is paradise, then what is the Alhambra? Heaven?"

Ode to Mumtaz

A similarly enchanting and paradisiacal sense of gardening seems also to have taken possession of the Mughal emperors of South Asia. Their founder was Zahīr un-Dīn Muhammad, generally known by the name Babur. He was born nine years before Christopher Columbus set sail for the Indies, and he was a maternal descendent of Genghis Khan. He was also the great-grandson of the Uzbekistani Emperor Timur, whose court in Samarkand was populated with a large garden bearing the names of the great Muslim cities: Shiraz, Baghdad, Damascus, and Cairo. Babur was much interested in literature, art, and music, and the "Gardener King" also followed his grandfather's horticultural interests. After losing his lands in Uzbekistan, he conquered and ruled parts of central Asia from the city of Kabul for more than twenty years. In and around this town, he built ten gardens, including the Bagh-e Babur, where his body was eventually interred. His memoirs teem with descriptions of his various gardens. In his description of the Bagh-e Vafa or Garden of Fidelity in Kabul, for example, he notes how he laid out the four garden beds of a paradise garden on a rise, fed by a reservoir of water, in which he planted orange and pomegranate trees. When he returned to the site eleven years later, the garden was fully mature:

> Its grass-plots were all covered with clover; its pomegranate trees were entirely of a beautiful yellow colour. It was then the pomegranate season, and the pomegranates were hanging red on the trees. The orange trees were green and cheerful, loaded with innumerable oranges; but the best oranges were not yet ripe. Its pomegranates are excellent, though not equal to the fine ones of our country. I never was so much pleased with the Bag-e-Vafa, as on this occasion.[15]

He also purchased a garden from his paternal uncle in the town of Istalif, eighteen miles north of Kabul, in an area still renowned for its physical beauty. In the process of upscaling the garden, Babur relates that

> a perennial stream, large enough to turn a mill, runs through the garden; and on its banks are planted planes and other trees. Formerly this stream flowed in a winding and crooked course, but I ordered its course to be altered according to a regular plan, which added greatly to the beauty of the place.[16]

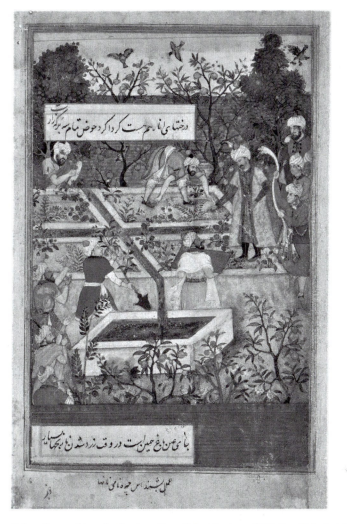

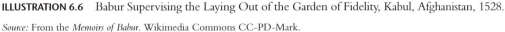

ILLUSTRATION 6.6   Babur Supervising the Laying Out of the Garden of Fidelity, Kabul, Afghanistan, 1528.

Source: From the *Memoirs of Babur.* Wikimedia Commons CC-PD-Mark.

Babur next turned his military attention eastward, came down the Himalayas via the Khyber Pass, and conquered Pakistan and northern India. He eventually settled in the cities of Delhi and Agra, and in the last city he laid out the Garden of the Eight Paradises. Yet Babur was only the first of a line of Mughal emperors, whose recreational and memorial gardens grew ever more lavish with each generation. He was succeeded by his son Humayun, who ruled for only nine years, yet his successor, Akbar the Great, is noted for his expansion of the empire and for his love of the arts. He built the first of the large mausoleum gardens for Humayun, situated in what is today New Delhi. The classic *chahar-bagh* is a walled square garden of more than a thousand feet on each side, divided by four avenues or axes with water channels and basins, with each of the four quadrants in turn divided into nine squares. The inner ninth square of each quadrant is overtaken by the first story of the red sandstone and marble mausoleum, which supports within it a large square superstructure capped by four small domes and a large Persian-inspired dome. It was also Akbar who moved the body of his grandfather Babur from a modest burial setting in Agra to the noted paradise garden in Kabul, designed with fifteen stepped terraces and a central water course.

Akbar's own mausoleum in Silkandra, outside of Agra, again raised the scale and grandeur of such projects. The thirty acres encompassed by Humayun's *chahar-bagh* are here expanded fourfold to 120 acres and named "Abode of Paradise." Both the gardens and the architecture of the tomb, the last with its many quotations from the Quran, were designed as a re-creation of the Garden of Eden. The inscription on the south gateway greets the visitor with these words:

> Hail, blessed space happier than the garden of paradise!
> Hail, lofty building higher than the divine throne!
> A paradise, the garden of which has thousands of Rizwans as servants,
> The garden of which has thousands of paradises for its land.
> The pen of the mason of the Divine decree has written on its court
> "These are the gardens of Eden, enter them to live forever."[16]

Later Mughal sovereigns were no less ambitious of their gardening and mausoleums, yet the hot and arid plains of Agra also led rulers to seek a summer retreat in the Vale of Kashmir, along the shores of Lake Dal at the base of the Himalayas. The area had long been known for its alluring beauty, and Akbar's son, Jahangir, described it in his memoirs in Edenic terms:

> Kashmir is a garden of eternal spring, or an iron fort to a palace of kings—a delightful flower-bed, and a heart-expanding heritage for dervishes. Its pleasant meads and enchanting cascades are beyond all description. There are running streams and fountains beyond count. Wherever the eye reaches, there are verdure and running water. The red rose, the violet, and the narcissus grow of themselves; in the fields, there are all kinds of flowers and all sorts of sweet-scented herbs more than can be calculated. In the soul-enchanting spring the hills and plains are filled with blossoms; the gates, the walls, the courts, the roofs, are lighted up by the torches of banquet-adorning tulips. What shall we say of these things or of the wide meadows (*julgahā*) and the fragrant trefoil?[17]

In 1620 Jahangir began work on his masterpiece, the Shalamar Bagh or "Garden of Bliss," in which water was channeled more than a mile from the foot of the mountains to the lake. The garden was dedicated to his Persian wife Nur Jahan, who would later play a major cultural role in the reign of her son and future emperor Shah Jahan, who in fact would complete the work. The garden's three major terraces demarcated levels of privacy. On the lower level was a building for giving private audiences, and above it, with the marble pavilion at its center, was a terrace reserved for the ladies' garden. The imperial household was housed on the top tier. The park with its oriental plane trees remains largely in place, but its current splendor only vaguely recalls its former majesty when, as earlier manuscripts record, the garden was planted with a multitude of smaller gardens filled with hundreds of different species of fruit trees, shrubs, and flowers. The marble pavilion within the complex contains the famous inscription: "If there is a paradise on earth, it is here, it is here, it is here." Shah Jahan was so seemingly enamored with his horticultural accomplishment in Kashmir that he later built a second "Garden of Bliss" in Lahore, Pakistan.

Yet the two Shalimar gardens of Shah Jahan were soon to be eclipsed by a third garden undertaken by the same emperor—that which contained the mausoleum of his lover and wife Mumtaz Mahal, who died three years after his ascension to the throne. Known as the Taj Mahal, the paradise and its buildings were built between 1632 and 1653 along the southern bank of the Yamuna River within a walled compound that is over 1,800 feet in length and 1,000 feet in width. A significant forecourt with its monumental gateway is appended to the south end. A single grand canal runs north-south, and an east-west crossing divides the garden in the conventional *chahar-bagh*, with each of the four sectors further divided into four gardens. The mausoleum sits atop a built plinth twenty-five feet above the garden, and its location at the north end of the precinct was seemingly a departure from other mausoleum gardens—that is, until a team of archaeologists in the 1990s discovered the remnants of another garden across the river, the "Moonlight Garden." It had the same width as the garden of the Taj Mahal, and was almost certainly its northern extension. Seen in this light, the Taj Mahal mausoleum now becomes centered within a much grander plan, rivaling in its scale the nearly contemporary garden at Versailles. The garden north of the river, however, was badly damaged by a flood in the seventeenth century and was shortly thereafter abandoned. The southern half of its footprint has since been erased by the silting of the river.

The closely mown lawns that run down the central axis of the Taj Mahal today originated under British rule, and the original garden, designed by Shah Jahan himself, was likely implemented by the same master gardener who laid out the garden in Kashmir. Earlier accounts of the garden again praise the beauty of its numerous trees and groves, together with the abundant and colorful varieties of flowers. The garden motif, in fact, does not stop at the mausoleum, because its white marble facade is delicately carved with a veil of naturalistic floral ornaments and intarsia inlays of colored marble, making it one of the most intensely detailed buildings in the world. At least one scholar has suggested that the floral designs, not widespread in Mughal architecture up until this time, may owe something to Western influences, notably the Jesuits, who were establishing contacts with officials late in the sixteenth century.[18] A few architectural histories have given little discussion to Mughal architecture and the Taj Mahal in particular, suggesting an inferiority when measured against comparable buildings in the West. Yet they are using the wrong measuring rod. The Taj Mahal is not a building but a memorial within a larger and more sensual Garden of Eden in all of its redolent essence and eschatological significance. In this regard, the Mughal rulers have no architectural peers, at least in their visions of the afterlife.

Academies in the Garden

In 1667 work began on the construction of the new library at Trinity College, Cambridge University. The baroque work would close off the second courtyard of Trinity College. By the time of its completion in 1695, the building was heralded as an early masterpiece of the nascent Palladian movement in Britain, a stylistic idiom that would rapidly spread across the British Isles, Scandinavia,

ILLUSTRATION 6.7   Wren Library at Nevile's Court of Trinity College, Cambridge University.

Source: Photo by Cmglee. Wikimedia CC BY-SA 3.0.

Russia, and North America. Yet within the Norman and Gothic context of seventeenth-century Cambridge, Christopher Wren's building hardly stands out. Its scale melds seamlessly with the surrounding college fabric, and perhaps there is a lesson here. Cambridge, like its sister town of Oxford sixty-six miles to the southwest, has remained, at least until recently, the paradigm of a livable city. In fact, by simply observing the amount of land given over to gardens and green areas, one can make the case that Cambridge and Oxford were the very first garden cities in modern times.

Every Eden seems to have its own original sin, and in the case of Oxford and Cambridge, the sins are many. Both began in the twelfth century as monastic settlements, yet the behavior of their students was not always Christian. There were many earlier conflicts within the towns, some quite bloody—the proverbial animosity between "the towns and the gowns." The Reformation in the sixteenth century led to an abrupt reversal of the ruling theology, again resulting in bloodshed. The English Civil War of a century later incited another round of political mayhem and burnings at the stake. And then there is the issue that for much of their existence, Oxford and Cambridge were closed to all people of non-Anglican faiths, as well as to individuals not attending the requisite preparatory schools. In short, the two universities, in their early years with their "legal monopoly" of English university education, came to epitomize the idea of snobbery. Notwithstanding, something very unusual and quite appealing took root in these two towns.

Cambridge antedates its rival city in its antiquity. Along the river Cam, just south of the eastern marshes of The Fens, the Romans built the town of Camboritum in AD 43 and enclosed it with masonry walls. With their departure at the start of the fifth century, it reverted to the native Britons, only to be conquered again by invading Anglo-Saxons, and later by the Danes who took the town in 875. They held it for a half century and transformed it into a trading center. After the Battle of Hastings in 1066, William the Conqueror built a castle on the left bank of the river, north of what would become the academic sector of the town. He also brought knowledge of the rudiments of the Norman or Romanesque style, to be incorporated into some of the first stone buildings in this part of England.

The frontier town of Oxford, situated between the historic kingdoms of Mercia and Wessex, had too endured the hand of the Danes and later the conquest of William, who also erected a castle there. William's governor set up the first monastic community in the town of roughly 100 houses, a precedent that would expand over the years with several monastic orders: the Augustinians, Benedictines, Cistercians, Carmelites, Gray Friars, and Black Friars. The year 1167 figured prominently in the town's development because Henry II, in a feud with the French crown, ordered home all English students studying in Paris. Many returned and resumed their studies in the monasteries of Oxford. In 1209, two students were hanged for a murder of a prostitute, which sent other students fleeing, some to take up studies in Cambridge. Nevertheless, the university charter granted by Henry III in 1248 set an important precedent, because it led to the monastic lecture halls being replaced by legally sanctioned colleges. University College was founded one year later, followed by Balliol College and Merton College. Cambridge University followed a similar path, in that lecture halls acquired the status of a university in the 1220s, and a papal bull in 1233 reinforced their teaching autonomy. Peterhouse, based on the model of Merton, was granted the status of a college in 1284, Clare College (originally University Hall) in 1321, and Trinity College (earlier King's Hall) in 1337.

One early decision became the key to the architectural development of the two towns. This was the transformation of the isolated lecture halls into the quadrangular or monastic model of buildings—that is, the integration of living quarters for students and fellows. A master's lodge, dining hall, student dorms, and a chapel formed a quadrangle of buildings around a common green area. This process began in the fourteenth and fifteenth centuries with the small quad at Merton College in Oxford. In 1379 William of Wykeham, in founding Oxford's New College, refined the idea by considerably expanding the scale of the quadrangle. Building along the remnants of the city's wall, he also saw to it that the college had additional space for food and pleasure gardens, making the campus in part self-sufficient.

The size of the quadrangle increased in dimension between the sixteenth and eighteenth centuries, and with it came the expansion of the number of colleges. In the city center of Oxford, which is more compact and urban than its sister town, we have an array of colleges along High Street and the area to the north. Among them are University College, Oriel College, Queens College, St. Edmund Hall, All Souls College, Brasenose College, Lincoln College, Jesus College, Exeter College, Hertford College, Balliol College, Trinity College, and Wadham College. Scattered among the colleges are the notable landmarks of St. Mary the Virgin Church, James Gibbs's baroque masterpiece of the Radcliffe Camera, the Bodleian Library, the Clarendon Building, and Wren's Sheldonian Theatre, the last being the venue for many university activities. It is a stunning array of buildings concentrated in a compact urban setting. All of these colleges have more than one quadrangle. St. John's College, to the north of this grouping, has six and employs a "Keeper of the Groves" to maintain its large gardens. At the east end of High Street along the river Cherwell is Magdalen College, the historic entrance to the city, which has vast lawns and a large grove to its north that supports a herd of deer. Across the Cherwell to the northeast of Magdalen is one of Oxford's famed meadows, the Water Meadow, a tract of nature between the two arms of the Cherwell. Inside the triangular form of the meadow is Addison's Walk, named after the prominent political and picturesque theorist who described it this way:

> Hence it is that we take delight in a Prospect which is well laid out, and diversified with Fields and Meadows, Woods, and Rivers; in those accidental Landskips of Trees, Clouds, and Cities, that are sometimes found in the Veins of Marble; in the curious Fret-work of Rocks and Grottoes; and, in a Word, in any thing this hath such a Variety and Regularity as may seem the Effect of Design, in which we call the Works of Chance.[19]

If this is insufficient green space to sharpen one's cognitive functioning, across High Street from Magdalen College is Oxford's Botanical Garden, spread over several acres, with green fields to the south and west. Nearby is Merton College, which expanded its single quadrangle into four courtyards, and then adjoined to the complex an unusually large Fellows' Garden, walled in for privacy. As one recent writer has described his late afternoon visit there, "the hibiscus bloomed white and

ILLUSTRATION 6.8   Aerial View of Oxford University, looking north. Christ Church College bottom left; Merton College bottom center; Botanical Garden bottom right, with Magdalen College and Water Meadow to its north.

Source: Photo by Chensiyuan. Wikimedia CC BY-SA 4.0.

blue against the college walls, and the wide borders teemed with wallflowers, lady's mantle, white tradescantia and red-hot pokers, while the sycamore of 1705 watched over them all."[20] To the west of the colleges of Merton and Corpus Christi is Oxford's best-known college, Christ Church. Its quadrangle is not only the largest in the city (with a Gothic gateway designed by Christopher Wren), but it also possesses its own cathedral. It was founded in 1525 by Cardinal Wolsey, who hoped to replicate the scale and beauty of his own Hampton Court. This was, however, before he had his falling out with Henry VIII, who subsequently took over Hampton Court and the college project as well. Christ Church, together with Corpus Christi and Merton, also share a view of Christ Church Meadow to the south, a scenic floodplain that is wedged between the Cherwell and Thames, almost the size of the historic town of Oxford.

Cambridge, with its parade of colleges running between its version of High Street and the river Cam, is not less paradisiacal in its display of greenery. From south to north from the Fitzwilliam Museum are Peterhouse College, Queens College, St. Catharine's College, King's College, Clare College, Old Schools, Trinity College, and St. John's College. King's College was founded by Henry VI in 1141, together with its feeder school, Eton, a degree from which was once required to enter the college. Five years later, work began on its complex of buildings that would take nearly a century to complete. Its Gothic chapel, an architectural masterpiece with the largest fan vault in the world, still today dominates the town's skyline. King's College has two rivals in Trinity College and St. John's College. Trinity was founded in 1546 by Henry VIII, but it was not until the mastership of Thomas Nevile, around the turn of the seventeenth century, that Trinity would challenge King's College in size and grandeur. Neville demolished several buildings and from the remnants laced together a "Great Court," one significantly larger than his rival. He also extended two wings west of the Great Court toward the river Cam, which would eventually be closed off by Wren's library along the river bank. Not to be outdone, the architect Nicholas Hawksmoor, in the first part of the eighteenth century, made plans for a second, larger courtyard at King's College, although it never came to fruition.

As if these courtyards in Cambridge were not sufficiently green, several of the colleges along the river purchased land on the opposite bank—known as "The Backs"—which they initially used for food gardens and pastures. It would not be long before some of these would be transformed into pleasure gardens and be connected to the colleges with private bridges. Perhaps the most famous of these are the three gardens of Clare College. The college built a Scholars' Garden and Master's Garden on the east side of the river and a luxurious Fellows' Garden on the west bank, connected to the school by a three-arched, classical bridge. The Fellows' Garden remains today a place for outdoor performances.

Not to be outdone, to the north of Trinity College reigns the larger complex of St. John's College. From its gateway at the eastern end, one passes through a historical sequence of three courtyards (from old to newer), before crossing the Bridge of Sighs (named for the Venetian bridge) and meeting with another series of courtyards, meadows, and gardens. From the two-story oriel windows of the building along the left bank of the river, one has a view of the occupied punts below, guided by gondoliers, as well as of the Master's Garden along the right bank. The latter, called "The Wilderness," was designed by Capability Brown, one of Britain's famed picturesque landscapers. In preparing his plans, he proposed bringing together all of "The Backs" and uniting them with a vast picturesque park with a lake and meandering paths—a plan unrealized. St. John's also has a Scholars' Garden and Fellows' Garden nestled within its groves.

Because of the application of the quadrangle or courtyard theme, the Oxford and Cambridge colleges have a very high percentage of green space versus built areas. In the smallest or most compact of the colleges, this ratio rarely falls below 50 percent, whereas in the larger colleges—even discounting attached groves, meadows, or riverbanks—this ratio increases to somewhere around 80 percent, a very decent ratio within the pedestrian scale of the towns. Moreover, the colleges,

ILLUSTRATION 6.9   Clare Bridge over the River Cam, with the Fellows' Garden to the left and the Scholars' and Master's Garden to the right.

Source: Photo by Rafa Esteve. Wikimedia CC BY-SA 4.0.

except in a few cases, are not contiguous—that is, they are spread throughout the city, allowing the supporting network of inns, shops with rented rooms above, bookstores, restaurants, pubs, and other businesses to fill in the urban fabric. All of the buildings are generally three or four stories in height, similar to the height of the colleges, and collectively they provide a rich urban texture of different materials, architectural styles, and local color. Moreover, all areas of the city are geared to the pedestrian, connected with an organically evolving system of lanes, alleyways, passages, places, and minor streets. In this regard they remained eminently accessible by foot or bicycle and, in many parts of the city, free of the automobile or the notorious car park. When one also takes into account the cultural amenities of prestigious libraries, museums, botanical gardens, athletic fields, theaters, and weekly musical performances held in many of the colleges—not to mention the satin shimmer of the Fellows' peacock gowns on a sunny day—one can only conclude that one has indeed entered Eden.

In the 1970s, the architect and planner Christopher Alexander, who had studied mathematics and architecture at Cambridge's Trinity College, compiled a *Pattern Language* for the design of towns. In his ideal city, there would be a four-story limit on building heights, a 9 percent limit on land given over to automobiles, streets would not be laid out in a checkerboard but in a relaxed manner, and the river would be safely protected with public parks ("life forms around the water's edge").[21] Cities would have activity nodes, promenades, and shopping streets, and there would be no sharp separation of residential from non-residential zones. The ideal city would also have open and abundant ponderance of green spaces for all to enjoy. One could enumerate a dozen or more patterns that Alexander gleaned from the experience of his college years in Cambridge, but this is because, by the 1970s, he had come to see Cambridge as the pattern for all cities to follow. It was for him a very humanized conception of the city.

But herein also lies the problem. The cores of both cities have today become virtual museums in their own right and are consequently overrun with tourists. Worse still, beginning in the 1970s and intensifying in the 1990s, both cities, inspired by the digital revolution, caught that sometimes deadly virus known as "building bug." The swelling of the local populations was forecast in Oxford in the late 1960s, when town and county officials, in seeking to mitigate the traffic problem of High Street, proposed a new four-lane highway across William Morris's sacrosanct Christ Church Meadow. The measure was defeated after intense opposition, although the boom of new buildings and research entities was only a few years down the road. And this is the lesson. Generations over centuries can construct a veritable paradise, and one generation of regents with towering endowments, with the best pedagogical intentions, can one day come along and pave it with new buildings, snarling traffic, and extraordinarily high living expenses. Swept into the utopian promise of the digital age, the silicon apple on the tree of knowledge proved to be far too enticing for these universities to pass on.

Notes

1. Jun'ichirō Tanizaki, *In Praise of Shadows*, trans. by Thomas Harper and Edward Seidensticker (Stony Creek, CT: Leete's Island Books, 1977), 18.
2. Matthew Stavros, *Kyoto: An Urban History of Japan's Premodern Capital* (Honolulu: University of Hawai'i Press, 2014), 43–74.
3. Jirō Takei and Marc P. Keane of *Sakuteiki: Visions of the Japanese Garden* (Tokyo: Tuttle, 2008), 151.
4. Ibid., 168–9.
5. Richard Neutra, "Foreword," to David H. Engel (ed.), *Japanese Gardens for Today* (Rutland, VT: Charles E. Tuttle, 1961), XII–XIII.
6. Takahiko Iimura, "A Note for 'MA: Space/Time in the Garden of Ryoan-JI,'" *Millennium Film Journal* 38 (Spring 2002). http://mfj-online.org/journalPages/MFJ38/iimura.html. Accessed May 2021.
7. Okakura Kakuzo, *The Book of Tea* (Boston, MA: Tuttle Publishing, 1956), 33.
8. Ibid., 106–7.
9. Christopher Tadgell, *The East: Buddhists, Hindus and the Sons of Heaven* (Abingdon: Routledge, 2008), 838.
10. *A Plain and Literal Translation of the Arabian Nights' Entertainments, Now Entitled the Book of the Thousand Nights and a Night*, trans. by Richard Burton (Burton Club, 1885), 4:113–18.
11. Ahmed Ibn Mohammed Al-Makkarí, *The History of the Mohammedan Dynasties in Spain; Extracted from the Nafhu-T-Tib Min Ghosni-L-Andalusi-R-Rattíb Wa Táríkh Lisánu-D-Dín*, trans. by Pascual de Gayangos (London: Oriental Translation Fund, 1840), 2:210.
12. Washington Irving, "Legend of Prince Ahmed Al Kamel; or The Pilgrim of Love," in *The Alhambra* (New York: Macmillan & Co., 1911), 217–58.
13. Ibid., 70.
14. Ibid., 111.
15. *Memoirs of Zehin-ed-Din Muhammed Baber*, trans. by John Leyden and William Erskine (London: Longman, Rees, Orme, Brown, & Green, 1826), 278.
16. Ibid., 147; Edmund W. Smith, *Akbar's Tomb, Sikandarah, Near Agra*, Archaeological Survey of India, Vol. XXXV (Allahabad, 1909), 34–5.
17. *The Tūzuk-i-Jahāngīnī, or Memoirs of Jahāngīnī*, trans. by Alexander Rogers (London: Royal Asiatic Society, 1909–14), 2:143–4.
18. See D. Fairchild Ruggles, *Islamic Gardens and Landscape* (Philadelphia, PA: University of Pennsylvania, 2008), 120–2.
19. Joseph Addison, *The Spectator* (London: George Routledge & Sons, n.d.), nos. 414, 597.
20. Peter Sager, *Oxford & Cambridge: An Uncommon History* (London: Thames & Hudson, 2005), 110.
21. Christopher Alexander, *A Pattern Language* (New York: Oxford University Press, 1977), 25. See in particular the patterns relating to towns.

7

SIMPLY BAROQUE

Conquest of Eden

Christopher Columbus departed the Spanish port of Palos de la Frontera on the morning of August 3, 1492, seeking a trade route to the East Indies. Scholars have noted that he had not read Marco Polo before this first voyage (he did later), but of course the Orient—Genghis Khan aside— had long been recognized as a land of exotic beauty, prosperity, and curiosity. He also likely did not believe he would discover the terrestrial paradise of Eden, although this thought was evidently not far from his mind. His first impressions of the new world were certainly idyllic in their tone. The "seven or eight kinds of palm trees," which he observed with his eyeglass along the north shore of Cuba, "like all the other trees, herbs, and fruits, considerably surpass ours in height and beauty." The landscape of Hispaniola was exceptional for its "mountains of very great size and beauty, vast plains, groves, and very fruitful fields, admirably adapted for tillage, pasture, and habitation." The island, moreover, had excellent harbors and its "rivers, so indispensable to the health of man, surpass anything that would be believed by one who had not seen it." The island's residents were also "well-formed," exceedingly handsome and liberal, and "exhibit great love towards all others in preference to themselves."[1]

On Columbus's third voyage to the New World in 1498, he had similar words for the island of Trinidad, which "was very beautiful, and as fresh and green as the gardens of Valencia in the month of March."[2] Its inhabitants, now named the Amerindians, were "tall, and elegant in their movements, wearing their hair very long and smooth, they also bind their heads with handsomely worked handkerchiefs, which from a distance look like silk or gauze." He goes on to report that "I call this place 'Jardines,' that is, 'the Gardens,' for the place and the people corresponded with that appellation."[3] It was only a few days later, in exploring the coastline of Venezuela near the multi-mouthed delta of the Orinoco River, that Columbus found the entrance to the Garden of Eden—or so he believed. He first speaks of the turbulence and "great impetuosity" of the water flowing into the ocean from the delta, then of holy scriptures and of the "fountain" from which the four principal rivers of Eden have their source. To support his contention in his official report, he cites the authorities of St. Isidore, Bede, Strabo, Petrus Comestor, St. Ambrose, and Duns Scotus—because "all the learned theologians, agree that the earthly paradise is in the east."[4] Although he was unable to penetrate the delta because of the

DOI: 10.4324/9781003178460-7

force of the waters being expelled into the sea, he was nevertheless convinced he was at the gate of Eden:

> I have never either read or heard of fresh water coming in so large a quantity, in close conjunction with the water of the sea; the idea is also corroborated by the blandness of the temperature; and if the water of which I speak does not proceed from the earthly paradise, it appears to be still more marvellous, for I do not believe that there is any river in the world so large or so deep.[5]

His discovery of Eden, however, evoked little stir upon his return to Spain, perhaps because the admiral had been brought back in chains after his arrest by the newly appointed governor of Hispaniola. He had been charged with mismanaging the colony. Another reason, certainly, was the scourge of gold-fever that had overtaken the Spanish court and nobility. Prior to Columbus's return from his third trip, in fact, several expeditions were underway to the New World—both officially and privately financed. All were in search of treasure.

Regarding the beauty of the New World, Columbus was not alone, for many other adventurers cited the region's idyllic climate, landscape, and the vigor of the local populations. In 1501, the Florentine Amerigo Vespucci (after whom, in 1507, the Baden cartographer Martin Waldseemüller named the new continent "America") set out on a Portuguese ship to explore the Brazilian coastline. He sailed south as far as the future Rio de Janeiro, and he recounted his travels in a letter to Lorenzo di Medici. The air of the country was "temperate and good," and "there are

ILLUSTRATION 7.1   Panel from Martin Waldseemüller *Universalis Cosmographia*, 1507. The designation "America" is placed in southern Brazil. US Library of Congress.

Source: Public domain.

never any pestilences or epidemics caused by bad air." Moreover, "the land is very fertile, abounding in many hills and valleys, and in large rivers, and is irrigated by very refreshing springs." The forests grow without cultivation, and "many yield fruits pleasant to the taste and nourishing to the human body." The people, who wear no clothing, are "gentle and tractable"—notwithstanding the mutilation of their faces and the occasional practice of cannibalism. Still, Vespucci was convinced that "if the terrestrial paradise is in some part of this land, it cannot be very far from the coast we visited."[6]

A multitude of similar observations are found in the first history of the Spanish explorations, *De Orbe Novo*, published in 1530 by Peter Martyr d'Anghiera. This scholar from Piedmont had been assigned by the papacy to the Spanish court as the official historiographer of Spain. In drawing upon firsthand accounts of the returning explorers, he repeatedly refers to the mildness of the local populations, the beauty of the scenery, and the fertility of the land. The soil of Hispaniola, he wrote, is so rich in nutrients that it allows an abundance of melons, pumpkins, and cucumbers, among other fruits and vegetables, just thirty-six days after sowing.[7] The landscape of present-day Columbia, "an Elysian country," is second to none:

> Spring and Autumn seem perpetual, for the trees keep their leaves during the whole year, and bear fruit. Groves of oak and pine are numerous, and there are seven varieties of palms of which some bear dates, while others are without fruit. Vines loaded with ripe grapes grow spontaneously amid the trees, but they are wild vines and there is such an abundance of useful and appetising fruits that nobody bothers to cultivate vineyards.[8]

Martyr records that when Pedro Arias Dávila first scouted the Columbian coastline, he had scared away the tribesmen of a Carib village and, upon disembarking, found "a piece of sapphire larger than a goose's egg," in addition to a collection of emeralds, chalcedony, jasper, amber, and gold—in addition to woven mats and cotton hangings depicting lions, eagles, and tigers. Inland, Dávila found well-cultivated gardens watered by ditches, just as they are in northern Italy. Martyr, in his descriptions, was similarly impressed with the "thousand" Caribbean islands surrounding Hispaniola, which he likened to "Nereid nymphs, fair, graceful, and elegant, serving as its ornaments like another Tethys, their queen and mother."[9] Virtually every early explorer believed there was something special, something biblical about this discovered paradise.

One of the rare diatribes that Martyr voices toward the end of his third report is vented not against the Europeans but those cannibal tribes in the region who prey upon the peaceful native populations: "These filthy eaters of men are reported to have killed myriads of their kind to satisfy their passion. Our compatriots have discovered a thousand islands as fair as Paradise, a thousand Elysian regions, which these brigands have depopulated."[10] More than 5,000 inhabitants of the island of Puerto Rico, he goes to report, have been carried off in the past few decades to fill "the appetites of these filthy creatures."[11] His point seems to be that God had indeed created a paradise in this part of the world, only to have a vile race of men rise from within and destroy it.

Of course, many present-day historians see these events and their exaggerations in a very different light. If the objective of Columbus's first voyage was to find a trading route to the Far East, the goal of the third voyage of 1498 was to explore the coastline of northern South America as well as to add a second Caribbean base to the one previously established in Hispaniola. From the beginning, the Europeans were quite content to divvy up the spoils and, almost as an afterthought, convert the local populations in their indentured servitude. The Treaty of Tordesillas of 1494, between Portugal and Spain, ceded Brazil to the Portuguese and the all the areas north of it to Spain. The race was on. Nicholás de Ovando, who in 1502 was replacing Columbus as the governor of Hispaniola, had sailed with thirty ships and 2,500 colonists. There he imposed the Spanish labor system of *encomienda*, whereby the locals were forcibly assigned to the Spanish explorers, nobles, and gentry, who had made the dangerous trip to extend their fortunes. With the death of Isabella in 1504, the lone dissenter to bonded labor, the slave trade emerged in full force.

The behavior of many of the appointed governors was ruthless. Ovando was particularly cruel in his treatment of the native Taino peoples of Hispaniola, and in five years he is reported to have reduced their population of 500,000 to 60,000. The governor of Cuba, Diego Velázquez de Cuéllar, was so upset with what he perceived to be the indolence of the locals that he introduced African slaves into the colony, a decision that would eventually make him the wealthiest Spaniard in New Spain. It was his subordinate, Hernán Cortés who, in defying Velázquez's order, amassed an expedition in 1519 to stake out a colony in the Yucatan and presumably seek greater glory for Spain. It would not take long for Cortés to understand that the real prize in Mexico was Tenochtitlán, a city of 200,000 inhabitants built on an island in the middle of Lake Texcoco—land now occupied by Mexico City. It was here that the supreme leader Montezuma controlled his vast Aztec Empire. Through a series of brilliant tactical maneuvers, Cortés orchestrated a rebellion of regional tribes against Montezuma and in 1521, through a subterfuge, actually held the king hostage in his own palace. In his letter to Charles V, he reported on Montezuma's vast gardens and pleasure houses—"so marvellous that it seems to me almost impossible to speak of their excellence and grandeur," and for which "there is nothing comparable in Spain." Of one house, he noted:

> there was a beautiful garden, with arbors overhanging it, of which the marbles and tiles were of jasper, beautifully worked. In this house there were apartments for two great princes, and all their servants. It had ten pools of water, in which were kept all the many and divers breeds of waterfowl found in these parts, all domesticated; for the sea-birds, too, there were pools of salt water, and for those of the rivers and lakes, there was fresh water, which for the sake of cleanliness, they renewed at certain times by means of pipes.[12]

The Aztecs—with their tall temples on which thousands of humans were sacrificed each year—were a warring people not without their own cruelties, but the destruction of the empire is reported to have resulted in more than a quarter of a million deaths in the battle of Tenochtitlán alone. Two waves of smallpox later in the century killed off nearly all of the remaining population. The destruction of the Inca Empire in Peru was on a similar scale of violence. A large portion of North America would also come under Spanish control, beginning with Juan Ponce de León's discovery of the coastline of Florida in 1513, and later (from Mexico) the Pacific coastline. León had fought the Moors at Granada in 1492, sailed with Columbus on his second voyage, and served as a conquistador under Ovando before taking over the governorship of Puerto Rico in 1509. León landed near St. Augustine along the Florida coastline, which he believed to be an island. He then sailed south along the coast, through the Keys, and explored a good portion of the Gulf Coast before giving up his search for the northern end of the island. His objective, in any case, was likely not the Fountain of Youth, but gold.

There were a few people who rose to the defense of native peoples of the Caribbean and Central and South America, chief of whom was Bartolomé de las Casas, the son of a landowner who arrived in Hispaniola in 1502 with Ovando and joined Velázquez in his bloody conquest of Cuba. After taking his vows in the Dominican Order, he underwent a spiritual awakening and became a passionate defender of the natives, the "most humble, most patient, most peaceful" people in the world. He made several trips back to Spain to plead for reforms, and although many mandates were issued, few were ever enforced. Beginning in 1516, Bartolomé set out in the first of his various writings to record the atrocities he had witnessed or gathered from others. In one report on the people of Yucatan, he commented on their destruction:

> The said kingdom has a circumference of about three hundred leagues. Its people were famous among all those of the Indies for prudence and cleanliness, and for having fewer vices and

sins than any other; and they were very well and worthy of being brought to the knowledge of God. A great town might have been built there by the Spaniards where they might have lived as in a terrestrial paradise had they been worthy; but, on account of their great avarice, stupidity and grave sins they were not; just as they have not been worthy to possess the many other countries that God has disclosed to them, in the Indies.[13]

The one positive thing to emerge from Las Casas's efforts was that his main work, *A Short Account of the Destruction of the Indies* (1552), was translated into Dutch, French, English, and German, raising the consciousness of what was taking place.

Spain and Portugal were not the only two countries staking claims in the New World. The Frenchman Jacques Cartier, in seeking a northwest passage to Asia, first explored the St. Lawrence River in 1534 and returned the following year to meet the natives along the Ottawa River: "people clad with cloth as we are, very honest, and many inhabited townes, and that they have great store of Gold and red Copper."[14] He returned in 1541 to search for the town of Saguenay, reportedly the source of this gold, but this quest proved fruitless. Samuel de Champlain later reclaimed the area for France in 1608 and set up trading posts in Quebec and Montreal, from whence French explorers would scout the Great Lakes region and the Mississippi Valley. The Dutch also brought settlers to the continent. In 1614 they explored the Hudson River valley and, in pursuit of fur, established a trading post near the later town of Albany. To protect this valuable merchandise from French and English raiding parties, they established a naval base at the tip of Manhattan in 1625, naming it New Amsterdam. It was destined to be taken by the British and renamed New York.

The other broker in the New World was of course Great Britain. John Cabot first laid British claims for North America in 1497 when landing in Newfoundland, but to little avail. Almost a century later, in 1584, Queen Elizabeth presented the dashing Walter Raleigh with a charter to colonize North America, those "remote, heathen and barbarous lands, countries, and territories, not actually possessed of any Christian prince nor inhabited by Christian People."[15] One purpose seems to have been to establish a stronghold for British "privateers" or pirates to carry out raids against Spanish ships carrying their presumed hauls of gold. Both of the two Roanoke Island colonies founded by Raleigh in North Carolina, however, carry the dubious distinction of being "lost." Raleigh is better known for his expeditions of 1595 and 1617 to Guyana and the Orinoco River basin in another fruitless search for the "golden city" of El Dorado, a theme that would later be memorialized in Voltaire's *Candide*.

The speculative colony of Jamestown in the Virginia Tidewater was founded in 1607 and was scarcely an immediate success. Only 38 of the 104 colonists survived the first year, and the mortality rate was even more grim for the second wave of settlers. Nevertheless, still more waves arrived and the production of tobacco eventually made the colony economically viable, so much so that the British crown cornered the European tobacco market by mid-century. With this prosperity also came the removal of the native populations, high taxes, rebellion, the burning of the town in 1676, and the acceptance of African slavery to replace the now removed or obliterated native populations.

Eventually, the underlying immorality of the exploitation would be called to account. Michel de Montaigne, in his 1580 essay "Cannibalism," weighed the lack of artifice of Brazilian natives—now the noble savage—against the treachery of their colonizers. To cite a passage that Shakespeare later enjoined in *The Tempest*:

[These people have] no Manner of Traffick, no Knowledge of Letters, no Science of Numbers, no Name of Magistrate, nor politick Superiority; no use of Service, Riches or Poverty; no Contracts, no Successions, no Dividends, no Properties, no Employments, but those of Leisure; no respect of Kindred, but common; no Clothing, no Agriculture, no Metal, no use of Corn or Wine; and where so much as the very Words that signify, Lying, Treachery, Dissimulation, Avarice, Envy, Detraction, and Pardon, were never heard of.[16]

He goes on to speak of the beauty of the county, "pleasant to a Miracle," with little or no disease, people neither "paralytick, blear-ey'd, toothless, or crooked with Age," who wage warfare "without clothing and with fearless obstinacy, with only bows and wooden spears." This is not savagery but "Nature," he concludes, which resides in these people "vigorous and spritely," and "which we have help'd to degenerate in these, by accommodating them to the Pleasure of our own corrupted Palate."[17]

In Praise of Folly

In Erasmus's book carrying the title of this section, the Dutch theologian, moralist, and friend of Thomas More presents us with Folly, a female offspring of the god of Wealth, who regularly consorts with several other minor deities, including Ignorance, Self-love, Flattery, Inebriation, Forgetfulness, Laziness, and Pleasure. Her role in the larger scheme of things, she believes, is to make people happy on earth. Yet this Lucianic account of her intrigues, published in 1511, is not what one would expect from this Rotterdam priest and Renaissance humanist. Folly "wasn't born on wandering Delos or out of the waves of the sea or 'in hollow caves,' but on the very islands of the Blest," whose fields grow "moly, panacea, nepenthe, marjoram, ambrosia, and lotus, roses, violets, and hyacinths, and gardens of Adonis to refresh the eye and nose." Nepenthe, incidentally, was the narcotic that Helen, in *The Odyssey*, had put into the wine of Menelaus, Telemachus, and Peisistratus to soothe their sad remembrances of the missing Ulysses: "a drug to quiet all pain and strife, and bring forgetfulness of every ill."[18]

Folly was making a fetching case for her own benefit to humankind. If she turns men witless in their old age, it is to set them free of the torment of their senses. If she gives women to men, it is for the male pleasure of gazing at female beauty and perpetual youth: "Isn't this the purpose of all

ILLUSTRATION 7.2 Folly in the Pulpit. Marginal sketch by Hans Holbein the Younger in Erasmus's *In Praise of Folly*.

their attention to their persons, all that make-up, bathing, hair-dressing, and all those ointments and perfumes, as well as the many arts of arranging, painting, disguising face, eyes, and skin?"—all of which is folly.[19] The happiest people in the world, Folly goes on to say, are idiots, fools, nitwits, and simpletons because they have no fear of death, no conscience, no shame, no ambition, no envy, and no love.[20] Invite an educated man to dinner and the evening will quickly become a bore; invite a poet and he will delight "the ears of the foolish with pure nonsense and silly tales."[21]

Erasmus's foreplay, as it were, is simply to prepare the reader for his real target, the folly of theologians, bishops, cardinals, and pontiffs. They either engage in frivolous and pointless disputes of terminology and doctrine or, much worse, surround themselves with luxury, buy their offices, or set about waging wars in the name of Christ. Such a lament plays into the pending Reformation, but Erasmus would not succumb to the pleas of his younger contemporary Martin Luther to join the cause. Erasmus's target was Pope Julius II, the warrior pope, who sought to reclaim the erstwhile Papal States. Julius, to his credit, also commissioned the rebuilding of St. Peter's in Rome, employed Raphael to paint the *School of Athens* in his private apartments, and ordered Michelangelo down from Florence to fresco the ceiling of the Sistine Chapel. His successor, Leo X, a close friend of Erasmus, was not much better in his ethics. He financed St. Peter's by selling indulgences, guaranteeing that those buying them would have reduced sentences in purgatory. These follies, among others, precipitated Henry VIII's and Luther's break with the church—the Reformation—and led to nearly two centuries of religious warfare throughout Europe.

Wars aside, Folly herself began making a rather flamboyant comeback by the start of the seventeenth century. Now we enter the period known as the baroque, the era of Borromini, Bernini, Bach, Caravaggio, Rembrandt, Vermeer, and El Greco. There were still wars, of course, but the baroque was also a period of great accumulations of wealth and extravagant sensorial delights, one in which Folly scarcely knew any bounds. It was a time for rethinking the scale of cities and gardens.

The use of the term "baroque" in urban histories generally begins with a single urban innovation: the long, straight avenue, sometimes cut through an existing urban fabric and generally designed within a larger geometric arrangement of similar streets. The wide avenue provided the convenience of faster movement, air, sunlight, and greenery, and it lent significant protection against the urban fires that were frequent in dense European cities. Sixtus V is sometimes credited with initiating this urban device (scarcely unknown in antiquity) when, in 1588, he commissioned Domenico Fontana to lay out a sequence of grand avenues for Rome. Fontana had made a name earlier by designing the vast gardens of Sixtus's own Villa Montalto. The garden has now disappeared, but—as the map of Giambattista Nolli of 1748 records—it was a wooded estate in Rome wedged between Santa Maria Maggiore and the Baths of Diocletian.[22] In plan, it encompassed 270 acres and consisted of a series of diagonal and gridded axes geometrically arranged. A young Gian Lorenzo Bernini, in fact, contributed a large fountain to the garden. Shortly after assuming the papal Seat, Sixtus began making preparations for the Catholic Jubilee in 1600, in which thousands of Christians were expected to visit the city. Fontana's task was to transform Rome into a "single holy shrine" by connecting the seven pilgrimage churches of the city with straight avenues and squares cut through the fabric.[23] Each landmark or square was highlighted by an obelisk to lead pilgrims visually from one church to the next along a lengthy spiritual circuit that visitors were expected to complete in a single day. In this way, the city now became centered on monuments via the spatial corridors linking them. The new avenues also made way for many new buildings in the latest style, not the least of which was Francesco Borromini's San Carlo alle Quattro Fontane and Bernini's Sant'Andrea al Quirinale. It also gave rise to new squares and street architecture, such as Francesco de Sanctis's "Spanish Steps," connecting the avenue leading in from the city's northern gate with a second avenue leading to the Basilica of Santa Maria Maggiore.

The Great Fire of 1666 that consumed much of London also led to a restructuring of that city. John Evelyn and Christopher Wren, among others, offered plans for the city's rebuilding, which were modeled on the strategy used in Rome. Wren's plan had two major avenues radiating east-ward from St. Paul's Cathedral, one connecting to the Royal Exchange, and the other running parallel to the river, and connecting a series of squares. On the west of St. Paul's, he proffered a large plaza of a scale imitating Bernini's new forecourt at the Vatican. Although his plan was not implemented, he did receive the nice consolation prize of the commission to rebuild St. Paul's Cathedral.

It was therefore left to Louis XIV, who assumed the French crown in 1661, to trumpet the vain-glorious tone of the new era. In the years before coming of age, his regent Jean-Baptiste Colbert planned the extension of the Louvre, France's royal palace. With great fanfare, Bernini was brought to Paris in 1665 to prepare the design—a grandiose undertaking that is said to have been scuttled by palace intrigues. It was also becoming clear at this time, however, that the youthful Louis had no intentions of living in Paris, or anywhere near the city and its masses. Folly, of course, stepped in to save the day with a trick of self-flattery. She no doubt whispered in Louis's ear the idea of transform-ing his existing hunting lodge in Versailles into a colossal Baroque palace with an even more sump-tuous royal garden. Louis's architect Louis Le Vau carried out the building design, but it was André Le Nôtre who took the laurel for the city's design and the garden. The city planner and landscaper created three, largely ceremonial tree-lined avenues radiating outward from the eastern forecourt of the palace at a sixty-degree angle, one leading to nowhere. It was between these avenues that the new city of courtiers would fill in over time. The most ornate part of his scheme, however, was the gardens he planned for the rear of the palace, which were certainly empyreal in their design and unprecedented in scale. A central *allée* structured a series of gardens, fountains, lawns, and canals, and opened a vista to the west more than a mile in length, mediated by a crossing axis of waterways. Overall, the forested park itself encompassed more than two square miles. In addition to the focal parterres in the foreground, there were a series of smaller and thematic gardens tucked away within

ILLUSTRATION 7.3   Pierre Patel, Chateau of Versailles, 1668. Museum of the History of France.

Source: Wikipedia, public domain.

the wooded areas. The park would also be graced with an impressive number of garden follies and architectural gems. Certainly, the most notable is Ange-Jacques Gabriel's design for the rococo Petit Trianon, built in the 1760s for Madame de Pompadour, the mistress of Louis XV. She is, however, better known for her intellectual salons attended by Voltaire, Montesquieu, and other Parisian notables. Her early death from tuberculosis in 1764, however, led her to the grave before the villa was completed.

The interiors of Versailles were also highly influential, as virtually every monarch in Europe of any self-respecting means attempted to replicate its florid appeal, albeit at a more modest scale. Perhaps the grandest of these efforts was the *Residenz* of Würzburg, begun in 1715 by the incomparable architect Balthasar Neumann. The building is noted for its grand staircase, which in turn is noted also for the glorious ceiling fresco by Tiepolo, the largest ceiling fresco ever attempted. Neumann, incidentally, was no less a genius at a smaller scale. His design of 1743 for the German pilgrimage church *Vierzehnheiligen*, or the Basilica of the Fourteen Helpers, has only one shortcoming, which is that Neumann may have been outperformed by the Zimmermann brothers and their contemporary rococo design for the *Wieskirche* in the Bavarian foothills of the Alps. Both churches pursued the paradisiacal instinct with great vigor and distinction.

Versailles also set a new standard for the baroque city and its gardens. It certainly encouraged Peter the Great, in 1703, to plan the new capital of St. Petersburg, situated on the Neva River at its entrance to the Baltic Sea. The Admiralty, the former headquarters of the Imperial Russian Navy, would now become the pivot point around which three avenues would eventually radiate, the most fashionable of which was the Nevsky Prospekt, a tree-lined avenue of the city crossing a series of belted canals similar to the layout of Amsterdam. Still another baroque city famed for the beauty of its buildings and gardens is Nancy, the former capital of the Duchy of Lorraine. Here, under the reign of the Polish king Stanislaus Leszczynski, a series of squares and promenades were built in the 1750s, northward along a lengthy axis from the Hôtel de Ville and culminating in the ornate hemicycle or square of the Palais du Gouvernement. The city itself sits amid vast tracts of forest to its north, west, and south, but city planners complemented the forest with a large parkland running parallel along much of the eastern edge of the governmental axis. Directly behind the palace were royal gardens of considerable size.

If the city of Nancy would have a competitor for its baroque beauty, it would have to be the German city of Karlsruhe, situated about a hundred miles to its east. It was founded by Margrave Karl Wilhelm of the German state of Baden. In 1715, the margrave decided to move his seat to a site within the Hardtwald Forest. His designer created a circular city, of sorts. The main body of the palace lies along the south edge of the circle's east-west diameter, with two wings fanning at a forty-five-degree angle. The palace, its governmental buildings, the formal garden, indeed the whole town resides within this southern ninety-degree segment of the circle. The genius of the design, one of Folly's greatest inventions, is that the other 270 degrees of the circle are given over entirely to gardens and forest—an inspired design of the grandest proportions. The inner belt of gardens, approximately 2,000 feet in diameter, was something akin to a curiosity garden, in that it contained pheasants, deer, goats, and tamed beavers. The larger outer belt of this design was originally left as forest, oddly scored by the radial pathways from the palace effectively leading nowhere. What is interesting about Karlsruhe, as with Nancy, is that many of these gardens and forested areas remain intact today, notwithstanding the expansion of the city.

In 1788, an American touring the Rhine Valley was taking notes and making sketches. On the fifteenth day of the month of April, having departed Speyer, Thomas Jefferson crossed the Rhine and arrived in Karlsruhe. He was complimentary of the Margrave of Baden's palace, which, he reported, "is built in the midst of a natural forest of several leagues diameter, and of the best trees I have seen in these countries." He goes on to discuss the Margrave's collection of wildlife and the beauty of the vegetation, the last of which he later advised American tourists to study "minutely."[24]

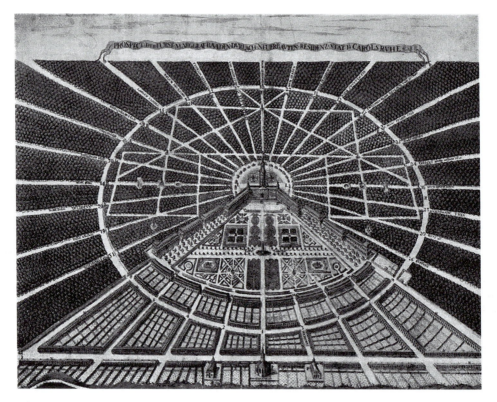

ILLUSTRATION 7.4   City Prospect of Karlsruhe, 1721. Copperplate by Heinrich Schwarz.

Source: Wikimedia, public domain.

His only negative remark, and a very legitimate one at that, was the reasoning for cutting radial *allées* through a pristine forest. Folly, no doubt, played a role in that decision as well.

A View of the Potomac

Folly, however, was still not done, and her next baroque creation is certainly a point of contention: the city of Washington. Charles Dickens, on his visit to the city in 1842, amended its popular moniker "City of Magnificent Distances" to "City of Magnificent Intentions," because its leading features were spacious avenues "that begin in nothing, and lead nowhere; streets, mile long, that only want houses, roads, and inhabitants; public buildings that need only a public to be complete; and ornaments of great thoroughfares, which only lack great thoroughfares to ornament."[25] When the poet and literary critic John Malcolm Brinnin hosted Dylan Thomas on his tour of the city a century later, before the city's infestation by lobbyists, the Welshman could still describe the city as "an abstraction."[26] Others have condemned its baroque symbolism. The American critic Lewis Mumford, for instance, lamented that the design of "the new capital was in every respect what the architects and servants of despotism had originally conceived."[27] Another historian went further by noting the "supreme irony that the plan forms originally conceived to magnify the glories of despotic kings and emperors came to be applied as a national symbol of a country whose philosophical basis was so firmly rooted in democratic equality."[28] Architects, to this day, generally assail the city's buildings and monuments. Nearly everyone decries its politicians. All of the commentary would seem to make the baroque city an odd one to appear in a study of paradise—unless one were willing to mull over the meaning of "Magnificent Intentions." For indeed a case can be made that no modern city was founded with more sincere aspirations than this modern-day Nineveh.

Its origins in the first term of George Washington grew out of a compromise. Two bills had been stalled in Congress. One was the federal assumption of the states' debt incurred during the Revolutionary War; the other was the location of the federal government itself. Before, during, and after the Revolutionary War, Congress had met variously in Philadelphia, Baltimore, Lancaster, York, Princeton, Annapolis, Trenton, and New York. Thus, the issue of a permanent seat was front and center, and naturally both the southern and northern states lobbied for their region—for the rather obvious reason that travel at this time was largely by horseback. At a dinner in New York hosted by Jefferson, the secretary of state sat down with James Madison and Alexander Hamilton, and the two Virginians agreed to forgo their opposition to the assumption bill in exchange for a location of the capital closer to the southern states, a compromise that resulted in the Residence Act of 1790. In January of the following year, President Washington selected a ten-square-mile tract along the Potomac River, five miles upstream from his estate at Mount Vernon. He viewed the river as the gateway to western development, and indeed ports were already active in Georgetown, Alexandria, and Bladensburg. Parcels of land of considerable size within the site were in private hands, a scattering of manors and agricultural lands in generally wooded areas.

Washington tapped Andrew Ellicott to undertake the task of surveying the land, and then made the inspired choice of Captain Pierre-Charles L'Enfant as the planner. The Frenchman had served on Washington's staff at Valley Forge, and he was wounded and taken prisoner during the Siege of Savannah. In an earlier letter to the president, he voiced his desire to become a useful citizen and "share in the Undertaking" of designing a city, and further suggested "that the plan should be drawn on such a scale as to leave room for that aggrandisement & embellishment which the increase of the wealth of the Nation will permit it pursue at any period however remote."[29] L'Enfant's credentials were indeed adequate. His father had been a court painter to Louis XV at Versailles and a member of the Royal Academy, and the son had studied at the Royal Academy of Painting and Sculpture in Paris. In private practice after the war, he renovated New York's City Hall, which became the seat of the first Congress. The scene was therefore set for a good outcome, but then Washington, for political reasons, designated a triumvirate of commissioners to overview the project—bureaucrats who, as Folly would have it, knew nothing about designing a city.

It is also here that Jefferson once again enters the picture, because Washington named his vice president as the point man on the project. Jefferson's architectural aspirations extended back to his years at the College of William and Mary in Williamsburg, where he dutifully read every architectural textbook that could be found while also criticizing the local architecture. Beginning in 1784, he lived five years in Paris as a minister and American ambassador in the period leading up to the French Revolution. In Paris, he leased an elegant townhouse on the Champs Élysées designed by the French architect Jean F.-T. Chalgrin, a short walk down to the Jardin des Tuileries, the city's much-admired park along the Seine. Across the river from it and under construction was the Hôtel de Salm, another elegant townhouse that would capture his fancy. In another letter to his confidante Madame de Tessé, the mistress of a Paris salon, Jefferson again noted that he was "violently smitten" with the building and would walk down to the Tuileries "almost daily" to study its great beauty.[30] This letter was three years prior to his trip to southern France, and his infatuation with the Maison Carrée in Nimes.

All of these architectural "affairs"—not to mention his miserly "peep only into Elysium," forced by his short stay in Italy on his trip south, on which he was unable to venture as far as Rome or Venice—would seem to make Jefferson an awkward but informed intermediary between George Washington and L'Enfant, a role that he indeed fulfilled. As L'Enfant was preparing his design, in March of 1791, Jefferson submitted his own design for a gridded street plan in the area of the present city bordering on Georgetown. What is interesting about the sketch is that both the President's

House and the Capitol were allotted three city blocks, whereas the "public walks," or urban promenade that joined these two areas, was given eight blocks. Neither Washington nor L'Enfant seemed much impressed with the gridded plan, and L'Enfant, in fact, referred to it privately in a memorandum to Washington as "tiresome and insipid . . . wanting a sense of the real grand & truly beautiful."[31] Yet Jefferson's "public walks" also alluded to something else with which L'Enfant was quite familiar: the promenade of the Champs-Élysées. Le Nôtre, the planner and landscaper at Versailles, had created the grand avenue in 1664 by inserting two rows of elm trees on each side for pedestrians to stroll along, with a roadway for carriages down the center. L'Enfant knew this mainstay of Paris and its history, and it may well have been out of respect for Jefferson's presence that L'Enfant wrote to Jefferson in April 1791 and asked for plans of major cities that would be useful for him to study. Jefferson responded, rather graciously, by sending him volumes from his own library containing the plans of Frankfurt, Amsterdam, Strasbourg, Paris, Orleans, Bordeaux, Lyons, Montpelier, Marseilles, Turin, Milan, and—quite naturally—Karlsruhe.[32]

The early design decisions—guided by an urban vision that "a powerful Empire ought to manifest"—were solid ones.[33] L'Enfant identified a ridge along the eastern part of the district, from which "a majestic aspect over the Country all round" could be obtained, and proposed it as a site for the Capitol at the edge of this ridge: "a pedestal waiting for a monument." He also, as with Versailles, directed three radiating avenues westward from the Capitol. One was Maryland Avenue, tracking southwest into a floodplain; the second was Pennsylvania Avenue, oriented northwest and leading to the President's House, allowing the president a view of the Capitol. For the third east-west axis, he placed his "Grand Avenue" or Mall, more than triple the width of the Champs-Élysées. It began at the congressional garden at the western base of Capitol Hill (featuring an unbuilt colossal waterfall) and extended to the Potomac more than a mile away. The Mall allowed carriages down

ILLUSTRATION 7.5 George Cooke, *City of Washington from Beyond the Navy Yard*, 1833. United States White House Collection.

Source: Wikimedia, public domain.

the center but it also had 400 feet of parkland on each side—reminiscent of the scale of Jefferson's "public walks." L'Enfant recommended that the edges of the parkland be lined along both sides with embassies.

L'Enfant, also emulating Versailles, proposed a north-south cross-axis of parkland to the Mall, running south from the President's House and garden, preserving an open view to the Potomac. At the river's edge was a public park, and at its intersection with the Mall, he proposed an equestrian statue of George Washington, a few feet from the present Washington Monument. There were other nuances to the plan that were well considered. All the avenues would crisscross one another in circles and squares. The Capitol with its garden would have no fewer than nine streets and avenues directed to it, and the President's House and Lafayette Park to its north would be the focus of eight. He also incorporated into his scheme a non-denominational church, five grand fountains ("intended with a constant sprout of water"), and locations for colleges, academies, and a playhouse.

The "Magnificent Intentions" of the new Capitol, as the reader might now guess, fell short in their realization. L'Enfant soon ran afoul of the pecunious commissioners, and barely into a year of service, in February 1792, he was dismissed for ignoring their advice. The other major flaw of the design process was the incomprehensible congressional decision not to fund the building of the new city. The states of Virginia and Maryland provided a small amount of operational monies to start the project, but the strategy was to have the large landowners cede one half of their land to the federal government for a nominal fee, and then have the right to develop the other half at their own profit. This decision quickly led to speculation at a large scale, ultimately to something akin to a pyramid scheme, and the city would not fill out for another century.

The young federal government also managed to botch its two major monuments: the Capitol and the President's House. Jefferson proposed a competition in 1792 for the former, which would have been acceptable except for one small matter. There were no trained or experienced architects in the young country. The details are of little significance, but neither the design nor the early construction proved satisfactory, and when America's first competent architect, Benjamin Latrobe, took over the project of the Capitol in 1803, he was forced to tear up much of the shoddy work. Latrobe, at this time, was now also being persistently nagged by President Jefferson, who challenged many of his design decisions for lacking antique precedent. Latrobe, in turn, took Jefferson to task for his bookishness and unwillingness to allow for artistic invention.[34] The issues, in any case, were rather graciously resolved by Folly in 1814, who saw to it that the British, in their march on the city, set the Capitol and President's House ablaze.

Jefferson also did not get his way on the President's House. In a letter to L'Enfant, he suggested that it be modeled on the Hôtel de Salm in Paris—for him, one of "the celebrated fronts of modern buildings" that had "received the approbation of all good judges."[35] The Irishman James Hoban won the competition with a Palladian-inspired design, beating out a smaller proposal that, by some accounts, Jefferson had submitted anonymously. Construction was slow, in large part due to the lack of funding. The building was still in a very crude state in 1800 when John Adams moved in during a cold November, and only in 1807 did Jefferson ask Latrobe to add a front porch and prepare a modest design for the rear garden, which had been so important to L'Enfant's plan. The building acquired the name "White House" after being rebuilt following its burning and being given a fresh coat of plaster.

The nation's capital also did not fare well throughout much of its early history. The plan was simply too grand for the population and size of government. The city's population in 1800 was all of 3,000 people, almost half of the population of Alexandria across the river. Moreover, the "Grand Avenue," or National Mall, proved to be a symbolic failing. The western edge was a tidal swamp, and the canal (an earlier creek) that ran through it in short order became foul and polluted. Sheep and cattle grazed on other parts of the Mall, and the area between it and Pennsylvania Avenue, near the Capitol, became known as "Murder Bay" for its crime and slum-like conditions. Sewers did not come to the city until the 1870s. One of Folly's last interventions was convincing Congress to run a rail line through it with a station at the base of the Capitol.

What ultimately turned the situation around was the McMillan Commission of 1902, which was formed under the leadership of Daniel Burnham, Charles McKim, and Frederick Law Olmsted, Jr. The commission attempted to reassert the spirit of L'Enfant's design and reiterated a strong processional parkland with groves of trees for the Mall. From the land reclaimed by dredging the Potomac, they created a site for the Reflecting Pool, the Lincoln Memorial, and groves of trees. L'Enfant's north-south axis running through the White House was reaffirmed, even strengthened, and pushed south to create a "Washington Common," a place for recreational events. Eventually it became the Tidal Basin and the site of the Jefferson Memorial. Fortified with aerial perspectives, the McMillan Report was a professional proposal in keeping with L'Enfant's earlier proposals, yet here again Congress managed to derail parts of the plan by locating a few buildings willy-nilly. Notwithstanding, it was through the efforts of the commission—revisited by federal planners in recent decades—that the city possesses the respectable baroque character it has today. From a few isolated spots in the city, if one looks closely, one can still sense the faint aura of L'Enfant's vision of an Edenic capital city.

Picturesque

When Henry VIII broke with the Catholic Church in the 1530s, it was also a break with the stylistic tendencies of the Renaissance, separating England politically and culturally from much of Europe. As renaissance and mannerist trends evolved into the baroque phase at the start of the seventeenth century, Reformational Britain again stood apart. There were exceptions, of course. The Englishman Inigo Jones traveled to the Veneto in 1606 to study the high classicism of Palladio, and seven years later he was appointed Surveyor of the King's Works and introduced the Renaissance's vocabulary to London with his designs for the Queen's House in Greenwich and the Banqueting House in Whitehall. Yet Jones's legacy was initially small. One later successor, the erudite Christopher Wren, was more eclectic in his reading of history. In addition to his Palladian-inspired library at Cambridge, his Oxford works include the Gothic Tom Tower at Christ Church College and the Sheldonian Theater, which drew upon Sebastiano Serlio's engraving of the ancient Roman Theater of Marcellus. His masterful design for St. Paul's Cathedral is classical in its styling but more influenced by recent French architectural tastes than Italian models. Wren's two talented successors, Nicholas Hawksmoor and John Vanbrugh, were generally classical in their outlooks but with highly personal baroque vocabularies bordering on genius, as we find in their two masterpieces started around 1700: Castle Howard in Yorkshire and Blenheim Palace in Oxfordshire. Some contemporaries, however, were not so kind. When Anthony Ashley Cooper, the Third Earl of Shaftesbury, issued his influential "A Letter Concerning Design" in 1712, he censured Wren, Hawksmoor, and Vanbrugh by name and called for an "improvement" in British taste, which he believed would be gained by founding a national academy for the arts, similar to the Académie des Beaux-Arts in France.[36]

Shaftesbury's plea would not be answered for another half century, because a series of events intervened—beginning in 1715 with the capture of the British Parliament by the Whigs. As with the Reformation, a distinct change of taste rapidly ensued in Britain, and the baroque vocabulary now associated with the Crown lost favor. In the same year, the Scottish architect Colen Campbell issued the first volume of his *Vitruvius Britannicus, or the British Architect*, which championed the purity of Inigo Jones's classicism and compared him in stature with Palladio. Later in the same year, Nicholas du Bois and Giacomo Leoni issued their translation of Palladio's treatise. Thus, almost a century and a half after the Paduan's death, a Palladian (high Renaissance) Revival sprang up in Britain.

By the mid-1720s, Richard Boyle, the Third Earl of Burlington, would emerge as the champion of the new movement. This wealthy aristocrat had made his first grand tour to Italy in 1714, but five years later, in sensing the new direction, he returned to explore firsthand the work of Palladio. Burlington was an admirer of Shaftesbury and espoused his artistic ideal of a *virtuoso*, or someone of breeding and politeness who "is careful to form his judgment of arts and sciences upon right models of perfection."[37] On his second trip to the south, Burlington began acquiring drawings by Palladio and his follower Vincenzo Scamozzi, as well as the papers that Jones and John Webb had collected. Eventually he assembled them in the Blue Velvet room of his Chiswick House, a library erected in the 1720s on his rural estate just west of London. The building is an erudite architectural homage to Palladio and Jones, and remains the jewel of his estate. He was assisted in this regard by the painter William Kent, who Burlington had twice met in Italy and then invited into his household to prepare a publication on Inigo Jones. The book appeared in 1727, followed three years later by Burlington's own book on Palladio's drawings. Burlington also lent support to Isaac Ware's *Designs of Inigo Jones and Others*, and he advised the historian Robert Castell on his proposed folio *Villas of the Ancients*. Over the next several decades dozens of Palladian villas were constructed across the country seats of Britain, feeding a classical spirit that for a while seemed indomitable. Yet even the best of these large and impressive estates, such as Kent and Burlington's design for Holkham Hall, did not rise to the level of a celestial production. Nevertheless, a very curious thing did take place. In the midst of this classical revival, garden designs shook off the baroque models of the Continent and acquired a distinctly naturalistic hue. Arguably, human sensibilities with respect to nature were changing in a somewhat radical, even paradisiacal way.

The English Garden, as it quickly came to be called, seemingly flew in the face of all that preceded it. The Italian gardens of the Renaissance were historical narratives of classical ideals meant to delight the upper crust of society. The gardens of Versailles and elsewhere extended this direction, but with a baroque sensibility that mandated extended vistas, long waterways and alleyways, and a strict geometric plan with a similarly geometric trimming of trees and shrubs. Yet Versailles, with its royal pretense, at the same time allowed no successors—if only for its sheer size and exorbitant maintenance cost. The English Garden, however, arose from a different way of thinking. In essence, it grew out of a developing notion of perception, one attributed to John Locke, by which we gain knowledge from the sensory experience itself rather than from conceptualization. It is a perspective that privileges the senses and emotions over such previously seen "innate" ideas such as beauty.

Hence, the geometrical order and rules of symmetry that dominated baroque thinking suddenly carried no aesthetic weight. They were replaced by feelings or flights of the imagination, in this case stirrings emanating from the forms of nature itself. This reasoning is already seen in such earlier British writers as Henry Wotton and Francis Bacon, but was better articulated in 1692 by the statesman William Temple, who, upon retiring to his country estate in Surrey and creating his own "Gardens of Epicurus," made these comments regarding Chinese garden design and its notion of beauty:

> But their greatest reach of imagination is employed in contriving figures, where the beauty shall be great, and strike the eye, but without any order or disposition of parts that shall be commonly or easily observed: and though we have hardly any notion of this sort of beauty, yet they have a particular word to express it, and where they find it hits their eye at first sight, they say the *sharawadgi* is fine or is admirable, or any such expression of esteem.[38]

Temple found his first apostle in none other than the classicist Shaftesbury, who in 1709 confessed that he could no longer resist his growing passion for the grandeur of raw nature:

> Even the rude rocks, the mossy caverns, the irregular unwrought grottos and broken falls of waters, with all the horrid graces of wilderness itself, as representing nature more, will be the more engaging, and appear with a magnificence beyond the formal mockery of princely gardens.[39]

Shaftesbury would pen his letter calling for an academy of art three years later, and this is the rub. Nearly all of the founders of the picturesque movement were classically minded aristocrats and students of Palladio, yet they consciously steered away from the "princely gardens" of France and Palladio's own preference for symmetry. One outlet for this new movement was the Kit-Cat Club, a gathering of Whig politicians, writers, and intellectuals, who shared their political and artistic viewpoints over food and fine wine. Among its participants were Burlington, Vanbrugh, Viscount Cobham, Joseph Addison, Richard Steele, John Locke, and occasionally Jonathan Swift. In this regard, the anti-royalist sentiments echoing in Shaftesbury's reference to "princely gardens" were known not only in Britain but were also understood elsewhere, as we shall see.

Particularly influential in advancing picturesque ideals were Addison's commentaries in the popular journal *The Spectator*, in which he noted that the "rough careless Strokes of Nature" are far bolder and masterly in their beauty than "the nice Touches and Embellishments of Art." The reason is that the beauties of formal gardens provide only "a narrow Compass," and thus the

> Imagination immediately runs them over, and requires something else to gratify her; but, in the wild Fields of Nature, the Sight wanders up and down without Confinement, and is fed with an infinite variety of Images, without any certain Stint or Number.[40]

In another article of 1712, he made the important aesthetic distinction between the "great," the "uncommon," and the "beautiful." He defined "greatness" similar to how Edmund Burke would later define the sublime—that is,

> huge Heaps of Mountains, high Rocks and Precipices, or a wide Expanse of Waters, where we are not struck with the Novelty or Beauty of the Sight, but with that rude kind of Magnificence which appears in many of these Stupendous Works of Nature.[41]

This line of reasoning not only provided a setting for the later writings of William Gilpin, Thomas Whately, Uvedale Price, and Richard Payne Knight, but it also characterizes the early gardening approaches of William Kent, Capability Brown, and Humphry Repton.

The movement came together in the 1720s within the Burlington circle. Robert Castell, in preparing his manuscript for *The Villas of the Ancients Illustrated*, had made the case that the Roman gardens of classical times evolved in three stages: the first in simply selecting a pleasing site, the second by imposing a model of symmetry, and the third and most refined stage by exploiting the attribute of visual irregularity. Burlington was already experimenting with this strategy at Chiswick, a garden that by his own admission was inspired by Hadrian's Villa at Tivoli. In Chiswick he brought in Charles Bridgeman to transform his formal garden into an irregular one, one that would have emotional appeal through its use of garden temples, follies, and statuary. In the 1730s he replaced Bridgeman with Kent, and the painter brought to the table the inspiration of the landscapes of Nicholas Poussin and Claude Lorrain. Another member of the Burlington circle was Alexander Pope, who during the same years was building a small villa along the Thames at Twickenham. At the rear of his house, he leased five acres of land north of the London roadway and designed a garden that included a theater, arcade, bowling green, and grove. To connect the garden with his house, he tunneled under the roadway with a naturalized grotto. One of his inspirations had been the gardens of Alcinous, the description of which he came across during his translation of Homer's *Odyssey*.

These efforts were soon overtaken by the English garden at Stowe, a 400-acre estate of Peter Temple, thirty miles north of Oxford. He had recently been elevated to Viscount Cobham for his services in the War of the Spanish Succession, an asset that he expanded by marrying a wealthy heiress. He was likely schooled in gardens at the Kit-Cat Club, and in fact one of his first acts was to commission Vanbrugh to make changes to his manor. Vanbrugh himself was another early theorist of the picturesque movement, of sorts. In his letter to the Duchess of Marlborough of 1709, for instance, he pleaded for the preservation of the ruins of old Woodstock Manor at Blenheim specifically for its picturesque qualities:

> And the Most Agreable Disposition is to Mix them, in which this Old Manour *gives so happy an Occasion for*, that were the inclosure filld with Trees (principally Fine Yews and Hollys) Promiscuously Set to grow up in a Wild Thicket. So that all the Building left, (which is only the Habitable Part and the Chapel) might Appear in two Risings amongst 'em, it wou'd make One of the Most Agreeable Objects that the best of Landskip Painters can invent."[42]

At Stowe, Cobham, possibly on the advice of Vanbrugh, hired Bridgeman to extend and transform the existing baroque garden and thereby create a political and classical narrative centered around natural vistas into which were inserted temples, churches, triumphal arches, obelisks, statuary, bridges, ruins, and a grotto—all connected with pathways tucked along the edges of groves. The allegorical script for the park seems to have been based upon Addison's "Vision of the Three Roads of Human Life," a short essay that he composed for *The Tatler* in 1709. In his dream, Addison described being in a vast garden park with many pathways, some leading to temples of lust ("labyrinths of coquettes"), others to vanity and avarice (political corruption), yet a third path leading to the temples of "honor and "virtue." The third path "was planted on each side with laurels, which were intermixed with marble trophies, carved pillars, and statues dedicated to lawgivers, heroes, statesmen, philosophers, and poets."[43] Upon reaching Stowe from the London road at the south end, the visitor also had a choice of paths, one leading to the Temples of Venus and Bacchus and the other leading to temples portraying virtue in politics and learning.

It took several decades for the work to be completed, and the strongest hand at play is that of Kent, who in the 1730s softened the formality of Bridgeman's initial design by relocating the trees aligned in rows, naturalizing the edges of the artificial lakes, and by crafting a series of smaller parks within the garden. His masterpiece is the Elysian Fields, an idyllic area of land along the banks of a stream, which features on one side the Temple of Ancient Virtue. It is a tholos or rotunda with an Ionic colonnade, inside of which are full-scale statues of Epaminondas, Lycurgus, Homer, and Socrates. Across the stream is the Temple of British Worthies, containing busts of prominent historical figures, divided into camps of heroic figures of "action" and those of "ideas." In the latter category are William Shakespeare, John Milton, Alexander Pope, Thomas Gresham, Inigo Jones, John Locke, Isaac Newton, and Francis Bacon. In his *Observations of Modern Gardening* of 1780, Thomas Whately describes the Elysian Fields with these words:

> Solitude was never reckoned among the charms of Elysium; it has been always pictured as the mansion of delight and of joy; and in this imitation, every circumstance accords with that established idea; the vivacity of the stream which flows through the vale; the glimpses of another approaching to join it; the sprightly verdure of the green-swerd, and every bust of the British worthies, reflected in the water; the variety of the trees; the lightness of their greens; their disposition; all of them distinct objects, and dispersed over gentle inequalities of the ground; together with the multiplicity of objects both within and without, which embellish and enliven the scene; give it a gaiety, which the imagination can hardly conceive, or the heart wish to be exceeded.[44]

A few hundred feet from the Temple of British Worthies is a Palladian Bridge, modeled after one of Palladio's unbuilt designs. As with many Italian and French gardens, the theme park of Stowe, by the 1740s, had become a tourist destination, complete with guidebooks so that the visitor would not miss its innumerable features and moral lessons.

ILLUSTRATION 7.6   Bridge and miniature Pantheon in the Gardens at Stourhead.

Source: Photo by Hamburg103a. Wikimedia CC BY-SA 4.0.

Stowe would soon be rivaled, if not surpassed, by later masterpieces of garden design, none more idyllic than Henry Hoare's transformation of his Palladian estate at Stourhead, mostly carried out in the 1750s. Here another large lake was created to highlight a series of Virgilian garden-follies, including a miniature Pantheon, Gothic cottage, Temple of Apollo, and a five-arch bridge spanning a very narrow portion of the lake. All were connected with a path that ran around the lake and through the forest.

Before leaving the picturesque movement in Britain, we should also comment on another inspired design from this period that also owes something to its ideas: the town of Savannah, Georgia. It was conceived by James Oglethorpe, the son of a wealthy English landowner and parliamentarian, who interrupted his studies at Oxford in 1716 to attend a military academy in Paris. From there, at the recommendation of John Churchill, the first Duke of Marlborough, he gained a position as an aide to Prince Eugene of Savoy, who would lead a successful European campaign to retake the city of Belgrade from Ottoman control. Oglethorpe fought there with distinction and, after making his way back to England, he won his father's Tory seat in the House of Commons. In the 1720s, Oglethorpe led a campaign against the overcrowded and filthy conditions of debtors' prisons in Britain, after his friend, the classical scholar Robert Castell, died of smallpox in one such prison due to debts he incurred while attempting to publish his book on Roman gardens. Together with John Percival, Oglethorpe was successful in passing a bill creating new cities in Georgia, where England's "worthy poor" could be relieved of debt and start a new and productive life in America. The proposal called for the assignment of fifty acres of land to each debtor, free passage, and the tools needed to start an agrarian life. George II granted a charter for the settlements in 1732.

From the British perspective, other considerations came into play. One was the desire to add another trading center south of Charleston, South Carolina, further strengthening Britain's connection with the Caribbean islands. Another was to fortify a line of defense against the Spanish interests in the south, based at St. Augustine but still holding a claim to southern Georgia. Notwithstanding, it was the humanitarian impulse that drove Percival and Oglethorpe to propose a model based on

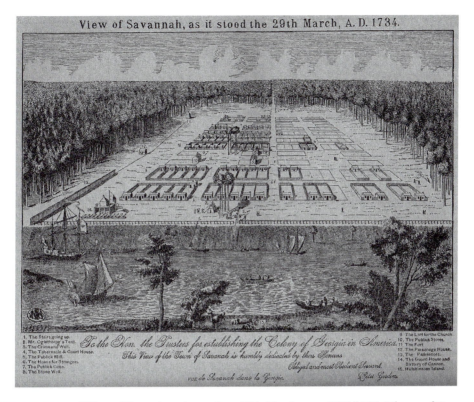

ILLUSTRATION 7.7   "View of Savanah, as it stood on 29th March, A.D. 1734." U.S. Library of Congress.

Source: Public domain.

ownership of land, a stable and reformed system of human rights under a secular administration, and a social system specifically banning slavery. The plan was also unique in that it encouraged impoverished or religiously persecuted members from other European countries to join in the migration. With these ideals in mind, Oglethorpe boarded a ship with 114 colonists in January 1733 and disembarked two months later in Charleston. Within a month, the site for the town along a Savannah River bluff was surveyed and 100 acres were cleared. Within a year the first fifty houses were built.

The plan for Savannah was unique in its conception. Each of the six wards or neighborhoods of the city was defined by its own green square, north and south of which were townhouses with walled gardens. To the east and west of the square were public and commercial buildings. The "garden aesthetic" of the square demanded that trees be preserved, and the area also served as a market on specified days. The town itself was to be surrounded with a green common that could be used for individual gardens and pasturing. Outside of the town was also a three-mile belt of farmland. Each person with a share in the colony was given a house lot, a five-acre food garden in the common, and forty-four acres of farm land to clear and cultivate. It was a noble experiment in creating a true garden city, and in fact two other sister cities—New Ebenezer and Darien—were settled, respectively by Protestant refugees from central Europe and the highlands of Scotland.

The noble experiment failed to live up to Oglethorpe's expectations for several reasons. One was that the climate was less suited for agriculture than was imagined abroad. The second was the need to divert resources to defend the town against Spanish incursions from the south, which ended only in 1742 when Oglethorpe led a successful counterattack—the Battle of Bloody Marsh—on St. Simon's Island, eighty miles to the south. The third was the simple presence of Charleston 100 miles to the north. The harbor town, with its belt of large plantations, had by the 1730s become a major trading center for Caribbean slaves and rum, and both (banned by Oglethorpe) proved to be too alluring to the "malcontents" of Savannah. Nevertheless, the plan of Savannah, with its bevy of parks, continues to serve as an instructive urban model. For those wards whose original size and character are still intact, it remains a humanly scaled city with walkable, tree-lined streets and green parks separated from each other by only a few blocks.[45] The town, it seems, was not entirely lost to Folly.

Notes

1. *Select Letters of Christopher Columbus, with Other Original Documents Relating to His Four Voyages to The New World*, trans. by R. H. Major (London: Hakluyt Society, 1847), 5–7.
2. Ibid., 114.
3. Ibid., 123–4.
4. Ibid., 136.
5. Ibid., 138.
6. *The Letters of Amerigo Vespucci and Other Documents Illustrative of His Career*, trans. by Clement R. Markham (New York: Burt Franklin, 1894), 48.
7. *De Orbe Novo: The Eight Decades of Peter Martry D'Anghera*, trans. by Francis Augustus Macnutt (New York: Putnam's Sons, 1912), 2 vols., I:87.
8. Ibid., I:318.
9. Ibid., I:358.
10. Ibid., I:341.
11. Ibid., I:342.
12. *Letters of Cortes*, trans. by Francis Augustus MacNutt (New York: G. P. Putnam's Sons, 1908), 265–6.
13. Bartholomew de Las Casas, "The Brevissima Relacion," in Francis Augustus MacNutt (ed.), *Bartholomew de Las Casas His Life, Apostolate, and Writings* (Cleveland, OH: Arthur H. Clark Company, 1909), 309–10.
14. *Early English and French Voyages, Chiefly from Hakluyt, 1534–1608*, ed. by Henry S. Burrage (New York: Charles Scribner's Sons, 1906), 72.
15. Ibid., 225.
16. *Montaigne's Essays in Three Books*, trans. by Charles Cotton (London: B. & B. Barker, 1743), I:229. See Shakespeare, *The Tempest*, Act II, scene 1.
17. Ibid., 228–30.
18. Desiderius Erasmus, *Praise of Folly and Letter to Maarten Van Dorp 1515*, trans. by Betty Radice (New York: Penguin Books, 1993), 16–17. *The Odyssey*, trans. by A. T. Murray, (Cambridge, MA: Harvard University Press, 1976), IV:220–3.
19. Ibid., 31.
20. Ibid., 54–5.
21. Ibid., 80.
22. See Kimberly Dennis, "Camilla Peretti, Sixtus V, and the Construction of Peretti Family Identity in Counter-Reformation Rome," *The Sixteenth Century Journal* 43:1 (2012), 71–101.
23. Sigfried Giedion, *Space, Time and Architecture* (Cambridge, MA: Harvard University Press, 1977), 92.
24. "Notes on a Tour Through Holland and the Rhine Valley, 3 March–23 April, 1788," *Founders Online*. https://founders.archives.gov. See also "Jefferson's Hints to Americans Travelling in Europe, 19 June 1788," *Founders Online*. Accessed March 2020.
25. Charles Dickens, *American Notes for General Circulation* (London: Chapman and Hall, 1850), 81.
26. John Malcolm Brinnin, *Dylan Thomas in America* (London: Readers Union, 1957), 36.
27. Lewis Mumford, *The City in History: Its Origins, Its Transformations, and Its Prospects* (New York: Harcourt, Brace & World, 1961), 407, 404–5.
28. John W. Reps, *Monumental Washington: The Planning and Development of the Capital Center* (Princeton, NJ: Princeton University Press, 1967), 21.
29. "To George Washington from Pierre L'Enfant," *Founders Online* (September 11, 1789), (note 24).
30. "Thomas Jefferson to Madame de Tessé," *Founders Online* (March 20, 1787), (note 24).
31. "Memorandum of Pierre-Charles L'Enfant," *Founders Online* (March 26, 1791), (note 24).
32. "Pierre Charles L'Enfant to Thomas Jefferson," *Founders Online* (April 4, 1791), (note 24).
33. "Memorandum of Pierre-Charles L'Enfant," *Founders Online* (March 26, 1791), (note 24).
34. "Latrobe's Letter to Thomas Jefferson, 21 May 1807," in Saul K. Padover (ed.), *Thomas Jefferson and the National Capital* (Washington, DC: United States Government Printing Office, 1946), 389–92.
35. "Thomas Jefferson to Pierre Charles L'Enfant," *Founders Online* (April 10, 1791), (note 23).

36. Third Earl of Shaftesbury, "A Letter Concerning Design," in Benjamin Rand (ed.), *Second Characters or The Language of Forms* (Bristol: Thoemmes Press, 1995), 21–2.

37. Third Earl of Shaftesbury, *Characteristics of Men, Manners, Opinions, Times*, ed. by Lawrence E. Klein (Cambridge: Cambridge University Press, 1999), 150.

38. William Temple, "Upon the Gardens of Epicurus; or, of Gardening, in the Year 1685," in Samuel Holt Monk (ed.), *Five Miscellaneous Essays by Sir William Temple* (Ann Arbor: University of Michigan Press, 1963), 30. See also Wotton's remarks in *Elements of Architecture* (1624) and Francis Bacon's essay "Of Gardens" (1625).

39. Third Earl of Shaftesbury, *Characteristics of Men, Manners, Opinions, Times* (note 37), 317.

40. Joseph Addison, Wednesday, 25 June 1712, *The Spectator* (London: George Routledge & Sons, 1888), 597.

41. Ibid., 23 June 1712, 595.

42. John Vanbrugh, "Letter to the Duchess of Marlborough (June 11, 1709)," in Geoffrey Webb (ed.), *The Complete Works of Sir John Vanbrugh*, 4 vols. (London: Nonesuch Press, 1928), 4:30.

43. "The Tatler," in George Washington Greene (ed.), *The Works of Joseph Addison*, 6 vols. (January 21, 1709), 4:131–6.

44. Thomas Whately, *Observations on Modern Gardening* (London: T. Payne, 1770), 221.

45. See Thomas D. Wilson, *The Oglethorpe Plan: Enlightenment Design in Savannah and Beyond* (Charlottesville, VA: University of Virginia Press, 2012); and Stanford Anderson, "The Plan of Savannah and Changes of Occupancy During Its Early Years: City Plan as Resource," *Harvard Architecture Review* 2 (Spring 1981), 60–7.

8

NEW ARCADIA

Prelude

In 1622, the wealthy Englishman Thomas Morton made an exploratory expedition to Massachusetts, during which he experienced rudeness from members of the Plymouth Colony. Nevertheless, he returned two years later and, with Captain Wollaston, set up a commercial trading settlement in what today is the Boston suburb of Quincy. In his book explicating his experiences, he waxed poetically of the area's great beauty:

> And when I more seriously considered of the beauty of the place, with all her fair endowments, I did not think that in all the known world it could be parallel'd, for so many goodly groves of trees, dainty fine round rising hillocks, delicate faire large plains, sweet crystal fountains and clear running streams that twine in fine meanders through the meads, making so sweet a murmuring noise to hear. . . . Fowles in abundance, Fish in multitude; and discovered, besides, Millions of Turtledoves on the green boughs, which sat pecking of the full ripe pleasant grapes that were supported by the lusty trees, whose fruitful load did cause the arms to bend: [among] which here and there dispersed, you might see Lilics and the Daphnean-tree: which made the Land to me seem paradise: for in mine eye t'was Nature's Masterpiece; Her chief Magazine of all where lives her store: if this Land be not rich, then is the whole world poore.[1]

Morton was not alone in describing the attractiveness of the landscape, but he was also not a typical visitor to the new world. This gentleman had studied law at London's Clifford's Inn and was a friend of Ben Johnson. He was known for his occasional outrageous behavior, as when he partied with others in London's bawdy theater district. Upon his arrival in Massachusetts, he set up, in contrast to his religious neighbors, what might be described as an alternative commune, one known for its orgies in which members of the Algonquian tribe participated. William Bradford, the leader of the Plymouth Colony, described Morton as the "lord of misrule," who "maintained (as it were) a school of Atheism." Equally bad, his band of followers

> also set up a May-pole, drinking and dancing about it many days together, inviting the Indian women, for their consorts, dancing and frisking together, (like so many fairies, or furies rather,) and worse practices. As if they had anew revived & celebrated the feasts of ye Roman Goddess Flora, or ye beastly practices of ye mad Bacchinalians.[2]

DOI: 10.4324/9781003178460-8

Morton's rowdiness became such an annoyance to Bradford that he ordered Myles Standish and his militia to enter Morton's camp, destroy the maypole, and put its leader in chains. He then exiled him to an uninhabited island.

Morton survived the ordeal and eventually sued the Plymouth Colony for his treatment, but with the ascension of Charles I to the throne in 1625 the colonies of New England took another turn. Charles had wanted to unify the Anglican Church, but through his clumsy efforts he only succeeded in pitting camps of Calvinists, Puritans, Presbyterians, Congregationalists, and Quakers against the high Episcopacy, controlled by bishops and the Crown. The "great migration" began in earnest in 1630 when John Winthrop gained a charter for the Massachusetts Bay Colony, and over the next decade as many as 20,000 Puritans crossed the Atlantic, landing in Massachusetts, Maine, New Hampshire, and Connecticut. The exodus was more than the free practice of religion; it was in some instances messianic. Winthrop, in a sermon, famously referred to his new settlement as a "Citty upon a Hill," an illusion to a gospel of Matthew. His sincerest hope was that his new colony would become the Christian "light" that would shine brightly for all the world to see.[3] The theologian Joseph Cotton in his sermon preferred to characterize the exodus out of England in Old Testament terms—by citing a verse of Samuel: "Moreover I will appoint a place for my people Israell, and I will plant them, that they may dwell in a place of their owne, and move no more."[4] As Charles Sanford reported in *The Quest for Paradise*, even the word "plantation" had an ecclesiastical connotation:

> Colonists were often explicit and detailed in developing the imagery of planting, especially since many of them were an agricultural people familiar with nature. They were planting the seed of the posterity of a new Adam and Eve in the rich, virgin soil of a new Eden, warmed by the Sun of Righteousness.[5]

Not everyone saw the roughness of the landscape in the same light as Morton. Bradford, when earlier stepping off the Mayflower, had described it not as New Jerusalem but as "a hideous & desolate wilderness, full of wild beasts & wild men."[6] Others saw the colony in political terms. Winthrop, for instance, viewed the effort as countering the "Diligence of the Papists" and the Spanish efforts in the South to enlarge "the kingdom of Antichrist."[7] Yet many of these colonies, with their strictness and dogmatism, fell short of theological idealism, as the Salem minister Roger Williams would soon discover. After questioning the right of the Massachusetts Colony to annex Indian lands without compensation in 1636, he was found guilty of heresy and sedition, and forced, in a bitterly cold winter, to self-exile across the Pawtucket River in a canoe with five others into Rhode Island. There, he set up that state's first colony, "Providence Plantations," to which others, also "distressed of conscience," soon fled.[8] And the situation in Massachusetts did not improve. Between 1659 and 1661, four members of the Puritan colony were hanged on Boston Common for espousing the principles of Quakerism. And in the 1690s there followed the infamous Salem witch trials. Puritanism rule proved to be far from paradisiacal.

The founding of Philadelphia by the Quakers was carried out with greater toleration and perhaps with a modicum of humanity. The Delaware River valley had been part of New Netherland until Britain took possession of it in 1664. Seventeen years later, Charles II offered William Penn a charter for the control of 45,000 square miles in Pennsylvania, in part to relieve Britain of the annoyance of the Quakers, the latest liturgical dissidents who were neither paying tithes nor swearing allegiance to the Crown. Penn was the son of a prominent nobleman and admiral, but he had been expelled from Oxford University for his religious beliefs and later served time in the Tower of London for writing pamphlets espousing the Quaker cause. In the 1670s he visited Ireland and Germany in search of converts, and all the while Charles II was becoming increasingly frustrated with religious opposition. Charles also owed a significant debt to Penn's late father, and the son, seeking compensation, accepted the grant of land with the promise that he would lead a large contingent of Quakers out of England. Other religious groups were also invited into the colony, among them Mennonites, Baptists, and smaller millennial sects, many of whom came to await the final days of the coming of Christ.

Penn, along with 2,000 others, sailed on twenty-three ships to the New World in 1682, and a similar number followed one year later. The first task in the interest of goodwill was to purchase land from a native tribe, which Penn believed, like many others at this time, was one of the ten lost tribes of Israel displaced by the Assyrians. Penn next surveyed the land and chose a location for his town, which was situated just north of the confluence of the Schuylkill and Delaware Rivers. The site for the city ran two miles wide along the river banks and one mile between the two rivers. Penn envisioned a town more rural than urban. He asked for the east-west streets to be uniform down to the water's edge, and with tracts of green space to run in the same direction. "Let every house be placed, if the person pleases, in the middle of its plat, as to the breadth way of it," he wrote, "that so there may be ground on each side for gardens or orchards, or fields, that it may be a green country town, which will never be burnt, and always be wholesome."[9]

The plan drawn up by his surveyor-general Thomas Holme in 1683 varied somewhat from Penn's advice, because it established a rectangular grid more urban in scale, with two main avenues crisscrossing in a ten-acre central square. The avenues divided the city into four quadrants with a public garden or park of eight acres in each sector. The latter gardens likely emulated those of London, which had been installed after the Great Fire of 1666. When Penn left the city for London in the summer of 1683, over 350 houses had been constructed, and within two years there were over 600 houses built. Even though the houses filled out less than half of the proposed plan, Philadelphia was on the way to becoming the largest city in North America. Penn's bylaws for the city were also quite novel and held some sway with later political developments in the country. As with Williams in Rhode Island, Penn mandated religious tolerance, freedom of expression, legal protections for property, and the elimination of capital punishment, except for treason and murder. However noble his intentions, the personal irony for Penn is that in building his paradise he exhausted his once-considerable fortune and died in England in a debtors' prison.

Pavilion IX

As Andrea Wulf has reminded us in her excellent study *Founding Gardeners*, the agrarian roots of the early settlers to the Atlantic seaboard of North America were still on prominent display a century later during the founding of the republic.[10] Benjamin Franklin owned a 300-acre farm in New Jersey and wrote several books on harvesting crops. The attorney John Adams similarly lived and maintained a farm outside of Boston. Both George Washington and James Madison did so in northern Virginia, at a much grander scale. And then there was the politician with perhaps the strongest ties to the land, Thomas Jefferson. For our purposes, he was also a builder, and by the end of his life he did manage to pursue his vision of paradise almost to its fulfillment in two works of high distinction: his estate at Monticello and his design for the University of Virginia.

Jefferson's fascination with architecture began during his years at the College of William and Mary, and intensified when he inherited 5,000 acres in Albemarle County upon the death of his father. The young law student chose to build not in a river valley with its ready access to water, as most people would do, but rather on a difficult, wooded hilltop knoll—one with a dramatic view of the Shenandoah Valley and the Blue Ridge Mountains. After the difficult tasks of finding water, cutting down trees, sawing wood, and mining clay for bricks, the modest three-room house he put up in 1770 was a respectable but by no means an exceptional design. Of course, political events would soon intervene, with the Boston Massacre of that same year and the Boston Tea Party three years later. The war followed and Jefferson faced his own peril when he eluded the cavalry force that General Cornwallis had sent to capture him. He fled south at the last moment to his Poplar Forest plantation.

Jefferson's *Notes on the State of Virginia* tells us a little more about his love of nature. He writes lovingly about America's trees, plants, fruits, minerals, and animal life. He counters specifically the ideas of the famed naturalist Georges-Louis Leclerc, the Comte de Buffon. The Frenchman had argued that the North American continent—its fauna, its wildlife, its native inhabitants—were in a state of ecological or evolutionary "degeneracy," far inferior to the peoples and landscapes of Europe.[11] Jefferson not only defended all of these features of North America, including the physical and mental skills of its indigenous populations, but during his ambassadorial duties in France, beginning in 1784, he took with him animal pelts to present to Buffon personally and argue on behalf of their evolutionary vigor.

The stay in France also formed the most important part of his architectural education, as several writers have noted. French architecture during this period was practiced at the highest level of design sophistication, and Jefferson simply marveled at its elegance. His consular duties commanded him to Versailles, but a trip he undertook in the spring of 1786 was more influential for his garden designs at Monticello. This was a tour that he and John Adams, the American ambassador to London, embarked upon—frantically—over a two-week period. They toured more than a dozen picturesque gardens, among them Chiswick, Hampton Court, Alexander Pope's garden at Twickenham, Woburn Farm, Wotton, Stowe, Blenheim, and Kew. Jefferson had studied them from afar years earlier, but he was manic to see them firsthand. His notes are succinct but insightful. He was dissatisfied with Burlington's estate at Chiswick, and he criticized the dome of the Chiswick Palladian showpiece for having "an ill effect" and the garden for showing "too much of art." At Blenheim, just outside of Oxford, he admired the lake that had been introduced by Capability Brown, which he described as "very beautiful, and very grand," and "the cascade from the lake is a fine one," but the garden had "no great beauties." One of his favorite stops was the Surrey estate of Woburn Farm, which, because it combined a pleasure garden with a working farm, was better suited to his own vision of what a rural estate should be. He was also much impressed with Stowe, in particular with the four levels of its ponds and the garden buildings.[12] Adams, incidentally, was put off at Stowe by the two temples dedicated to Bacchus and Venus, as "quite unnecessary as Mankind have no need of artificial Incitements, to such Amusements." He did note that the "Temples of ancient Virtue, of the British Worthies, of Friendship, of Concord and Victory, are in a higher Taste."[13]

Jefferson's later three-month tour of southern France and northern Italy, during which he fell in love with the Maison Carrée, was also notable because the trip's purpose was in large part to study the region's agriculture. Among his interests was the cultivation of the olive tree and the caper, but not the grape, because "those who cultivate it are always poor."[14] Poverty, however, did not stop him from visiting the major wineries of Burgundy, the Rhone Valley, and Bordeaux, and making substantial purchases. Another of his pursuits was Piedmont rice, which the French compared favorably with American Carolina rice. Upon finding it in Italy, he was told that its export was illegal under penalty of death. Not to be deterred, Jefferson hired "a muletier to run a couple of sacks across the Appenines to Genoa," and then, fearing they would not arrive, carried on his person "as much as my coat and surtout pockets would hold."[15] He sent the rice to South Carolina for planting.

He returned to the United States in 1789 and joined Washington's cabinet as secretary of state, and later served as vice president before, in 1800, beginning his two terms as president. Monticello never left his mind. Within a few years he decided to take down the eastern or front wall of his now five-room villa and more than double the area of Monticello's footprint. It was a costly and time-consuming decision that would meet with major difficulties, not the least of which would be disassembling and realigning the segmented stone columns of the front portico. Dismantling the house's roof also revealed that many of the earlier roof beams had rotted and needed to be replaced. His debts were mounting and he was not able to order the sheet-lead to finish the new roof until

ILLUSTRATION 8.1   Jane Braddick Peticolas, View of the West Front of Monticello and Garden, 1825.

Source: Wikimedia, CC-PD-Mark.

1807. The house and its interiors (now twenty-one rooms) were by then impeccable in their design and sophistication, although the porch remained uncompleted until 1822.

What elevates Monticello to idyllic proportions were the surrounding gardens, where his vision of paradise came into sharp focus. He had been toying with its design since the early 1770s—building and removing a deer park, deciding whether or not to build a grotto and cascade, whether or where to add orchards and groves—and between 1804 and 1807 he wrote a new memorandum for improving the grounds. It called for a series of dells, ravines, glens, hollows, and glades, the leveling of gardens, building a ha-ha, turning the spring into a cascade, digging a fish pond visible from the house, and converting "all of the farm grounds of Monticello" into orchards of cider, apple, and peach trees, with "orchard grass cultivated under them." Overall,

> the canvas at large must be a grove, of the largest trees (poplar, oak, elm, maple, ash, hickory, chestnut, linden, Weymouth pine, sycamore) trimmed very high, so as to give it the appearance of open ground, yet not so far apart but that they may cover the ground with close shade.

These areas "must be broken by clumps of thicket," such as privet and mountain laurel, allspice, lilacs, and honeysuckle, planted "such as the open grounds of the English are broken by clumps of trees." Equally interesting, in drawing upon his English tour, were his choice of garden ornaments—a "turning Tuscan temple" with the proportions of the Pantheon, "Demosthenes' lantern," and two Chinese pavilions, similar to those at Kew Gardens. In another notation he calls for a "model of cubic architecture," which likely was a classical temple.[16]

None of these architectural follies were built, but significant parts of his landscape plan were realized, and before his death in 1826 Monticello would become one of the largest gardens in the country, and one of the few dedicated to horticultural research. On the south side of his manor on a terrace, he built a vegetable garden of more than a thousand feet in length, which became his experimental seed laboratory for newly identified species or for different varieties of known species.

Below this level, over a much larger area, he placed orchards, which contained more than 125 varieties of fruit trees.[17] In a letter to Charles Willson Peale of 1811, he wrote that

> I have often thought that if heaven had given me choice of my position & calling, it should have been on a rich spot of earth, well watered, and near a good market for the productions of the garden. No occupation is so delightful to me as the culture of the earth, & no culture comparable to that of the garden.[18]

These words were also written after two other major accomplishments: the Louisiana Purchase of 1803 and the Lewis and Clark Expedition. Jefferson tapped his personal secretary Meriwether Lewis, together with William Clark, to head the exploration, which departed from Saint Louis in 1804 with two intentions. One was to explore the headwaters of the Missouri River and seek a

ILLUSTRATION 8.2   Lawn of University of Virginia, with the library at the top.

Source: Photo by author.

northwest passage to the Pacific Ocean. The scientific reason, however, was to discover new species of animals and vegetation, in addition to fathoming the "soil and face of the country." The bald-headed eagles and grizzly bears piqued their sense of awe, but so did "those monsterous trees" with Mount Hood and Mount St. Helens serving as backdrops.[19] To sharpen Lewis's botanical skills, Jefferson sent him to Philadelphia for a year to study botany, zoology, and celestial navigation in preparation. Clark was chosen for his skills as a frontiersman, engineer, and geographer.

By 1815, and largely due to the cost of building Monticello, Jefferson was facing bankruptcy. The sale of his precious library in that year to the Library of Congress did not ease his financial slide. His building instinct, however, would not waver. He had earlier put forth a proposal to the Virginia legislature to fund a new university, which would offer the highest tier of education. In a letter of 1805 he spoke of the importance of education for holding together the fragile democracy, especially to train those individuals "to whom nature has given minds of the first order."[20] He envisioned a university that would be strong in the useful branches of science, and he criticized the colleges at

ILLUSTRATION 8.3   Pavilion IX on the lawn at the University of Virginia.

Source: Photo by author.

Oxford, Cambridge, and the Sorbonne for being a century behind the science of their age. Five years later, he proposed that the new university should have ten professorships with sufficiently endowed salaries as to "draw the first names of Europe to our institution." His final and most radical point was that the plan for the university should not consist of large buildings—which "are always ugly, inconvenient, exposed to the accident of fire, and bad in cases of infection"—but be a village, or a grouping of individual houses for each professor, with quarters in the rear for students.[21]

He went to work on a plan for the new university, which took the form of ten lodges with family quarters upstairs and a lecture hall below. They were to be joined by a colonnaded walkway along their fronts and form a U-shape campus plan, opening onto a lawn with trees. The lawn originally provided a view of the Blue Ridge Mountains before it was blocked by a later building. Behind each pavilion, a short distance away, were student dormitories, connected to the lecture pavilions by gardens enclosed within serpentine brick walls. Jefferson believed vegetation and fresh air were essential for the educational and moral success of the institution.

Yet the genius of Jefferson's scheme lay also with the quality of its architecture. In his proposed plan, he had consulted with the architects William Thornton and Benjamin Latrobe. The retired president accepted Latrobe's suggestion for a focal building and responded with a one-half scale model of the Roman Pantheon at the top of the plan—the Rotunda—set on a high basement with three oval rooms on the first level and his domed library hall above. The professors' pavilions step down toward the south, and all are individually designed. Yet one pavilion in particular stands out for its unclassical simplicity and for what it reveals of Jefferson's personality: Pavilion IX. It is a brick cube with an apse inserted into the front wall containing the central doorway; the horizontal line of the colonnade crosses the front of the house at the springing of the apse's arch.

It is an unusual design because the source for the apse with a crossing entablature derives from a Parisian townhouse built in 1772 by the architect Claude-Nicolas Ledoux for the celebrated ballerina at the Paris Opera, Marie-Madeleine Guimard. The dancer was known for her many love affairs with the wealthiest suitors in the city, who seem collectively to have financed her mansion known as the "Temple of Terpsichore." On top of the crossing entablature in Paris was a statue of the muse of dance being crowned by Apollo, and in bas-reliefs across the front were scenes of Amours and Bacchantes. Adjacent, in the forecourt, was a private theater seating 500 people. Guimard is said to have hosted three lavish dinner parties every week: one for the aristocrats and court officials, one for artists, and one to which she invited the most attractive young women of the city. Such a lifestyle could hardly sustain itself, and in time she was forced to sell her luxurious mansion through a public lottery—coinciden-tally, just as Jefferson was assuming his ministerial duties. It is unlikely that the Virginian had any direct dealings with the dancer and courtesan, but he certainly would have been familiar with the design of her Parisian townhouse. Back in Charlottesville, the source of the architectural motif employed at Pavilion IX was likely unknown. Yet for Jefferson, who was approaching his eightieth birthday, the building was no doubt a reminder of his youth, of his many memories of Parisian social life, memories inevitably stamped with his own paradisiacal flirtations with both buildings and people.

New Harmony

In 1803 the millennial Pietist Georg Rapp, with 900 Lutheran dissenters from the Swabian Duchy of Württemberg, crossed the Atlantic and set up a German settlement in Pennsylvania. For more than twenty years the orthodox Rapp had been preaching against the ceremonies of the Lutheran church and seeking a return to Christian communalism, all the while viewing himself as a prophet of the second coming of Jesus Christ. After several trials in Swabia and one brief period in jail, he wrote to Napoleon Bonaparte in 1802 seeking permission for him and his followers to resettle in Louisiana, but the territory was soon sold to the United States. In a personal meeting with Jefferson in 1804, Rapp bartered for the purchase of 40,000 acres of land in Ohio, a deal that Jefferson sup-ported but for which he ultimately failed to obtain congressional approval. In October of the same year, Rapp was successful in purchasing 4,500 acres of land from a private owner twenty-six miles north of Pittsburgh, where he began to reassemble the members of his community. He named the community Harmony, and the Harmony Society became the legal entity into which all members placed their goods in common—an association that would prosper for the next century.

   Almost all of the mass immigrations to the young country were religious minorities fleeing Europe. Some were large and well-organized groups, such as the Puritans and the Quakers, whereas others were smaller sects seeking refuge from the perpetual religious wars of Europe. Of the latter, a number of sects were millennial in orientation, in that they believed the day of reckoning was near and they wished to prepare themselves for the transition to paradise through a community of like-minded peo-ple in the New World. Rapp, an excellent organizer and competent builder, was of this persuasion. He preached a form of communism not unlike the Shakers, in which individuals would surrender all property, work on behalf of the community, and take vows of celibacy, even within marriage. Harmony soon thrived in its economic production. Its streets filled out with log cabins, soon to be replaced with timber and brick buildings. Gardens were widespread, and the goods produced in orchards, vineyards, distilleries, and manufacturing facilities created an abundance of wealth. Rapp then decided to build another town in a more temperate location, one that would have river access to larger markets. In 1814, he purchased 20,000 acres of virgin land along the Wabash River in scenic southwestern Indi-ana. The river connected to the Ohio River, and the latter to the Mississippi River, offering an inter-national market. He wanted to implement the utopian ideas of his fellow Swabian Johannes Andreae in *Christianopolis*, a utopian vision that placed a high value on industry and education.

   The town of New Harmony was laid out around a town square, and within a few years the Rap-pists again were successful in cultivating the surrounding fields and vineyards. Mills and workshops were set up for the production of silk, wool, cotton, hemp, and leather goods, from which clothing, shoes, and rope were made. A distillery produced spirits for export and a brewery made a heavy beer for both residents and for export. New Harmony's beer, in fact, became a much sought-out com-modity throughout the region and was exported as far as St. Louis. The town buildings were noted

ILLUSTRATION 8.4   Karl Bodmer, Detail from the painting *New Harmony on the Wabash River*, 1832–33. Printed in *Reisen in das innere Nordamerikas 1832–1834* (1840–41).

Source: Wikimedia, public domain.

for their high quality. The insulated houses were built with a modular system and skillful carpentry. Two churches were constructed, the second in a cruciform plan, whose upper central story was supported with twenty-eight columns of walnut, cherry, and sassafras. Again, it was exquisitely crafted.

The education system was progressive. Girls and boys were given coequal education, including vocational training from the ages of six to fourteen—almost unprecedented on the frontier. Music and song were prominent within the curriculum, and adults were offered evening classes. Also notable were the town's gardens. One was a botanical garden that became a place for medicinal research. Another was a hedge-and-shrub labyrinth set within a five-acre pleasure garden. It was "arranged with such intricacy," as one visitor reported, "that without some Daedalus to furnish a clue, one might walk for hours and fail to reach a building erected in the center."[22] At its core was a circular temple of rough logs draped with grapevines and morning glories. It was a rustic allegory of the "peace and harmony" of afterlife achieved through the toil and suffering on earth.

As the community prospered, it also gained political influence. Indiana territory was admitted to the Union in 1816, and Rapp's uniform voting block held sway across the sparsely populated state. At one point, he was even asked to prepare a plan for the new state capital at Indianapolis. The community, meanwhile, acquired an international reputation, and several social reformers, among them the Scotsman Robert Owen, wrote to Rapp to ask the secret of his success. Yet New Harmony's economic and political dominance would also have its downside. Many Hoosiers living nearby, in the economic downdraft of the War of 1812, became jealous of the town's success and there was a riot in 1820 over the use of the city's lumber mill. The policy of celibacy was also reducing the population, even as settlers from Württemberg were still arriving. Finally, in 1824, Rapp decided to return his followers to Pennsylvania and commissioned the Englishman Richard Flower to sell the entire town—its 180 buildings—through advertisements in American and European newspapers.

Rapp's fortunes waned after his relocation, as he failed to heed the lesson of his fellow Pietist Johann Jacob Zimmermann, who once had falsely predicted the end of the world. The failure of the world to end on September 15, 1829, scared off many of Rapp's followers, and he died five years later.

Yet this is only the first chapter in the saga of New Harmony. Flower did not have to work hard to sell the town, because after his return to England he simply made his way to the Scottish town of New Lanark, where he met Rapp's distant admirer Robert Owen. Flower pitched the manufacturing town as the perfect place to put his own communitarian theories to a test. Owen was intrigued, and, after visiting New Harmony in 1824, he made the decision to purchase the town. Within the next year, 900 new residents of New Lanark would make their way to the town, although with a more secular perspective on paradise.

Owen was perhaps the quintessential utopian socialist, although Karl Marx and Friedrich Engels, in *The Communist Manifesto*, were not hesitant to point out his compassionate socialism was not without a high degree of idealism and naiveté. Concluding his formal education at the age of ten, Owen was sufficiently industrious over the next eleven years to become a manager of a textile mill in Manchester. In the following year, 1793, he was elected to the Manchester Literary and Philosophical Society, and six years later he moved to Scotland to marry Anne Dale, the daughter of the owner of one of the country's largest cotton mills. By the turn of the century, Owen had amassed a considerable fortune and felt compelled to address the appalling conditions of his mill workers. He reduced working hours, limited the use of child labor, and built housing for working families. His most notable innovation, attracting the attention of social reformers and politicians, was the educational program for New Lanark. Here he created a preschool for children with a focus on dance and music. He also built a second school for children five to ten years of age, which was in effect a primary school followed by continuing schooling and learning a trade. Owen drew upon the educational reforms of Johann Heinrich Pestalozzi. In his curriculum, the Swiss educator took a child-centered approach to teaching by acknowledging differences in the pace of learning. Pestalozzi emphasized sensory perception, or hands-on learning, and shunned the use of physical or verbal punishment. Children should be taught, as Owen also reasoned, to approach all others with loving-kindness. This idea reached to the core of Owen's thinking, because by withdrawing praise, blame, reward, and punishment from the child, by acknowledging the influence of the surroundings upon their development, the child, and later the adult, a rational proceeding "by which the earth can be laid out and made to become a terrestrial paradise and all its inhabitants made to become good, wise, united, and happy."[23]

Owen's utopian aspirations soon grew grander. Between 1813 and 1817, he lobbied on behalf of his socialist program by suggesting that he had gained a key insight into human nature; namely, that the character of each individual is entirely malleable, "that the character of man is, without a single exception, always formed for him; that it may be, and is chiefly created by his predecessors," who form his ideas, habits, and code of conduct.[24] In essence, one is shaped entirely by family, education, and living environment. The solution, then, is for all societal forces to be directed at training children in good practical habits that will contribute to good character. Ideally, such a program would also entail new departments of government, a nationalized system of education, and seminaries to train teachers. Only by redirecting societal resources to this end, in fact, could a "second creation or regeneration of man" be brought forth, one that will acknowledge his "natural faculties, qualities and powers, which will imbue him with a new spirit, and create in him new feelings, thoughts, and conduct, the reverse of those which have been hitherto produced."[25] If the present social system of Britain has led us into pandemonium, Owen concludes, "the new leads direct to a perpetual paradise on earth,—to the true practical Millennial state of human existence."[26]

Owen was a master publicist, and he soon put forth a plan to create a series of self-sustaining communities for indigent workers across Britain. These were to be manufacturing and agricultural towns for 1,200 people, and the shape of the town was a parallelogram, in which separate housing for couples and children defined the perimeter. Centered within the courtyard were a public kitchen and dining hall, a church, a nursery, and a primary school. Groves and places for exercise and recreation surrounded these communal buildings. Additional kitchen gardens were placed outside the perimeter rowhouses, and beyond them were the manufacturing facilities and farmland. Philanthropic industrialists and politicians listened politely to Owen's proposals, but politically the scheme was entirely unrealistic. Owen was therefore very amenable to Flower's visit. He sold his mill in New Lanark in 1825 and emigrated to the United States with the lofty ambition to create "The New Moral World," one based on a rationalist egalitarianism that would purge workers of their bad habits. It was thus with pomp and circumstance that Owen marked his arrival with a lecture tour, beginning in Philadelphia. There he was greeted warmly by a circle of educators and scientists connected with the Academy of Natural Sciences, who knew his ideas well. Among them were the school reformers Marie Duclos Fretageot and William Phiquepal. Observing from abroad was the academy's president and America's leading geologist, William Maclure, who had earlier, with similar educational interests, convinced two schoolmasters to transfer their Pestalozzian schools from Paris to Philadelphia. In the previous year, Maclure had in fact visited Owen in New Lanark.

In Washington, Owen addressed not one but two joint sessions of Congress in February and March, both attended by the newly elected President John Quincy Adams. Owen outlined the philosophy and ambitions behind his new Eden and displayed a drawing and a model of the new city he hoped to build in Indiana, prepared by the architect Thomas Stedman Whitwell. The plan of the new town was similar to his proposal of 1817, and it was to be situated on a bluff three miles south of the town of New Harmony, with a prospect of the river.[27] Owen also visited James Madison at Montpelier and Jefferson at Monticello, and the latter apparently confided in Owen that he welcomed his reforms because he too had become disappointed that the character of the American people had not improved under the new constitution.[28] The same or later model was exhibited the following November in New York and Philadelphia, and was put on display inside the White House for six weeks.

Only toward the end of April 1825 did Owen and his entourage finally arrive in New Harmony, no doubt with a feeling that his near-lifelong ambition would be realized. He was welcomed by the 900 or so individuals that had already arrived, most of whom were attracted to his socialist ideals. Surprisingly, the salesman Owen, fresh off his publicity tour, brought no specific plans for organizing the political structure at New Harmony—neither a strategy for governing nor for screening new members, both of which would undermine his efforts. Instead, he formed a Preliminary Society or "halfway house" with provisional committees to plot the future direction of the community. Even more inexplicably, Owen left the community in June, barely two months after his arrival to return to Scotland and bring back family members. The spirited proselytizer once again loaded the front and back ends of the trip with lectures and only arrived back to New Harmony in January.

His return, however, was not planned without theatrics. In Pittsburgh he boarded a "Boatload of Knowledge," a keelboat of forty notable scientists and artists who had committed to his cause, and who had dared the inclement weather and icy waters to move their labs and studios to this idyllic community. The trip, arranged by Owen and Maclure, nearly proved a disaster when it got stuck in the icy waters of the Ohio River near Beaver, where it was rescued—as it turned out, by Rappists. Numerous other luminaries were aboard the boat, among them the mineralogist Gerard Troost, the entomologist Thomas Say, the physician William Price, the naturalist Charles Lesueur, and the artist Balthazar Abernasser. Not only did a significant percentage of America's best scientists move to the distant wilds of Indiana, but they also brought with them their curricula, instruments, and libraries. Inspired by the efforts of the scientists, Owen's two sons—David Dale and Richard—both became geologists; the former the first president of Purdue University, and the latter a congressman who authored the bill creating the Smithsonian Institution. It is debatable, however, if the early staff of this institution matched the expertise Owen had assembled in New Harmony.

It was largely through these educators, scientists, and artists that New Harmony gained its global reputation.[29] Yet New Harmony would also become notable in other respects. Many of its residents championed equal rights and the abolition of slavery. The suffragette Frances Wright was a prominent voice in both campaigns, and political discussions in general were prominent within the community. The Thespian Society, organized by William Owen, also won accolades. All in all, it seemed on paper to be an ideal society with all of the trappings of high culture, set within an idyllic setting. Yet problems soon ensued. With the number of new arrivals, the living accommodations were stretched beyond their limits, and, aside from the upper tier of scientists and artists, there was a shortage of skilled tradesmen or experienced workers to run the various mills, workshops, and farms. There was also the issue of freeloaders. The amount of financial credit rendered for one's labor was a contentious issue that nagged the town, and once again no workable policy was in place. Owen, who ran a large mill in Scotland with great skill and competence, seemed unable to make the most basic business decisions.

These tensions were already evident when Owen returned in January, and he soon convened a convention to end the Preliminary Society and draft the permanent constitution. He did offer specifics on some policies regarding membership, but he did not address other important issues such as the ownership of property. Upon the completion of the constitution in early February, people were given three days to affix their signatures, which itself became an issue of contention. Various groups made objections to the document, and some soon splintered from the town to found new communities elsewhere. At first Owen was fine with these dispersals because they eased the shortage of living space, but at the same time they removed some of the town's best workers. The economy of the town, in part because of Owen's lengthy absences, never gained a solid footing, and there were few who could manage or run the various manufacturing operations that had been a financial boon to the Rappists. In May, frustrated residents insisted on seeing the model of the new city that Owen had promised he would build, but Owen refused to display it. In September, Owen made another attempt to write a general constitution, yet this only delayed the end of the experiment for a few months because a sharp rift had opened between Owen and Maclure over the pedagogical program. Owen wanted the curriculum to emphasize "character" formation, whereas Maclure, who was in charge of the schooling, adhered to his Pestalozzian beliefs. Because Maclure had also made a sizable financial investment in the town, this dispute led to a bitter lawsuit.

Owen delivered his farewell address to the town in late-May 1827, after which he returned to Scotland. The town remained, yet with only a few of its founding ideals. Over the next several decades, Owen would continue to proffer schemes for townships or socialist communities, but they were met with a declining audience of listeners, as a new generation of utopian thinkers began to emerge. Ralph Waldo Emerson once referred to Owen as "the most amiable, sanguine and candid of men," yet he was someone who "had not the least doubt that he had hit on a right and perfect socialism, or that all mankind would adopt it."[29] At New Harmony he also proved to be a better salesman of utopia than a leader, but perhaps this is because human nature, against his most basic tenet, is in fact not so malleable.

As an afternote: New Harmony in the 1950s underwent a renaissance through the efforts of Jane Blaffer Owen, a distant granddaughter of Robert Owen.[30] Several historic buildings were restored and a new visitor center was built, along with four new parks. One is a labyrinth based on a recreation of the labyrinth in Chartres Cathedral—a gesture to Rapp's labyrinth. Another is a grove dedicated to Jane's spiritual mentor Paul Tillich, which is formed with two outer earth mounds planted with 300 spruce trees, and two inner and smaller rings planted with hemlocks and spruces. The grove, with its shadowy, tunnel-like mulch pathways, is reminiscent of a labyrinth, and its thematic intention is to emphasize our womb-like connection with nature. These gardens, in a way, underscore another important point. The town is today virtually synonymous with Owen's ideology of progressive socialism, which was a short-lived and failed experiment. Much less attention has historically been given to Rapp's bucolic or harmonist sensibilities toward nature, which, when invested with human labor, survived more than a century in the three successful towns that he founded.

Emersonian Iterations

It is not surprising that the mythology of an American arcadia, first voiced by Puritans in the seventeenth century, would carry forward for much of the next two centuries, but a poignant counterpoint was voiced in 1782 by J. Hector St. John de Crèvecoeur, the son of a Norman aristocrat. In his book *Letters from an American Farmer*, which appeared three years before Jefferson's *Notes on Virginia*, he shares many of the Virginian's scientific and agrarian sentiments. St. John's topics are far-ranging, such as geographical and cultural descriptions of Nantucket and Martha's Vineyard; the city of Charleston and his aversion to slavery; the living habits of bees, snakes, and hummingbirds; and a visit to the Philadelphia botanist John Bartram. Yet the book's popularity today rests with a single chapter titled "What Is an American?" He begins his case in the guise of a Pennsylvania farmer by noting the myriad secrets and beauty of nature, and the peaceful quality of an agrarian society, in which one shares a community with one's neighbors. Arcadia may lack great manufacturers and refinements of luxury, he goes on to say, but America nevertheless has an abundance of fair cities and substantial villages, decent houses, good roads and bridges, ripe orchards, and scenic meadows. Moreover, its multiethnic people are liberated from the hostile arm of gentry, courts, kings, bishops, and ecclesiastical dominion. It is ruled only "by the silken bands of mild government" and a code of self-reliance. "Here individuals of all nations are melted into a new race of men," he reports, one that will eventually lead to "great changes in the world." What, then, is an American? He is someone "who acts upon new principles; he must therefore entertain new ideas, and form new opinions."[31] This is the American.

Yet there is one troubling aspect to St. John's arcadia, which is summarized in his final chapter, "Distresses of a Frontier-Man." Until three years earlier, St. John had been the owner of a prosperous farm sixty miles north of New York City, and over the previous nineteen years he had cultivated his lands with his American wife and children in a pastoral setting—a bucolic life disrupted by the Revolutionary War. Arcadia had now given way to the anxieties of plundering British troops on the one hand and similar attacks by Native American raiders. In effect, the final chapter was his apology for surrendering arcadia and seeking a new start in old Europe. His plan was to travel to France and England (where he eventually published his book), find a new country seat, and return to move his wife and children there. Attempting to sail from New York, however, he was delayed in his travels first by his arrest by the British as a suspected spy, and later by a shipwreck that landed him in Ireland. Only upon his return to New York in 1782 did he learn of the murder of his wife, the scattering of his children, and the burning of his homestead. His Eden had been relocated to Hades.

Ralph Waldo Emerson, born in 1803, came of age after the War of 1812 had concluded, and therefore he lived in a different America that enjoyed relative peace. There were, it need not be said, disruptions and ethical lapses everywhere: the westward expansion of American settlers, the displacement and depopulation of Native American tribes, and the curse of slavery. Still, there was another factor that worked against the pastoral spirit that Emerson embraced, which was industrialization and its damage to the natural landscape. In the last regard Emerson, a graduate of Harvard's Divinity School and erstwhile pastor at Boston's Second Unitarian Church, chose to respond. After resigning his ministry in 1832, he would within a few years launch the transcendental movement and become the most influential American intellectual of the nineteenth century.

There are many facets to Emerson's naturalistic philosophy—first voiced in his essay "Nature" of 1836—not the least of which was his desire to create a new and independent American culture grounded in the primeval landscapes of new arcadia and free of the cultural trappings of Europe. It was the sentiment of adolescent nationhood voiced in his essay "The American Scholar," and it was a position of independence expressed most eloquently four years later in the opening pages of his essay on self-reliance: "There is a time in every man's education when he arrives at the conviction that envy is ignorance; that imitation is suicide; that he must take himself for better, for worse, as his portion." The great man is only "he who in the midst of the crowd keeps with perfect sweetness the independence of solitude."[32] Again, it was a posture echoed at the start of his talk, "The Young American," when he observed that "America is beginning to assert itself to the senses and to the imagination of her children, and Europe is receding in the same degree."[33] Effectively, Emerson's vision for America was both eschatological and revelatory, in that he viewed the new country as destined to play a leading role in the redemptive story of humanity. Moreover, the wellspring from which this self-sufficiency could be imbibed was not an intellectual one. Arcadia was to be found in the fountainhead of nature: the garden.

In "Nature," three currents of this wellspring are evident: the transcendental ethic, the role that commerce must play, and the cultural interface of beauty and art. Transcendentalism, born of the theology of Unitarianism, has always been a difficult term to define, and Emerson portrays it as an awareness or intense spiritual experience in which people shed their egotism and recognize that they are only a small part—"a god in ruins"—of a much grander universe: "I become a transparent eye-ball: I am nothing; I see all; the currents of the Universal Being circulate through me; I am part or particle of God."[34] Yet opening the human mind to the "light and power" of nature is not simply ecological, because it carries with it a vital dimension. Nature is there for humans to study and learn its "ministry to man," and only from this understanding can humans apply nature's principles to the building of our "cities, ships, canals, and bridges."[35] Effectively, Emerson's vision is one of paradise, although, as Leo Marx has argued, one allowing material progress.[36] In 1844 he made the case that the tools of industry, "now that steam has narrowed the Atlantic to a strait" and "the nervous, rocky West is intruding a new and continental element into the national mind," will assist in leading us back to the garden. He urged Americans to use these tools to cultivate the land and beautify it even more so: "How much better when the whole land is a garden, and the people have grown up in the bowers of a paradise."[37]

The keynote of his naturalist philosophy is love of beauty, or what he refers to as "the plastic power of the human eye." It too unfolds on three levels. First there is the simple delight or biophilic enjoyment of nature—outline, color, motion, grouping—the medicinal tonic that repairs and refreshes the body and soul through its ever-changing tapestries of seasons. This stage only forecasts a higher dimension of nature, which is the spirituality and virtue that it bequeaths humans. "Every rational creature has all nature for his dowry and estate," he observes.[38] One may reject it or creep into a corner and, like most men, abdicate his entitlement, but beauty is an entitlement for the taking. The dimension of beauty exercised by the poet, painter, sculptor, musician, and architect constitutes the third level:

> The world thus exists to the soul to satisfy the desire of beauty. This element I call an ultimate end. No reason can be asked or given why the soul seeks beauty. Beauty, in its largest and profoundest sense, is the expression of the universe.[39]

Moreover, it was to be found not by adopting the cultural pretensions of Europe or its aesthetic measuring rod, but by cultivating a uniquely American aesthetic found in the uniquely American ethic of fitness or lack of pretense. "Our houses are built with foreign taste; our shelves are garnished with foreign ornaments; our opinions, our tastes, our faculties, lean, and follow the Past and the Distant," he laments at one point. "And why need we copy the Doric or the Gothic model?"[40]

The Emersonian circle began to coalesce with the inaugural meeting of the Transcendental Club in 1836, which took place in the living room of Sophia and George Ripley. The latter was a

Unitarian minister and, in addition to Emerson, Amos Bronson Alcott, Margaret Fuller, and Orestes Brownson attended. The first issue of their literary journal, *The Dial*, appeared four years later, with Fuller assuming the lead editorial role. In its inaugural issue, the editors invoked the name *Dial* not as

> the Gnomon in a garden, but rather as is the garden itself, in whose leaves and flowers and fruits the suddenly awakened sleeper is instantly apprised not what part of dead time, but what state of life and growth is now arrived and arriving.[41]

The journal had a four-year run, during which Henry David Thoreau published his first writings. Emerson had met Thoreau in 1837, shortly after the latter's graduation from Harvard, and Emerson employed him to serve as a tutor to his children. It was also on Emerson's forested property, adjacent to Walden Pond, that Thoreau built his small cabin in 1845 and vowed to live the simple life, "to live deliberately, to front only the essential facts of life, and see if I could not learn what it had to teach and not, when I came to die, discover that I had not lived."[42] Although his visual range was limited by the surrounding woods, there was "pasture enough for my imagination," enough to dedicate his ritual morning bath in the pond to the Roman goddess Aurora, to have noonday visions of the Ural steppes of Tartary, and to settle in the evening under the watchful eyes of the seven daughters of the Titan Atlas, transformed by Zeus into the constellation Pleiades.[43] The journal recording his voluntary sabbatical from the human world within the embrace of nature was his literary masterpiece *Walden*, which appeared in 1854.

If Thoreau's disengagement from society represented one interpretation of the transcendental ethic, the Transcendental Society soon proffered another. It was the building of an egalitarian community—a "Paradise anew," in the somewhat sarcastic words of Nathaniel Hawthorne.[44] The failure of such earlier communities as New Harmony in the 1820s only temporarily subdued interest in such ventures, because the financial crisis induced by the Panic of 1837 led to a severe seven-year economic recession. It was within this economic context that a 480-page book appeared in 1840, setting before an American audience the ideas of Charles Fourier. We will consider his theories in the next chapter, but his American interpreter, Albert Brisbane, in any case took care to downplay or eliminate Fourier's more exotic proposals regarding sexuality and other sensory delights. Brisbane had spent two years in Paris studying under Fourier, and upon his return to New York he had converted Horace Greeley, the owner of the *New York Daily Tribune*, to the cause. It was a significant conversion because Greeley would allow Brisbane to write a regular column on Fourier in what was the most widely read newspaper in the country. The book's and column's leading theme, quite simply, was "INDUSTRY CAN BE RENDERED ATTRACTIVE."[45]

The book did not escape the attention of *The Dial*, which its October issue praised for raising the question of the relationship between labor and capital, and the reviewer even lauded Fourier who "may be placed at the head of modern thinkers." There was a caveat, which is that some of Fourier's views are "so exclusively adapted to the French character" that they might prejudice "persons of opposite habits and associations."[46] This seems to have been the case, because when the Ripleys later proposed to the Transcendental Club that they collectively purchase a 175-acre dairy farm in a wooded area of West Roxbury, near the Charles River, they did so without any ideological overlay other than transcendentalism. Both Emerson and Fuller were sympathetic to the cause but declined to participate financially. Joining the Ripleys, however, was the young Hawthorne, for whom *The Scarlet Letter* and fame was still a decade away. Hawthorne used the commune as the setting for his later book *The Blithedale Romance*, although he resigned from the community a year into its founding.

Initially, Brook Farm had modest success. As with New Harmony, an important part of the commune was the school and kindergarten, both inspired by Pestalozzi's theories. Sophia Ripley supervised the program and taught German, Italian, and history, and her husband taught philosophy and mathematics. A Harvard student, Charles Dana, came to teach Greek and German. This curriculum itself tells us why many of the early members of the commune were abolitionists, artists, feminists, and intellectuals—notwithstanding the expectation to perform manual labor. Emerson and Fuller, both of whom sent relatives to the school, came and lectured on occasions. A wagon was on standby in the evening to transport members nine miles into the city of Boston for cultural events, and by the end of 1843, Brook Farm had over 100 residents, a greenhouse, and orchard. The one drawback, and a significant one, was that the composition of the soil was not good for agriculture. Hence, the community, from the beginning, struggled to break even.

It was around this time that Brisbane and Greeley entered into the picture. They had formed a Fourier Association in New York City and were encouraging a number of new Fourier-inspired communities in several states, none of which had the resources to build what Fourier had called a phalanstery, or a single large building to house the community and its activities. They viewed Brook Farm as the best opportunity to see the community building realized and, with some persistence, they convinced the Ripleys—much to the dismay of Emerson—to have Brook Farm join the association. In the summer of 1844, the residents of Brook Farm marshalled their meager resources and began building an ample three-story building with sheltered porches at each level. Such a project would have been no problem for many of the religious groups with their cadres of skilled tradesmen, but this was, after all, largely a community of intellectuals. Notwithstanding, the framing of the walls and roof was complete when work was shut down for the winter of 1845. As the snow began to give way in early March, they restarted work and brought in a wood stove to aid in finishing the interiors. A fire broke out one night and rapidly consumed the entire wooden structure. By morning it was clear that the bucolic experiment of a transcendentalist paradise, now crushed by debt, had abruptly ended.

In the end, the enkindling of Brook Farm proved to be only a propitiation deposited near the altar of Emerson, because the latter's naturalist's philosophy would expand in more significant ways over the course of the century. One was his influence on architecture and the arts. "We feel, in seeing a noble building, which rhymes well, as we do in hearing a perfect song," he wrote for the first issue of *The Dial*, "that it is spiritually organic, that is, had a necessity in nature, for being, was one of the possible forms in the Divine mind, and is now only discovered and executed by the artist, not arbitrarily composed by him."[47] Informing him in this regard was the sculptor Horatio Greenough. The latter had graduated from Harvard in 1825, four years after Emerson, and moved to Italy to study sculpture under Bertel Thorwaldsen and Lorenzo Bartolini. Emerson met Greenough in 1833 in Florence, and they corresponded regularly thereafter. Greenough's general claim to fame were his sculptural works, among them his marble work of George Washington with a nude chest, commissioned for the rotunda of the Capitol in 1840. Yet Greenough also had strong views on architecture. Already in the 1830s he was a harsh critic of the Greek Revival or the mimicking of Greek forms, and in the following decade his views evolved into a credo on behalf of organic functionalism—that is, instead of using a stylistic language to house various functions, one should simply allow the functions and the nature of the site to dictate the design. This mandate opened a line of thinking that in America would track down to the efforts of Louis Sullivan and Frank Lloyd Wright, as we will see.[48] Emerson championed similar views. In his book *English Traits* of 1855, he reflected on meeting the now-deceased Greenough in Florence, and characterized him as "a superior man, ardent and eloquent, and all his opinions had elevation and magnanimity," someone who "announced in advance the leading thoughts of Mr. Ruskin on the *morality* in architecture."[49]

Emerson's views on nature also fell in line with the Hudson River School of painters, although here the cross-pollination was mutual. The school's founding artist was Thomas Cole, who had been born in England and emigrated to Philadelphia in 1818. He came of age, as it were, in New York City in the mid-1820s, in the literary and artistic circle of James Fenimore Cooper, William Cullen Bryant, John Trumbull, William Dunlap, and Asher Brown Durand. His views on the landscape, however, were also formed from his reading of British picturesque writers. When he co-founded the National Academy of Design in 1826, he was already producing his first masterpieces—*Sunday Morning on the Hudson River, The Clove, Catskills*, and *Sunrise in the Catskill Mountains*. The reach of his early ambition can be measured by two large-scale canvases he crafted in 1927, *The Garden of Eden* and *Expulsion from the Garden of Eden*, in which he attempted, somewhat boldly, to portray the celestial fields. In the latter painting, he contrasted the blissfully idyllic landscape with a visually terrifying and darkened world into which a pitifully mournful Adam and Eve were stumbling.

Cole—coincidental with Emerson's essay on nature—published his "Essay on American Scenery" in the same year, in which he speaks to the "quickening spirit" of untamed nature as "an unfailing fountain of intellectual enjoyment, where all may drink, and be awakened to a deeper feeling of the works of genius, and a keener perception of the beauty of our existence."[50] After discussing in some detail the painterly elements of the American landscape—its wildness, mountains, lakes, rivers, and sky—he expresses with a note of sorrow how quickly "the most noble scenes are made desolate" by the "ravages of the axe," preventing future generations from enjoying such beauty. He concludes with a plea: "Nature has spread for us a rich and delightful banquet. Shall we turn from it? We are still in Eden; the wall that shuts us out of the garden is our own ignorance and folly."[51]

He penned his essay after his three-year tour of Europe, where he met several English painters, among them J.M.W. Turner. He also spent six months in Florence, whose galleries "are paradise to a painter," where he also met and befriended Greenough.[52] Back in New York, his paintings took on a somewhat more philosophical tenor. His planned quintet of paintings, "The Course of Empire," was a majestic statement on the birth and decline of human civilization, with large panels depicting *The Savage State* of nature; *The Arcadian or Pastoral State; The Consummation of Empire*, with its richly rendered classical city; *The Destruction*, or the sacking of this city; and *The Desolation*, portraying the ruins now overrun by vegetation. In all five paintings, craggy mountaintops loom in the background, a granite reminder of the invincible force of nature as opposed to ephemeral human

ILLUSTRATION 8.5 Thomas Cole, *The Course of Empire: The Arcadian or Pastoral State*, 1834. Collection of the New York Historical Society.

history. In a letter to Cole's biographer Louis Noble, the novelist Cooper referred to "The Course of Empire" as "the work of the highest genius this country has ever produced."[53] Cole went on to produce several other allegorical paintings before his death in 1848, among them his stunningly beautiful *Dream of Arcadia*.

Emerson's influence, later in the century, is also found in the work of Frederick Law Olmsted, who was about to enter Yale College in 1822 when an eye affliction forced him to withdraw. He then worked as a sailor, merchant, and part-time journalist before his wealthy father purchased a farm for him on Staten Island. After returning from a walking tour in England in 1851, he received an offer from the publisher George Putnam, his neighbor, to write a book about his experiences. In planning his effort, he set out to meet the picturesque theorist Andrew Jackson Downing at his Hudson Valley estate in Newburgh. The meeting proved pivotal to his future.

Downing's outlook too had been strongly shaped by Emerson, and with the publication of *A Treatise on the Theory and Practice of Landscape Gardening* in 1841, Downing became America's leading horticulturalist. His vision, however, went beyond writing a landscape primer fitted to American soil and climate. In a loose association with the architect Alexander Jackson Davis, he wrote sections on "The Improvement of Country Residences" and "Remarks on Rural Architecture." The frontispiece of the book is Davis's bucolic rendering of his design for the Robert Donaldson estate along the Hudson, *Blithewood*, near Barrytown. Downing expanded architectural themes in two other volumes, *Cottage Residences* (1841) and *The Architecture of Country Houses* (1850). Both were design handbooks for building suburban and rural houses. The latter book also included his ambitious introductory essay "The Real Meaning of Architecture," in which he stresses the social value and moral influence that good housing has on the individual. It was Downing's belief that the character of each individual can be read through the habitats one builds, and therefore "it is evident that Domestic Architecture is only perfect when it is composed so as to express the utmost beauty and truth in the life of the individual."[54] Downing then won the competition for the Washington Mall

ILLUSTRATION 8.6   Andrew Jackson Davis, *Blithewood*, frontispiece to Andrew Jackson Downing, *A Treatise on the Theory and Practice of Landscape Gardening*, 1841.

Source: Metropolitan Museum of Art, Harris Brisbane Dick Fund.

with a picturesque plan, although the project stalled with his tragic death in 1852. He was aboard a steamer on the Hudson River when a fire broke out and he drowned in trying to save a life.

Olmsted's visit to Downing the year before was important because there he met Downing's new partner, the architect Calvert Vaux, who would inherit the landscape and architectural practice. The visit may have inspired Olmsted to imagine bigger things, because a few years later he decided to sell his farm and purchase a partnership with the new owners of *Putnam's Monthly Magazine*. Over the next five years, he published three extended essays on his travels to the antebellum South and Texas—material later gathered into books. It would seem that he had settled into a profession, but in 1857, at a Connecticut resort, he met by chance Charles Elliott, who had studied gardening under Downing. Elliott was a member of the New York City commission that was considering the design of Central Park. The board was looking for a superintendent to manage the construction of the park, and Elliott encouraged Olmsted to apply for the position. Downing had been a strong advocate for a major park in the city, and the idea had also gained the support of William Cullen Bryant. Although lacking experience, Olmsted rushed to the city to apply for the position and was successful in gaining it. The design of the new park, in the upper half of Manhattan, was nominally under the control of Colonel Egbert Viele. Olmsted's task was to manage the 700 laborers who were draining the swamps and clearing the land of vegetation and existing homes.

The park's design, however, was at a standstill. Viele wanted a contract to proceed and a number of prominent citizens and architects, led by Vaux, insisted on an open design competition. The park board finally agreed and, in the fall of 1857, announced a competition with a due date of March. Vaux, in need of someone with knowledge of the terrain, invited Olmsted to join him in submitting a scheme. Vaux himself was a talented designer and, as a recent émigré, he was personally familiar with English picturesque gardens. Olmsted, although lacking experience in design, had horticultural knowledge and was similarly familiar with British picturesque efforts as well as the writings of Emerson. If Vaux and Olmsted needed another edge, it was that Vaux was married to the sister of the Hudson River School painter Jervis McEntee, who assisted in the final rendering of the plans. At the required scale, the site plan was ten feet long by two feet wide, and in its professional rendering it far outpaced the other thirty-three entries.

It is of course impossible to know what parts of the conception can be attributed to which partner, although certainly Vaux designed all of the bridges, archways, and ancillary buildings. Yet Olmsted by this time knew the existing landscape very well and had a sense of how it could be manipulated and watered. Although most projects of such grand scale would only slowly come to fruition, Central Park was the exception. Parts of it were already in use at the end of 1858, and within a few more years its 800 acres would become an idyllic masterpiece. One of the earliest decisions was to submerge the four required crossing roads to preserve the views of nature within the park. This necessitated protective fencing and vegetation to conceal the roadways but also an abundant use of explosives to extricate the shallow bedrock. The competition brief also required a prospect tower and a parade ground. Vaux and Olmsted ignored the first requirement by deferring it to a later time and shrunk the latter—the Mall—into a shortened straight line (the only straight line of the scheme) leading to a terrace and music pavilion. All of the pathways for horse-drawn carriages, walkways, and riding paths were curvilinear and framed the natural meadows, playgrounds, ponds, and lakes. The lowered cross-roadways provided some of the soil for turning the marshes into meadows and adjusting the topography, but large quantities of soil were also brought to the site. Three hundred thousand trees were planted, as were "tons" of grass seed. The soil around existing rock outcroppings was often trimmed away to dramatize these features, and new outcroppings and material for the roadways were created from the bedrock fragments. Olmsted's favorite part of the park, the Ramble, was a stroke of genius and the heart of the design. Constructed along the north shore of the lake, it is a thirty-six-acre "wild garden" consisting of forested pathways, coves, flower gardens, ponds, and Vaux's stone arch—all far removed from the noise and grime of the city.

The urban park, more generally, was not seen by Olmsted as an exercise in gardening, but something very essential to America's collective soul and the survival of its political system. Like the public parks in Europe, he argued that parks promoted democratic values, in the sense that they brought together people of every social class. Parks also held recreational benefits for the urban poor who could not escape to country homes for weekend or summer jaunts. In fact, the expanse of cities like New York put the countryside out of reach of all families who did not possess a horse and buggy. Health was another very important factor in Olmsted's thinking, in particular the importance of clean air and exercise. In a report for Brooklyn's Prospect Park, for instance, he cited the grim statistic that the average age of death in nineteenth-century Liverpool (140,000 people per square mile) is seventeen years, whereas the average age of someone in London (50,000 people per square mile) is twenty-six.[55] Part of the reason for this disparity is the communication of disease, but Olmsted also realized—presaging what we know today—that time in natural settings has enormous restorative benefits for the human organism. Parks with their natural scenery, fresh air, exposure to sunlight, and physical activities, he notes, "employs the mind without fatigue and yet exercises it; tranquilizes it and yet enlivens it; and thus the influence of the mind over the body, gives the effect of refreshing rest and reinvigoration to the whole system."[56] Above all, parks make people happy. In speaking of the small and large families who gather every Sunday in Central Park on Sundays, he made this observation:

> Tables, seats, shade, turf, swings, cool spring water, and a pleasing rural prospect stretching off half a mile or more each way, unbroken by a carriage road or the slightest evidence of the vicinity of the town, were supplied them without charge, and bread and milk and ice cream at moderate fixed charges. In all my life I have never seen such a joyous collection of people, I have, in fact, more than once observed tears of gratitude in the eyes of poor women, as they watched their children thus enjoying themselves.[57]

Olmsted's efforts were not only intended to exalt the superiority of bucolic life but also to counter what Georg Simmel later referred to as the "intensification of nervous stimulation" of the metropolis and its "affront to the natural rhythm of life."[58] If the promise of an American arcadia had been rudely shoved aside by industrialization, geographic expansion, and the growth of large cities, the situation was not entirely beyond repair, Olmsted seemed to argue. Arcadia's essence could still be recaptured in a bottle, as it were, with a little money and a basic understanding of human affinity with natural settings. Olmsted's efforts and ideas were quite persuasive and he went on to apply his gospel of urban parks (to name but a few) to Brooklyn, Buffalo, Chicago, Detroit, Louisville, Milwaukee, Montreal, and Albany. He graced Boston as well with the garland of its Emerald Necklace. Yet perhaps the more prefigurative of his efforts to create an ideal community was a small, planned suburb he designed nine miles southwest of downtown Chicago: the town of Riverside.

The process of suburbanization is generally frowned upon today by many urban theorists, but Olmsted viewed it from a different time and perspective. He envisioned the "civilized refinement" of the suburb not as "a retrogression from, but an advance upon" the city, because "no great town can long exist without great suburbs."[59] He even buffered this claim by citing a paper presented to the British Association for the Advancement of Social Science, which argued that the city's congested housing—a "prolific source of morbid conditions of the body and mind, manifesting themselves chiefly in nervous feebleness or irritability and various functional derangements"—could only be relieved by "removal to suburban districts."[60]

Olmsted also saw something more in his design—an Edenic community of like-minded people of different economic levels. In this instance, the suburb was not so much an escape from the city as a quasi-paradise of living within nature, a perfection created by the artful human hand. The site along the winding Des Plaines River, its "groves of trees consisting of oaks, elms, hickories, walnuts, limes, and ashes," its clean water and access to boating, its green commons, its allowance for residents to ride, walk, and simply take fresh air along the forested parks of the riverbanks—all demanded a natural solution far removed from the gridiron plan. In this case, "we should recommend the general adoption, in the design of your roads, of gracefully-curved lines, generous spaces, and the absence of sharp corners, the idea being to suggest and imply leisure, contemplativeness and happy tranquility."[61] He went so far as to lower the street elevations so that neighbors across from one another would have a visual expanse of continuous lawns and vegetation; setbacks were implemented to keep the community pastoral. Turf, foliage, and birds should abound, he argued, and to this end he insisted on bringing in more than 30,000 deciduous trees and 7,000 conifers. Moreover, the town's one existing structure, a resort hotel that once served the boisterous needs of Buffalo Bill Cody, was a stagecoach stop that in 1868 would become a station for "a great train line" that would provide transportation to the city. This artery, however, did not stop Olmsted from proposing a roadway into town, for those with a preference for the slower pace of the horse and buggy. From the vantage point of the human experience, Eden it was—even a few decades before Louis Sullivan and Frank Lloyd Wright would bring their considerable design talents to embellish the township.

"Lying Out at Night under Those Giant Sequoias. . . "

At the time of Cole's death in 1848, a now-vibrant Hudson Valley School of painters was expanding its geographic range of interests. In the 1850s and 1860s, for instance, Cole's student Frederic Church made trips to Ecuador, Colombia, and Jamaica to explore the natural beauty of those countries. Westward expansion in the United States, ushered in by the first transcontinental railroad, opened these territories to painters. Albert Bierstadt, for one, followed a survey team to Wyoming and Colorado in 1859 to record some of the first vistas of the Rockies. On a trip to the Sierra Nevada Mountains in 1863, Bierstadt, in several paintings, revealed the awe-inspiring grandeur of Yosemite to an American audience. In a letter to Abraham Lincoln's private secretary John Hay,

ILLUSTRATION 8.7 Albert Bierstadt, *Looking Down the Yosemite Valley*, 1865.

Source: Google Art Project Works. Gift of the Birmingham Public Library.

Bierstadt noted, "We are here in the garden of Eden, I call it. The most magnificent place I was ever in, I employ every moment painting from nature."[62]

These paintings, together with the invention of daguerreotypes, led to the federal designation of national parks. Yellowstone National Park, tucked into the northwest corner of Wyoming, became the first protected area in 1872. Although parts of it had been visited by members of the Lewis and Clark Expedition, it was only in 1869 that a party was able to find a route into the center of the park and survey Yellowstone Lake. Yosemite was first ceded to the State of California by Congress in 1864, but it took the efforts of John Muir to provide it and its surroundings with federal protection.

Muir was a native Scotsman whose family had immigrated to the United States. He was a rambler, naturalist, geologist, botanist, and philosopher. After settling in California in 1868, he built a remote cabin—emulating Thoreau—along and partly over Yosemite Creek, which served as his base for his treks and studies into the highlands. He would take with him some tea, bread, and a copy of Emerson to read under the stars. By 1871 Muir's fame had grown to the point that Emerson himself sought him out on his visit to Yosemite, where the New Englander offered him a professorship at Harvard. Muir declined and in 1874 began writing a series of articles titled "Studies in the Sierra," putting forth his theory that Yosemite's valleys were formed by glacial pathways (rather than earthquakes), leading to such odd geological formations as the Half Dome. He later teamed up with the editor Robert Underwood Johnson to write a series of essays prodding Congress into designating Yosemite a National Park, which it did in 1890. Muir was also struck by the size and beauty of Yosemite's trees, in particular "the noblest of a noble race," the Giant Sequoias. Their size, he noted in a paper of 1876, could have a diameter of up to 25 feet and approach 300 feet (or thirty stories) in height.[63] Muir later wrote: "All these colossal trees are as wonderful in the fineness of their beauty and proportions as in stature, growing together, an assemblage of conifers surpassing all that have yet been discovered in the forests of the world."[64] Incidentally, the name given to these redwoods, *Sequoia sempervirens*, was bequeathed by the Cherokee leader Sequoyah, a warrior, silversmith, and painter who invented an ingenious Cherokee system of writing by using symbols for syllables taken from the English, Greek, and Hebrew languages. In 1903, President Theodore Roosevelt visited the park and, because it was a perfunctory tour, he approached Muir and asked to be shown the real Yosemite. The two men set off hiking on an overnight trek into the backlands of Glacier Point; the hike became one of Roosevelt's most memorable moments. He now fully understood the need for their preservation:

> As regards some of the trees, I want them preserved because they are the only things of their kind in the world. Lying out at night under those giant Sequoias was lying in a temple built by no hand of man, a temple grander than any human architect could by any possibility build, and I hope for the preservation of the groves of giant trees simply because it would be a shame to our civilization to let them disappear. They are monuments in themselves.[65]

Roosevelt's comments were published in 1906, the year in which Louis Sullivan wrote a letter to Carl Bennett, the president of the National Farmers' Bank of Owatonna, Minnesota, on a dissimilar yet not distant matter. In announcing his intentions for the design of the bank, he confessed that he was up at five in the morning to study the effects of morning light on wild grasses, and how his "whole Spring is wrapped up just now in the study of color and out of doors for the sake of your bank decorations." He goes on to say that "I don't think I can possibly impress upon you how deep a hold this color symphony has taken upon me."[66] It was a letter from an architect who had been without work for two years, a destitute architect yet one of the greatest design talents of the nineteenth century. Sullivan, two years younger than Roosevelt, was born of a generation of American architects—among them Henry Hobson Richardson, Frank Furness, and Stanford White—who had viewed their task as one of creating the uniquely American architecture that Emerson had heralded. His famous catchphrase, "form ever follows function" was borrowed from Greenough, although it has been woefully misinterpreted by historians of architecture writing from a twentieth-century perspective—Sullivan was the antithesis of Le Corbusier or Mies van der Rohe.

Born in Boston, Sullivan briefly attended the newly founded Massachusetts Institute of Technology, worked briefly in the Philadelphia office of Furness (cut short by the Economic Panic of 1873), and then made his way to Chicago. Shortly thereafter he left for studies in Paris, and a few years after his return, in 1883, he partnered with Dankmar Adler. In short order the firm became one of the busiest in the booming American Midwest. Sullivan produced scores of masterful designs, among them the Auditorium Building in Chicago and the Wainwright Building in Saint Louis. Yet success is sometimes fleeting. The Economic Panic of 1893 brought with it a precipitous decline in building activity, and in the following year his partnership with Adler foundered. Sullivan's practice survived for a while, but by the turn of the century he would find himself with fewer and fewer clients. He died in 1924 in a Chicago flophouse, an alcoholic, still immensely talented but largely broken in spirit.

Sullivan was also a serious thinker and writer. His personal library (later auctioned with his bankruptcy) was strong in the areas of physiology and psychology, and Sherman Paul has documented his familiarity with the efforts of John Dewey, who arrived at the University of Chicago in 1894.[67] Sullivan's Emerson grounding is also well established and it flows through his writings. His essay "Inspiration," presented to an architectural audience in 1885, is nothing less than an Emersonian rhapsody on the beauty of nature—its growth and noble decay, how a new art can only form when the "sympathetic soul" of the artist attunes and amplifies his spirit with the animating "rhythms of nature."[68] He actually sent a copy of the speech to Walt Whitman, but he received no response.

The same theme runs through his *Kindergarten Chats*, a series of didactic conversations taking place at the turn of the century with a novice architect. Here he speaks of the "living force" and "vital spirit" that resides within all creative endeavors, and that "the real function of the architect" is "to vitalize building materials, to animate them collectively with a thought, a state of feeling, to charge them with subjective significance and value, to make them a visible part of the genuine social fabric."[69] The designer does not do this alone but only through the emissary of the Over-Soul:

> For Nature is ever the background across which man moves as in a drama: that dream within which man, the dreamer, moves in his dream; that reality which is man's reality. For all life, collectively is but one vast drama, one vast dream, and the soul of man its chief spectator.[70]

It was a metaphor that he put into practice, as we see with his design for the National Farmers' Bank. Impressionistic polychromatic effects, particularly in his interiors, had been a preoccupation with Sullivan with earlier designs such as the Auditorium Building, but his focus in Owatonna, in collaboration with Louis Millet, had now sharpened. Drawing upon the color theories of Ogden Nicholas Rood, the two sought to exploit impressionistic effects such as opalescence, fluorescence, and phosphorescence, although with quiet or subdued tones—what Richard Etlin once referred to as Sullivan's "life-enhancing symbiosis of music, language, architecture, and ornament."[71]

For the interiors, Sullivan decided on a color scheme "of early spring and autumn, predominantly, with the steadying note of green throughout the entire scheme."[72] The decorative patterns painted on the walls above the wainscoting, "a glory of luxuriant color and form," were carried out in soft tones of red, red-orange, yellow, and green, with some gilding. The massive, half-circular stained-glass windows on two sides, intensifying the opalescent effect, had muted tones of green, yellow, blue, and orange, creating a "general effect of rich variegated green." Other interior fixtures reinforced these tones. The wainscoting, for instance, was formed of "Roman bricks of a rich, red color, capped with an ornamental band of green terra cotta." The aim was to create a conventionalized garden of color with each carefully chosen tint of nature playing its part in the symphony.

ILLUSTRATION 8.8   Louis Sullivan, National Farmers' Bank, Owatonna, Minnesota, 1906.

Source: Photo by Tim Waclawski. Flickr CC BY-ND 2.0.

Bennett, in assessing the result, wrote that "all the colors, when seen from a distance, blend into a general impression of soft red and green, while at close range they maintain their strong and beautiful individuality."[73] Sullivan rendered the exterior with no less prismatic passion. The brickwork was banded with a small but variegated framework of painted tiles and a larger band of green terra-cotta modeled into intricate floral patterns with acorn color notes. In his specifications to the brick supplier, Sullivan insisted that the ground of the brick should be coarser than usual, and its formwork should have cutting wires to impress on each face "a texture with a nap-like effect, suggesting somewhat an Anatolian rug; a texture giving innumerable highlights and shadows, and a moss-like softness of appearance."[74] For the brick colors, he sought a variation of hues,

> from the softest pinks through delicate reds, yellows, (varying the intensity) through the light browns, dark browns, purples and steel blacks—each of these colors with its own gradations and blendings—the possibilities of chromatic treatment are at once evident.[75]

The bank, renovated in recent years, is certainly among Sullivan's more impressionistic works. It is a paradise planted on the unpretentious grasslands of an agricultural prairie. The building is a far cry from the ancient redwoods of Yosemite, but the design is no less tall in its grandeur.

Notes

1. *The New English Canaan of Thomas Morton* (Boston, MA: The Prince Society, 1883), 179–80.
2. William Bradford, *History of Plymouth Plantation*, ed. by Charles Deane (Boston, MA: Privately Printed, 1856), 237.
3. Winthrop voiced these words in his sermon "A Model of Christian Charity," written in 1630 aboard the ship *Arbella*. The verse of Matthew is 5:14.
4. Joseph Cotton, "God's Promise to His Plantations," in *Old South Leaflets* (London: William Jones, 1630), #53, 4. See 2 Samuel 7:10.
5. Charles A. Sanford, *The Quest for Paradise: Europe and the American Moral Imagination* (Urbana, IL: University of Illinois Press, 1961), 104.
6. William Bradford, *Brandford's History of "Plimoth Plantation"* (Boston, MA: Wright & Potter, 1901), 1:195.
7. "Winthrop's Conclusions for the Plantation in New England," in *Old South Leaflets*, #50 (Boston, MA: Old South Meeting House, 1894), 25.
8. See James D. Knowles, *Memoir of Roger Williams, the Founder of the State of Rhode-Island* (Boston, MA: Lincoln, Edmands and Co., 1834).
9. William Penn, "Instructions . . . to . . . My Commissioners for the Settling of the . . . Colony . . ." Cited from John Reps, *Town Planning in Frontier America* (Columbia, MO: University of Missouri Press, 1980), 143.
10. Andrea Wulf, *Founding Gardeners: The Revolutionary Generation, Nature, and the Shaping of the American Nation* (New York: Vintage Books, 2011).
11. "Notes on the State of Virginia, Query VI," in *Thomas Jefferson: Writings* (New York: The Library of America, 1984), 180–91.
12. Jefferson, "Notes of a Tour of English Gardens, [2–14 April] 1786," *Founders Online*. https://founders.archives.gov. Accessed March 2020.
13. John Adams, "Notes of a Tour of English Country Seats, &c., with Thomas Jefferson, 4–10? April, 1786 [from the Diary of John Adams]," *Founders Online* (note 12).
14. "From Thomas Jefferson to George Wythe," *Founders Online* (September 16, 1787), (note 12).
15. "From Thomas Jefferson to Edward Rutledge," *Founders Online* (July 14, 1787), (note 12).
16. Thomas Jefferson, "Monticello: notebook of improvements," page 2 of 14, 1804–1807. *Thomas Jefferson Papers: An Electronic Archive* (Boston, MA: Massachusetts Historical Society, 2003). www.thomasjefferson-papers.org/. Accessed March 2020. See also Jack McLaughlin, *Jefferson and Monticello: The Biography of a Builder* (New York: Henry Holt and Company, 1988), 342–6.
17. Wulf, *Founding Gardeners* (note 10), 173–86.
18. "Thomas Jefferson to Charles Willson Peale," *Founders Online* (August 20, 1811), (note 12).
19. The phrase "those monstrous trees" in cited in their journal, November 9, 1805. *The Journals of Lewis and Clark*, ed. by Bernard DeVoto (Boston, MA: Houghton Mifflin Company, 1981).
20. Letter to Littleton Waller Tazewell, 5 January 1805, in *Thomas Jefferson: Writings* (note 11), 1149–52.
21. "An Academical Village," Letter to Messrs. Hugh White and Others, 6 May 2010, in *Thomas Jefferson: Writings* (note 11), 1222–3.
22. Robert Dale Owen, cited in George Browning Lockwood, *The New Harmony Communities* (Marion, IN: The Chronical Company, 1902), 40.
23. Robert Owen, "Important Public Meeting to Advocate an Entire Change in Forming the Character of Man and Governing Society," in Appendix to *Address on Opening the Institution for the Formation of Character, at New Lanark, Delivered on the 1st of January, 1816* (London: Home Colonization Society, 1841), 13.
24. Robert Owen, *A New View of Society: Or, Essays on the Formation of the Human Character* (London: Longman, Hurst, Rees, et al., 1816), 90–1.
25. Robert Owen, "Socialism, or, the Rational System of Society," in Appendix to *Address on Opening the Institution for the Formation of Character* (London: Three Lectures Delivered in the Mechanics' Institute, 1840), 15.
26. *The Life of Robert Owen: Written by Himself* (London: Effingham Wilson, 1857–58), 1:238.
27. On the address and the model, see Donald F. Carmony and Josephine M. Elliott, "New Harmony, Indiana: Robert Owen's Seedbed for Utopia," *Indiana Magazine of History* 76 (September 1980), 201–2.
28. Lockwood, *The New Harmony Communities* (note 22), 83.
29. Ralph Waldo Emerson, "Historic Notes of Life and Letters in New England," *American Transcendentalism Web*. https://archive.vcu.edu/english/engweb/transcendentalism/authors/emerson/essays/historicnotes.html. Accessed May 2021.
30. See *Avant-Garde in the Cornfields: Architecture, Landscape, and Preservation in New Harmony*, ed. by Ben Nicholson and Michelangelo Sabatino (Minneapolis: University of Minnesota Press, 2019).
31. J. Hector St. John de Crèvecoeur, *Letters from an American Farmer: Describing Certain Provincial Situations, Manners, and Customs . . . of the British Colonies in North America*, 2nd ed. (London: Thomas Davies, 1783), 52–3.
32. Ralph Waldo Emerson, "Self-Reliance," in *Ralph Waldo Emerson: Essay & Lectures* (New York: The Library of America, 1983), 259 and 263.

33. Emerson, "The Young American," in *Ralph Waldo Emerson* (note 32), 213.
34. Emerson, "Nature," in *Ralph Waldo Emerson* (note 32), 10.
35. Ibid., 13.
36. Leo Marx, *The Machine in the Garden: Technology and the Pastoral Ideal in America* (Oxford: Oxford University Press, 1964).
37. Emerson, "The Young American," in *Ralph Waldo Emerson* (note 32), 216.
38. Emerson, "Nature," in *Ralph Waldo Emerson* (note 32), 16.
39. Ibid., 19.
40. Emerson, "Self-Reliance" (note 32), 278.
41. *The Dial* 1:1 (July 1840), 4.
42. Henry David Thoreau, *Walden or, Life in the Woods* (New York: Milestone Editions, n.d.), 83.
43. Ibid., 80–1.
44. "Paradise anew" is a reference to Brook Farm by Nathaniel Hawthorne, in *The Blithedale Romance* (Boston, MA: Houghton, Mifflin and Company, 1900), 8.
45. Albert Brisbane, *Social Destiny of Man: Or, Association and Reorganization of Industry* (Philadelphia, PA: C. F. Stollmeyer, 1840), VI.
46. *The Dial: A Magazine for Literature, Philosophy, and Religion* (Boston, MA: Weeks, Jordan, and Company, 1841), 1:265–6.
47. Ralph Waldo Emerson, "Thoughts on Art," *The Dial* I (January 1841), 375.
48. See Horatio Greenough, "'American Architecture' and 'Structure and Organization,'" in Harold A. Small (ed.), *Form and Function: Remarks on Art, Design, and Architecture* (Berkeley: University of California Press, 1947).
49. Ralph Waldo Emerson, *English Traits* (Cambridge, MA: Harvard University, 1966), 2–3.
50. Thomas Cole, *The American Monthly Magazine*, New Series, Vol. I (Boston, MA: Otis Broaders & Co., 1836), 1–2.
51. Ibid., 12.
52. A comment in a letter to Mr. Gilmore, January 29, 1832, cited in Louis Legrand Noble, *The Life and Works of Thomas Cole*, ed. by Elliot S. Vesell (Hensonville, NY: Black Dome Press, 1997), 101.
53. *The Letters and Journals of James Fenimore Cooper, 1845–1849*, ed. by James Franklin Beard (Cambridge, MA: Belknap Press, 1968), 5:398.
54. A. J. Downing, *The Architecture of Country Houses* (New York: Dover, 1969), 25.
55. Olmsted, Vaux & Co., *Observations on the Progress of Improvements in Street Plans, with Special Reference to The Park-Way Proposed to Be Laid Out in Brooklyn* (Brooklyn Vanden's Print, 1868), 17.
56. F. L. Olmsted, "The Value and Care of Parks," (1856), reprinted in Roderick Nash (ed.), *The American Environment: Readings in the History of Conservation* (Reading, MA: Addison Wesley, 1968), 22.
57. Frederick Law Olmsted, "Public Parks and the Enlargement of Towns," in *Public Parks: Being Two Papers Read Before the American Social Science Association in 1870 and 1880* (Brookline: No Publisher, 1902), 46–7.
58. See Georg Simmel, "The Metropolis and Mental Life," in Kurt H. Wolff (trans. and ed.), *The Sociology of Georg Simmel* (New York: The Free Press, 1964), 410.
59. Olmsted, Vaux & Co., *Preliminary Report Upon the Proposed Suburban Village at Riverside, Near Chicago* (New York: Sutton, Bowne & Co., 1868), 7.
60. Ibid., 6.
61. Ibid., 17.
62. Letter to John Hay, 22 August 1863. Cited from Elizabeth Mankin Kornhauser, *Hudson River School: Masterworks from the Wadsworth Atheneum Museum of Art* (New Haven: Yale University Press, 2003), 28.
63. John Muir, "On the Post-glacial History of Sequoia Gigantea," *Proceedings of the American Association for the Advancement of Science* 25 (August 1876), 242–52.
64. John Muir, "The Treasure of the Yosemite," *The Century Magazine* XL:4 (August 1890). www.yosemite.ca.us/john_muir_writings/the_treasures_of_the_yosemite. Accessed March 2021.
65. *A Compilation of the Messages and Speeches of Theodore Roosevelt, 1901–1905*, ed. by Alfred Henry Lewis (Washington, DC: Bureau of National Literature and Art, 1906), 410.
66. Cited from Richard Etlin, "Louis Sullivan: The Life-Enhancing Symbolism of Music, Language, Architecture, and Ornament," in Marlies Kronegger (ed.), *The Orchestration of the Arts—A Creative Symbiosis of Existential Powers* (Dordrecht: Kluwer Academic Publishers, 2000), 174.
67. Sherman Paul, *Louis Sullivan: An Architect in American Thought* (Englewood Cliffs, NJ: Prentice-Hall, 1962), 98–9.
68. "Essay on Inspiration," in Robert Twombly (ed.), *Louis Sullivan: The Public Papers* (Chicago, IL: University of Chicago Press, 1988), 26.
69. Louis Sullivan, *Kindergarten Chats and Other Writings* (New York: Witterborn Art Books, 1947), 140–1.
70. Ibid., 159.

71. On Sullivan's color theory, see Lauren S. Weingarden, "The Colors of Nature: Louis Sullivan's Architectural Polychromy and Nineteenth-Century Color Theory," *Winterthur Portfolio* 20:4 (Winter 1985), 243–60.
72. Carl K. Bennett, "A Bank Built for Farmers: Louis Sullivan Designs a Building Which Marks a New Epoch in American Architecture," *The Craftsman* 15:2 (November 1908), 184.
73. Ibid.
74. Louis Sullivan, "Artistic Brick," in *Public Papers* (note 68), 202.
75. Ibid., 203.

9

EDEN REVISITED

Unfulfilled Phalansteries

Arcadia aside for the moment—the splenetic nature of the French Revolution created a tendentious divide as sharp as almost any in modern political history. It was one that not only put an end to the patrician system that had long prevailed in Europe but also tamped down the excesses of baroque and rococo architecture, which few would deny was in need of interdiction. The architect Jean-Nicolas-Louis Durand made this point explicit in 1802 when, in commenting on the three Vitruvian principles of "Commoditie, Firmness, and Delight"—to use Henry Wotton's 1624 translation—he expunged the last idea of any consideration by noting:

> It is evident that pleasure can never have been the aim of architecture nor can architectural decoration have been its object. Public and private utility, the happiness and the protection of individuals and of society: such is the aim of architecture.[1]

This formulation, opening a Haussmannian boulevard for twentieth-century functionalism to proceed down, dispensed with this frivolous notion of delight, or so it seemed within the darkened eye of the storm.

Yet pleasure or delight can never be put away so easily. It would have its restitution in the coming years, but two other pre-revolutionary incidents are also important for presaging what would unfold, both then and today. One was the "discovery" of Greek architecture in the 1750s by separate French and British expeditions to Athens, a city that had been off-limits to Western travelers during its centuries of Ottoman rule. In the opinion of David Le Roy, the Frenchman who breached the political citadel to publish the first images of the Parthenon, classical Greek architecture was superior to Roman architecture, which had long been the model of the French Academy of Architecture. It was superior not because of the old sawhorse of proportions but because of the way their heavier columnar masses were perceived or corporeally experienced. Such an idea naturally sent palpitations through the body of classical theory, yet it had other implications. In drawing on the physiological aesthetics of picturesque theorist Edmund Burke, Le Roy made the observation that when we walk along a colonnade with its dramatic contrast of light and shadow, our optic nerve is stimulated in a way that resonates throughout the entire bodily organism.[2] It was a profound insight into our physical relationship with the built environment, yet unfortunately it would, with a notable few exceptions, be ignored for much of the next two centuries.

DOI: 10.4324/9781003178460-9

The second incident was a relatively little-known book by Nicholas Le Camus de Mézières that appeared in 1780, *The Genius of Architecture*. It was one of the last exhalations of the Rococo spirit, and it explored an idea that would also be put away in post-revolutionary times—the idea that every architectural environment has a particular atmosphere or conveys a mood. It is true that the Scottish architect Robert Adam had earlier raised the idea of a "sentimental" architecture, one that appeals directly to the senses.[3] Yet Le Camus insisted that the purpose of design was "to arouse emotion," which the talented architect does by engaging both the heart and the soul.[4] Each room in a house, he wrote, should have its unique mood. A boudoir, for instance, should be an "abode of delight," allowing the lady to "yield to her inclinations," a room in which all is "subordinate to luxury, comfort, and taste."[5] In the design of a dining room—if one is to entice "fair Hebe" to grace the meal with her presence and "dispense the nectar of the gods"—one should "let gaiety, freshness, lively colors, and the character of youth and beauty set the tone of the decoration."[6] Although these views were directed to the upper class, the same principle can also be applied to a modest dwelling.

Le Camus's book falls in line with the work of the so-called visionary architects, most notably Étienne-Louis Boullée and Claude-Nicholas Ledoux. The latter was the architect of Mlle Guimard's Temple of Terpsichore, which had so transfixed Thomas Jefferson, but Ledoux designed a number of other fashionable townhouses with similar aristocratic and allegorical flair. Unfortunately, he also designed a few other things that later were not so well received. One was the Jeremy Bentham–inspired, half-circular salt production facility in the eastern province of France-Comté, in which its indentured residents worked under the (potentially) constant supervision of someone in the director's attic perch at the radius point of the arc. Michel Foucault would later write his own allegory on this theme in *Discipline and Punish*. Ledoux in the 1780s also designed a score of much-hated toll houses circumventing Paris, which nearly cost him his head during the Reign of Terror. In retirement, the apologetic designer transformed his salt works into his "ideal city" of Chaux—whimsical and imaginative in parts but scarcely paradisiacal.

The more interesting Boullée enjoyed fame in his early years for designing Parisian townhouses, and none more idyllic than the Hôtel Be Brunoy. Its lush rear gardens fronted the Champs-Élysées, where they too would have been admired by Jefferson on his daily walks. The principal motif of the garden facade was a temple front with six Ionic columns, behind which was an arcade with fully arched French doors. The walls of the side wings were covered with planted trellises, and the pyramidal roof culminated with a statue of the seated Flora—the Roman goddess of flowers and fertility. Boullée later explored the themes of mood, atmosphere, and light in his stupendous drawings and the posthumously published monograph *Essay on Art*, where he defined a building's character as "the effect of the object that induces some kind of impression on us."[7] The most famous of his dramatic renderings are those of his Cenotaph to Isaac Newton, a spherical building of vast proportions, both mysterious and powerful in its Masonic image of the cosmos. The upper part of the dome was to be pricked with tiny windows to project a starry sky inside. After confessing his inability to find a form worthy of Newton, Boullée, in his description, noted that he decided to grace the exterior of his sphere only with flowers and cypress trees.[8]

The Revolution and the ensuing Reign of Terror would soon put an end to such frivolity, yet unrest and wars would continue until Napoleon's defeat at Waterloo in 1814. The Congress of Vienna restored an unpopular Bourbon monarchy in France, beginning with Louis XVIII. He died in 1824 and the reign of his successor, Charles X, ended badly with the July Revolution of 1830. It is within such a context that we can consider the first of two significant utopian thinkers with at least a pretension of paradisiacal thinking. Charles Fourier, whose influence we have already seen in America, was born into a respected family and, after an apprenticeship with a silk merchant in Lyon, he took half of his patrimony in 1793 and set up his own business. When the revolutionaries arrived in southeastern France, Fourier defended the city before its fall, was arrested, and had his assets seized. For the rest of his life, he moved from lowly job to lowly job, living on a small subsistence.

ILLUSTRATION 9.1   Étienne-Louis Boullée, Hôtel de Brunoy, View from the Champs-Elysées by Jean-Baptiste Lallemand, c. 1780.

Source: Wikimedia, public domain.

ILLUSTRATION 9.2   Étienne-Louis Boullée, Cenotaph to Newton, 1784.

Source: Wikimedia Creative Commons CC0 License.

This explains in part why he turned his energies to conceiving a world in which everyone would live harmoniously in a state of bliss. The setting for this paradise was a commune or phalanstery—a secluded world in which one was free to pursue a range of manual, intellectual, and sexual interests, have fresh flowers on the table every evening to accompany gastronomical delights, and even the "poorest laborer" would be served a Burgundian wine superior to the finest vintage of Romanée-Conti.[9] The last was certainly the most outrageous revolutionary promise ever made in the history of the human race.

There was, of course, a method to his madness, one that he expounded in dozens of volumes, in which he continually reformulated his ideas. He formed his social vision around two suppositions. One, an indisputable fact, is that the present world is rife with waste and corruption, not to mention the horrors of poverty and warfare. The second, presaging in an interesting way Sigmund Freud's notion of Eros, is the belief that civilization and its discontents are the result of the repression of the paradisiacal instinct, although he did not specifically use this term. In pursuing the theme of emotional well-being, no Frenchman before him—neither Rousseau nor Diderot nor Montesquieu—had ventured down such an adventurous psychological path. Perhaps Walter Benjamin summarized Fourier's thought best when he wrote that his "phalanstery is designed to restore human beings to relationships in which morality become superfluous."[10]

Fourier's discovery, which he believed was on a par with Newton's discovery of the modern laws of physics, was what he termed the principle of "passionate attractions and repulsions." Succinctly, it is the belief that many, if not all, of the social problems of the world are the result of unfulfilled or conflicting human passions, or the efforts of "civilization" (as with Rousseau, a pejorative term) to tamp down or suppress normal human behavior, chiefly our aesthetic and sensual passions. These repressive mechanisms are what stand in conflict with and distort our natural behavior and lead to all manners of social discord. His novel approach was not directed to modifying or altering human behavior, but to accept who we are and allow our natural instincts to play out within a social structure planned to accommodate their expression. He identified twelve human passions that need to be harmonized, and the phalanstery is the environment in which this new society is to evolve. Fourier counted no fewer than 810 personality types, and thus the ideal phalanstery with a gender balance should house 1,620 people on three square miles of land. It is best located in a temperate climate on a hilly site, such as one finds in the area around Lausanne, in itself a heavenly landscape along the north shore of Lake Geneva at the base of the Alps. It is, however, no socialist utopia, because Fourier did not believe it was possible to change human behavior by decree. Existing social structures therefore remain in place, and people would buy into his communities at various levels of investment and have different standards of living. Nevertheless, all contribute to the community with their labor.

Perhaps the most interesting of his twelve passions is the butterfly passion, the papillon rule, or the need for a periodic change of scenery and perceptual stimuli. Because of this passion, people work as many as three or four different jobs a day, and workplaces are always clean and elegant. The objective is to make labor fun and interesting. Working in a field, for example, was likened to a country outing, where workers would be accompanied by decorated wagons carrying musicians, with a bevy of servers to offer an array of snacks and drinks. The workers would be outfitted in overalls, but even these garments were to be enhanced with colorful borders, belts, and plumes. The one exception to manual labor allowed by Fourier were artists and scientists. In the distant future, when interconnecting phalansteries covered the earth and the global population reached three billion people, Fourier reasoned, "the earth will have, on an average, thirty-seven million poets equal to Homer, thirty-seven million geometricians equal to Newton, and thirty-seven million comedians equal to Molière, and the same with all other imaginable talents."[11]

Another unusual feature of the phalanstery is that gardens are everywhere about, and not just because Fourier himself had a special penchant for flowers. The richness and sensual variety of nature, he believed, is central to human happiness, and our abuse of nature in the city and the countryside is one of society's greatest failings. Free love is another feature of the phalanstery. Women are afforded absolute equality, and although marriage was allowed, polygamy was encouraged for all because of the papillon rule. The intention is to unfetter sexual desire and allow everyone to pursue their particular interests without fear of failure. For instance, rituals were enacted for all men and women choosing polygamy, so that there would be no embarrassment incurred by a rejected suitor. Committees, overseeing a special troupe of Bacchantes or their male counterparts, would also see that every man and woman would be entitled to a "sexual minimum," including the older segment of the population. The sexual experience, Fourier observed, "is no longer, as it is with us, a recreation which detracts from work; on the contrary it is the soul and the vehicle, the mainspring of all works and of the whole of universal attraction."[12]

The image of Fourier's phalanstery, depicted by his disciple Victor Considerant, displays a building loosely based on Versailles with twice the floor area. The central wing, defined by a tower serving as an observatory and optical telegraph, houses a temple, dining areas, stock exchanges, meeting halls, and libraries. Immediately behind the central wing is a courtyard with gardens and parade grounds, used for daily performances. One wing of the complex has the noisy workshops, and the other wing contains the caravansary with its ballrooms and halls for visitors. More shielded are the private apartments in which the "passional series" or amorous relations take place each evening. This separation of spaces, as Fourier informs us, is different from other places of assembly, even royal palaces, "where everyone is thrown together pell-mell according to the holy philosophical principle of equality." Such an idea, he says, is "completely intolerable in Harmony."[13]

One of the more interesting features of the phalanstery is the "street-gallery" running through the complex, which seems to have been modeled on the iron-and-glass shopping arcades cropping up in France. Benjamin saw Fourier's arcade, populated at all times of the day, as "the architectural canon of the phalanstery."[14] It was a skylighted, three-story, air-conditioned gallery, with cafés and shops, also allowing the evening goer to visit "the theater and the opera in light clothes and colored shoes without worrying about the mud and the cold." It would possess a "charm so novel that it alone would suffice to make our cities and castles seem detestable."[15]

Fourier placed a very high value on employing luxurious materials and artful decorations, as a kind of atmospheric dressing. Even the meanest workshop was to be built of beautiful materials—not just to make the worker happy but to instill manners and refinement through the sumptuous environment itself. Luxury, he argued, leads to social intercourse and the cultivation of taste, and it therefore heightens one's self-esteem. In the same way, a vital part of the evening's festivities, which were varied, was the opera, by which he means every type of choreographic exercise or theatrical production. Children would begin training in this "semi-religious exercise" at an early age, because "training in material unity will direct them toward passionate unity."[16] Therefore the opera would be as necessary to the success of the phalansteries as plows and machinery.

Aspects of Fourier's new and amorous vision of the world can today be seen as fantastical, yet there is one insight that cannot be faulted. This was the realization that the human instinct for happiness was not an abstraction but something that could be given tangible form. He understood that the physical and social environments condition human behavior, as we see today in an obverse way with so many of our failed cities. The gardens, joyous labor, amorous liaisons, artistic performances, fine meals, superior wine, and good manners—all are ways, in Fourier's playbook, to cultivate a refined pleasure and enrich human happiness. What certified bon vivant could disagree with such a premise?

Aux Artistes

If Fourier saw the future of French society as building a new order from the ground up, his slightly older contemporary, the Comte de Saint-Simon, imagined utopia as a trans-European union led by a vanguard of artists, scientists, and industrialists. A son of an aristocrat, Saint-Simon fought alongside General Washington at Yorktown, was injured by a cannonball, captured by the British, and upon his release traveled to Mexico to speak with the viceroy about building a canal between the two oceans. He later suggested to Spanish authorities that they should create a canal from Madrid to the Atlantic. Back in France, he enjoyed a good life, and an even better one in the early days of the Revolution, when he made a small fortune by purchasing confiscated church properties with the ever-inflating *assignats* or revolutionary currency. At one point he, together with Talleyrand, even pondered purchasing the Cathedral of Notre-Dame and selling it for scrap. During the Reign of Terror, however, he was forced to renounce his title, imprisoned, and escaped execution (as did Ledoux) only because of Robespierre's arrest. Over the next decade he managed to lose his once-considerable wealth.

His life took a different turn in 1802 when, after a failed marriage, he visited Madame de Staël at her chateau on Lake Geneva. De Staël was already quite renowned for a publication of a few years earlier, in which she had argued for a new "science of society" to bring order to a world fitfully disordered. Saint-Simon responded by writing a pamphlet to the citizens of Geneva in which he too proposed a trans-national theology or society consisting of three classes: a Newtonian council, property owners, and workers. All three should wield some political power, but the first is the most fanciful because the council, in supplanting both the state and the spiritual role of the church, is to be run by mathematicians, physicists, chemists, physicians, authors, and painters.[17] It should have its own temple, which in his description seems to have been influenced by Boullée's Cenotaph to Newton. Inside the mausoleum is an underground temple accessible only to the anointed. Surrounding the monument, whose exteriors should command a "majestic and brilliant spectacle," are laboratories, workshops, colleges, and a library limited to 500 volumes—all that was needed to inform this new and efficient world.[18]

Over the next two decades Saint-Simon's social theory would evolve and waver between the poles of positivism, forming a science of human society, and his socialist theology. In all of his many variations, power would be withdrawn from the "idlers" of society (politicians, gentry, and soldiers) and devolve to a new class of savants, accomplished scientists, artists, and entrepreneurs of industry—the latter having mastered the art of producing goods and accomplishing large tasks. A few of his proposals even exhibit a paradisiacal air. For instance, in 1819 he called for replacing the current monarchy with a House of Commons with three houses: Chambers of Invention, Examination, and Execution. The first of these would consist of 300 members (civil engineers, writers, artists, architects, and musicians), who would be responsible for building public works and staging public festivals. Here he proposes turning the whole of French soil "into a superb English park, adorned with all that the fine arts can add to the beauties of nature." These gardens would house museums of locally produced goods and rival the design of princely gardens in former times. "Luxury," he decides in a manner similar to Fourier, "will become useful and moral when it is enjoyed by the whole nation."[19] As Saint-Simon also notes in the same text, *"Let artists transport the earthly paradise into the future, presenting it as the consequence of the new system's foundation, and this system will be established without delay."*[20]

Saint-Simonism became a major political and religious movement in France only after the leader's death in 1825. Five years later, by one estimate, there were as many as 40,000 converts to the movement, which included prominent French intellectuals, such as Pierre Leroux, Charles Augustin Sainte-Beuve, George Sand, and Hector Berlioz, in addition to a number of international admirers, among them Franz Liszt, John Stuart Mill, Thomas Carlyle, and Heinrich Heine. Yet this utopian fervor would not survive for long. Its moment of inflection came when one of Saint-Simon's closest disciples, Barthélemy Prosper Enfantin, proclaimed himself to be the "supreme Father" of the socialist movement, whereby he assembled forty costumed monks at his Ménilmontant estate and reformulated its theology to be the rehabilitation of the flesh, emancipation of women, and free love. Enfantin even dispatched one disciple to the Middle East to find the "female Messiah" to himself. As he discerned her in a vision, she was a Jewish woman attached to a harem in Constantinople. It proved to be a step too far for many Saint-Simonians, as well as for political authorities, who arrested the sect at Ménilmontant for flouting public morals.

This notwithstanding, the cult of Saint-Simonism did have at least one positive effect, which was the challenge it posed to both architecture and art. In summoning artists and architects to the cause in his polemical tract of 1830, *Aux Artistes*, Émile Barrault expanded upon Saint-Simon's view of history as a cycle of two revolving epochs: the organic and the critical. The apogee of the two organic epochs in design practice were the temples of ancient Greece and Gothic cathedrals. Greek architecture was grand in conception, deep in imagination, and expressed the sentiments of vigorous designers. Gothic architecture was harmonious in form and meaning, large in scale, and spiritually profound. Surrounding these two organic eras, however, were the interregna of critical eras in which societies were culturally unstable or lacked unity. If the art of the organic epochs was authentic, the art of critical eras, including the present, was little more than narcissistic. Barrault judged contemporary architecture to be "pleasing" to the public, but artificial and insignificant in the sentiments it conveys. One may observe "agreeable and elegant combinations, but one finds in their inanimate forms no *poésie*."[21]

Aux Artistes appeared at a time when French artistic education was in the midst of a crisis. The problems went back to the shuttering of the Royal Academy of Architecture in 1793, and its reconstitution within the Académie des Beaux-Arts in 1819, under the leadership of its *secrétaire perpétuel* Antoine-Chrysostome Quatremère de Quincy. He was another fascinating revolutionary figure: a sculptor and scholar, a friend of the painter Jacques-Louis David and Robespierre, and, conversely, a supporter of Lafayette, which caused him to flee France on one occasion with a death sentence on his head. In his artistic tastes, he was a strong admirer of Greek Neoclassicism, which became increasingly unpopular with students as Saint-Simonian ideas filtered into the ateliers. The ambition of architecture students—in the face of Quatremère de Quincy's historicism—was to usher in a new "organic" era of design, and the seedbed of this *petit revolution* was the French Academy housed at the Villa Medici in Rome, where the prize-winning students of each year's design competitions in Paris were awarded graduate studies.[22]

It was in the midst of this chaos that Victor Hugo intervened, as Neil Levine and others have so well documented.[23] After witnessing the boisterous students during the July Revolution of 1830, Hugo decided to add a chapter to *Notre-Dame de Paris* (*The Hunchback of Notre Dame*), titled "Ceci tuera cela" ("This Will Kill That"). It recounts a medieval conversation of Archdeacon Claude Frollo with a disguised Louis XI, when the priest, in looking to the cathedral outside his window and then pointing to a new printed manuscript on his desk, makes the comment, "This will kill that." Hugo's preferred interpretation of the comment is that the invention of the printing press had made architecture obsolete as a cultural purveyor of ideas, because the teachings of the church could now be learned from the printed book rather than from the costly outfitting of churches. In short, architecture no longer had a role to play in shaping modern society. He then invited one of the student leaders of the *petit revolution*, Henri Labrouste, to confer and comment on his chapter.

Labrouste's definitive response would be delayed for a few years, but in two competitions in the 1830s for an asylum and a prison, he displayed his interest in the "healing" power of design, the role that a building's atmosphere can play in mediating or balancing the passions of which Fourier spoke.[24] It was this interest that he also brought to his remarkable design of the library or Bibliothèque Sainte-Geneviève in Paris, a university library that was notable because its gas lamps both allowed nighttime study and kept students (in theory) out of taverns. The site was on a prestigious square opposite Jacques-Germain Soufflot's Church of Ste.-Geneviève, the last of which was transformed in revolutionary times into the Panthéon for France's civic heroes. The bodies of Voltaire and Rousseau, among others, still lie there in state. The theme of Labrouste's library design was the

Platonic "academy" in the garden, a point that he made explicit in later remarks when he noted that, at the entrance, he had wanted to create a large garden with trees and statues

> to prepare those who come there for meditation. A beautiful garden would undoubtedly have been an appropriate introduction to a building devoted to study, but the narrowness of the site did not permit such an arrangement and it had to be foregone.[25]

Instead, he moved the garden into the entry foyer, where one, after entering, passes through a dark forest of thick stone piers supporting branches of curved iron trusses originally painted green, against a sky-blue ceiling. Along the side walls are garden murals, as if one is indeed strolling through a garden. At the end of this passage, by means of a luxurious staircase (and passing by a large reproduction of Raphael's *School of Athens*), one ascends to the upper level and enters the lofty twin barrel-vaulted reading room, supported at the center with sixteen tree-like, cast-iron columns sprouting limbs of open arcuated trusswork. A white, veil-like (terra-cotta) ceiling seems to hover above the iron branches. By day, the room is brilliantly illuminated with a series of arched windows above the two stories of bookcases on the two long sides of the building; by evening, the atmosphere narrows to the halo that the gas light places on the tables.

It is truly an inspired paradise dedicated to enlightenment, but Labrouste would build upon a building's atmospheric power in 1854, when he received the commission to re-house the largest library in the world, the Bibliothèque Nationale of France. The building was placed within an existing masonry shell of the courtyard of the Hôtel Nevers and the former Palace of Cardinal Mazarin, into which Labrouste designed a reading room more than doubling the size of his earlier library. The Edenic instinct—the garden—is also given a more heavenly flight of imagination. Labrouste's reading room, nine bays in plan, consists of a light cast-iron structure inserted into an existing

ILLUSTRATION 9.3   Henri Labrouste, Ceiling of the Reading Hall of the former Bibliothèque Nationale, now the National Institute for Art History (INHA), Paris.

Source: Photo by Adelphilos. Wikimedia CC BY-SA 4.0.

shell, forming a ceiling of nine billowing, translucent domes of eggshell-white enamel panels. Each is adorned with colored decorative pleats and a central skylight, which collectively produce diffused natural light for readers below. The domes are supported on tall, incredibly thin cast-iron columns, and they have, in fact, the structural logic of a fragile hoopskirt (and indeed they were likened to crinolines by the popular press). Yet Labrouste's theme is easily discernible to the hundreds of readers seated below: the joyous sensation of reading a book in a park. To emphasize this point, the lunettes above the book walls on two sides of the room present rather detailed images of treetops and sky, painted by the same artist of his earlier library. As the historian David van Zanten has described the room's evocative atmosphere:

> The space is thus opened on three sides to a great fictive park while the breeze which might be imagined rustling the surrounding sea of leaves also seems to be holding aloft the billowing white, clothlike domes of the room as if they were awnings, tied down by the spindly iron columns rather than held up. Just as Labrouste's imaginative cutting of the stone exterior of the Bibliothèque Sainte-Geneviève makes it seem heavier and more solid, here the illusionistic elaboration of the iron construction makes the interior seem lighter and opens before the readers' minds quiet, reassuring vistas.[26]

Libraries are easy to design, or so it seems, based on the evidence that there are so many great libraries in architectural history—from that of Michelangelo in Florence to Wren at Cambridge to Fischer von Erlach in Vienna. The design of a library seems to peak the paradisiacal spirit of gifted architects. Few libraries, however, match the atmosphere and contemplative solitude of this imaginative masterpiece of Labrouste, now fittingly refashioned into the National Institute for Art History.

Venetian Interlude

> *SINCE first the dominion of men was asserted over the ocean, three thrones, of mark beyond all others, have been set upon its sands: the thrones of Tyre, Venice, and England. Of the First of these great powers only the memory remains; of the Second, the ruin; the Third, which inherits their greatness, if it forget their example, may be led through prouder eminence to less pitied destruction.*[27]

With such somber and steely authority, not to mention well-practiced fervency, John Ruskin opened his literary masterpiece *The Stones of Venice*. A few pages later, he made the Mosaic reference more explicit by naming Ham as the enchanter of the architectural shaft, Japheth the bestower of the arch, and Shem as the spiritualizer of both. Beautiful Venice, notwithstanding its state of near ruin in the mid-nineteenth century, was thereby invested with biblical apodicticity based on the paradisiacal perfection of its Gothic architecture between the years 1180 and 1418.[28] All else of the city's glorious building history, according to Ruskin, fell short of perfection.

Ruskin, of course, was not the first or last traveler to be enchanted by the beauty of *La Serenissima*, the "most serene" city by Byzantine proclamation. Its profound artistic aura has been interpreted by visitors with every hue of the rainbow. Shakespeare employed the costumed fabric of the city as the setting for *The Merchant of Venice* and *Othello*. Goethe on his *Italian Journey* spoke glowingly of the city's theaters, churches, music, and art. Henry James wrote much of *The Portrait of a Lady* from his room on the Riva Schiavoni, where

> the waterside life, the wondrous lagoon spread before me, and the ceaseless human chatter of Venice came in at my windows, to which I seem to myself to have been constantly driven, in

the fruitless fidget of composition, as if to see whether, out in the blue channel, the ship of some right suggestion, of some better phrase, of the next happy twist of my subject, the next true touch for my canvas, mightn't come into sight.[29]

Marcel Proust, whose modest success as a writer in 1896 rested on a collection of short stories, decided in the following year to take a novitiate and delve into the gospel of Ruskin. He began with a French translation of Ruskin's *The Bible of Amiens*, a book focused on this quondam "Venice of France." At the start of the new century, Proust reached deeper into Ruskin's "religion de la Beauté" with a translation of *Sesame and Lilies*, which served as a primer for his novel *Remembrance of Things Past*.[30] The specter of Ruskin and Venice haunts many of its thousands of pages, although the city as a venue does not materialize until the sixth volume. In the seventh and final volume, it erupts with the geological force of Vesuvius when—after the loss of his lover Albertine, a period in a sanitarium, a lengthy stay of literary lassitude and despair—the narrator stumbles upon two uneven flagstones in a residential Parisian driveway. They recall for him two uneven stones on which he had similarly stumbled years earlier in the baptistry floor of St. Mark's in Venice, and the memory leads him to experience a resuscitating catharsis, a "dazzling, elusive vision" that ultimately frees him to pursue his literary craft. More so, the involuntary memory of Venice unlocks for him the profound secret of consciousness itself, the "true nature" of life, the fact that our existence is stitched together by a web of such fluid yet ephemeral memories.[31] The flagstones of the baptistry exposed not only the "bare and barren impressions" of Venice but they also allowed him to recapture with lucidity all other sensations and memories of that day: the church, the piazza, the *imbarcadero*, and the canal.

> But let a sound already heard or an odour caught in bygone years be sensed anew, simultaneously in the present and the past, real without being the present moment, ideal but not abstract, and immediately the permanent essence of things, usually concealed, is set free and our true self, which had long seemed dead but was not dead in other ways, awakes, takes on fresh life and it receives the celestial nourishment brought to it.[32]

From the heightened perspective of Proust, Gustav von Aschenbach's melancholic obsession with the boy Tadzio, as portrayed in Thomas Mann's *Death in Venice*, reads pathetically grim. Conversely, what is more aesthetically uplifting than Joseph Brodsky's encomium on Venice—the city as "being itself a work of art, the greatest masterpiece our species produced."[33] He conflates Venice's "paradisiacal visual texture" with "a fine-boned, long legged" and stunningly attractive Vladimir Mayakovsky scholar he had just met, dressed in "paper-light suede and matching silks," wearing a nutria coat and a string of pearls (thirty-two strong), all "redolent of mesmerizing, unknown to us, perfume." Fittingly, the beatific conflation takes place on an overcrowded Venetian vaporetto under "the scattered silver of the Milky Way."[34]

Yet the writer with the strongest fixation on Venice was Ruskin, whose first visits came in 1835, 1841, 1845, and 1846. Yet his two stays in 1848 and 1851–52, a combined stay of fifteen months, demonstrate his iron assiduity—not just with the prolixity of words found in the three volumes of *The Stones of Venice*, but with his manual activities in the shivering temperatures on the ground. His ambition was nothing short of sublime: to survey and document with drawings and photographs every Byzantine and Gothic building in this "Paradise of cities" and its surrounding islands, in the midst of their ruined condition and imminent demise.[35] In words written from Verona in 1852, words that ring true to the soul of every architect, "I should like to draw all St. Mark's and all this Verona stone by stone, to eat it all up into my mind, touch by touch.[36]

The Republic of Venice, founded in 697, had come to an ignominious end in 1797 when Napoleon and Austria fought over its possession, with the French general looting the four bronze horses atop the porch of St. Mark's. It was likely divine payback for Venice's somewhat inglorious plunder of Constantinople during the Fourth Crusade of 1204, when Venice and the Crusaders (ostensibly on a mission to take Cairo) sacked the byzantine city instead and carted away its gold and precious works of art, much of which found their way into St. Mark's Basilica. If the deities needed still another reason, there should be some retribution for the fact that it was the Venetians who bombarded the Athenian Parthenon in 1687 in their seemingly never-ending wars with the Ottomans. Austria, in any case, took the city with the peace of 1815—that is, until 1848, when the Venetians drove out the Austrian garrison in a rebellious spring. The Austrians responded by laying siege to the city and bombarding it with cannon fire. Numerous casualities, starvation, cholera, and destroyed buildings ensued, and the Venetians were forced to surrender in the late summer of the following year. Shortly thereafter, Ruskin and his coterie circled around closed roads and remnants of barricades to be among the first non-combatants to enter the ruined city. He and his wife Effie were quartered together with Austrian military officers (much to the delight of Effie and her companion Charlotte Ker) in the fashionable Denieli Hotel at the head of the Grand Canal, also on the Riva Schiavoni. It was at the time Venice's finest hotel, scarcely more than a hundred yards from the Doges Palace and St. Mark's Square.

Yet Ruskin, now liberated from the social duties of his unconsummated marriage, was in fact ill-prepared for his ordeal. It was a bitterly cold fall and winter, and the art critic, in amassing his many thousands of pages of notes, measurements, elevations, daguerreotypes, and detailed drawings, spoke despairingly of the devastation of the city: the displaced inhabitants living on the streets, destroyed churches, the "lonely and stagnant canals, bordered for the most part by the dead walls of gardens, now waste ground; or by patches of dark mud, with decayed black gondolas lying keel upmost, sinking into the putrid and black ground gradually."[37] The extremity of the chill and the tedious nature of his work were equally lamentable, especially the "pain of frost-bitten finger and chilled throat as I examined or drew the window-sills in the wintry air." In drawing his floor plans, he also scampered over roofs and dangled from ladders, and on a daily basis, during his visit of 1851, he had to salve the protestations of his "gondoliers, who were always wanting to go home, and thought it stupid to be tied to a post in the Grand Canal all day long, and disagreeable to have to row to the Lido afterwards."[38] Nevertheless, he persevered and began the first volume upon his return to London in March of 1850. Yet the scope of the work demanded a return to the city in September of the following year and ten more months of "watchful wandering." Only in October of 1853 did the third volume appear.

Ruskin painted his paradisiacal portrait of Venice around the "central building of the world," which we will return to momentarily, but the spirit of his study is far more encompassing. One starting point of his Venetian discourse is a geological history—not of Venice but of the Matterhorn, the Alpine peak with which he, in his regular travels to the South, had often visited and sketched. Ruskin used the sheer wall of its eastern face, "hewn down, as if by the single sweep of a sword, from the crest of it to the base," to make an architectural statement. For this "most noble cliff in Europe," with its "stain-less ornaments of the eternal temple," is no monolith of stone but geological strata of different materials, variable in their hardness and coloration, horizontally built up from intense and timeless geological forces. And it is from this "universal law of natural building" that he posits his key architectural idea of the "wall veil," whereby the wall formed of imperfect and inferior materials, such as brick, can be strengthened "by introducing carefully laid courses of stone," thereby lending textural effects to the wall fabric.[39] Almost simultaneously and quite coincidentally, a German refugee living in London, the architect Gottfried Semper, was developing his notion of *Bekleidung* (the wall dressing), the idea that the architectural wall developed from (and still symbolically evokes) the primitive wall mats of the earliest spatial enclosures.[40] From the hardness of Alpine quartz to the soft vegetable fibers of mats, the effect in its application to architecture was one and the same: the wall veil.

Ruskin's focus on Venice, like his exquisite sketches, was giving shape to history. In his view, Tyre, "as in Eden, the Garden of the God," preceded *La Serenissima* in her beauty, and Tyre had its downfall. The passage of Ezekiel to which Ruskin alludes, is also suggestive of the fading glory of Venice that he will lay out:

> *Thou hast been in Eden the garden of God; every precious stone was thy covering, the sardius, topaz, and the diamond, the beryl, the onyx, and the jasper, the sapphire, the emerald, and the carbuncle, and gold: the workmanship of thy tabrets and of thy pipes was prepared in thee in the day that thou was created.*

Yet sadly Venice, "like her in perfection of beauty," has entered the final stage of her decline. She is but "a ghost upon the sands of the sea, so weak—so quiet,—so bereft of all but her loveliness, that we might well doubt, as we watched her faint reflection in the mirage of the lagoon, which was the City, and which the Shadow."[41]

His description of the region is similarly infused with melancholy. The gondola ride across the shallow yet black lagoon, the "white moaning seabirds," the steady ocean tide on "whose bosom the great city rested so calmly," the sunset transforming the "angry pallor" of the island of St. George of the Seaweed "into a field of burnished gold"—all speak to Venice's beginnings as an exarchate of Ravenna, its glorious rise as a preeminent sea and trading power, now giving way to the "adversity of nature and the fury of man."[42] The basilica of Santa Maria Assunta on the island of Torcello, seven miles north of Venice, is a fitting place to begin his saga. This early Romanesque church was founded in 639 by settlers escaping the raiding parties of the Huns on the mainland. Its mosaics date from the ninth century, and church height was raised two centuries later with the addition of two side aisles. For Ruskin, Torcello represented all that is grand with early Christianity: its stark exterior plainness, the quality of its sculptural fields, the acanthus leaves of its Corinthian capitals, and the mosaics applied to the interiors. Equally instructive was the Church of San Donato on Murano, in particular the exterior apse wall of the church with its wall veil of red and yellow bricks, divided between stories with double trefoil bands. Ruskin was fascinated with the fact that the trefoils of the upper band were two inches higher than the lower, providing the optical illusion of being lighter in their proportions.

ILLUSTRATION 9.4   Basilica of St. Mark's, Venice, in Gentile Bellini, *Procession in the Piazza San Marco*, 1496.

Source: Wikimedia CC BY-SA 4.0.

He similarly admired the archivolt at the end of the northern aisle, "the curious zigzag with which the triangles die away against the sides of the arch, exactly as waves break upon the sand."[43]

His description of these churches, over fifty pages in length, are merely to set the reader in a proper mood for his survey of Venice, which largely focused on two buildings. The first is the Basilica of St. Mark's, which, as Ruskin reports, can only be properly approached from the darkened alley off the Bocca di Piazza, allowing one to enter St. Mark's Square at the northwest corner. Only from this angle "there opens a great light" when the church comes into full view, and the emotion upon gaining sight of the church is emphatically transcendental:

> a multitude of pillars and white domes, clustered into a long low pyramid of coloured light; a treasure-heap, it seems, partly of gold, and partly of opal and mother-of-pearl, hollowed beneath into five great vaulted porches, ceiled with fair mosaic, and beset with sculpture of alabaster, clear as amber and delicate as ivory,—sculpture fantastic and involved, of palm leaves and lilies, and grapes and pomegranates, and birds clinging and fluttering among the branches, all twined together into an endless network of buds and plumes; and in the midst of it, the solemn forms of angels, sceptred, and robed to the feet, and leaning to each other across the gates, their figures indistinct among the gleaming of the golden ground through the leaves beside them, interrupted and dim, like the morning light as it faded back among the branches of Eden, when first its gates were angel-guarded long ago.[44]

It does not take the reader too many more pages to discern the reasons for Ruskin's ebullience. If European architecture is handed down from Greece through Rome, the architecture of St. Mark's, and Venice more generally, exudes its radiant feeling because it is byzantine—that is, the wall-veiled architecture of incrustation. Because the island nation was built on sand, remote from quarries, its early builders had to build in brick, although the human heart cannot be stilled by such emotional indifference. The shiploads of building materials brought to the island thus had to be as costly as possible: gold and porphyry, alabaster and mother-of-pearl, marble, and amber. Hence the "muscular power of its brickwork is to be clothed with the defence of the brightness of the marble," and if one does not understand the gist of Ruskin's artistic hypothesis, he makes himself more explicit: "the school of incrusted architecture is *the only one in which perfect and permanent chromatic decoration is possible.*" Let us "look upon every piece of jasper and alabaster given to the architect as a cake of very hard colour, of which a certain portion is to be ground down or cut off, to paint the walls with."[45]

These efforts compelled Venetians to import artists from Constantinople, and Ruskin pursues every facet of the basilica with scrupulous detail: the depth of the sculptural fields, the fact that no tesserae in any mosaic are ever of the same tint, that green tesserae (as Viollet-le-Duc had noted with glass) is never used without blue, that the apse of the central doorway rests on no fewer than four highly ornate archivolts, each of which he sketches. Some of these drawings speak of details now effaced with time, a tribute to his archaeology. Ruskin goes on to particularize the church's lily capitals, the two majestically carved marble pillars outside the baptistry door, and the two columns in the Piazzetta, the extension of St. Mark's square to the sea, on which is perched the winged-lion of St. Mark and the statue of St. Theodore standing atop a crocodile. Yet Ruskin did not point out to the reader that the same two pillars also frame, across the cyan lagoon, a view of Palladio's white-marbled church of San Giorgio Maggiore.

After Ruskin later scours Venice's Byzantine and Gothic palaces along the canals and then pens his popular essay of volume two, "The Nature of Gothic," one would think that his subject had been exhausted, yet there remains "the central building of the world," now more majestically earmarked as the "Parthenon of Venice."[46] With its two principal facades facing the Grand Canal and the Piazzetta, the Ducal Palace is a much simpler fabric, one in which Ruskin discerns "exactly equal proportions" of Roman, Lombard, and Arab influences. Its history begins in 813, the year in which

ILLUSTRATION 9.5 Detail of the facade of St. Mark's.

Source: Photo by author.

Charlemagne died, but only a few traces of its Byzantine predecessor, adorned with "ornaments of marble and gold," survive. The Gothic phase of the work began early in the fourteenth century and underwent several renovations. With a loggia and gallery below, the upper decorated facade is encrusted with a diaper pattern of white and pale-rose marble, which Ruskin had described in *Seven Lamps* as "the purest and most chaste model that I can name (but one) of the fit application of colour to public buildings."[47] The one exception is Giotto's Campanile in Florence. Even the one minor flaw in the canal facade of the Ducal Palace—the two windows on the right dropped lower than the others—is turned by Ruskin into a meritorious stroke: "In this arrangement there is one of the most remarkable instances I know of the daring sacrifice of symmetry to convenience, which was noticed as one of the chief noblenesses of the Gothic schools."[48] It seems hardly coincidental that in the building's floor plan, it is the Great Council Chamber that commands the taller window placements, and the chamber's wall separating it from ancillary rooms with the two lowered windows, contains the massive canvas of Tintoretto's *Paradise*, for Ruskin, "the most wonderful piece of pure, manly, and masterly oil-painting in the world."[49]

The bulk of Ruskin's saintly description next turns to the carvings embodied in the loggia and gallery stories, fashioned from Istrian stone brought from the Dalmatian coast. Literally, he leaves no stone untouched. The featured pieces are the two end sculptures at the corners of the sea elevation, *The Fall of Man* and *The Drunkenness of Noah* with two of his sons. In both subjects, Ruskin is enamored with the foliage, "a remarkable instance of the Gothic Naturalism." It is even more so in the *Noah* piece (fashioned in 1317), where the sculptor, although overstepping the limits of his art, "has literally carved every rib and vein upon them in relief; not merely the main ribs which sustain the lobes of the leaf, and actually project in nature, but the irregular and sinuous veins which chequer the membranous tissues between them," all of which produces a "peculiar tessellated effect upon the eye."[50]

ILLUSTRATION 9.6   Ducal Palace, Venice. Started 1340.

Source: Photo by author.

Ruskin devotes lesser attention to the three arch-angels above these works at the gallery level, but he writes much lengthier accounts of the column capitals, where, in an act bordering on obsession, he chronicles all eight faces (when surviving) of each of the thirty-five column capitals of the lower story, all of which personify Virtues and Vices. He ventures into this narration so that the "reader may both happily and profitably rest for a little while," and "review the manner in which these symbols of the virtues were first invented by the Christian imagination," and what they say "of the state of religious feeling in those by whom they were recognized."[51] Such an effort underscores the fact that Ruskin saw his efforts as both archaeological *and* missionary.

The third volume of *The Stones of Venice* is devoted to Renaissance architecture, which Ruskin characterizes as a period of decline—not for the perfection of its execution but because in the demand for "dexterity of touch," the architects "gradually forgot to look for tenderness of feeling; imperatively requiring accuracy of knowledge, they gradually forgot to ask for originality of thought." This approach proved "more fatal and immediate in architecture than in any other art," not only because it was "less consistent with the capabilities of the workman" but also because it was "utterly opposed to that rudeness or savageness on which, as we saw above, the nobility of the elder schools in great part depends."[52] Nevertheless, this "pestilent art of the Renaissance" in Venice is not entirely without merit, as he recounts with a few examples, but by far the most interesting of his many condemnations of Renaissance design is Palladio's Church of San Giorgio Maggiore, across the lagoon from the Ducal Palace. If architectural historians have long praised the transposition of pedimental forms in its main facade, Ruskin opined that it was "impossible to conceive a design more gross, more barbarous, more childish in conception, more servile in plagiarism, more insipid in result, more contemptible under every point of rational regard."[53] This was only the beginning of a lengthy paragraph, in which the English author went on to castigate the church's many other faults.

ILLUSTRATION 9.7 Palladio, Church of San Giorgio Maggiore, 1566.

Source: Photo by author.

Ruskin's opinions, archaeology, and masterful drawings aside—the power and fascination of Ruskin remains with his prose, his ability to portray Venice with a passion and imagery that no author has matched before or since. For instance, in concluding the second volume (after another favorable reference to Tintoretto's *Paradise*), he reflects more generally on his fervor for the city:

> sometimes when walking at evening on the Lido, whence the great chain of the Alps, crested with silver clouds, might be seen rising above the front of the Ducal Palace, I used to feel as much in awe in gazing on the building as on the hills, and could believe that God had done a greater work in breathing into the narrowness of dust the mighty spirits by whom its haughty walls had been raised, and its burning legends written, than in lifting the rocks of granite higher than the clouds of heaven, and veiling them with their various mantle of purple flower and shadowy pine.[54]

This passage exposes the depth of his love for Venice, but Ruskin's ultimate genius is the zeal with which he imbibed every detail of his Eden with eyes that no one before him had seen, "stone by stone." Moreover, those who visit Venice after reading him now see his paradise with eyes that they did not before possess. And like many people today, he too feared the "fast-gaining waves, that beat like passing bells," which continue to threaten the stones of the city.[55]

The Red House

It has been noted that Ruskin began writing the second volume of *Stones of Venice* on the first of May, 1851, the day that the "Great Exhibition of the Works of All Nations" opened in Hyde Park, only a few blocks from his home in Mayfair. It was for him a transgressive if not malevolent symbol of Britain's industrialization. Joseph Paxton and Charles Fox's iron-and-glass exhibition building encompassed more than twenty-six acres, including several fully mature trees. The expanse of its interior, by far the largest building in the world, simply had no precedent. And it is little wonder that many of the 30,000 people who attended its grand opening, including the queen and prince consort, were concerned with whether the glass ceiling would shatter with the royal salute fired from a model frigate moored on Serpentine Pond. Nevertheless, the size of the Crystal Palace was not its most impressive engineering feat. It was the fact that its 1,000 cast-iron columns and 100,000 square yards of glass had been manufactured, shipped, and erected within a span of eleven months. Matthew Digby Wyatt, the architect in charge of construction, hailed it as the beacon of the industrial age, "the universality of development attained by combining the division of labour in manufacturing with the aggregation of its results in commerce."[56] Ruskin, of course, viewed it in another light:

> The quantity of thought it expresses is, I suppose, a single and very admirable thought of Sir Joseph Paxton's, probably not a bit brighter than thousands of thoughts which pass through his active and intelligent brain every hour—that it might be possible to build a greenhouse larger than every greenhouse was built before. This thought, and some very ordinary algebra, are as much as all that glass can represent of human intellect.[57]

From a paradisiacal perspective, however, the great novelty of the "magical glass" cabinet—containing 100,000 articles from over 14,000 exhibitors—was that the wares displayed were from countries across the globe both industrial and "primitive." It was certainly the grandest ethnological collection ever assembled at the time, featuring a "Caraib Hut" from Trinidad, Native American birch canoes, Oriental carpets, grass skirts from Africa, and hedge-like lattice works of aboriginal tribes from the South Seas. Artistic and industrial products of the entire world were on display side by side. Richard Redgrave, in his official "Supplementary Report on Design," pounded the machine-made products of his countrymen and then went on to goad architects for their stylistic eclecticism.[58] Conversely, Owen Jones lauded the "repose of color and form" found in the textiles of India, Tunis, Egypt, and Turkey. He later recast his analyses into the thirty-seven design principles in his *Grammar of Ornament* of 1856.[59] Jones, just a few years earlier, had recorded the wonders of Moorish architecture with his astonishing renderings of the artwork of the Alhambra.

It should also be reported that Ruskin's star, redirecting architects along quite a different path, was at this moment ascending. In his *Seven Lamps of Architecture*, written before his book on Venice, he had spoken glowingly of the Gothic lamps of Sacrifice, Truth, Power, Beauty, Life, Memory, and Obedience as moral precepts clad in the mantle of Mosaic commandments. The architect William Butterfield felt sufficiently swayed by the book to jettison his former church designs of gray ragstone and produce the polychrome splendor of the church of All Saints on Margaret Street in London. Its interior—its flooring tiles, walls, gilded timberwork, and painted ceilings—is a veritable paradise of color, matched only by his later chapel at Keble College, Oxford. Another architect to see the light was George Edmund Street. Upon reading *The Stones of Venice* in 1852, he, together with Philip Webb, embarked on a tour of northern Italy to trace Ruskin's footsteps, out of which he produced a 400-page study filled with his sketches, some tinted with wash. In it, he underscores Ruskin's "brilliant advocacy of many laws and truths in which every honest architect ought gladly to acquiesce," and then concludes with the question "Why should we not be equally remembered three centuries hence?"[60] The talented Street went on to become a prominent designer, but he is also known for an apprentice who briefly interned in his office, an Oxford student with rebellious instincts saturated with medieval sensibilities: William Morris.

Born into a family of wealth, Morris in 1853 entered Exeter College, where he befriended the future-painter Edward Burne-Jones. The two initially enjoyed their literary explorations of Arthurianism and medieval poetry, but it was *The Stones of Venice* that molded Morris's outlook most profoundly. In his section titled "The Nature of Gothic," Ruskin with usual passion condemned the linearity and geometrical perfection of classical ornaments because they dehumanize the laborer who must paint or carve them, whereas the "living soul" of Gothic architecture, allowing for human imperfections, resides precisely in such unclassical qualities as savageness, changefulness, natural-ism, and grotesqueness. If classical architecture was only able to invent five orders, Ruskin boasted, "there is not a side chapel in any Gothic cathedral but it has fifty orders, the worst of them better than the best of the Greek ones, and all new."[61] Ruskin's writings appealed to Morris not only because of their concern for the laborer but also for the necessity to bring beauty into everyone's life. It was in his momentary inebriation induced by the apostolic language of Ruskin that Morris entered the studio of Street in 1856 to become an architect, although it would only be a short stay. Burne-Jones had meanwhile moved to London and apprenticed himself to Dante Gabriel Rossetti and he was soon successful in luring Morris to London, where Morris was warmly received by the Pre-Raphaelite painters, in part because he also had the financial resources to buy their works. Painting, however, was not one of Morris's strengths, and he turned a new page in 1861 when he, with six others, founded the decorative arts firm of Morris, Marshall, Faulkner & Company, the cornerstone of the Arts and Crafts movement. It was largely financed by Morris and based in the Red House, which Webb had designed for Morris near Bexleyheath, just outside of London. The house with its medieval air remains a relic of its revered specter, yet the "honest" design of Webb, with interior brick arches and oak accents, was also known in its day for its setting amid idyllic gardens of sweetbriar and wild rose, with a bowling green and orchard walks "amid gnarled old fruit-trees."[62]

The firm's Prospectus of 1861 defined it as a guild of "Fine Art Workmen in Painting, Carving, Furniture and the Metals." The idea of a guild had been tried before by Augustus Welby Pugin, and it was not far from the mind of Prince Albert when, following the Great Exhibition of 1851, he founded a college of art manufacturers in South Kensington, which became the Victoria and Albert Museum. Yet Morris's efforts were different. With Ruskin's medieval ethic, he and his fellow artists circled around the mantras of natural materials and hand craftsmanship to find redemption within

ILLUSTRATION 9.8 Philip Webb and William Morris, "Red House," 1859, Bexleyheath, England.

Source: Photo by Ethan Doyle White. Wikimedia CC BY-SA 3.0.

the industrial currents of modern life. The firm eventually prospered and outgrew the Red House. Morris initially did much of the overseeing of the firm, but he was soon active with weavings, dyes, printed fabrics, wallpapers, chintzes, and eventually book printing, in addition to his voluminous writings. In a lecture given at the Working-Men's College of 1881, he, like his mentor, spoke of the need to bring beauty into everyday life as a way to cultivate quiet sensitivity or personal calm. In speaking of carpet designs, he encouraged his students to study the Eastern models, but also noted his personal axiom:

> I, as a Western man and a picture-lover, must still insist on plenty of meaning in your patterns; I must have unmistakable suggestions of gardens and fields, and strange trees, boughs, and tendrils, or I can't do with your pattern.[63]

The garden, in fact, was the thread woven through his writings, and this fabric of his thought has been understated by some historians. Leaving aside his preoccupation with natural landscapes in his poetry, we find the same sensibility on nearly every page of his novel *News from Nowhere*, which appeared in 1890. The book is almost always characterized as "utopian" in line with Morris's socialist inclinations, yet the garden trumps his politics entirely. The novel reads lovingly as Morris's phantasmic return to the Garden of Eden.

Morris was not alone in this regard. In 1888, the Hungarian economist Theodor Hertzka published *Freeland: A Social Anticipation*. The book—more a plan for a real community than a utopian fantasy—contains a heavy brew of economic theory, but only because Hertzka believed he had discovered an economic principle that had eluded Adam Smith, David Ricardo, Henry George, and Karl Marx. It was the value of a competitive market system that functions through voluntary "productive" associations favoring innovation and new technologies. The inexplicable site for his proposed community was equatorial Africa, the highlands surrounding Lake Victoria, and the details of Hertzka's Eden, as narrated by the novel's Italian diplomat, are threefold: the city's gardens, its liberated women, and its architecture. Here is the interpolator's first impression upon his arrival:

> Imagine a fairy garden covering a space of nearly forty square miles, filled with tens of thousands of charming, tastefully designed small houses and hundreds of fabulously splendid palaces; add the intoxicating odours of all kinds of flowers and the singing of innumerable nightingales—the latter were imported from Europe and Asia in the early years of the settlement and have multiplied to an incredible extent—and set all this in the framework of a landscape as grand and as picturesque as any part of the world can show.[64]

The men of the settlement have managerial and artistic prowess, but the women, who will also be the heroines for Morris, outstrip them. The hostess of the diplomat is forty-five years old but looks half her age. She is "brilliantly beautiful, but is rendered specially charming by the goodness and nobility of mind impressed upon her features." Her three daughters, who move with cheerful grace and aristocratic poise, possess no less "indescribable charm," but we soon learn that two are actually pupil-daughters—that is, initiates who refine their manners and intellect by entering the household of a "superior woman" for at least a year.[65]

Eden lake, around which the city is centered, is bordered by a fourfold avenue of palm trees, and a large portion of it is taken up by luxurious bathing establishments surrounded by shady groves, interspersed among which are sixteen theaters, operas, and concert halls. The library of Eden Vale plays the role that the Forum did in ancient Rome. With its 980,000 books, it attracts 5,000 readers per day and also serves as a kind of social cafe. All of the houses, "half-Moorish half-Greek," have lush gardens with choice trees and beautiful flowers, statuary, and fountains. The architectural gem, however, is the National Palace of Freeland, which surpasses the physical extent of the Vatican, with cupolas taller than the dome of St. Peter's. The building, we are told, was born of "a new style of architecture," which in the nobility of its forms rival the best of Greek and Egyptian monuments.[66]

It is quite possible that Morris knew of Hertzka's book, although the English translation appeared only in 1891, but Morris was very familiar with Edward Bellamy's *Looking Backward*, for which he wrote a critical review. The insomniac Bostonian in the American novel is induced into a trancelike sleep in an underground vault in 1887, and he awakens 113 years later in a vastly transformed political world. The social unrest and the economic downturns that plagued the nineteenth century have now been put to rest in a blissful socialist society, in which poverty and crime have been eliminated and working hours drastically shortened. Morris, in his review for *Commonweal*, took issue with the author's genteel and commercialized vision of the socialist ethic, and was even more hostile to the idea that human happiness could be purchased by limiting one's unhappy working hours—in his words, to the "reduction of *labour* to a minimum," rather than "to the reduction of *pain in labour* to a minimum." He rightly saw Bellamy's bourgeois society with the visual tedium of attractive yet commonplace buildings as frivolous, absent any serious aesthetic sensibility. Moreover, in this pre-Soviet era, Morris countered that "the variety of life is as much an aim of true communism as equality of condition," and in this regard art "is not a mere adjunct of life which free and happy men can do without, but the necessary expression and indispensable instrument of human happiness."[67] These remarks are expanded by Morris two years later in his preface to John Ruskin's "The Nature of Gothic," printed as a stand-alone edition by Morris's Kelmscott Press. Here he reports how Owen and Fourier sought to recast labor as a pleasurable activity by creating a beautifully constructed workplace and by amplifying its atmosphere through forms of incidental entertainment. Whereas these efforts might "lighten the burden of labour," Morris observed, in the end they "would not procure for it the element of sensuous pleasure."[68] It was Ruskin, Morris argued, who solved the problem, because he saw that beauty was actually the result of labor pleasurable unto itself; that is, when "beauty is once again a natural and necessary accompaniment of productive labour."[69]

This is also the message of *News from Nowhere*, which is set in London along the River Thames around the start of the second millennium. The problem of labor has been solved because government has devolved into local units of management run by the communes, wards, and parishes. People choose to work because "the freedom for every man to do what he can do best" is the adage that everyone follows, happily contributing to the success of the non-coercive system.[70] Effectively, the fellowship of humankind has receded back to its medieval roots (not without some difficulties or political experimentation), yet retains the rich treasury of the literary and plastic arts. Even the use of pre-revolutionary industrial machinery has largely been discarded, not because of contempt for the machine but because it was found that sowing the fields or scything the hay by hand is a far more festive activity than conventional agriculture could ever be. All are happy and age well due to their native felicity and regular physical exercise. The women are extraordinarily beautiful. One of the first women that the time traveler meets at the morning Guest House is forty-two years old, although the protagonist believes she is twenty:

> I stared at her, and drew musical laughter from her again; but I might well stare, for there was not a careful line on her face; her skin was as smooth as ivory, her cheeks full and round, her lips as red as the roses she had brought in; her beautiful arms, which she had bared from her work, firm and well-knit from shoulder to wrists. She blushed a little under my gaze, though it was clear that she had taken me for a man of eighty.[71]

In dress, the women are no longer "upholstered like armchairs" but wear clothes in a style somewhere "between that of the ancient classical costume and the simpler forms of the fourteenth century garments," of light and gay materials suited to the seasons.[72] The clothes of the oarsman that he meets also reflect those of the fourteenth century, yet his simple shirt of blue cloth is highlighted with a belt clasp of "damascened steel beautifully wrought. "In short, he seemed to be like some specially manly and refined young gentleman, playing waterman for a spree, and I concluded that this was the case."[73] And it is not just the people and their costumes that are anachronisms, because the city of London too has reverted to its medieval condition. On the protagonist's horse-drawn wagon ride into town from west of Hammersmith, he first spies Westminster Abbey along the glade of a forest. The orchard now planted in Trafalgar Square is spotted from among its surrounding "whispering trees and odorous blossoms," and the British Museum is first seen from a "narrow lane between the gardens," opposite a "wide space of greenery, without any wall or fence of any kind."[74] All of London, in fact, has transformed itself into an Edenic setting, and the few surviving historic buildings, all considered "ugly" by the present residents, are left standing only because they provide adequate housing, or have, like the British Museum, the historical curiosities of a grand library. The House of Parliament, in this social system without a government, is fittingly being used as a dung-market.

This is the reason why architecture plays such a minimal role in Morris's saga. The people already reside in the Garden of Eden, and buildings should not detract from the overwhelming beauty of the garden. The cast-iron bridges of the past have been replaced with more modest ones of stone or timber. The houses of residents are simple cottages, seemingly plucked from *The Poetry of Architecture*, Ruskin's very first literary publication. Here is how Morris describes the houses along the river Thames:

> Both shores had a line of very pretty houses, low and not large, standing back a little way from the river; they were mostly built of red brick and roofed with tiles, and looked, above all, comfortable, as if they were, so to say, alive and sympathetic with the life of the dwellers in them. There was a continuous garden in front of them, going down to the water's edge, in which the flowers were now blooming luxuriantly, and sending delicious waves of summer scent over the eddying stream.[75]

The buildings surrounding the market of Hammersmith again take on a Ruskinian caste. One, with its low walls and steeply pitched roof, he reports, "seemed to me to embrace the best qualities of the Gothic of northern Europe with those of the Saracenic and Byzantine, though there was no copying of any one of these styles."[76] Another octagonal building, resembling the Baptistery of Florence, was also "most delicately ornamented," and the protagonist's humble tour guide, the earlier oarsman, proudly admits to having a hand in casting the damascened bronze doors of the village's theater. As with Fourier, people in this paradise have a proficiency in multiple professions.

It is traveling within the garden along the Thames that Morris meets the Elysian female persona of wisdom who will initiate him in the rites of paradise. She is a woman of "strange and almost wild beauty," and she effortlessly transfixes his heart and soul. At one minute she can flirtingly admit that, in a country of so many beautiful women, she has often "troubled men's minds disastrously." The next minute she asks,

> don't you find it difficult to imagine the times when this pretty country was treated by its folk as if it had been an ugly characterless waste, with no delicate beauty to be guarded, with no heed taken of every fresh pleasure of the recurring seasons, and changeful weather, and diverse quality of the soil, and so forth? How could people be so cruel to themselves?[77]

It is also she who, with her "last mournful look," must reveal to the protagonist that his blissful time in Eden has ended and he must return to his own century. If there is one experience that betokens his newly acquired knowledge, it is when, at sunset, his boat passes Oxford's river meadows, which are now rid of the squalidness incurred by the "stir and intellectual life of the nineteenth century," and

> had once again become as beautiful as they should be, and the little hill of Hinksey, with two or three very pretty stone houses new-grown on it (I use the word advisedly; for they seemed to belong to it) looked down happily on the full streams and waving-grass, grey now, but for the sunset, with its fast-ripening seeds.[78]

This observation is scarcely utopian, but one deeply rooted in a revelatory moment of the paradisiacal instinct.

Notes

1. J.-N.-L. Durand, *Précis of the Lectures on Architecture*, trans. by David Britt (Los Angeles, CA: Getty Publication Programs, 2000), 84.
2. See Julien-David Le Roy, *The Ruins of the Most Beautiful Monuments of Greece*, trans. by David Britt (Los Angeles, CA: Getty Publication Programs, 2004), 372. See also Edmund Burke, Part 4:13, "The Effects of Succession in Visual Objects Explained," in *A Philosophical Inquiry into the Origin of Our Ideas of the Sublime and the Beautiful*.
3. A letter to Lord Kames, see John Fleming, *Robert Adam and His Circle in Edinburgh and Rome* (London: John Murray, 1962), 303.
4. Nicholas Le Camus de Mézières, *The Genius of Architecture; or, The Analogy of That Art with Our Sensations*, trans. by David Britt (Santa Monica, CA: Getty Publication Programs, 1992), 71.
5. Ibid., 115.
6. Ibid., 136.
7. Étienne-Louis Boullée, *Architecture: Essai sur l'art*, ed. by Jean-Marie Pérouse de Montclos (Paris: Hermann, 1968), 74.
8. Ibid., 137–8.
9. See Frank and Fritzie Manuel, *Utopian Thought in the Western World* (Cambridge, MA: Belknap Press, 1979), 667.
10. Walter Benjamin, *The Arcades Project*, trans. by Howard Eiland and Kevin McLaughlin (Cambridge, MA: Belknap Press, 1999), 5.
11. Charles Fourier, *Oeuvres complètes, Théorie des quatre mouvements et des destinées générales* (Paris: Bureau de la Phalange, 1891), 1:124.
12. Charles Fourier, draft to *Nouveau monde amoureux*, cited from Jonathan Beecher and Richard Bienvenu, *The Utopian Vision of Charles Fourier* (London: Jonathan Cape, 1971), 59.
13. Charles Fourier, *Théorie de Unité universelle*. Cited from Beecher and Bienvenu, *The Utopian Vision of Charles Fourier* (note 12), 242.
14. Benjamin, *The Arcades Project* (note 10), 5.
15. Fourier, *Théorie de Unité universelle*. Cited in Beecher and Bienvenu, *The Utopian Vision of Charles Fourier* (note 12), 245.
16. Ibid., 260.
17. Henri Saint-Simon, "Letters from an Inhabitant of Geneva to His Contemporaries," in Keith Taylor (trans. and ed.), *Henri Saint-Simon (1760–1825)* (London: Routledge, 2015), 198–206.
18. Ibid., 79.
19. Henri Saint-Simon, *L'Organisateur* (November 1819), cited from Taylor, *Henri Saint-Simon* (note 17), n. 203.
20. Saint-Simon, *L'Organisateur*, cited from Neil McWilliam, *Dreams of Happiness: Social Art and the French Left 1830–1850* (Princeton, NJ: Princeton University Press, 1993), 41.
21. Émile Barrault, *Aux Artistes: Due Passé et de L'Avenir des Beaux-Arts* (Paris: Alexandre Mesnier, 1830), 19.
22. Letter of Léon Vaudoyer to A.-L.-T. Vaudoyer, 20 July 1829. Cited in Barry Bergdoll, *Léon Vaudoyer: Historicism in the Age of Industry* (New York: The Architectural History Foundation, 1994), 293, n. 47.
23. See Neil Levine, "The Book and the Building: Hugo's Theory of Architecture and Labrouste's Bibliothèque Ste-Geneviève," in Robin Middleton (ed.), *The Beaux-Arts and Nineteenth-Century French Architecture* (Cambridge, MA: Massachusetts Institute of Technology Press, 1982), 138–73.
24. A point made by Martin Bressani and Marc Grignon in "The Bibliothèque Sainte-Geneviève and 'Healing' Architecture," in Corinne Bélier, Barry Bergdoll, and Marc Le Coeur (eds.), *Henri Labrouste: Structure Brought to Light* (New York: The Museum of Modern Art, 2013), 97–101.
25. Cited from David van Zanten, *Designing Paris* (Cambridge, MA: Massachusetts Institute of Technology Press, 1987), 238.

26. David van Zanten, "Henri Labrouste," in Adolf K. Placzek (ed.), *Macmillan Encyclopedia of Architects* (New York: The Free Press, 1982), 2:595–6. See also Marc Le Coeur, "The Bibliothèque Nationale: Between Rationalism and Illusionism," in *Henri Labrouste* (note 24), 135–63.
27. John Ruskin, "The Stones of Venice," in E. T. Cook and Alexander Wedderburn (eds.), *The Complete Works of John Ruskin* (London: George Allen, 1903–4), Vol. 10:17.
28. Ibid., 34.
29. Henry James, "Preface," to *The Portrait of a Lady*.
30. See Daviel Simon, "Translating Ruskin: Marcel Proust's Orient of Devotion," *Comparative Literature Studies* 38:2 (2001), 142–68.
31. See Russell Epstein, "Consciousness, Art, and the Brain: Lessons from Marcel Proust," *Consciousness and Cognition* 13 (2004), 213–40.
32. Marcel Proust, "The Past Recaptured," in Frederick Blossom (trans.), *Remembrance of Things Past* (New York: Random House, 1932), 2:996.
33. Joseph Brodsky, *Watermark: An Essay on Venice* (New York: Penguin Books, 1992), 116.
34. Ibid., 9–12.
35. John Ruskin, *Praeterita: Outline of Scenes and Thoughts* (Sunnyside, Kent: George Allen, 1887), 2:102.
36. Ruskin, "The Stones of Venice" (note 27), 10:XXVI.
37. Ibid., 9:XXVI.
38. Ibid., 9:XXVIII.
39. Ibid., 9:86–8. See Lars Spuybroek, *The Sympathy of Things: Ruskin and the Ecology of Design* (Rotterdam: V2 Publishing, 2011), 78–80.
40. See Gottfried Semper, *The Four Elements of Architecture and Other Writings*, trans. H. F. Mallgrave and Wolfgang Herrmann (New York: Cambridge University Press, 1989), 103–4.
41. Ruskin, "The Stones of Venice" (note 27), 9:17. The passage from Ezekiel is 28:13.
42. Ibid., 10:9.
43. Ibid., 10:56.
44. Ibid., 10:82–3.
45. Ibid., 10:98.
46. Ibid., 10:340.
47. John Ruskin, "The Seven Lamps of Architecture," in *The Complete Works of John Ruskin* (note 27), 8:183.
48. Ruskin, "The Stones of Venice" (note 27), 10:334.
49. Ibid., 10:438.
50. Ibid., 10:361.
51. Ibid., 10:365.
52. Ibid., 11:15.
53. Ibid., 9:381.
54. Ibid., 11:438–9.
55. Ibid., 9:17.
56. Matthew Digby Wyatt, *The Industrial Arts of the Nineteenth Century* (London: Day & Son, 1851), 1:VII.
57. Ruskin, "The Stones of Venice" (note 27), Appendix 17, 9:456.
58. Richard Redgrave, "Supplementary Report on Design," in *Report by the Juries* (London: William Clowes & Sons, 1852).
59. Owen Jones, "Gleanings from the Great Exhibition of 1851," *Journal of Design and Manufactures* 5 (June 1851), 93.
60. "First Preface," in *Brick and Marble in the Middle Ages: Notes on Tours in the North of Italy*, 2nd ed. (London: John Murray, 1874), XVIII and 407.
61. Ruskin, "The Stones of Venice" (note 27), 11:110.
62. The words of a visitor, cited from Aymer Vallance, *William Morris: His Art, His Writings, and His Public Life* (London: George Bell and Sons, 1897), 49.
63. *The Collected Works of William Morris* (London: Longmans Green and Company, 1914), 22:195–6.
64. Theodor Hertzka, *Freeland: A Social Anticipation*, trans. by Arthur Ransom (London: Chatto & Windus, 1891), 190.
65. Ibid., 191.
66. Ibid., 202.
67. William Morris, "Looking Backward," *Commonweal* 5:180 (June 22, 1889), 194–5.
68. William Morris, "Preface," to *The Nature of Gothic by John Ruskin* (London: Kelmscott Press, 1892), IV.
69. Ibid., I–II.
70. William Morris, *News from Nowhere* (Cambridge: Cambridge University Press, 1995), 96.
71. Ibid., 20.
72. Ibid., 16.
73. Ibid., 9.

74. Ibid., 44 and 52.
75. Ibid., 10–11.
76. Ibid., 26.
77. Ibid., 196.
78. Ibid., 193.

10

BRAVE NEW WORLD

Modern Cities

Paris is famously known as the cultural capital of the nineteenth century, and few would dispute this claim. From its Académie des Beaux-Arts to its École Polytechnique, from its ateliers of painters and sculptors to its literary salons, from its operatic performances to its musical recitals, from its shopping arcades to its *haute couture*—Paris had no serious peer. Yet the physical city itself, as its many visitors know it today, was in large part the creation of the second half of the nineteenth century. It is true that the city had a start somewhere in its Gallic or Celtic past, and that Julius Caesar's lieutenant Titus Labienus set up a garrison town on the Left Bank of the future city. The Frankish Clovis chose the city as the capital of his Merovingian dynasty in 508, and the Vikings came to Paris for an unwelcome visit in the ninth century. Yet by the end of the first millennium, Paris had pretty much established its prominence and longevity. The modern city and much of its artistic character, however, needed the impulse of the revolutions of 1789, 1830, and 1848 to materialize. The barricades, the coup d'état, and the installation of Napoleon III in 1852 as the crowned head of the Third Empire—all were factors in rebuilding the modern city, almost from the ground up.

And just as Achilles needed the intervention of Thetis and Hephaestus to fashion his new armor, so Paris needed the administrative abilities of Baron Georges-Eugène Haussmann to remake the city. Napoleon gave the prefect not only significant authority, but also a map of the city on which he had crayoned the lines of new avenues he wished to slice through the existing urban fabric. The emperor and his prefect created more than twenty miles of tree-lined boulevards, new squares, and new bridges. There was an occasional mark of high inspiration, such as the creation of the Avenue de l'Opéra to frame the masterpiece of Charles Garnier's magnificent new building at its culmination. Sightlines within the once-cramped city were quite important. The new train station of the Gare de l'Est was placed atop the new boulevard that stretched more than a mile south to the Ile de la Cité. On the island, a dome was shifted on one of the many new government buildings under construction to provide a fitting terminus. The entrance bridge to the island was graced with two new theaters. Similarly, from the hill above the city on the left bank, the Boulevard Saint-Michel swept down past the Luxemburg Gardens to the same island, where its vista culminated with the Gothic spire of Sainte Chapelle. Nearby new buildings were added to the Académie des Beaux-Arts, including the glazed roofing of the former courtyard of the Palais des Etudes. The Rue de Rivoli, running along the north side of the Louvre and the Tuileries garden was upgraded with hotels in preparation for the International Exposition of 1855, which followed in the footsteps of the London Exhibition of

DOI: 10.4324/9781003178460-10

ILLUSTRATION 10.1   Camille Pissarro, *Avenue de l'Opéra, Morning Sunshine*, 1898. Philadelphia Museum of Art. Gift of Helen Tyson Madeira, 1991.

Source: Wikimedia PD-Art Photographs.

1851. With the close of the event, the planner Adolphe Alphand would outfit the surrounding park with new structures to house summer concerts, cafés, restaurants, playhouses, playgrounds, concession stands, and street lighting. His plan was such a success that, from the testimony of foreigners, he boasted that the grand avenue "is once again without rival in the world."[1]

The largely medieval city, with many parts overcrowded, unsanitary, and crime-ridden, was remade on a massive scale. To help fund the project, Napoleon incorporated into the city several surrounding suburbs to increase the tax base and doubled the physical area of the city while increasing its population fourfold. Large sections of the city were gutted, following guidelines that controlled every detail of new construction, including the width of streets and height of buildings, cornice lines, the size of doors, windows, and railings, the width of sidewalks, the design of tree grates, benches, newsstands, fountains, and kiosks. Major civic ceremonies celebrated each of these initiatives, as the city became the global symbol for the new era canonized by Charles Baudelaire with the word of *modernité*. A cadre of talented painters—Édouard Manet, Camille Pissarro, Pierre-Auguste Renoir, and Claude Monet—rushed to present their artistic impressions of the new metropolis.

The most idyllic of the new developments, however, was a vast new park system requiring the planting of over 600,000 trees. It began at the local level with small parks in every neighborhood. Large new parks were added to the north and south sides of the city; existing ones were redone. The two largest interventions, however, were the Bois de Boulogne and Bois de Vincennes on the west and east sides, respectively; both were over 2,000 acres, or twice the size of New York's Central

Park. They were picturesque creations of Alphand, effectively a series of theme parks, with allées, canals, cascades and grotto, plantings, recreational areas, restaurants, architectural ornaments, and multiple lakes. The scale of Bois de Boulogne, with its popular Longchamp horse-racing course, even demanded its own tree-lined avenue of exceptional width stretching west from the refashioned parkland around the Arc de Triomphe. All was documented in a beautifully illustrated volume, *Les Promenades des Paris*, with its nearly 500 engravings. The scale, pace, and cost of rebuilding, of course, could not continue indefinitely, and in 1869 Haussmann was forced to resign. In the following year, Napoleon III foolishly engaged Bismarck in the Franco-Prussian war, which ended abruptly with the embarrassed emperor himself being captured at the Battle of Sedan.

Paris, nevertheless, provided the model of modernity that many European cities would emulate. Vienna, the seat of the Habsburg Empire with its own imperial pretensions, had a fortified urban core—the "old town"—which had remained essentially unchanged since the twelfth century. Over the centuries, thirty-four suburbs had gathered around it—at a distance. In 1857, Emperor Franz Josef made the decision to tear down the city's ramparts with its broad glacis, and replace them with a tree-lined Ringstrasse or ring boulevard, circling around the old city to the banks of the Danube River. The roadway fed a profusion of new monuments on both sides, including a new church, city hall, parliament, university, opera, and a theater. It was also crossed by a vast cultural forum formed by a curvilinear extension to the Hofburg Palace (two extensions were planned) and a pair of museums designed by Gottfried Semper for natural history and art history. Remaining areas along the avenue were filled in with Parisian-style apartment buildings. Within a generation, the baroque city with its new avenues, planned neighborhoods, and mass-transit routes had become another paradigm of European modernity.

What happened next, however, was not unexpected for a city shortly to become famous for its psychiatry. In 1889, the architect Camillo Sitte published his book, *City Planning According to Artistic Principles*, which not only challenged the Parisian model but drew upon Aristotle's remark that "a city must be so designed as to make its people at once secure *and happy*."[2] Sitte broached the issue of living in a city from both a physiological and psychological perspective. One issue he raised was the newly minted condition of agoraphobia, the "yawning emptiness and oppressive ennui" experienced by the new migrants to the metropolis, accustomed to the cozy scale of village life.[3] This problem, Sitte argued, was not only the fault of "geometers" who lay down their tedious and mentally fatiguing avenues and open spaces, but also of planners who fail to heed the artful lessons of the past. The organic growth of gently curving streets and well-scaled, enclosed town squares were important lessons to be learned, Sitte felt, because they reflected the trusted intuition of their original builders. Yet Sitte was no simple romantic. He provided readers with dozens of classical, medieval, and Renaissance examples of successful urban squares, which should be studied for the ideas that lay behind them:

> Modern living as well as modern building techniques no longer permit the faithful imitation of old townscapes, a fact which we cannot overlook without falling prey to barren fantasies. The exemplary creations of the old masters must remain alive with us in some other way than through slavish copying; only if we can determine in what the essentials of these creations consist, and if we can apply these meaningfully to modern conditions, will it be possible to harvest a new and flourishing crop from the apparently sterile soil.[4]

Semi-enclosed town squares of the past are appealing because "old planning was not conceived on the drafting board" but rather on the ground, ruled by the optical limits of the human eye.[5] Because the eye is the apex of a visual pyramid, he reasoned, the world around us unfolds in a concave manner, which is why enclosed urban space imparts to us a sense of comfort and pleasure. The wide avenues and isolated buildings of modern times bleed away this concavity and produce convexity, or a lack of spatial enclosure, destroying the relationship of human scale to the urban environment.[6] People, he insisted, prefer well-scaled urban squares and gently curving streets.

Sitte delved into other factors as well. In turning his attention to landscaping and gardens, for instance, he points out that there is another "psychological factor, rooted in the imagination" at play—the fact that

> the melancholic city dweller suffers from a partly imaginary, partly real sickness rooted in a longing or nostalgia for unfettered nature and its clean air. This ailment, which can be aggravated to the point of the loss of the work ethic, is best cured by the sight of greenery, by the presence of beloved Mother Nature.[7]

Olmsted, as did Alphand in Paris, had earlier made a similar case in arguing on behalf of urban "lungs," but Sitte's solutions are different. He eschews the tree-lined boulevard for a number of reasons, both practical and visual, and he turns instead to small-scale solutions: flowers on balconies, rose gardens, the introduction of water into landscapes, and he waxes most eloquently on "the great significance of the *poetic*, the imaginative, or, as it is understood in our day, the *picturesque* in town planning."[8] This calls for a greater visual variety in the urban environment, but also for replacing the tree-lined boulevards with smaller urban parks, and in a few cases the use of a "single tree" well situated within a built area. In his words, "the imagination does not need massive stimuli, but only a touch or hint."[9] Sitte's preferred solution is, however, the enclosed garden or the paradise, bounded not by open fences but by solid walls. The open urban park, particularly at a small scale, can be infested with the dust and dirt of the city and is exposed to the wind, the rattling of carriages, odors, and other distractions. The enclosed courtyard or semi-private garden, however, shields one from these intrusions: "Here one is isolated from the big city and its clamor. One lives as in the country, and all around the court in suites and rooms are places of intellectual pursuit and the workshops of artisans, provided with good light, sunshine, and a view into the green."[10]

Although Sitte's book would cause considerable stir within city-planning circles across the continent, he would have little success in Vienna. His nemesis was Otto Wagner, city planner and professor of architecture at the Vienna Academy of Fine Art, who in 1896 published his highly influential book *Modern Architecture*. He could not have been more Parisian in his tastes, having once remarked—against one writer recounting the pleasure of Alpine hikes—that his ideal stroll would be from the Place de la Concorde to the top of the Champs-Élysées. His view of the city was similarly straightforward: "our realism, our traffic, and modern technology imperatively demand the straight line."[11] Against those who take the "painterly" approach of Sitte, he argued, that if they

> would only open their eyes they would soon be convinced that the straight, clean, practical street leading up to our destination in the shortest possible time—occasionally interrupted by monumental buildings, appropriately designed squares, beautiful and meaningful perspectives, parks, etc.—is also the most beautiful.[12]

Wagner's paper "The Development of the Great City" was written for a conference held at Columbia University in 1911.[13] It was presented, fittingly, alongside Daniel Burnham and Edward Bennett's grand plan for Chicago.

The remaking of Paris had certainly aroused the imagination of Burnham. He made this point in directing the World's Columbian Exposition of 1893, when he invited five Beaux-Arts-trained American architects to design the main pavilions. They were built along the central spine of the main canal, with two separate side canals. Burnham, as we have seen, was also a member of the McMillan Commission, which in 1902 attempted to re-deploy parts of L'Enfant's original design for Washington, DC. Over the next few years, Burnham and Bennett also prepared Paris-inspired proposals for Cleveland, San Francisco, and Manila, before producing their masterplan for the city of Chicago in 1909. The folio itself is a work of art, with its large and stunning bird's-eye perspectives of the future city by Jules Guérin. The authors preface their remarks with a history of city planning, which included the plans for Paris, Vienna, and Washington. Chicago, as the authors begin their proposal,

> is now facing the momentous fact that fifty years hence, when the children of to-day are at the height of their power and influence, the city will be larger than London; that is, larger than any existing city. Not even an approximate estimate can be ventured as to just how many millions the city will then contain.[14]

The two authors proposed a continuous belt of green parks along the shore of Lake Michigan, and four major parks surrounding the city, connected with radial green parkways. At the city's center is a towering city hall set within a large plaza, roughly in the location where today two freeways come together and dump thousands of suburbanites into the city each morning. In Burnham and Bennett's plan, however, there was no such profanity. Congress Street, leading from city hall to Lake Michigan, is a formal dual-lane boulevard culminating with Grant Park fronting Michigan Avenue, east of which is a parklike setting with a library, science museum, and art museum. The lake, with its broad gardens, piers, marinas, and pleasure boats, becomes the thoroughly appealing *pièce de resistance*. The modern city unfolds as hundreds upon hundreds of fashionably attired strollers out and about, occasionally parting a path for a horse-drawn carriage or that newfangled contraption of the automobile. Yet the imagery at the same time seems mislaid or eccentric. This is not the Chicago of slaughterhouses or the shantytowns that Sullivan once referred to as the "backyards of urgent commerce."[15] This is a cultural rendering of what Thorstein Veblen had portrayed five years earlier as

ILLUSTRATION 10.2   Jule Guérin, Michigan Avenue Looking towards the South. The focal point of the rendering is a facsimile of Charles Garnier's Paris Opera.

Source: From Daniel Burnham and Edward Bennett, *Plan of Chicago* (Chicago: The Commercial Club, 1909), Plate CXVIII.

the society of the "leisure class." It is Paris's seventh or eighth arrondissement magically transported to the shores of Lake Michigan without the fiery history of the Bastille or the bohemian charm of Montmartre. It is not paradisiacal but utopian in its alienating largesse. The park that Burnham envisioned along the lake, however, was built and remains today the city's greatest strength.

Garden Cities

The nineteenth century alternative to the "great city," with its massive scale, arteries, and *flâneurs* was the garden city or bucolic suburb, such as Olmstead had envisioned for Riverside. There were also a few American predecessors, among them Llewellyn Park, New Jersey (1853), Lake Forest, Illinois (1857), and Ridley Park and Short Hills, New Jersey (1872, 1877). Frederick Olmsted Jr., who laid out the garden suburb of Forest Hills in Queens in 1909, portrayed it as ideal for "people of moderate income and good taste"—who, in contrast to the "the monotony of endless straight, wind-swept thoroughfares which represent the New York conception of streets" will prefer narrower, curvilinear streets allowing "garden-like neighborhoods, each having its own distinctive character."[16]

In urban histories, however, the garden city is synonymous with the ideas of the Englishman Ebenezer Howard. The modest thinker was born in London in mid-century and, after some teenage training as a shorthand clerk, he emigrated to the United States, where he took up farming in Nebraska. This was before he realized that he lacked a green thumb. He then migrated to Chicago, where, in the 1870s, he worked as a reporter for the courts and press. He certainly studied the communities of Riverside and Lake Forest before he moved back to England. He was also familiar with Morris and his take on paradise, to which he was sympathetic. Yet perhaps the individual with whom he was most in tune was Ruskin, who, in *Sesame and Lilies*, had expressed his vision of the idyllic city:

> no festering and wretched suburb anywhere, but clean and busy street within, and the open country without, with a belt of beautiful garden and orchard round the walls, so that from any part of the city perfectly fresh air and grass, and sight of far horizon, might be reachable in a few minutes' walk.[17]

Howard used a longer version of this passage as an epigraph to his first chapter.

Howard's book, *To-Morrow: A Peaceful Path to Real Reform*, appeared in 1898. Four years later he issued a second edition retitled *Garden Cities of To-Morrow*. For someone without a planning background, he nevertheless succeeded in sparking a revolution in urban thinking that still resonates across the globe today. The book is not a planning primer but is rooted in his apolitical paradisiacal desire to reform society by relieving overcrowded cities and providing the alternative of bucolic, self-sufficient communities on commonly owned land surrounded by greenbelts. He provides no drawings but very effective diagrams. The stellar concept is his analysis of the city and country, and their features. The city provides jobs, social opportunities, and places of amusement, but it also is plagued with high rents, slums, long working hours, unemployment, foul air, and the expense of maintaining a costly infrastructure. The countryside provides fresh air, sunshine, the beauty of forests and meadows, and low rents, but it also offers little employment outside of agriculture, few social opportunities, and no amusements. The garden city is the implementation of all of these positive features and the elimination of all of the negative ones.

Howard supplies a bounty of administrative details to inform his plan, quite simply "the spontaneous movement of the people from our crowded cities to the bosom of our kindly mother earth, at once the source of life, of happiness, of wealth, and of power."[18] The social reformation begins with a like-minded coalition of trustees or shareholders willing to lease or purchase 6,000 acres of land, of which 1,000 acres will be settled by 32,000 residents. The schematic or conceptual plan of

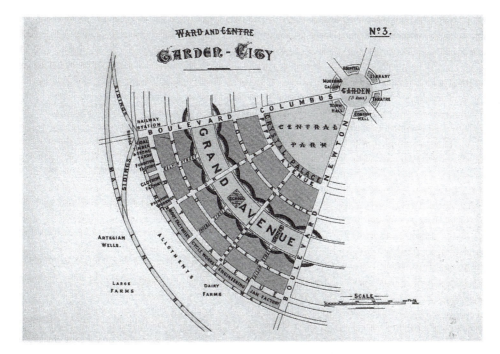

ILLUSTRATION 10.3   Diagram 3, from Ebenezer Howard, *To-morrow: A Peaceful Path to Real Reform* (London: Swan Sonnenschein & Co., 1898).

the garden city is circular, with rings of different activities. At the heart is a five-acre garden or village green surrounded by the town hall, museum, hospital, library, theater, and concert hall. These facilities are rimmed, in turn, by another 135-acre central park for recreational use. The next layer is the crystal palace, a glass arcade used for places of business and assembly, as well as other amusements such as winter gardens. Surrounding it are the residential neighborhoods with some lots larger than others, some sharing common gardens and kitchens. The next tier continuing outward is Grand Avenue, a wide greenbelt on which are located the schools, churches, and other local facilities. Along the outermost ring are the places of employment. The distance from the outer ring to the cultural core of the city is a mere 600 yards, and the other 5,000 acres surrounding the city remain as rural landscapes with farms, wildlife areas, cemeteries, and occasional philanthropic institutions such as convalescent homes or schools for the blind. Howard also envisioned a larger constellation of garden cities joined by rail lines and canals, together housing 250,000 people. He was scrupulous about each and every business detail, including the makeup of the municipal boards and the precise cost or savings of each of the utilities.

Howard's idea could not have been better fitted with the time. A number of factory towns were being built around the turn of the century in the earlier tradition of Robert Owen. In 1888, the Lever Brothers built Port Sunlight across the river from Liverpool to support their soap manufacturing works. The garden town of Bournville, now a part of the city of Birmingham, was larger and more detailed in its planning. It was built in 1895 by George Cadbury for workers of his nearby chocolate factory, and its streets were designed for rowhouses, duplexes, and single houses, all with gardens in front and rear. A park along The Bourn still today weaves its way west through the community, leading down to a heath with a pond. Ample recreational and green areas are also scattered among the housing estates, a picturesque town with many Edenic qualities.

In 1902, Barry Parker and Raymond Unwin teamed up to design the small community of New Eastwick, outside of York, which integrated the idea of a garden suburb within the stylistic norms of the Arts and Crafts movement. Ranks of houses were proposed, owing much to the relaxed style made popular by Baillie Scott and Charles Voysey. Parker and Unwin's design soon caught the attention of Howard, who a year earlier had formed the Garden City Association with interested parties. They were in the process of purchasing 3,800 acres of land with the idea of creating the first Garden City at Letchworth, thirty-five miles north of London. As Unwin later explained his design strategy, he was much enamored with the "German school of town planners," who—following Sitte—were drawing upon the informality of medieval cities such as Rothenburg and Bruges.[19] This may be true, but at the same time the designers fitted Letchworth with a strong axial spine and a series of diagonals converging at the main municipal square at the center. Areas for housing, commercial, industrial, and recreation were zoned separately, a decision that would eventually turn the town over to the automobile. Notwithstanding, Letchworth has some very appealing aspects. A larger North Common, with seventy acres of woodlands, was preserved north of the rail line. The town's main recreational area, Howard Park, lies adjacent to the commercial quarter, and with its serpentine pond and children's splashing pool, it remains a much-valued feature of the town. Unwin in fact stressed the importance of water, not only because it injects "life, light, and colour" into parks but also because

> the pond can be so placed that the rosy hues of the sunset will be reflected in the water, and be seen from different streets or groups of houses as the sun changes its setting point with the changing seasons, a natural decoration of the greatest beauty will be provided.[20]

Another strength of Letchworth, aside from the town's generally green character, is its housing, the earliest of which were designed by Parker and Unwin in a simple Arts-and-Crafts style. Abundant open green areas were also designed throughout the straight and curved residential streets.

The town, however, proved to be undercapitalized and fell short of its projected growth in its early years. The start of World War I also played heavily into the delay. Howard lived in the town until 1920, when he moved to the second garden city of Welwyn, fifteen miles to the south. The beaux-arts or formal spine of Louis de Soissons's master plan—double streets separated by double rows of trees and a central green—again seems out of character with the idea of an informal garden community, and it also creates unusable open space and expands the walking distances well beyond what Howard had envisioned. A tram was planned to alleviate this problem, but it never materialized. A railway line still divides the city into western and eastern sectors, which also became problematic. The better neighborhoods formed on one side, whereas parts of the working-class communities on the other were cut off from the commercial center by the industrial zone.

Welwyn, like its sister city, was slow in developing, and the town had only a third of its projected residents by 1938. One failing of both towns was the fact that the anticipated industrial base did not develop as planned, and these sectors went through some rough building patches in the middle decades of the twentieth century with the blight of modern factory design. With the lack of a strong industrial base, most residents today commute to work in London or the surrounding areas. In effect, the two cities had morphed into garden suburbs.

The unsurprising key to a garden city or suburb is the enchantment of its location, and if one is seeking to create such a paradise, one can do no worse than to find a historic tract of land already approximating the ideal of Elysium. And in the fair land of Britain, few ancient landscapes can compete with Hampstead Heath. Its vast woodlands, ponds, and grasslands sit astride a sandy ridge that, from a hill at the south end, affords a legally protected view over London. The grounds are also inculcated with history. It is rumored that a tumulus near the Men's Bathing Pond (there is also a Ladies' Bathing Pond and a Mixed Bathing Pond) is the burial site of Queen Boudica and her 10,000 Celtic warriors who were defeated by the Romans in AD 61. The ruler Ethelred, "the Unready," gifted five hides of "Hemstede" to a servant in 986, and both the friars at Westminster Abbey and the Crown at times owned parts of the heath; the latter used it as a hunting preserve. In the sixteenth and seventeenth centuries the heath was known for its exotic herbs and healthy air, as parts were devolving into private hands. Even then, it did not suffer. The heath still retains one of Britain's finest architectural gems, the stately Kenwood House designed by the incomparable Robert Adam. It was only natural, then, that the communities around the heath began attracting artists and writers, those known for possessing or pursuing the paradisiacal instinct.

Yet one particular community around the heath stands out. In 1896, the London transit authority, in forecasting the path of suburban development northward, considered extending its municipal "black line" one station north of its former terminus at Hampstead. The proposed station at Golders Green was met with joy from real estate developers but with alarm from Dame Henrietta Barnett, the wife of Canon Samuel Barnett, the vicar of St. Jude's, Whitechapel. The East London parish was a poor one and Henrietta had seen firsthand the poverty and lamentable living conditions of the inner city. Equally important, she and her husband owned a weekend home somewhere east of Eden, overlooking Hampstead Heath. She successfully orchestrated a campaign to halt the construction of the station temporarily, and over the next several years (by personally writing 13,000 letters) she managed a campaign to create the Hampstead Garden Suburb Trust to purchase land east and north of the proposed station, including eighty acres for the extension of the heath northward. Unwin was hired to prepare a low-density plan, one that would preserve the existing forested areas, avoid the uniformity of row houses, respect each renter's "outlook," and separate the lots with hedgerows rather than fences. A great many other details were written into the covenants. By a special Act of Parliament, the interior roads were limited in width—20 feet for those not exceeding 500 feet in length. These alleys reduced the areas consumed by roads from 40 percent to 17 percent of the land, and still today their narrowness represses the desire to own an automobile. Houses were limited to an average of eight per acre, allowing larger areas for gardens. Many houses were formed around a common green, and the corners of some street intersections were planted with shrubs and trees. One of the stated objectives of the covenants was to bring about "the intermingling of the different classes" by providing housing for workers, partially subsidized by the rents of wealthier home owners.[21]

Barnett's efforts and Unwin's design were eminently successful, and over the next several years the trust continued to purchase land. By 1914, it had acquired a sizable portion for later development, and by 1936 the suburb had approached much of its present level of development. In 1969, the entire suburb, with its heath extension and forested Big Wood Nature Reserve, was designated a "conservation area" by special parliamentary legislation. Today, this quiet community with its boundary roads lined with fashionable shops of every kind, like the town of Hampstead itself, is one of the more affluent areas of London. This success also reveals one of the fundamental laws of paradise design. All people understand the difference between idyllic environments and acceptable or substandard environments. However much one might try to tip the scales in the interest of economic fairness, people with means will drive up real estate prices in order to live within the gates of Eden. The only solution to this problem, it would seem, is to create more Edens, preferably each with its own heath.

Eurythmic Cities

Historians of the modern city generally begin a discussion of Barcelona by considering Idelfonso Certá's city plan of 1858. Over the previous four years, in a state of political unrest, the old walls of Europe's densest city came down and, after a failed competition and some backroom discussion, Certá's plan for Barcelona was accepted. It was a legitimate effort to create a more attractive city, aided by his knowledge of Haussmann's work in Paris and infused as well with Saint-Simonian fervor. Six grand avenues intersected at a central square of the now ungirdled city, street corners were chamfered to create social and commercial areas, and the square blocks used for housing were to be built only on two sides of the squares and thereby allow ample spaces for shops, gardens, parks, and public spaces. Certá was insightful, as the success of his later book *General Theory of Urbanization* (1867) suggests. The only issue is that, although much of the street plan was adopted, subtle but significant changes came to the city over the following century. The running gardens connecting blocks gave way to interior courtyards, and the height of buildings doubled in size. This is not to say that the city is not among Europe's most charming. Its native beauty, however, lies less with the plan and more with the legacy of the city's most extraordinary resident architect—Antonio Gaudi. To every visitor to the Catalonian capital, his efforts are inseparable from the image of the city.

Consider the sinuous and anthropomorphic forms of the Casa Battló, started in 1906. The blue-green tile and stucco facade reads like a coral reef in a shallow bay, and the osteal forms of the first two stories, together with the wraparound Venetian carnival masks fronting the balconies above, give even the most distracted passersby a reason to pause. The variegated roof tiles osculate from a clayey red to powder blue before concluding in turquoise. Meanwhile, the overall roof form takes the outline of a scaly dragon, and its circular turret with its four-square cross at one end has been interpreted as the spear of St. George (the patron saint of Barcelona) slaying the loathsome creature—a metaphor for Catalonian independence.

ILLUSTRATION 10.4   Antonio Gaudi, Casa Battló, Barcelona.

Source: Photo by ChristianSchd. Wikimedia CC BY-SA 3.0.

The undulating corner facade of the Casa Milà, designed a few years later and known locally as the *La Pedrera* or "the stone quarry," presents a more benign appearance with its thirty-two swelling balconies and leaf-like balustrades worked into twisted wrought-iron forms. Yet behind the facade are some of the more variegated and spectacularly conceived interiors to be found anywhere on earth, all exquisitely handcrafted. The two interior courtyards are treated figuratively and literally as gardens, and the anthropomorphic collection of chimneys on the roof is often referred as the "Garden of the Warriors," designed no doubt to keep evil spirits at bay.

And then, of course, there is Gaudi's most famous building in the city, the Sagrada Familia or Roman Catholic Basilica, which, with its conical towers soaring 300 feet into heaven, defies any verbal description. It is perhaps the grandest work of art and architecture ever attempted in modern times. Gaudi began the design in 1883, and it remained with him for the rest of his life. He planned a total of eighteen spires or towers, representing the twelve apostles, the four evangelists, Mary and Jesus. Only the first four of the Nativity Porch were nearing completion at the time of his death, but with the resumption of work in recent years, the genius of the design is beginning to material-ize in an empyreal fashion. The interior, allegorically, is a spiritualized forest of arborescent columns of different heights, diameters, and materials (porphyry, basalt, granite), branching at the top into shallow hyperbolic vaults—columns of stunning polymorphic character and height. The colorful

ILLUSTRATION 10.5 Interior nave of the Sagrada Familia.

Source: Photo by Math Pinto. Wikimedia CC BY 3.0.

light admitted in the nave, side aisles, and skylights is absolutely enchanting in its overall effects. The exterior is no less transcendent. The glacial forms of the Nativity Porch, dedicated to the allegories of faith, hope, and charity, compose a veritable botanical manual. Among its garden elements, scholars have identified Egyptian papyrus, Indian lotus flowers, water lilies, violets, passion flowers, pickle weed, Surinam purslane, bulrush, thistle, aloe, false arcadia, a Judas tree, hydrangea, wisteria, palms, alfalfa, olive, peach, cherry, and apple trees.[22] At the pinnacle of the central porch, between twin towers, is a Greek cypress serving as the Tree of Life. The Garden of Eden has never been so well portrayed in lithic forms.

One place to admire the Sagrada Familia in Barcelona is from the terrace and undulating glazed bench of Park Güell, another surreal creation of Gaudi that actually began as a design for a garden suburb. It was commissioned by Eusebi Güell, a wealthy textile manufacturer and friend of Gaudi. Because of his trade, Güell often traveled to England, where he became familiar with the ideas of Ruskin and Morris. In 1899 he purchased thirty-seven acres of steep hillside west of the city. The site was known as *Montanya Pelada*, or "peeled mountain," because it had been used for ore mining and largely deforested. Gaudí first introduced oaks, pines, mimosas, eucalyptus, and palm trees. The site's very steep slope also made roadways very difficult and expensive. With the engineering assistance of Joan Rubiò, Gaudí laid out the cutback roads, large parts of which were supported on viaducts or bridge-like structures supported by a continuous linear vault of rough stone, open on one side and supported by inclined piers. The ordinance that Gaudí and the owner drafted restricted all lots and roadways to 50 percent of the land, and buyers could build on no more than one-sixth of their land, with the rest to be cultivated as gardens. No trees could be cut, and existing views of neighbors had to be preserved. Integrated within the roadway vaults were pedestrian paths with stairs to the next level.

Gaudí's assistant, Francisco Berengeur, built a model home, and Gaudí designed the rubblework administrative center and a caretaker's lodge at the entrance. Both, with their undulating, richly patterned tile roofs sprouting mushrooms, are seemingly taken from a child's fairytale book. Between the two houses is a monumental staircase with three gardens set within it. The stairs lead to a large structure that was intended to be a hypostyle hall, an open-air community market, but today it exists simply as a concrete structure with a roof supported—astoundingly—on eighty-six Doric columns. The underside of the slab is not flat but takes the form of a honeycomb pattern, giving it spatial depth. Gaudi conceived the top of the hall as the main public square, and it was originally planned to have a Greek theater on the innermost side. Yet, then, World War I intervened. In 1914 only two of the proposed sixty lots had been sold, making the community a colossal economic failure. In 1923, the entire hillside was sold to the city as a public park, and today Parc Güell has become a UNESCO World Heritage Site, whose "show home" is the Gaudí Museum. The gardens are visited daily by thousands, who come to see the creative hand of one of the more remarkable artistic talents of modern times.

If Europe had a pretender to Parc Güell at the start of the new century, it would have to be the Mathildenhöhe, or the Darmstadt Artist Colony. It is, to be sure, a somewhat pretentious attempt by the Grand Duke of Hesse, Ernest Ludwig, to build a shrine to Jugendstil or Art Nouveau consciousness, but the site of the colony on the scenic Mathildenhöhe overlooking the city could not have been better chosen. Fueled with Nietzschean fervor, the colony led to the building of a number of modestly successful houses, including the grand Exhibition Hall and the colossus of the "Wedding Tower," a celebratory landmark to the Grand Duke's marriage to Princess Eleonore in 1905. Both the tower and the exhibition building were designed by Joseph Maria Olbrich, the unapologetic Austrian secessionist. Nevertheless, the swaggering aura of a colony built exclusively for artists, albeit with many pleasing aspects, cannot come close to matching Germany's most idyllic community and arguably the most overlooked paradisiacal experiment of the early twentieth century: the garden city of Hellerau. The experiment ended cruelly with an assassin's bullet in 1914.

Many factors played into Hellerau's conception: the difficult unification of Germany in 1871, a small but growing middle class, and the need for a historically fragmented country to define a unifying culture and make that difficult passage to an industrial society. The idea of a garden city was also not alien to a country still largely rural, and the British Arts and Crafts movement had many followers in Germany. Yet Hellerau also brought a unique twist to the idea of a garden city, which is the manner in which it was conceived. Underpinning it was a superb university system, which over the course of the nineteenth century had been conducting pioneering research in the areas of human physiology, psychology, and perception. Johann Friedrich Herbart, Hermann Helmholtz, Gustav Fechner, and Wilhelm Wundt had prepared the groundwork, and toward the end of the century this new knowledge was being shaped into aesthetic theories.

Robert Vischer, in drawing upon the philosophical discourse of his father Friedrich Theodor, published a doctoral dissertation in 1873 in which he coined the word *Einfühlung*, or "feeling-into," translated into English near the start of the twentieth century as "empathy." Vischer was seeking to explain how the process of artistic perception works. We may approach the visual arts through optical stimulation, he reasoned, but this visual experience also has an emotional and visceral underlayment engaging multiple biological systems. Every artistic experience therefore involves an "intensification of sensuousness"; that is, "a person harmoniously feeling oneself into a kindred object or space, or as humanity objectifying itself in harmonious forms."[23] Thus our conceptual understanding of artistic forms is inherently physiological and emotional. We perceive the world not only with our eyes but as a fully embodied experience. Vischer's dissertation appeared one year prior to Wilhelm Wundt's pathbreaking *Principles of Physiological Psychology*.

The idea of a physiologically based empathy unleashed dozens of volumes in response, and in 1886 the art historian Heinrich Wölfflin gave it a slightly different interpretation with his doctoral dissertation, "Prolegomena to a Psychology of Architecture." He characterized the embodied experience of a building as a kind of vestibular *Formgefühl*, or "feeling-for-form," arising only "because we ourselves possess a body."[24] We animate forms because our optic nerves and the sensory area of the brain work sympathetically and in unison with our internal organs. Through our own body's sense of balance, for instance, we know the basic conditions of gravity, force, resistance, rhythm, and other corporeal experiences by internalizing them, and architectural forms become beautiful when they accord with "basic conditions of organic life."[25] Wölfflin's professorial German competitor in the art history world, August Schmarsow, characterized architecture with a similar argument but from a contrary viewpoint. He defined the essence of the architectural experience as a *Raumgefühl*, or "feeling-for-space." And this feeling, like Wölfflin's feeling-for-form, is similarly complex. Presaging our contemporary understanding of embodiment—spatial perception is experienced by "the residues of sensory experience to which the muscular sensations of our body, the sensitivity of our skin, and the structure of our body all contribute."[26] The discovery of mirror neurons or mirror systems in the 1990s effectively documented the correctness of these hypotheses, and Hellerau was a precocious attempt to create an artistic society through the training of the body.

The town was the creation of the entrepreneur, naturalist, and social reformer Karl Schmidt. Following the lead of William Morris, Schmidt founded the German Workshops for Handcrafted Art in Dresden in 1898, bringing together skilled craftsmen and designers to make high-quality furniture for Germany's emerging middle class. By 1906 his business had become so successful that he needed to consolidate his various workshops, and with this need came the idea of building a town to house workers. With a few other investors, he purchased a sizable tract of rolling, wooded land seven miles north of Dresden, and brought together three architects to design it. The town in its physical appearance was not unlike other garden cities. Curvilinear streets followed natural contours, and there was a modest town square. The scale of the town was eminently walkable, and the architectural quality of its housing was high, as one would expect from a town of cabinetmakers. Standards were drafted to improve natural light and ventilation, in-house laundries were mandated,

ILLUSTRATION 10.6 "A Plastic Exercise," a dance form.

Source: From M. E. Sadler (ed.), *The Eurhythmics of Jaques-Dalcroze* (Boston, MA: Small Maynard and Co., 1913).

and cooperatives were set up for food. Private gardens were strongly encouraged for food and pleasure, and the town itself was woven within an existing forest. In short, it was an Edenic endeavor with a view of Saxony's colorful Sandstone Mountains to the south. Yet, there was one other factor that would make this town unique.

One of the town's co-founders was a young and ambitious Wolf Dohrn, the son of a noted marine biologist with a keen interest in the arts. Moreover, he had just completed his dissertation under the noted psychologist Theodor Lipps, who had constructed a school of psychology built around Vischer's notion of *Einfühlung*, or the way we feel our way into or connect with our built environments. Dohrn's desire was somewhat simpler: to create a "German Olympus" or a place dedicated to fostering human happiness. The key was to create an educational system grounded in the arts, and to this end he contracted with the Swiss musicologist Émile Jaques-Dalcroze in 1909 to inaugurate the Institute of Eurythmics. Here children would be trained in music and dance routines intended to bring into harmony one's emotional, nervous, and motor systems. Dohrn had a theater and campus built in 1911 to house both teachers and visiting students, where children and adults would master an instrument and receive this rhythmic bodily training. "For the body," as Dalcroze once noted, "can become a marvellous instrument of beauty and harmony when it vibrates in tune with artistic imagination and collaborates with creative thought."[27]

What happened over the next few years was one of the great cultural spectacles of the twentieth century.[28] A new concept of a theater, one mingling the audience and dance performers, was designed by Adolphe Appia. It opened for the summer music festival of 1912 to an audience of over 4,000 people. A repeat performance of Christoph Gluck's *Orpheus and Eurydice* in the following year attracted more than 5,000 visitors. In 1913, the year the musical hall and dormitories were fully operational, 495 musicians, young and old, were in residence at the institute, but what is most astounding were the artists and intellectuals who made their way to this relatively remote

Saxon city to see this social and cultural experiment in person—among them Ebenezer Howard, Martin Buber, George Bernard Shaw, Max Reinhardt, Serge Diaghilev, Thomas Mann, Stefan Zweig, Oskar Kokoshka, Rainer Maria Rilke, Emil Nolde, Hugo Ball, Heinrich Wölfflin, Max Klinger, Wilhelm Wörringer, Julius Meier-Graefe, Franz Kafka, and Upton Sinclair. Architects and their spouses were similarly well represented. Alma Mahler, widow of the composer Gustav Mahler and future wife of Walter Gropius, visited Hellerau, while Ada Bruhn, the future wife of Mies van der Rohe, was a student in the program. Perhaps the most curious visitor, however, was Charles-Édouard Jeanneret, who had yet to adopt the pseudonym Le Corbusier. He visited the town on four occasions, in part because his brother (by his own admission, his mother's favorite child) was a musical instructor at the institute. Dalcroze's elaborate eurythmic dance performances, tucked into a town situated in the serene and green Saxon hillside, had captured the world's attention. In retrospect, the town of Hellerau perhaps represented the closest the twentieth century came to creating an earthly paradise through its many dimensions. Yet this most remarkable experiment came to an abrupt end in the autumn of 1914 with a few bullets discharged from a gun in Sarajevo. World wars and more than three decades of death and turmoil would follow, and the noble experiment was soon forgotten under the ponderous weight of human misery.

Capital Cities

It has been said on occasion that historians are captive to the whims of the present, and if we look at the plans of three cities in the years leading up to World War I, in light of their earlier assessments, it is hard to dispute this fact. Let us briefly consider Tony Garnier's *La Cité industrielle*. It has been generously praised by many historians as a socialist "utopia" or harbinger of modernity, largely because of its exclusive use of reinforced concrete. Yet it was an academic exercise started by a Beaux-Arts student at the French Academy in Rome in the late 1890s, and the idea was to

ILLUSTRATION 10.7   Tony Garnier, "Terrace over the Valley," *Une Cité Industrielle* (1918).

Source: Museum of Fine Arts of Lyon. Wikimedia CC BY-SA 4.0. Public domain.

design, on paper, a regional capital situated in a mountainous Rhone River valley—politically informed by the ideas of Fourier, Saint-Simon, and Émile Zola. The exquisite drawings prepared by Garnier indeed have a striking visual appeal, but its importance for this study has little to do with its politics, materials, or methods of production. It is of interest because, as Dora Wiebenson has suggested, it was a pedagogical effort to design a city based on the ancient city of Pergamon, a city on the citadel with the industrial factories pushed into the valley below it.[29] If Pergamon had a gymnasium, Garnier's upper city had a running track and athletic field, adjacent to the city baths. If Pergamon had its amphitheater, Garnier planned a massive assembly building, a lozenge-shaped open-air canopy seating 3,000 people, a theater, and smaller meeting rooms for political re-education. If Pergamon had its famed library, Garnier's city had its Temporary Exhibition Hall modeled on Pergamon's Altar of Zeus. And if Pergamon had a Temple of Asclepius below the town, the industrial city had its hospital or heliotherapeutic facility on a ridge above the elevated city. There is even an uplifting William Morris moment found in Garnier's industrial city. In the entablature of the Assembly Hall, Garnier cites a passage from Zola, which lyrically speaks of the day when technology and socialism has relieved humankind of all but the most noble of its labors:

> It was decided that the festivities should take place out-doors, near the town, in a great field where tall stacks of wheat should be erected to resemble the columns of a gigantic temple; these stacks shone like gold when the rays of the sun fell upon them. Far off the columns of stacks of grain stretched to the horizon, proving the inexhaustible fertility of the soil. There they sang, there they danced, in the sweet perfume of the ripened wheat, in the midst of that vast fertile plain, from which the work of men who had become reconciled drew bread enough to satisfy them abundantly.[30]

By contrast, the new capital city of New Delhi, whose foundational stone was laid in 1911 by King George V, emits no such romantic flights of imagination. It was designed as the new imperial capital of India, and its planner Edwin Lutyens, with the assistance of Herbert Baker, saw to it that it had all of the imperial trappings of British rule. Set upon the ridge above the Mughal city of Delhi, the Baroque plan, with radiating avenues and circles, is overwhelmed by the colossal central axis that begins with the Viceroy's House (today the Presidential Residence) and proceeds two miles east to the India Gate. To the west of the exceedingly large and domed Viceroy's House is a garden in the tradition of the Mughal emperors. Versailles could be set down within the vast city and appear mean by contrast. Indeed, Humayun's Tomb, built by Akbar the Great at the eastern edge of the city, appears little more than a backyard garden. There is nothing paradisiacal about New Delhi. It is in fact difficult to imagine any city plan more alien to its time, or to the political tremors about to quake.

There was, by contrast, another new capital planned during these very same years, one scarcely noted by urban historians in its day, but one arguably with paradisiacal aspirations. It is only in the last few decades that the Australian capital of Canberra has come to be appreciated for the beauty of its design. The Commonwealth of the new country was officially proclaimed on January 1, 1901, and the first issue was where to locate the capital. Sydney and Melbourne jockeyed for the prize, but, after deliberation, a political compromise was reached to locate the new capital in the intermediate Yass-Canberra region. In April 1911 an international competition was announced, and 137 entries were submitted. Yet, few of the well-known city planners participated, because both the Royal Institute of British Architects and the American Institute of Architects boycotted the competition because of the paltry prize money. This decision, as it turns out, opened the door to imaginative thinking. In May, the jury awarded the second prize to the town planner Eliel Saarinen, but first prize was given to a husband-and-wife team living in Chicago with no major planning experience. In a press release given to the *New York Times* after the announcement, Walter Burley Griffin and

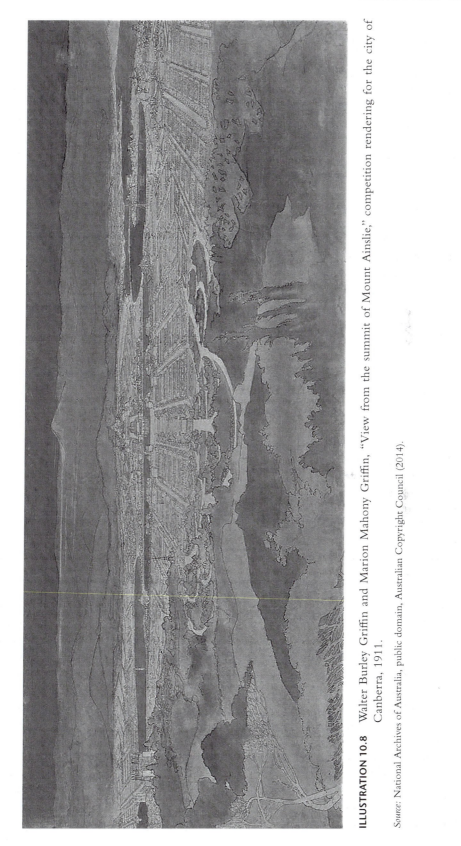

ILLUSTRATION 10.8   Walter Burley Griffin and Marion Mahony Griffin, "View from the summit of Mount Ainslie," competition rendering for the city of Canberra, 1911.

Source: National Archives of Australia, public domain, Australian Copyright Council (2014).

Marion Mahony Griffin promised to build "a city not like any other city in the world," and they actually set out to do it.[31] The dramatic watercolor presentation drawings, largely by the hand of Marion, would certainly have impressed the jury. Some were eight feet by thirty feet in dimension.

The Americans were little known outside of Chicago but were scarcely short of talent. Marion, older than her husband by five years, was the first employee hired by Frank Lloyd Wright in 1895, one year after she had received a degree in architecture from the Massachusetts Institute of Technology. Hers was the artistic hand behind several of the renderings of Wright's designs that found their way into the *Wasmuth Portfolio* of 1910, which brought him international fame. When Wright, a year earlier, decided to leave Chicago for Italy, he offered Marion the charge of the Oak Park studio, but she declined. Walter was a graduate of the University of Illinois in Urbana-Champaign, and in 1901 he also went to work for Wright. After a dispute with his boss regarding his office responsibilities, he quit in 1906 and started his own practice. Marion joined him in marriage and design partnership in 1911. The newlyweds also had two other things in common. Both were descended from the Emersonian Unitarian tradition, and Walter, in particular, was deeply impressed by the transcendental thread that wove its way through Thoreau and Whitman and into the lyrical soul of Sullivan. The second thing was that both had a deep respect for nature; both were informed botanists and master landscape designers. Walter, in Wright's office, had been in charge of all landscape designs, in part because he and Wright shared the same high regard for the legacy of Olmsted. Both assets were brought to Australia in 1913, when the two made their move halfway around the world.

It was their sensitivity to the features of the Canberra landscape that elevated their design above all others, in a way similar to how the river and the topography influenced L'Enfant's plan for Washington. The site possessed the sloping shape of a bowl, with Mount Bimberi fifteen miles to the south and the smaller yet dominant Mount Ainslie just to the north of the proposed city. A river ran through the middle of the capital, which the Griffins transformed into a series of natural and curvilinear basins or lakes, embellished with generous areas given to parks. The main north–south axis—Prospect Parkway—aligned with the two topological peaks of the mountains north and south, allowing nature itself to take the dominant hand in designing out the city. The Griffins described their site as an amphitheater with Mount Ainslie at their back: the land sloping down to the river and rising again on the southern shore. The downward incline was the auditorium, the river the arena, and the upward terraces on the opposite shore a stage with

> government structures sharply defined rising tier on tier to the culminating highest internal forested hill of the Capitol; and with Mugga Mugga, Red Hill, and the blue distant mountain ranges, sun reflecting, forming the back scene of the theatrical whole.[32]

Scarcely could a better description of their intentions have been written. The government buildings on the south side of the river unfolded in three terraces or tiers, with the Capitol occupying the highest, the Parliament house just below it, and other governmental agencies the bottom tier along the basin. In plan, the Capitol also formed the apex of the triangle extending to the opposite shore and two major squares at the triangle's apexes, the civic center and commercial center. Wrapped within the base of the triangle connecting these two centers, along the north shore of the basin, were cultural institutions, such as museums, galleries, the library, and the university—all set within a picturesque landscape or parkland. The main north-axis parkway positioned by the axis of the Capitol on the south side ramps up to the foot of Mount Ainslie with additional walking routes to the top. At the base, the Griffins placed a casino, viewing it as a major recreational area. Green areas and nature preserves were elsewhere planned in abundance, such as in the Yarralumla valley west of town, which offers "open areas for a maximum of outdoor life."[33] The planners also located five garden suburbs (each given indigenous floral names) along secondary axes, again governed by the topography. These would be, as they noted in their explanatory report, "characterized by society, clubs, and church assemblages for that large social group of special character peculiar to a national capital," and were laid out with both green spaces and separate pedestrian and vehicular paths.[34]

The biophilic plan was indeed inspired, which of course made it imperative for politicians and bureaucrats to intervene and fiddle with changes. Some argued that its plan, with its axes, was not true to the idea of a garden city; others argued that the abundant green areas made the city too diffuse or an overly green garden city. Even before the Griffins made their way to Australia, governmental authorities within the bureaucracy were preparing a counter plan, insidiously and unethically assembling a pastiche of ideas taken from several of the other entries. With the outbreak of war in 1914, the Griffins' designs even came to be seen somehow as "Germanic," although it is difficult to imagine any reason for this odd interpretation. Although Walter, shortly after his arrival a year earlier, was given the title "Federal Director of Design," the ten federal ministries overseeing his activities sought to undermine him at every turn, forcing him to resign his commission by 1920 with little if anything accomplished. Only in 1923 did the country actually commit to building the new capital, yet the only building constructed over the coming decades was a provisional Parliament, standing virtually alone in a barren landscape.

As it turns out, all of these delays helped to save the Griffins' plan by allowing time for its merits to be better understood. In 1957, almost a half-century after the competition, work began on transforming the river into a series of lakes, following the Griffins' proposed layout but contoured in a more natural way. As work on the capital proceeded over the coming decades, the locations of many of the major buildings shifted from their original spots, yet none for the worse. In 1978, a competition was held for a new Parliament to be placed on the site of the proposed Capitol. The winning scheme was a sensitive and imaginative design by the Philadelphia office of Mitchell/Giurgola, with the assistance of the landscape architect Peter Rolland. Much of the building was placed *under* a hyperbolic section of lawn rising toward the crown of the site with pyramidal skylights over the central Members Hall below. Carved out at the north end of its main axis is an elegantly detailed plaza or "Great Verandah" with a forecourt and pond, offering a spectacular view across the lakes and parkway to Mount Ainslie. Wide niches along the east and west sides allow the cascading of house and senate chambers down the hillside interspersed among "whispering trees and odorous blossoms"—to borrow a phrase from Morris. Cultural amenities also soon filled out the heart of the city within a parklike setting, and over the last few decades, in particular, Canberra has become a true garden city, standing above all other capitals in this regard.

One reason why city officials did not abandon the original plan was the simple fact that the Griffins did not leave Australia but subsequently built a successful practice there. They designed two other garden cities—Griffith and Leeton—and a number of garden suburbs. Perhaps their finest building complex was Newman College in Melbourne, planned in 1915. It remains an attraction today for its extensively detailed landscape of flowers and shrubs organized for the seasons, in the words of one historian "a botanical colour symphony" of oranges, scarlets, yellows, salmons, coppers, silvers, pinks, and blues.[35] On the outskirts of the city, they also designed the garden suburb of Eaglemont, which is known for the Griffins' effort to preserve the local red-gum trees, a species of eucalyptus native to Australia. As with Hampstead, artists and architects prefer to live there.

North of Sydney, where the Griffins also maintained an office, they planned the 640-acre community of Castlecrag on land they themselves purchased and largely controlled. It remains a scenic peninsula of hilltops extending into Middle Harbor on land that had been previously degraded. Once again, the Griffins separated the roadways from pedestrian paths, and organized the latter around a system of twenty-eight parks or natural areas with vistas—in addition to the green stretch of land preserved along the waterfront. Collectively, the works of the Griffins in the postwar years of the 1920s and early 1930s stand out as bucolic acts of design sanity amid the gathering storms.

Walter died in India in 1937 while designing a university there, and Marion shortly thereafter returned to Chicago in retirement. She died in 1971, unfortunately before the parliamentary capstone could be installed as the focal point of her urban design.

Cities of Glass

The great Impressionist Claude Monet was an avid botanist. He designed and constructed his extensive gardens in Giverny almost from scratch and even purchased additional land to build the water meadow with its Japanese bridge, which he filled with water lilies and variegated cultivars imported from South America and Egypt. At one point he needed seven gardeners to carry out his daily instructions. By everyone's account, Giverny today remains a national treasure and a true paradise, unparalleled in its visual passion and design.

In 1918, as World War I was coming to a close, Monet approached his friend, the Prime Minister Georges Clemenceau, and expressed his wish to offer something to the fallen French soldiers. He followed through by painting eight colossal panels of water lilies, more than 6 feet in height and nearly 100 feet in length. The murals were initially to be placed in the Rodin Museum, but Clemenceau determined that the old Orangery along the Seine, adjacent to the Garden of the Tuileries, could be retrofitted to accommodate them better. Monet proposed two large oval rooms to accommodate the paintings, and the recent renovation of the building today provides a stunning location to display these paradisiacal works under natural light.

Monet was not alone in his artistic endeavors during the war years, and perhaps it is unfair to place the works of this great master alongside the watercolor images of Bruno Taut, but it is also true that paradise can have many interpretations. Taut in 1918 was a relatively unknown architect. He had participated in the design of two garden cities prior to the war, but he is first noted in architectural histories for a small and quite unusual glass pavilion representing the Luxfer glass manufacturer at the German Werkbund Exhibition of 1914. What makes the Cologne glass pavilion interesting, aside from its unusual "asparagus dome," are the circumstances from which it sprang. During the pre-war years, Taut had formed a close friendship with the writer Paul Scheerbart, a surrealist or "astral phantast" as one historian has referred to him.[36] Scheerbart's first book was titled *Paradise: The Home of Art*, and in 1914 he collected thirty aphorisms under the title "Glass Architecture," which he dedicated to Taut. The opening aphorism reveals his intention:

> We live for the most part in enclosed spaces. They form the milieu out of which our culture has grown. Our culture is, to some extent, a product of our architecture. If we wish to raise our culture to a higher level, then we need to change our architecture, for better or worse. And this will only be possible if we open up the rooms in which we live. We can only do so by turning to glass architecture, which admits the light of the sun, moon, and stars, not with just a few windows but with as many glass walls as possible—with colored glass. The new milieu that we shall thereby create will bring with it a new culture.[37]

The idea that the design of the built environment can have a transformative effect on the culture in which we live was certainly a pertinent observation, but Taut's glass pavilion sought to magnify this point. The structure, whose construction was partly financed by Taut himself, was a late admission into the exhibition. The provisional building sat on a concrete base, and its thin square columns supported an entablature, which carried a few aphorisms by both Taut and Scheerbart, such as "building in brick only does us harm," and "colored glass destroys hatred." The walls between the columns were filled in with glass blocks, and the "polyhedral lamellar dome structure" was pieced together from rhomboid sheets of glass.[38] The interior, of which only a couple of black-and-white images survive, was quite unworldly in its conception. Nearly the entirely building was made of glass, and to the interior walls Taut attached colored glass panes and even translucent paintings. Under the dome of the upper cupola room, he placed a chromatic glass canopy with prisms to filter the spectral light, and beneath the canopy was a cascade of water to add movement and sound to the intended kaleidoscopic effects.

The Cologne Werkbund Exhibition is better known for the ideological showdown that pitted Muthesius (one of the architects at Hellerau) and Henry van de Velde (the director of two schools at Weimar). Van de Velde was backed in the debate by two young guns, Taut and Gropius. The latter at the last minute was given the design for a "model factory" at the Werkbund event, one that also would define early modernism's factory "aesthetic" of steel and glass. As it turned out, the debate over artistic freedom would soon prove moot by the tragedy at Sarajevo, and yet the war effectively allowed a passing of the guard, as it were. Muthesius, at the close of the Werkbund event, would retire to private practice. Van de Velde would be placed under house arrest as a Belgian citizen, and Gropius, who was drafted into military service and seriously wounded, would take over his two schools and rename them the Bauhaus. Taut declared himself a pacifist and sat out the conflict, all of which makes his alliance with Gropius seemingly an odd one.

With the war underway, Taut cloistered himself in his studio and assumed his new calling as an "imaginary architect"—envisioning not utopias but colorful chimeras in a number of note-book sketches. The results of these Trappist efforts were four published volumes, beginning in 1919. In the first of these, *Die Stadtkrone* or "Crown of a City," he argues for architects to move beyond functional considerations and address themselves to the inner life of people, which in his view revolves around play and sensory pleasure.[39] He insists that a city should be designed around a single dominant element or spiritual landmark, a point he makes with images of Mont Saint-Michel, the Athenian Acropolis, and Angkor Wat, among others. He then goes on to present a schematic design for a circular garden city, nearly five miles in diameter for 300,000 people. Large tracts of land along all four axes are carved out with swaths of forests, and even the repetitive rowhouses display large garden areas in their rear. The most curious feature of the city is the town core, which consists of a series of four buildings and parks stepping upward in a pyramidal fashion, culminating with the "Crystal House" at the center. The crown is nothing other than a non-functional yet "astonishingly beautiful room, reached from the theater and smaller community buildings by staircases and bridges."[40] Its "cosmic" mood is intended "to dissolve the spell of reality" and, as he further describes it,

> Here all tender and great feelings are awakened when the full sunlight spills into the tall space and splinters into endless fine reflections, or when the evening sun fills the upper vault with its crimson glow, enhancing the rich effervescence of the glass images and sculptural works.[41]

Again, "the soul of the artist transcends all that was formerly figurative and natural, and rediscovers the glow and the shimmer of colorful materials, metals, precious stones, and glass in every part of the room, evoked by the play of light and shadow."[42] Taut evokes Master Eckhart to justify his crystal room, but his sensibilities are closer to Abbot Suger's vision for the altar of Saint-Denis.

This theme is further developed in two illustrative works, *Alpine Architecture* and *The Dissolution of the Cities*. Neither has a printed essay. Instead, there is a handwritten text worked into his drawings, serving as a running theological commentary espousing both the religion of Mother Earth, and a protest against an era whose creative endeavors have been reduced to the inventions of battleships and nerve gas. In *Alpine Architecture*, thirty watercolor drawings are arranged in five parts, and the crystal house once again appears, but it is now transposed to an Alpine setting. In some drawings, the buildings take on a floral or crystalline configuration; in others, the

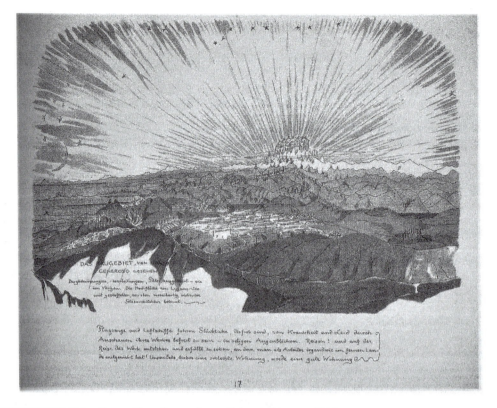

ILLUSTRATION 10.9   Bruno Taut, Image from *Alpine Architecture*, 1919.

Source: Wikimedia, public domain.

habitations rest peacefully within the wildflower fields at the foot of the mountains; in still others, peaks such as the Matterhorn and Monte Rosa are refashioned into new crystalline shapes or fitted with new meanings. This theme is reaffirmed in *The Dissolution of Cities*, where he rejects altogether the modern-day metropolis. The antibody for Taut is simply a return to the good earth and making peace with one another within the calming serenity of nature. Appended to the book are several printed excerpts analyzing the reasons for a now-defeated German society in the freefall of financial bankruptcy and political revolution. He draws at length on the writings of Peter Kropotkin, but there are shorter citations from Leo Tolstoy, Novalis, and Friedrich Nietzsche. Interestingly, Taut concludes the appendix with a single line from Emerson ("Cities give not the human senses room enough"), and then offers a large part of Walt Whitman's poem *Pioneers! O Pioneers!*

All of these efforts would have passed into history with little commentary, except that in 1921 Taut returned to the real world by accepting a post as the director of planning for the town of Magdeburg. He threw himself into the task, and one year later the British architectural critic Herman George Scheffauer, in surveying the accomplishments of this "constructive fantast and mystic of a higher order," reported that Taut

> took the grey old city and began to infuse it with architectural life, movement, and colour. He strove to break up the tone and contours of much immovable hideousness by hiding and scattering it under a veil of colour, as in his expressionistic surface treatment of house fronts and such things as cast-iron pillar-clocks in public squares.[43]

Protests greeted Taut's early efforts, but at least some of the antagonists were soon won over. Taut succeeded, as Scheffauer records, by returning

> to the grey industrial town the joy in colour that marked the peasant's house, the coloured facades of old patrician houses, the medieval church, the bright colour scheme for which Nature herself sets the keynote in the brilliant viridian patina with which she turns the copper roofs of old steeples and cupolas into purist jade.[44]

Taut made many more proposals for office buildings, a festival hall, green terracing of the banks of the flood-prone Elbe River, and a memorial to fallen soldiers, but the lack of political support from the city council eventually forced him to resign.

Yet he soon gained an important post in Berlin as an architect for the Berlin public housing cooperative, where he had the support of the city architect Martin Wagner. The American Dawes Plan of 1924 had stabilized the German currency and allowed the financing for reconstruction to begin. The following year, Taut began work on the so-called *Hufeisen Siedlung* or Horseshoe Estate in Berlin. The settlement has many garden-city touches, but its defining feature is a large apartment complex shaped like a horseshoe that folds around a "crystal" lake, with a central common area lined with block gardens—all viewed from the recessed balconies above. Surrounding this feature are row houses, some in plan tilted or gently curving away from the narrow streets to provide a sense of enclosure and green space. The houses are also given generous green areas in the rear. Another feature is his play with color. His pre-war project for a housing estate at Falkenberg was dubbed by critics as the "paint-box colony" for his bold use of color.[45] At Hufeisen, Taut continues to offer shades of blue, green, ochre, white, and red—all conceived both to humanize the projects and, psychologically, to give the owners a sense of gaiety. It was designed as a low- or modest-income project, but the quality of the work soon inflated demand. With its continuing success, the estate in 2008 was recognized as a UNESCO World Heritage Site.

No less successful was Taut's design for Berlin-Zehlendorf, generally referred to as *Onkel Toms Hütte*, or "Uncle Tom's Cabin," a name taken from a local tavern and Harriet Beecher Stowe's anti-slavery novel. Again, it is a richly chromatic work of row houses and apartments by an artistic hand, only here, unlike at Hufeisen, Taut and his landscaper laid out the estate within an existing pine forest and retained as many trees as possible. Taut, with the assistance of Hugo Häring and others, also gave the buildings both a modern design vocabulary and a greater articulation and individuality of form. Tuberculosis and influenza were the great scourges during these years, and much of the simplification of design (flat planes and large windows) was intended to open up the living space to as much light and air as possible while eliminating dust-collecting surfaces. In his design primer of 1924, *The New Dwelling: The Woman as Designer*, Taut called attention to these details as well as to the role that women were playing in housing design. Notable in this regard were the designs of Grete Schütte-Lihotsky, the architect of the "Frankfurt kitchen," and her American counterpart Christine Frederick, whose book, *Household Engineering*, was translated into German in 1920.

In retrospect, all of these efforts to create better housing for the middle classes would be overtaken by the Weissenhof Exhibition held in Stuttgart in 1927, whose design importance at the time has, in my view, been over-emphasized by historians. There is as well a somewhat tragic end to Taut at the height of his design powers. With the rise of the National Socialists, Taut, like many of his colleagues, would leave Germany—in his case, to work in the Soviet Union. Yet the relocation would prove disastrous for all Germans who ventured to labor under Josef Stalin. Unable to return to Germany with growing hostilities, Taut traveled to Japan and wrote three books on Japanese architecture and its culture, the artistic simplicity of which he felt offered important lessons for European modernists. Although he would practice for a few years in Turkey before his death in

1938, his creativity did not survive wartime circumstances. He was one of many of his generation to find the gates of paradise closed by the cataclysmic misalignment of the stars.

Notes

1. Adolphe Alphand, *Les Promenades des Paris* (Paris: J. Rothschild, 1867–73), 210.
2. Camillo Sitte, "City Planning According to Artistic Principles," in George R. Collins and Christiane Crasemann Collins (eds.), *Camillo Sitte: The Birth of Modern City Planning* (New York: Rizzoli, 1986), 141.
3. Ibid., 183.
4. Ibid., 249.
5. Ibid., 187–8.
6. Ibid., 271.
7. Ibid., 307.
8. Ibid., 309.
9. Ibid., 308.
10. Ibid., 317–18.
11. Otto Wagner, "Generalregulierungsplan," in Otto Antonia Graf (ed.), *Otto Wagner: Das Werk des Architekten* (Vienna: Hermann Böhlaus, 1985), I:94 (trans. mine).
12. Ibid., 93. He was responding to Karl Henrici's article "Langgeweilige und kurzweilige Strassen," *Deutsche Bauzeitung* 27:44 (June 1893), 271.
13. Otto Wagner, "The Development of a Great City," *The Architectural Record* 31 (May 1912), 485–500.
14. Daniel H. Burnham and Edward H. Bennett, *Plan of Chicago Prepared Under the Direction of The Commercial Club* (Chicago, IL: The Commercial Club, 1909), 33.
15. Louis Sullivan, *The Autobiography of an Idea* (New York: Dover Publications, 1956), 242.
16. Frederick Law Olmsted Jr. in Nelson P. Lewis, *The Planning of the Modern City* (New York: John Wiley & Sons, 1916), 311–12.
17. John Ruskin, *Sesame and Lilies*, in *The Works of John Ruskin* (London: George Allen, 1905), 18:183–4.
18. Ebenezer Howard, *Garden Cities of To-Morrow* (London: Swan Sonnenschein, 1902), 15.
19. Raymond Unwin, *Town Planning in Practice: An Introduction the Art of Designing Cities and Suburbs* (London: T. Fisher Unwin, 1909), 104.
20. Ibid., 287.
21. Ibid., 204.
22. Francesca Navés Viñas, "The Parks and Gardens of Gaudí," Maria Antonietta Crippa, in *Living Gaudí: The Architect's Complete Vision* (New York: Rizzoli, 2002), 71. She cites the earlier scholarship of Isidro Puig-Boada and Joan Bergós.
23. Robert Vischer, "On the Optical Sense of Form," in H. F. Mallgrave and Eleftherios Ikonomou (trans.), *Empathy, Form, and Space: Problems in German Aesthetics, 1873–1893* (Santa Monica, CA: Getty Center Publication Programs, 1994), 117.
24. Heinrich Wölfflin, "Prolegomena to a Psychology of Architecture," in *Empathy, Form, and Space* (note 23), 151.
25. Ibid., 160.
26. August Schmarsow, "The Essence of Architectural Creation," in *Empathy, Form, and Space* (note 23), 286.
27. M. E. Sadler, *The Eurhythmics of Jaques-Dalcroze*, trans. by P. & E. Ingham (Boston, MA: Small Maynard and Company, 1913), 21.
28. See Marco De Michelis and Vicki Bilenker, "Modernity and Reform: Heinrich Tessenow and the Institut Dalcroze at Hellerau," *Perspecta* 26 (1990), 143–70. Didem Ekici, "'The Laboratory of a New Humanity': The Concept of Type, Life Reform, and Modern Architecture in Hellerau Garden City, 1900–1914" (Ph.D. dissertation, University of Michigan, 2008).
29. See Dora Wiebenson, *Tony Garnier: The Cité Industrielle* (New York: George Braziller, 1969), 26.
30. Cited from Émile Zola, *Travail: Labor* (New York: Harper & Brothers, 1901), 485–6.
31. *New York Times*, May 24, 1912.
32. *The Federal Capital: Report Explanatory of the Preliminary General Plan* (Commonwealth of Australia, 1913), 2.
33. Ibid., 12.
34. Ibid.
35. See Christopher Vernon, "The Landscape Art of Walter Burley Griffin," in Anne Watson (ed.), *Beyond Architecture* (Sydney: Powerhouse Publishing, 1998), 97.
36. See Dennis Sharp, *Modern Architecture and Expressionism* (London: Longmans, 1966), 85.
37. Paul Scheerbart, "Glasarchitektur," *Projekt Gutenberg.de*. www.projekt-gutenberg.org/scheerba/glas/glas.html (trans. mine). Accessed June 2021.
38. See Marcus Breitschmid, "Glass House at Cologne: Bruno Taut," in David Leatherbarrow and Alexander Eisenschmidt (eds.), *Twentieth-Century Architecture* (Malden, MA: Wiley Blackwell, 2017), 61–72.

39. Bruno Taut, *Die Stadtkrone, with Contributions by Paul Scheerbart, Erich Baron, Adolf Behne* (Jena: Eugen Diederichs, 1919).

40. Ibid., 67.

41. Ibid., 67–8.

42. Ibid., 68–9.

43. Herman George Scheffauer, "Bruno Taut: A Visionary in Practice," *Architectural Review*, LII:313 (December 1922), 155.

44. Ibid., 156–7.

45. On Falkenberg and other aspects of Taut, see Rosemarie Haag Bletter, "Expressionism and the New Objectivity," *Art Journal* (September 1983), 108–20. See also her dissertation, "Bruno Taut and Paul Scheerbart's Vision: Utopian Aspects of German Expressionist Architecture" (PhD diss., Columbia University, 1973).

11

CHARTEUSE INTERMEZZOS

Silence and Civility

One would scarcely expect to find paradisiacal thinking between the years 1914 and 1945 for rather obvious reasons. Bare survival, not the tending of gardens, was the order of the day. Therefore, during these years we have to be content with smaller manifestations of the human creative instinct, and a fitting place to begin is with a cemetery—specifically, the Woodland Cemetery set within rolling hills a few miles south of Stockholm. The design competition of 1917 was won by two young architects, Erik Gunnar Asplund and Sigurd Lewerentz, and this hallowed and wooded preserve retains its silence today. Only a few minor roads lead into discrete parking areas nestled along the perimeter, allowing the grounds to be designed primarily for the visitor to wander its solitary paths. One enters the grounds from the nearby metro station by passing through a grove of trees, which opens onto a grassy knoll, whose most notable feature, at a distance, is a colossal granite cross. It is an act of consolation said to be inspired by Casper David Friedrich's painting *The Cross beside the Baltic*. Approaching the cross, other features of the site soon come into view, including a chapel, a pond with garden islets, and a fieldstone pavement serving as a place for outdoor memorials. The dominant feature of the knoll, however, is placed off to the side and situated at the apex of the hill. It is a square stand of twelve weeping elm trees composing the Meditation Grove. What the trees enclose is a raised garden with benches, and at the garden's center is a small well. It is a place for inward reflection, but it is also a spot offering doleful views over the cemetery's burial sites, which still lie ahead and are mostly tucked into the wooded landscape. The path leading down from the Meditation Grove more than vaguely suggests a descent into the underworld.

One feature accentuating Woodland's serene and bucolic character is that many of the headstones within the wooded groves are placed on lawns yet irregularly spaced between the mature spruce trees of the forest. Nature, not geometry, prevails. At the far end is a Resurrection Chapel, built in a classical style, and there are as well two other chapels along pathways. One is a "primitive hut" tucked off into a thicket. Its large pyramidal roof of black shingles has a front porch under it, supported on twelve white timber columns. Inside is a room with a raised floor for a casket, surrounded by eight columns supporting a dome and oculus. The other major chapel, the Crematorium Chapel, nearer to the cemetery's entrance, has a sculptural grouping of figures, reminiscent of Rodin, making the transition from the horizontal position of death to vertical salvation with raised arms.

DOI: 10.4324/9781003178460-11

ILLUSTRATION 11.1   Erik Gunnar Asplund and Sigurd Lewerentz, Woodland Cemetery, Stockholm, 1917.

Source: Photo by Natalie Maynor. Wikimedia CC BY 2.0.

Asplund is known as a "metaphysical" architect, in the sense that his buildings seem to emerge from meditation. This is true of his design for the Stockholm City Library, set within a large park along Stockholm's main avenue. Its circular reading room is, in effect, a raised tholos originally set within a square of three flanking wings. There is an emotional drama to the work. One ascends to the luminous circular drum of the reading room with its three tiers of books by means of a darkened staircase. The thin metal rails of the two upper tiers allow the books themselves to command the visitor's attention, upon stepping into the light. Above the beautifully crafted bookcases is a white, textured wall of stonework, giving another dimension to the purposely tall drum. Asplund's personal style is sometimes referred to as Romantic or Nordic modernism, which is distinctly different from the white, functionalist icons of European modernism in the 1920s. This romantic ideal with its focus on emotion seems to be eminently suited to the light-deprived northern landscapes of Scandinavia, in which the brief southern light of winter arrives almost horizontally across the horizon. Skylights and clerestories are designed not so much for their prospects as they are instruments to gather in as much solar radiation as possible, and reflections of light within a building are palpable manifestations of the designer engaging with the human instinct for play.

Alvar Aalto was another architect with a similar demeanor and sense of play. In his early years the Finnish designer flirted with the functionalist vocabulary of the day, but after winning the competition in 1929 for the tuberculosis sanitorium in Paimio, his design instincts shifted. He began to view design as something more than arbitrary artistic expression, as something that should be rooted in the human needs of its users. In the case of a hospital, these needs are quite specific. He studied the spectral ranges of artificial illumination and noise transmission between and inside rooms. He became cognizant of the fact that architectural design generally assumes a vertically oriented person, whereas a hospital room is experienced by the patient lying in a bed.[1] This supine position inspired different design strategies—such as that lighting should not be placed in the center of the ceiling or in the line of vision of a supine person. He redirected the heating system toward the foot of the bed and lowered windows to provide the patient with a view of nature. Aalto used colorful accents throughout to enliven the hospital itself, and he and his wife Aino even designed bentwood hospital chairs in which the curvature of the back-rest was contoured to facilitate the breathing of a tubercular person. This idea would also prompt Aalto to create a company manufacturing bentwood chairs and stools, because he disliked the coldness of modern Bauhaus-inspired metal chairs against human skin.

Over the course of the 1930s, Aalto's work continued to veer away from the rationalist and utopian bent of early European modernism, as we see in his writings. In addressing the Swedish Society of Industrial Designers in 1935, he emphasized the failings of modern design. Not only does the simplified, boxlike styling of early modernism fail to connect with many people on an emotional level, he argues, but the results, born of industrial methods of production, at times even suffer "from a flagrant inhumanity."[2] He closed his talk to designers by stressing the need to study nature, its luxurious forms and combinations, and he praised, in particular, Japanese culture, whose love of flowers, plants, and natural motifs also promoted a virtuosity in the handling and treatment of natural materials.

We see the first mature realization of this shift in design sensibilities with the Villa Mairea in 1937, a summer home for two artistically inclined clients. Set within a wooded landscape, the villa is bucolic in its conception and detailing. The L-shape layout of the living areas is extended along the north with a loggia leading to a sauna and a kidney-shaped pool giving spatial definition to the garden courtyard. On the south entrance side, he placed a rustic *porte-cochere* supported on narrow poles to define the entry. Upon entering the house, one meets with another collection of poles supporting an open stair. It is actually an allegorical play with the private courtyard beyond. As Juhani Pallasmaa has observed, the view transforms "the interior into a metaphorical forest punctuated by columns and wooden poles; conversely, the courtyard, a clearing in a pine forest, has a very sheltered atmosphere."[3] The living room to one side is warmly outfitted with natural tones and purposely tactile in its detailing—the fireplace anchored within a whitewashed brick wall, deep red floor tiles, a ceiling of pine slats assembled into squares, the woven textures of the rugs, and the rattan wrapping around the black columns. All create a softened interior of civility, warmth, and intimacy. Incidentally, one of Aalto's initial inspirations in his design was Frank Lloyd Wright's Fallingwater.

Aalto would go on to match this effort in his design for the Säynätsalo Town Hall in the late 1940s, an unpretentious complex situated on a rugged island south of Jyväskylä. Its motif is once

ILLUSTRATION 11.2 Alvar Aalto, Villa Mairea, Noormarkku, Finland, 1938–39.

Source: Photo by Ninara. Wikipedia CC BY 2.0.

again a courtyard or clearing within the forest, now elevated above the surrounding landscape by two flights of stairs, one of grass with timber risers. The grass court with its pool is defined by the seemingly disparate functions of a library, administrative offices, and caretaker's apartment. The dominant wing of the council chamber, like a sculpture on its podium, is reached by another stair-case with brick steps, brick walls, and a tall timber ceiling lit by upper clerestories. The drama is fully revealed only when one enters the chamber room with its wood and leather furnishings designed by Aalto. Its whimsically canted roof is supported by uniquely designed, fanned timber trusses. It is a masterful civic chamber for a small community.

Another factor enhancing Aalto's sense of design was his interest in anthropology, and in par-ticular the anthropological theories of Yrjo Hirn. In the latter's book of 1900, *The Origins of Art*, Hirn pondered the human instincts for play and making art, ideas that Aalto similarly embraced. For Aalto, in fact, play was the second most compelling aspect of the design process. He extracted his designs through hours and hours of sketching, allowing both an incubation and maturation of ideas. We have already noted his most important design ethic: "Architecture, too, has an ulterior motive always lurking behind the corner, the idea of creating paradise."[4]

Soothsayers and Idealogues

The Austrian Adolf Loos has been a darling and bête noire of modern architectural historians; his is a story that has its beginning in fin-de-siècle Vienna. In one essay penned in 1908, "Ornament and Crime," he equated ornament in architecture with tattooing the human body. With pre-Dada irony, he observes that the "modern man who tattoos himself is either a criminal or a degenerate. There are prisons in which eighty percent of the inmates show tattoos. The tattooed who are not in prison are latent criminals or degenerate aristocrats."[5] The Atticism of many of Loos's oracles has been interpreted in many ways. After the early assessment of Loos as the conscience of modern architecture, he was later criticized as a voluptuary enamored with his interiors employing striking marbles, furs, shag rugs, and Oriental carpets. Still later, in the postmodern era, he was heralded as a born-again classicist, quite willing, like his latter-day historicists, to ransack the past for a pleasing Doric column or two. By the time of the poststructural era of the 1990s, his personality was deemed so complex that he needed to be sanctioned for his Derridean slippages, among other things.

Psychoanalysis and philosophy aside (they really don't mix here), Loos becomes interesting as an architect when one actually steps inside his buildings, but one must also start with a basic under-standing of the man. It starts with his fancy for everything sartorial. In 1898 he was commissioned by Vienna's major newspaper to write reviews of the Vienna Jubilee Exhibition, during which he focused much of his attention on clothing. The modern man, he often suggested, should be impeccable in his attire. The outer jacket should be an inconspicuous black frock coat of fine wool, exquisitely cut, shaped, and sewn. Socks are to be preferred to leg wrappings, and shoes should be laced patent leather, unstylized, and fitted. Underwear is better knitted than woven. The sophisti-cated gentleman should purchase his top hats only in London, because he feared the English were exporting bowlers of lesser quality abroad. Dickeys and pre-tied ties should forever be banned. Loos even wrote an occasional essay on ladies' fashion. In one, he opened with images of lustful desires, tormented men, cracking whips, and yes, the Marquis de Sade—all as a prelude to his argument that women should be allowed to wear pants and thereby relieve their dependency on men.[6] In 1903 Loos founded a newspaper titled *The Other: A Paper for the Introduction of Western Culture into Austria*. He promised a regular column on proper etiquette and advice on such things as how to prepare a dinner party, phrase an invitation, and observe the proper protocol for social visits. Of course, other issues such as masturbation, death, cooking, and sex were also placed on the table.

It was therefore hardly a coincidence that his first major commission was for Goldman & Salatsch, Vienna's high-end gentlemen's clothing store. The building stands on a busy corner opposite the

ILLUSTRATION 11.3   Adolf Loos, Looshaus on the Michaelerplatz, Vienna.

Source: Photo by Thomas Ledl. Wikimedia CC BY-SA 4.0.

Hofburg Palace in Vienna, and was fiercely opposed by code officials and members of the public when—after the scaffolding and protective tarps came down—the four upper stories of the building were rendered in plain white stucco. Loos, after much litigation and an incipient ulcer, was able to attain the occupancy permit only by adding flower boxes to the facade. At least the code officials understood a paradisiacal gesture when they saw one. The lower stories that housed the prestigious tailoring firm did not suffer from such ignominy. It was fashionably wrapped in panels and columns of Cipollino marble, for which Loos (no doubt at the expense of his client) likely traveled to the Greek island of Euboea to obtain. Not to worry, Loos probably returned his architect's fee with due haste in restocking his wardrobe over the next few seasons.

In 1898 Loos also wrote another essay titled, "The Principal of Dressing." It concerns not clothing but the German notion of *Bekleidung*, a principle introduced by Loos's intellectual mentor Gottfried Semper. The latter, as we have seen, had argued that the textile "dressing" was a primeval motive for design, a descendant of the woven mats or animal hides hung vertically as a shelter against wind. When more solid walls were built, the wall dressing nevertheless remained as a symbolic vestige, as we find in the painted textile patterns found in Egyptian tombs. It is in understanding the primacy of this motive, Loos argues, that separates "some architects" from "*the architect*." The former design a room and then look around for a suitable wall covering, whether paneling, paint, or wallpaper. *The architect*, however, operates in a reverse way: "the artist, the architect, first senses the effect he wishes to produce and then envisions the space he wishes to create."[7] These effects may range from reverence in a church to a sense of homeyness in a dwelling, and when the effect is determined, only then does the designer choose the appropriate materials. In short, architecture is evocative and must appeal to human sentiments; it exists to create moods for those who dwell.

Loos also went out of his way to insist that the design of a house should not be an artistic exercise; rather, it should primarily appeal to one's innermost feelings and sense of comfort. "Man loves everything that serves his comfort," he once noted, "he hates everything that wants to shake him from his safe and secure position and trouble him. He therefore loves his home and hates art."[8] This principle, articulated in the era of Gustav Klimt, explains his many colorful interiors and fondness for expensive marbles and Persian rugs—tattooing, as it were. It also explains a house he designed in Paris in the mid-1920s. There, Arnold Schoenberg had introduced Loos into Dadaist circles, and the architect even designed a house for Tristan Tzara. More intriguing, however, is a design he prepared for Josephine Baker, the black American dancer who had enthralled the Parisian avant-garde with her dance performances, some lavishly staged by Jean Cocteau. Whether it was a real or imagined commission is still a mystery. Baker grew up in a ghetto in Saint Louis dancing on street corners for pennies, and after some success in New York she went to Paris and became an overnight sensation. Baker was not a simple person but possessed both acumen and sophistication, especially with her newfound wealth. As Loos's third wife Claire Beck later records Loos's account of the design commission: "It was in Paris. She came to me and was in a bad mood. Just think, Loos, she pouted, I want to do big, big remodeling in my house and do not like plans of architects." Loos responded, "What, you did not come to me first? Don't you know that I can design the most beautiful plan in the world for you?" Loos in his memoirs then reflected on the quality of his design, "I consider it one of my best. The exterior wall is covered with white and black marble slabs—diagonally striped. The most beautiful thing in the house is the swimming pool—with its ethereal lighting".[9]

The rectangular house with a cylinder inserted into one corner (as Labrouste had done at the Bibliothèque Nationale) was intended for a fashionable Paris neighborhood. The ground story serves as a white marble plinth for the main stories above, which are clad in horizontal (not diagonal) bands of white and black marble, seemingly a little over a foot in depth. The black and white bands have been interpreted in every conceivable way, but I doubt if it had any particular meaning for Loos. And the horizontal layering of contrasting bands of stonework certainly had ample precedents in Renaissance architecture. In any case, it is the interior that is intriguing. One would have entered beneath the corner tower and climbed a grand staircase, before arriving at a sizable antechamber. There, one would have two options. One could turn left into an equally grand salon or theatrical stage designed for social intermingling and accommodating fifty spirited guests. The second option would be to continue forward and ascend a circular staircase leading up to a spacious dining room. In the room next door was the "ethereal" swimming pool set under a skylight.

The idea of placing the weight of the pool and seven feet of water on the top level of a building, supported only by columns on the first floor, was not the most structurally efficient thing to do, but Loos's intention was clearly theatrical. A pool within a residence is in itself scarcely controversial; indeed, Baker had a small pool installed in her house on the Champs-Élysées. Yet what makes this pool an object of much discussion is what Loos did on the level below the pool. Into the pool's side walls, he inserted four windows and a passage around the pool, effectively turning it into an aquarium and allowing guests to watch other guests swimming. On the outer walls of the corridor, he also aligned four windows to bring light (not exterior views) to the aquatic display. This design has evoked considerable debate as to its motive, but one might also consider that the guests of Baker were either associated with the theater or the artistic avant-garde. In any case, we should also note the "most beautiful plan," had little chance of being realized; it was a momentary exercise in paradisiacal thinking.

Le Corbusier, who was born Charles-Édouard Jeanneret, was no less infatuated with Baker. The Swiss architect would have seen Loos's design for her house on display at the Salon d'Automne in Paris in 1929, and in November of that year Jeanneret, returning from São Paulo, found himself a fellow passenger with Baker aboard a ship. Back in Paris they were seen frequenting costume balls together and likely had a more intimate relationship. Le Corbusier's personality, however, was seemingly the polar opposite to that of Loos. Early in life, there may have been some levity in his bearing, but it seems to have been well guarded. If Loos was cosmopolitan and proper in his manners, Jeanneret was obsessive, megalomaniacal, and possibly autistic—albeit gifted with boundless energy.

Jeanneret was born in a Swiss watchmaking town nestled in the Jura Mountains, a little over a mile from the French border. He played with Fröbel blocks as a child and attended the local art school, the director of which pointed him toward architecture. In his early twenties he traveled throughout Europe, and in 1910 he landed a job with the architect Peter Behrens in Berlin, where he stayed for five months. It constituted the sum of his architectural training. Afterwards, he made an extended trip to Greece and Turkey, recording his experiences in notebooks and travel sketchbooks. Jeanneret began practicing architecture in his hometown during the war, but his lack of professional training soon caught up with him, and under the cloud of malpractice he left for Paris at war's end. There, he met the painter Amédée Ozenfant and took up painting. Ozenfant was leading a machine-inspired artistic movement known as "Purism," and he was also at the time seeking financial backing to launch the journal *L'Esprit Nouveau*. It quickly became a voice within the Parisian art world and covered a range of topics from the arts to literature, psychology, and cinematography. Jeanneret proved himself to be a talented writer and polemicist. Adopting the sobriquet of Le Corbusier, he wrote numerous articles relating to architectural design, and then in 1923, he assembled the essays into a best-selling book, *Toward an Architecture*. The book's release could not have been better timed, because it appeared when there was little building activity in Europe. Thus, with only

ILLUSTRATION 11.4   Le Corbusier, Cover to *Vers une architecture* (Toward an Architecture), 1923.

Source: Author's library.

a slender portfolio of built works—none particularly inspiring—Le Corbusier suddenly found himself a celebrity within European architectural circles.

The book's famous but unhappy metaphor, "a house is a machine for living in," strips it of any paradisiacal pretension, and the book's provocative utopian character would haunt design discussions for the rest of the century. Hyperbolic polemics abound. He concludes one early chapter, for instance, by noting that American grain silos were the "magnificent FIRST FRUITS of the new age. AMERICAN ENGINEERS AND THEIR CALCULATIONS CRUSH AN EXPIRING ARCHITECTURE."[10] Three themes come to the fore. First, architecture needs standards of design; second, these standards should be predicated on the mass production of housing; and third, the alternative is revolution—that is, if the first two criteria are not met. Given the recent revolutions in Russia and Germany, the threat was not too much of an overreach. The book flutters with other lofty language, the idea that a great era has dawned, one with a new spirit and modern state of mind, one that makes the "styles" of the past a "lie." The new spirit is best represented in the paradigms of ships, airplanes, and automobiles, particularly in the standardization of their components and rapid factory assembly. The book engages the reader with a multitude of photographs and drawings, and the image he adopts for the book's cover is a view down the deck of the Cunard Line's vessel *Aquitania*. The image is described inside with these words: "To Architects: The value of a long promenade, a volume that's satisfying and interesting; unity of materials, beautiful arrangement of the structural elements, soundly set out and combined into a unity."[11] He then admits that such an aesthetic may not be accepted by all but nevertheless concludes, with true Saint-Simonian fervor,

> [the] art of our era is in its rightful place when it addresses itself to the elites. Art is not a popular thing, still less a deluxe whore. Art is a necessary foodstuff only for elites that must reflect so as to be able to lead. Art is in its essence elevated.[12]

Mass production, with all its utopian underpinnings, becomes the hallmark of the new era, and only industry can rescue the ailing European city. For this to happen, however, we must drop our biases as to what constitutes a dwelling. And, if we look at the housing problem objectively, "we will come to the house tool, the mass-production house that is healthy (morally, too) and beautiful from the aesthetic of the work tools that accompany our existence."[13] It does not matter that people may not want these assembly line productions, nor that his offered designs have sub-minimal standards for cooking and bathing (requiring hotel-like communal services). And if this reconstitution of the entire social structure is now called into play by his righteous hand, he at least assures us that it "provides the solution to the servant crisis (a crisis that is just beginning and is an ineluctable social fact)."[14] The alternative to his ideas is of course revolution, which is the outgrowth of the great discord that "reigns between a modern state of mind that is an injunction and the suffocating stock of centuries-old detritus." Society today, he assures us, longs for this great transformation in living standards, the architect is simply the agent coming to the rescue of our faltering political and social structure. And if we do not cede to the demand to invest the architect (preferably Le Corbusier himself) with supreme authority—well, the closing words of the book makes the alternative explicit:

Architecture or revolution.
Revolution can be avoided.[15]

Even before the book appeared in print, the urban proposals of Le Corbusier demonstrate that he had become smitten with utopian fever. In his 1922 proposal for a capitalist city for three million inhabitants, for instance, he converged four freeways and train lines on a central complex of twenty-four cruciform glass towers, sixty stories tall, which served as a commercial and administrative hub. Outside of this zone, he placed ten- and twelve-story zigzag housing blocks for workers, monotonous and maniacally dystopian in their repetition. He later designed a schematic variation on the theme and placed his new city on the right bank of the Seine River—leveling a significant portion of Paris. Such a proposal might be taken for an act of madness, but Le Corbusier was always comfortable in his world. After his publication *La Ville Radieuse* in 1933, his ideas came to be known to the English-speaking world through the euphemism "Radiant City." Trouble would follow wherever the idea was interpreted.

The Inalienable Wright

In contrast to the poverty and political turmoil of much of Europe, the United States entered the 1920s with buoyant optimism. It had invested relatively little in the war yet had gained much in talented exiles, growing wealth, high spirits, and the country's emergence as a major military and political power. It was a decade of excesses and contradictions, of prohibition and speakeasies, women's suffrage and the Flapper, the Model T, radio, talking movies, the Cotton Club, Art Deco, and the craze of the Charleston. It was the period in which F. Scott Fitzgerald, Sinclair Lewis, William Faulkner, Eugene O'Neill, and Ernest Hemingway defined a modern American literature. Musically, it was the era of Louis Armstrong, Duke Ellington, Jelly Roll Morton, and George and Ira Gershwin. Architecturally, it was the utopian competition to build ever more Icarian skyscrapers, which would reach a feverous pitch before the stock market crash in 1929 melted the wings of the contestants.

The tall building was partly in place before the war, but it took a different form in Manhattan with the new zoning ordinance in 1916, which required a system of setbacks to allow at least a crack of sunlight onto the sidewalks below. It was generally well received. The architect Irving J. Pond saw it as a psychological appeal to human sentiment, in which horizontal and vertical elements "are introduced into the structure in such manner that each may make its own appeal to the emotions and be held in restraint by the other."[16] The delineator Hugh Ferriss saw the ziggurat form prescribed by the ordinance as a way to drop decorative motifs altogether, and for architects to view themselves instead as sculptors.[17] A second turning point in tall-building design was represented in the Chicago Tribune Tower competition of 1922. It attracted entries from American firms, but also many from European designers idled by the war. Although the winning scheme was the Gothic design from the office of Raymond Hood, other schemes questioned why this new urban paradigm needed a stylistic dressing at all. Both Walter Burley Griffin and Bernard Bijvoet presented interesting and original alternatives, as did the second-place finisher Eliel Saarinen, who in fact used the second-place prize money to emigrate to the United States. He would later design the Edenic campus of Cranbrook Academy, and his son became a major architect. The shallow bedrock of Manhattan also allowed the tall building to become a legitimate skyscraper, which, with the occasional Art Deco charms of Ely Jacques Kahn, would culminate later in the decade with the Chrysler Building of William van Alen. The graceful and spirited building cannot claim to be millennial, but the ingenious architect, with the support of Walter Chrysler, attempted with his scalloped, chromium-nickel-steel headdress to match the metallic sleekness of automobile design.

There were at least a few early voices raised in opposition to these buildings. Louis Sullivan at the start of the century had attacked the commercial buildings of lower Manhattan as "barbarian," noting that "as they increase in number and uproar, make this city poorer and emptier, morally and spiritually; they drag it down and down into the mire. This is not American civilization; it is the rottenness of Gomorrah. This is not Democracy—it is savagery."[18] Sullivan's later supporter, Claude Bragdon, raised the issue in 1918, albeit with a little more moderation. In *Architecture and Democracy*, he argued there are two types of architecture: *arranged* (artificial, bookish, composed, self-conscious, and prideful) and *organic*, which springs from an inner necessity for self-expression, as when the Emersonian spirit "draws near to the surface of life" and design becomes truly creative.[19] The tall building is the vehicle for the first type, he goes on to say, but it does have certain positive features, such as a more extensive use of glass to admit sunlight into offices, although to the detriment of the street below. It is also a product of a building culture and economy that allows little deviation from standard practices. Bragdon, like Sullivan, seeks his Olympia in "the index of the inner life of those who produced it" and through the embrace of the ornamental values of light, color ("the sign manual of happiness"), and the geometries of nature.[20]

Sullivan and Bragdon lead us into the mind of Frank Lloyd Wright, certainly one of the century's most prodigious talents. He was born in 1867 in rural Wisconsin and was raised in his early years in rural Massachusetts, where his Unitarian mother instructed him in the kindergarten methods of Friedrich Fröbel. They emphasized not only playing with geometric blocks but also music and trips into nature. The latter was to be further understood by working in gardens. The family returned to Wisconsin when Wright was eleven, and one of his first commissions, at the age of twenty, was to design Hillsdale Home School for his aunts, Ellen and Jane Wright. It was a farming and industrial school established for children to learn, again, directly from nature through excursions into the countryside. After two semesters at the University of Wisconsin, Wright made his way to Chicago in 1887 and soon found his way into the office of Adler and Sullivan, where his first job was to prepare contract drawings of Sullivan's designs for the Auditorium Building. He much admired the talent of Sullivan, his *lieber Meister* (dear master), but a dispute in 1893 over Wright's bootlegged residential designs led to their separation.

Wright then opened his own office in the suburb of Oak Park, and in the 1890s he absorbed the influence of the Arts and Crafts movement as well as the machine—the "peerless Corliss tandems whirling their hundred ton fly-wheels" in nearby Gary, Indiana. He then believed that they would ultimately "emancipate human expression" and fulfill Whitman's longing for democracy.[21] Yet these merely were stepping stones in his passage to the "Prairie Style" and a return to his Emersonian roots, which he would cultivate in earnest around the turn of the century. In the first exposition of his design ideas in 1908, "In the Cause of Architecture," he starts with the leitmotif of "Nature" as the lodestar to good design. He, with his growing interest in Japanese culture, even draws attention to the word *edaburi*, which he translates as "the formative arrangement of the branches of a tree."[22] The image is proffered as a "civilized" metaphor for how an architect should think about a design, which he reduces to six principles. First and foremost is simplicity and repose, which is achieved through low and gently sloping roofs with quiet skylines. He follows with individuality of expression, and shaping a building to harmonize with the surroundings of nature. He calls for the use of "soft, warm, optimistic tones of earths and autumn leaves" in addition to emphasizing the nature of the materials. Finally, there is the quality of sincerity, which seems to derive from a number of factors, among them design integrity, simple lines and forms, and an "atmosphere as pure and elevating in its humble way as the trees and flowers are in their perfectly appointed ways."[23] Interestingly, all of these parameters could have been adduced by studying the houses and gardens of Kyoto.

Yet this very productive period of his life came to an abrupt end in 1909 when Wright, at the age of forty-one, abandoned his family and departed for Europe with Mamah Cheney, the wife of one of his clients. He returned to the United States the following year—not to Chicago but to Wisconsin, where he began the construction of what would become the estate of Taliesin in Spring Green. It became the site of a terrible calamity in 1914 when a servant (on a day when Wright was in Chicago) set the house ablaze and murdered Mamah, her child, and five others working in his office. Wright's career then lay in shambles, but he endured. He designed the Imperial Hotel in Tokyo in 1919 and in the early 1920s in Los Angeles he built several extraordinary houses, among them the celestial La Miniatura or Millard House in Pasadena, built on what Wright described as a "ravishing ravine" with "two beautiful eucalyptus trees."[23] It was constructed in the same year that Le Corbusier published *Toward an Architecture*, and Wright's use of "textile blocks" vaguely approaches the idea of prefabrication. The two distinctions are that they were manufactured on the site and, more

ILLUSTRATION 11.5   Frank Lloyd Wright, La Miniatura or Millard House, Pasadena, 1923.

Source: Photo by Levi Clancy. Wikimedia CC BY-SA 4.0.

importantly, they were cast in patterned molds with the sand and gravels extracted from the site—bonding the coloration of the house with the landscape in a classic statement of design individuality.

During the 1930s, the decade of the Great Depression, his creativity was perhaps at its apogee, with such well-known works as Fallingwater, a mountain retreat in Pennsylvania, and Taliesin West, the winter's desert retreat for him and his fellowship of students. His first sketches for the Guggenheim Museum in New York came in the mid-1940s, when he was in his late seventies. Nevertheless, another of Wright's contributions to the theme of paradise, little discussed, was his reconceptualization of the city, views that were initially proffered in response to the urban proposals of Le Corbusier.

In a lecture given at Princeton University in 1930, Wright opened with an interesting question: "Is the city a natural triumph of the herd instinct over humanity, and therefore a temporal necessity as a hangover from the infancy of the race, to be outgrown as humanity grows?"[24] The question of dispersing the city into the countryside, which he had been pondering over the previous year, may have bemused his audience of students and academics, yet as the Great Depression was descending Wright would more and more come to the view that the modern city—a "mobocracy," as he referred to it—was trapped within a death spiral, asphyxiated by overcrowded and unsanitary conditions. Two years later, in *The Disappearing City*, Wright offered his alternative by expanding on the idea of a garden city, yet this time with an interesting twist of logic. For now, it is the automobile that can transport us to Eden. His "Broadacre City" calls for the dispersal of urban populations to regional centers in the salutary countryside, where each family would have a minimum of one acre of land, fresh air and fresh vegetables, and an automobile. These regional rural centers would provide jobs and the production of goods in noiseless, smokeless, and scaled-down factories needing only to meet regional needs. Wright did not see this plan as socialist but rather as a new version of "the least government"—an iteration, in his argument, deriving from the ideas of Jefferson, Hamilton, Washington, Emerson, Lincoln, William Lloyd Garrison, and John Brown.[25]

This new Elysian is born of the fruits of the modern age. The machine, he argues, provides electrification, the combustion engine (collapsing spatial distances), refrigeration, and new building materials. With these tools, basically everything can literally become a garden in Wright's vision of the community, which will be self-sufficient and without urban dependencies. The scenic highways stringing together these housing areas are three lanes wide and without telephone poles or billboards. Hospitals would be reduced to smaller clinics set within spacious gardens with ample sunlight. A few tall apartments buildings, based on his St. Mark's Towers project, would be allowed but they would be surrounded by large parks. The cultural amenities of cinema, drama, opera, concerts, and lectures could be taken in the comfort of one's home, over radio, or through the promising new medium of television. All corporate work could be done from home, eliminating the need for office buildings.

Among the most interesting of his proposals are those for schools and homes. Schools would be situated in the "choicest part of the countryside, preferably by a stream or by a body of water." Classrooms would hold no more than ten children, and

> enough ground for a flower and vegetable bed for each pupil would be alongside, with large play-spaces beyond that. Each pupil would learn of the soil by working on it and in it, and he would educate his hand to draw what his eye might see, and learn to model it equally well. Eye-minded is modern-minded. So the school building should be developed by artists and architects as, in itself, a free work of art.[26]

The home should also be radically reconsidered in design. As with Le Corbusier, its functional parts are to be prefabricated, but now carefully attuned with the landscape and the new patterns of living:

> Steel and glass will be called in to fulfill their own—steel for strength, durability and lightness; translucent glass, enclosing interior space, would give privacy yet make of living in a house a delightful association with sun, with sky, with surroundings gardens. The home would be an indoor garden, the garden an outdoor house.[27]

Wright also created his Fellowship at Taliesin in 1932, the same year in which his book appeared. As Jennifer Gray has pointed out, architectural training was only secondary to the commune. Disciples would be trained in the ways of the landscape first by working daily in the fields and gardens, instilling them with a grander horticultural ethic, a "better way of life."[28] The fellowship, altered and expanded to Taliesin West outside of Scottsdale, continues to this day, but Wright was less successful with Broadacre City, the model of which was first displayed in Rockefeller Center in 1935. Although paradisiacal in conception, it also proved to have a little too much utopian spirit and received only lukewarm support even from sympathetic architects and planners, and less from others. Part of the reason for this was that the media establishment and other practitioners were already galvanizing around a very different vision of the city, predicated on the principles of the International Style. Wright's Camelot was politely dismissed as a vision of a quixotic romantic.

Descent Into High Modernism

In looking at architectural production in Europe and North America in 1914 and comparing it stylistically with the buildings designed after 1945, the year in which high modernism becomes fully manifest, one might at first be perplexed at how dramatically the face of design could alter itself over the course of a single generation. This transition also presents a historiographic problem that has haunted many writers. What were the roots of modernism before its full manifestation? What exactly were the factors that caused such a decisive change of expression? Why did the track of design, driven by these new construction methods and materials, take the particular path that it did?

The architectural historian Nikolaus Pevsner was one of the first to chronicle the origins of modernism. In his influential book of 1936, *Pioneers of the Modern Movement*, the German refugee living in England offered the thesis that architectural modernism had four sources: the Arts and Crafts movement led by William Morris, French painting in the 1890s, Art Nouveau, and nineteenth-century engineers. Problems with this analysis become evident, however, when he compares the "effortless mastery of material and weight" of the Fagus Shoe Factory—in his view modernism's first mature manifestation—with the chapel of Saint-Chapelle and the choir of Beauvais.[29] Polemics aside, nothing in the Fagus factory, designed by Gropius in 1911, suggests the influence of William Morris (who abhorred the use of metal), French painting, or Art Nouveau. The only credible lineage of this new "factory style" of design then would be engineers, a fact to which Pevsner himself acknowledges during an oddly illuminating moment toward the end of his book (removed from later editions), when he notes that

> the warm and direct feelings of the great men of the past may have gone; but then the artist who is representative of this century of ours must needs be cold, as he stands for a century cold as steel and glass, a century the precisions of which leave less space for self-expression than did any period before.[30]

In Sigfried Giedion's first historical study of modernism of 1928, he too had advanced nineteenth-century engineering as the source for modernism, specifically the market halls, railway stations, and exposition buildings of France. Yet Giedion taps Le Corbusier, rather than Gropius, as the prophet or antihero of modernism. He can be called such because the "architect" no longer exists in this new and modern era. The "constructor" now reigns supreme in the process of collective design.[31] Giedion, to his defense, was trained as an engineer and it is quite natural that he

ILLUSTRATION 11.6 Walter Gropius and Adolf Meyer, Fagus Factory, Alfeld on the Leine, Germany, designed 1911.

Source: Photo by Olrik66. Wikimedia CC BY-SA 4.0.

would view modern architecture in such a light. In his best-selling book of 1941, *Space, Time and Architecture*, the Swiss historian would expand the zeitgeist of modernism to include abstract modern painting and sculpture as well as the relativity theories of modern physics.

Many other historians have since weighed in on modernism's origins, but I will spare the reader some time by offering a simpler explanation. It is true that new materials and constructional techniques played significant roles in shaping architectural practice before and after 1945, but there was another, rarely mentioned factor that came into play: office politics. These were the political talents of a few individuals who organized themselves and set down rules of the game and, in the process, brooked no apostasies. Modernism in Europe began in earnest in 1928 with the creation of the International Congress of Modern Architecture (CIAM), which grew out of a housing exhibition of the previous year on a hillside above the city of Stuttgart.

The housing exhibition of Weissenhof Estate, which I mentioned earlier, was initiated in 1925 by Gustaf Stotz, the regional director of the Baden-Württemberg branch of the German Werkbund. He wished to put on display recent housing trends. The Berlin architect Mies van der Rohe was appointed by the national office of the Werkbund to manage the event, and it was his decision to transform it into an international showcase and invite a number of prominent designers from outside Germany. The event, despite its cost overruns, delays, and sloppy construction, turned out to be a polemical success largely because of the extensive publicity campaign that preceded it.[32] One of the books written to coincide with its opening, Walter Curt Behrendt's *The Victory of the New Building Style*, opened with this stirring zeitgeist proclamation: "Influenced by the powerful spiritual forces in which the creative work of our time is embodied, the mighty drama of a sweeping transformation is taking place before our eyes. It is the birth of the *form of our time*."[33]

Weissenhof, however, was also a place for intrigue. Before the exhibition opened, Mies had said to Giedion and others that the "movement must now be cleaned up" through "a secret purification." Mies wanted to present a unified front of modernism by limiting membership to a select group of architects, which he referred to as the "seven lamps." In letters to the Dutch architect J.H.P. Oud, Giedion informed him that he was one of the lamps and disclosed that the other six were Mies, Gropius, Mart Stam, Le Corbusier, Hans Schmidt, and Cornelis van Eesteren.[34] The purification, however, did not take place because of friction within the group. As a result, Giedion then began to have conversations with a wealthy Swiss woman, Hélène de Mandrot, who offered her castle at La Sarraz as a venue for the meeting of select architects. This offer, however, presented another problem for the continent still torn by the war, which was the issue of who would write the agenda for the meeting: one of the Germans, Swiss architects, or Le Corbusier? The last, as a provision for his attendance, received the nod and, interestingly, neither Mies nor Gropius attended. The La Sarraz Declaration, announcing the creation of CIAM, demanded—among other things—that architects be given absolute authority, that clients subvert their interests to "the new conditions of social life," and that prefabrication replace skilled labor in practice. The redistribution of private land also became "the indispensable preliminary basis for any town planning."[35]

Other CIAM conferences followed in the pre-war years, two of which were notable. At the follow-up conference in Frankfurt in 1929, the Germans, with intramural factions of socialists and communists, seized the agenda and proposed the now-infamous "minimum dwelling" standards for housing, the minimal amount of living space needed for a family to live. It would become the model for low-cost row housing. Gropius, in response, presented an interesting sociological argument. Pointing to the rise of divorce rates, he argued that "the large apartment building satisfies more nearly the sociological requirement of present-day industrial populations with their symptomatic liberation of the individual and early separation of the children from the family."[36]

Yet the most significant of the early conferences took place in 1933, after the rise of National Socialism in Germany had precluded German architects from attending—many, in fact, had already moved to Russia to support Josef Stalin. CIAM also had grown. Le Corbusier leased a passenger ship to take the delegates from Marseilles to Athens, on which over a hundred participants hashed out the details of what became "The Athens Charter."[37] It is unknown how accurately the new charter captured the details of the conference, because Le Corbusier did not write the articles until the early 1940s. Its ninety-four propositions, based on studies of thirty-three cities, were nevertheless monumental in defining the next decades. There were, as one might expect, numerous worthwhile reflections on the nature of the present city and its failings, but the charter also gave full support to his idea of the Radiant City.

The story of modernism's beginning would end here, except for the growing influence of the United States, which had been excluded from these European discussions. Fortunately (or unfortunately) there was one entity to step in and save the day: the newly founded Museum of Modern Art (MoMA). Its founding director in 1929 was the art historian Alfred H. Barr, who regularly visited Europe to pursue his interest in European painting. Barr wanted a department of architecture and asked Philip Johnson, another wealthy heir, to be the curator. Johnson at the time knew little about architecture, but on his many tours of Europe, one specifically coinciding with the Weissenhof Exhibition, he had in fact met Le Corbusier, Gropius, and Mies van der Rohe. Johnson was also accompanied on trips by his schoolmate and fellow Europhile Henry-Russell Hitchcock, who was writing a book on modern architecture. In 1932 Barr, Johnson, and Hitchcock decided to hold an architectural exhibition to showcase recent European trends, titled "The International Style: Architecture since 1922." The exhibition catalogue proclaimed that "today a new style has come into existence. The aesthetic conceptions on which its disciplines are based derive from the experimentation of the individualists."[38]

The coterie quickly decided upon displaying the work of Le Corbusier, Gropius, and Mies, but then there was the suggestion to add an American architect. In the background loomed the figure of Wright, whose nature-centered approach to design was in sharp conflict with the white, cubic style fashionable in Europe. The New Yorkers did not want him in the event, but it was difficult to leave him out. At one point, Wright pulled himself from the show when he was relegated to the inferior status of a "pioneer," although in the end he remained. Nevertheless, we now have the quite curious situation in which two cultural elites without architectural training—Hitchcock and Johnson—were writing the design criteria for the new "International Style," which American architects should master to keep up with the times.

Astonishingly, the principles of this new style were reduced to three: volume, regularity, and the absence of applied decoration. Volume mandated simplified forms made from industrial materials, such as glass, metal, tile, or marble facings (materials generally without surface texture). Natural materials, such as wood, brick, and stone, were frowned upon, although not strictly excluded. Regularity demanded a standardization of parts and a boxlike simplification of forms, as well as an avoidance of symmetry. The absence of decoration required that ornamentation now be replaced with "detailing," or how the junction of industrial materials come together and is expressed. Although decoration is disallowed, it was permissible to use isolated works of abstract sculpture and painting as decorative objects, here and there, to complement the new simplified forms.

There is, however, an interesting subtext to Hitchcock and Johnson's book. They reject a purely functionalist architecture (which only a few Europeans had advocated) in favor of a more "aesthetic" approach to design. In starting down this path, the two authors, perhaps for the first time in architectural history, based the quality of a building's design not on its fitness for purpose, its setting within a landscape or a national culture, or its compatibility with human wishes. They reduce the building instead to an object of art devoid of any human meaning other than its symbolic modernity. This diminution is most evident in the final chapter, where they describe the minimalist character of European housing estates built during the postwar housing crisis, which, they argue, are superior to the individualized homes of (presumably culturally backward) Americans. This peculiarly American excess of "sentimentality" (which we will see again shortly) should be purged in favor of the "universal" spirit kindling the new style. In other words, it is not up to clients who commission or rent housing to decide what they want or like. The authors even admit that departing from historical or local traditions may be difficult for some designers to accept, but they also stress that the architect's utopian task is nothing less than to reform or remake a nation's aesthetic sensibilities. Their only caveat is that this new standard of housing should not be "functionally so advanced that they are lived in under protest."[39] Of course the views of Hitchcock and Johnson would change over time. The former would co-author with Wright a monograph of his work, and Johnson would— after World War II—return to school, take a degree in architecture, and enjoy a successful practice. Yet to an embittered Wright in 1932, they were an impolite rejection of all of his values.

A Brief Excursus on Dystopias

It is perhaps no coincidence that during these same years, the genre of dystopian literature first appears. Wars, genocide, and economic depressions tend to have this disheartening effect. It is therefore of some interest to raise the question of how dystopian novels depict architecture. Do they recognize a connection between the imposition of a totalitarian order and the designed environment that it spawns?

Aldous Huxley's *Brave New World* (1932) is the easiest to deal with because there is so little description of the built environment. The most vivid passage, in fact, appears on the very first page, when Huxley recounts the details of the Central London Hatchery and Conditioning Centre, a "squat grey building of only thirty-four stories," whose enormous fertilization laboratory on the ground floor faces north. The "glass and nickel and bleakly shining porcelain" present in the laboratory reflect a "wintriness" responding to the cold outside. We learn later that London is a city of "huge table-topped buildings," some sixty stories and some with 4,000 rooms. All are separated from satellite suburbs by a six-kilometer parkland.[40] Huxley seems to have been aware of Le Corbusier's urban proposals.

By contrast, George Orwell's *1984*, published in 1949, is vivid with sensory details of nightmarish London. The hallway of Winston Smith's tenement house smells of boiled cabbage and old rag mats, the elevator is broken, and electricity is spotty. From his window, he views London's rotting nineteenth-century houses, their sides shored up and their broken windows patched with cardboard. The battered doorways of the houses bring to mind "rat holes," and puddles of filthy water collect around the cobblestones in the streets. At a distance, Winston, from his room, can also see the "enormous pyramidal structure of glittering white concrete," certainly an allusion to modernism, "soaring up, terrace after terrace, three hundred meters into the air."[41] It is just possible to read the Party's slogan on its walls:

WAR IS PEACE

FREEDOM IS SLAVERY

IGNORANCE IS STRENGTH

Later in the novel, Orwell makes another mocking allusion to the postwar visions of the early twentieth century by characterizing the socialist elites of the future society as "rich, leisured, orderly, and efficient—a glittering antiseptic world of glass and steel and snow-white concrete."[42] Every room in Winston's world is quite the opposite. The "low-ceilinged" office canteen is buried underground and is "deafeningly noisy"; the stew spews forth a "sour metallic smell."[43] The office carpet of his antagonist O'Brien is silent, and the ruby wine poured for Winston and his lover Julia barely has a taste. The room in which Winston and Julia regularly meet is above a junk shop in an impoverished part of town. And although the mahogany double bed of their lovemaking, a remnant from the past, is infested with bedbugs, "It did not seem to matter. Dirty or clean, the room was paradise" compared to governmental workplaces.[44]

Of course, the decrepit world of this soulless dystopia has its antithesis in the Golden Country outside of London, in which Julia and Winston arrange their first illegal tryst. It is literally a paradise with the bluebells underfoot, the dappled light and shade, the greenness of leaves, the sweetness of the air that "seemed to kiss one's skin," and "the grassy knoll on which they lie, surrounded by hazel bushes and elm trees," whose boughs "swayed just perceptibly in the breeze, and their leaves stirred faintly in dense masses like women's hair."[45] The stealth treasure Julia brought her would-be lover, a favor long denied to lowly party members, was a piece of chocolate.

Yevgeny Zamyatin's masterful dystopia *We*, written in 1920, precedes by more than a decade Huxley's gray London high-rises, and its architecture is what makes his book particularly fascinating. His is a city of glass, but it is no Tautian fantasy. Zamyatin had participated in the first Russian Revolution of 1905 and was twice arrested and exiled to Siberia. He eventually completed his studies in engineering and served in the Russian navy as a shipbuilder stationed in England. He was a supporter of the October Revolution in 1917, but then, as the iron rule of the Bolsheviks began to play itself out, his attitude changed. His novel falls in line with the Constructivist proposals for glass towers, and it was a time of great energy and enthusiasm among writers and artists anticipating the new communist society. The novel in fact depicts a "perfect" society, a perfectly controlled, ultra-rational society of spiritual automatons under constant surveillance with no tolerance of fantasy or imagination. The "One State" assigns people numbers rather than names, and the protagonist—D–503—in one instance listens to a friend reflect on the "ancient legend of paradise," the choice offered to Adam and Eve between happiness without freedom or freedom without happiness. Those "morons," his friend relates, chose the latter, leading D–503 to reflect on his happiness without the least desire for individual freedom: "And again we are simple-hearted and innocent like Adam and Eve. No mess about what is good and what is evil: Everything is very simple, heavenly, childishly simple."[46]

Life in the city-state of One Nation, founded sometime after a 200-year war that decimated all but 2 percent of the earth's population, is tightly regimented. The day for each citizen, in his or her gray uniform, is dictated to the minute, with compulsory times for working, eating, political marching, and sleeping. Daily educational lectures are mandatory, and everyone is assigned a profession. D–503 is a mathematician and engineer in charge of designing a rocket ship, the *Integral*, which will launch hundreds of his comrades into space in search of denizens of other planets to convert to their ideology. He writes his daily memoirs to have something of himself to accompany the flight on its expedition.

Every citizen of One Nation is also tested for sexual hormones and, based on the results, is awarded regular visits by an assigned sexual partner. Only with the proper voucher for such a visit can one close the curtains in one's glass apartment. D–503 is quite happy with his assigned partner, O–90, and he is quite content with everything else—that is, until he meets I–330, the female heroine. And here is where architecture plays the dominant role. One nation is "a glass city of unalterable straight streets, the glass pavement splashing rays of light, divine parallelepipeds of transparent dwellings," a city surrounded by a diamond-like glass perimeter wall, a glass city without a speck of nature.[47] Even a cloud in the sky, for D–503, mars the perfection of the city's geometry. It is a sterile city of linear perfection, allowing the engineer, as he writes in his journal, to "feel like a tower; I am afraid of moving my elbows so that the walls, domes and machines do not shatter."[48] And here is the rub. Glass, which for Taut and the avant-garde mystically defined the philosopher's stone of modernity, became for Zamyatin the instrument of aesthetic and sensory oppression, exposing every thought and movement one makes to the view of others. Glass is static, colorless, transparent, hard, and it can be manufactured into rigid geometric shapes. It is the antithesis of nature.

It is within this context that I–330, a sensuous Eve, "slim, sharp, stubbornly lithe like a whip," comes into the life of D–503, seemingly by accident.[49] He sees her at a concert playing an ancient instrument, dressed in a closely fitting black dress, an antique costume from the past, which sharply delineates the whiteness of her shoulders and breasts. She takes him to see the "Ancient House," a museum curiosity on the edge of town encased in glass, next to the Green Wall. The museum is a relic of the solid dwellings of the ancients, and there the flirtatious I-330, after slipping out of her uniform, bedazzles him by sipping a liqueur in her yellow silk dress with tall black stockings.[50] Unassigned and forbidden sex, as powerful as any magnet in D-503's propulsion laboratory, seems inevitable, and the temptress eventually leads him—now troubled by his desires, feelings, and dreams—into a world he had never imagined. The green wall surrounding the city, he soon learns, is not green, but its translucency displays the green flush of nature outside. Once he secretly crosses the barrier, he discovers more. Accustomed to walking only on perfectly flat planes of glass, he initially stumbles and falls on the uneven terrain. And then in this post-apocalyptic landscape he confronts the remnants of the ancient human race—the simple people. They are naked and the men have body hair. The women have faces "delicately pinkish and hairless, with "large, firm breasts of beautiful geometrical form."[51] That evening he partakes of the fruit of this atavistic Eden.

D-503 swoons, but to little avail. He, blemished with inward desire, has been lured into a revolutionary plot in which I-330 and others will highjack his ellipsoid spaceship and transport themselves and the simple people to a new life on another planet. Yet the plan is discovered by the city's "Benefactor" (Orwell's Big Brother) and foiled. Eve, with her timeless sensibilities, refuses to recant her actions and is executed, while Adam commits to brain surgery to remove those areas dealing with imagination and emotions. In the end, the reformed and once again complacent engineer returns to his city of glass, where all is clear, rational, and right.

George Orwell once suggested that Aldous Huxley drew his inspiration of *Brave New World* from Zamyatin's novel, yet the architectural backdrops of the two books are too severe to make such a comparison.[52] The glass architecture of Zamyatin is more than a metaphor; it is the setting that also sculpts the actions of the participants with transparency and planar precision, as does the "gloomy, untidy space" of a room in the Ancient House, where, as the protagonist relates:

> It held a strange "grand" musical instrument and some wild, unorganized, insane motley of colors and forms just like their music. A white ceiling rose above dark-blue walls with red, green, and orange covers of ancient books; yellow bronze candelabras, a Buddha's statue, and the furniture lines distorted by epilepsy, unfit of any equations.[53]

It is perhaps too easy to compare Zamyatin's geometry of glass with Orwell's depraved world of torture and thought police, yet the imagination of good novelists rarely fails to touch upon something obvious, which is that human behavior indeed bears a symbiotic relationship with the environment in which we dwell. When architects, after 1945, resumed practice around the globe with their new industrial materials, they sincerely believed that they were improving the world by replacing Zamyatin's "Ancient House" with newer, cleaner, and more transparent glass boxes, forever brooking subterfuge and political intrigue. These were certainly noble intentions, but, as Zamyatin's novel also demonstrates, when one reduces the world to formulae one also runs the risk of suppressing something very fundamental to human nature—those powerful emotional sensibilities that pervade our very cognitive cores. "Man still breathes both in and out," the architect Aldo van Eyck once noted: "When is architecture going to do the same?"[54]

Notes

1. Alvar Aalto, "The Humanizing of Architecture," in Göran Schildt (ed.), *Alvar Aalto in His Own Words* (Helsinki: Otava Publishing Company, 1997), 103.
2. Alvar Aalto, "Rationalism and Man," in *Alvar Aalto* (note 1), 89–93.
3. Juhani Pallasmaa, "From Tectonics to Painterly Architecture," in Peter MacKeith (ed.), *Encounters 1: Architectural Essays* (Helsinki: Rakennustieto Publishing, 2012), 219.

4. Alvan Aalto, "The Architect's Dream of Paradise," in *Alvar Aalto* (note 1), 215.

5. Adolf Loos, "Ornament and Crime," in Ulrich Conrads (ed.) and Michael Bullock (trans.), *Programs and Manifestoes on 20th-Century Architecture* (Cambridge, MA: Massachusetts Institute of Technology Press, 1975), 19.

6. Adolf Loos, "Ladies Fashion," in Jane O. Newman and John H. Smith (trans.), *Spoken into the Void: Collected Essays 1897–1900* (Cambridge, MA: Massachusetts Institute of Technology Press, 1982), 99–103.

7. Adolf Loos, "Das Prinzip der Bekleidung," in *Ins Leere Gesprochen, 1897–1900* (Vienna: Georg Prchner, 1921), 140. (trans. mine)

8. Adolf Loos, "Architektur," in *Trotzdem, 1900–1930* (Vienna: Georg Prachner, 1931), 101.

9. Claire Beck Loos, *Adolf Loos: A Private Portrait*, ed. by Carrie Patterson (Los Angeles, CA: Doppel House Press, 2011), 6–7.

10. Le Corbusier, *Toward an Architecture*, trans. by John Goodman (Los Angeles, CA: Getty Publications, 2007), 106.

11. Ibid., 154.

12. Ibid., 157.

13. Ibid., 254.

14. Ibid., 273.

15. Ibid., 307.

16. Irving K. Pond, "Zoning and the Architecture of High Buildings," *Architectural Forum* 35 (October 1921), 133.

17. Hugh Ferriss, "The New Architecture," *The New York Times Magazine* (March 19, 1922), 8.

18. Claude Bragdon, *Architecture and Democracy* (New York: Alfred A. Knopf, 1919), 147. Bragdon, with the original manuscript in hand, gives a different phrasing from that published in Sullivan's *Kindergarten Chats*, remarks likely toned down by the newspaper editor.

19. Ibid., 56.

20. Ibid., 68.

21. Frank Lloyd Wright, "The Art and Craft of the Machine," in Bruce Brooks Pfeiffer (ed.), *Collected Writings* (New York: Rizzoli, 1992), I:69.

22. "In the Cause of Architecture," *Collected Writings* (note 21), I:86.

23. Frank Lloyd Wright, *Frank Lloyd Wright: An Autobiography* (New York: Horizon Press, 1977), 268.

24. "The City," *Collective Writings* (note 21), Vol. II:69. On Wright's larger urban views, see Neil Levine, *The Urbanism of Frank Lloyd Wright* (Princeton, NJ: Princeton University Press, 2016).

25. Frank Lloyd Wright, *The Disappearing City* (New York: William Farquhar Payson, 1932), 12.

26. Ibid., 79–80.

27. Ibid., 45.

28. Jennifer Gray, "Teaching Gardens: The Sociology of Plants," in *Frank Lloyd Wright Quarterly* 29:2 (Spring 2018), 10–17.

29. Nikolaus Pevsner, *Pioneers of Modern Design: From William Morris to Walter Gropius* (Hammondsworth, Middlesex: Penguin, 1960), 216.

30. Cited from the first edition of the book (London: Faber & Faber, 1936), 205–6.

31. Sigfried Giedion, *Building in France, Building in Iron, Building in Ferro-Concrete*, trans. by J. Duncan Berry (Santa Monica, CA: Getty Publication Programs, 1995), 91.

32. Richard Pommer and Christian Otto, *Weissenhof 1927 and the Modern Movement in Architecture* (Chicago, IL: University of Chicago Press, 1991), 131–44.

33. Walter Curt Behrendt, *The Victory of the New Building Style*, trans. by H. F. Mallgrave (Los Angeles, CA: Getty Publications, 2000), 89.

34. Events cited in Pommer and Otto, *Weissenhof 1927* (note 33), 158 and 273 n. 1. Giedion's letter to Oud was dated November 17, 1927.

35. For La Sarraz Declaration, see Ulrich Conrads, *Programs and Manifestoes of 20th-Century Architecture* (Cambridge, MA: Massachusetts Institute of Technology Press, 1975), 109–13. For CIAM, see Eric Mumford, *The CIAM Discourse on Urbanism, 1928–1960* (Cambridge, MA: Massachusetts Institute of Technology Press, 2000).

36. Walter Gropius, "Sociological Premises for the Minimum Dwelling of Urban Industrial Population," in *Scope of Total Architecture* (New York: Collier Books, 1974), 91–102.

37. *The Athens Charter*, trans. by Anthony Eardley (New York: Grossman Publishers, 1973).

38. Henry-Russell Hitchcock and Philip Johnson, *The International Style* (New York: The Norton Library, 1966), 19.

39. Ibid., 94.

40. Aldous Huxley, *Brave New World*, chapter 4, part 1.

41. George Orwell, *1984* (Boston, MA: Houghton Mifflin Harcourt, 2003), 91.

42. Ibid., 264–5.

43. Ibid., 132.

44. Ibid., 228.
45. Ibid., 203.
46. Yevgeny Zamyatin, *We*, trans. by S. Viatchanin (New York: New York Concept, n.d.), 53.
47. Ibid., 6.
48. Ibid.
49. Ibid., 7.
50. Ibid., 25.
51. Ibid., 134–5.
52. George Orwell, "Preface," to *We* (note 47), I.
53. Zamyatin, *We* (note 46), 23.
54. Aldo van Eyck, "Kaleidoscope of the Mind," in *Miracles of Moderation* (Zurich: Eidgenössische Technische Hochschule, 1976), 2.

12

THE PASSAGE OF MODERNISM

Urban Kakotopias

Optimism was quite high in North American design studios following World War II. A score of talented architects had migrated to America over the previous fifteen years, and the steel-and-glass style of high modernism was, for tall buildings at least, eminently suited to an industrial economy making the transition from wartime production to a global economy. The expanded labor force also led to rapid expansion and innovations in the manufacturing of glass and metals. Mies van der Rohe had planted his first "factory-style" building at Illinois Institute of Technology in Chicago in 1942, and six years later he designed the first two glass-and-steel towers on Lake Shore Drive. Eero Saarinen combined modernism's detailing with a colorful glazed brick in his buildings for the General Motors Technical Center near Detroit, begun in 1949, and the following year, Gordon Bunshaft designed an impressive glass tower in Manhattan, the Lever House. The following year Walter Gropius, who had founded The Architects Collaborative, completed the Graduate Center at Harvard University, very much in the style of his apartment buildings of the late 1920s. The larger scale of the new commissions also demanded a commensurate increase in the size of architectural offices, and hence we have the transition to larger corporate practices with specialists to assure generally high standards of detailing and a relatively uniform style of practice.

It was with urban theory, however, that significant problems first became apparent. Quite simply, the design imperatives of the International Style were too limited in their vocabulary to meld harmoniously with existing cities, despite the best efforts of the media and politicians to defend high modernism as a sign of progress. The first crack in the modernist facade came in 1947 when Lewis Mumford penned a piece for *The New Yorker*, titled "Bay Region Style." In it, he touted the "new winds" that were gaining strength on the American West Coast, winds that would eventually reach "even backward old New York." These winds would deal a cruel blow to "those academic American modernists who imitated Le Corbusier and Mies van der Rohe and Gropius, as their fathers imitated the reigning lights of the Ecole des Beaux Arts." The pollen carried by these winds was the seed of a "native and human form of modernism," one that was "a free yet unobtrusive expression of the terrain, the climate, and the way of life on the coast."[1]

We will return to the West Coast shortly, but Mumford's article indeed proved traumatic to the East Coast establishment, long accustomed to controlling issues of politics and culture. MoMA, barely fifteen years after setting down stylistic principles, responded in 1947 with a symposium, "What Is Happening to Modern Architecture?" The event was attended by architects and historians

DOI: 10.4324/9781003178460-12

who came to debate, or rather to reaffirm, the precepts of the International Style. In addition to the heretical Mumford, there was also the phenomenon of "New Empiricism" noted in the Scandinavian countries. The term referred to a thoughtful piece published in the British journal *Architectural Review* in 1947, in which J. M. Richards praised modern Swedish housing for employing local materials such as wood and brick, which preserved the handicraft tradition and resonated with the sensibilities of Nordic peoples.[2]

The first to take the microphone in New York was Barr, who began the evening by emphasizing the stylistic latitude of the International Style. He assured the nervous audience that the International Style was not "conceived as a kind of rigid strait-jacket requiring architects to design cubistic, white stucco boxes on Lally columns, with flat roofs and glass walls."[3] He then went on, with no small condescension, to label the Bay Region houses that Mumford had praised as a kind of domesticated "International Cottage Style," expressive of a "*neue Gemütlichkeit*" or new (excessive) sentimentality. This was a play on the locution *Neue Sachlichkeit* in modern art, "New Objectivity" as it was known to art historians.[4] That he used the German language to express this somewhat awkward idea is puzzling, because it essentially flattened his argument. Hitchcock and Gropius, in any case, followed him to the podium with a coordinated defense. Opposing them was the designated defender of "New Empiricism," Gerhard Kallmann, who upheld the Scandinavian movement because it considered the psychological needs of occupants—precisely the "sentimentality" in which Hitchcock and Johnson had warned American architects not to indulge. Kallmann set the stage for Mumford, who was the final speaker of the evening. As the clock was striking eleven, the New Yorker made the case that

> people, when they ask for a building, do not ask for it in any style. That is the healthy state that we should have in every part of the world. To me, that is a sample of internationalism, not a sample of localism and limited effort.[5]

The evening, as one might expect, settled nothing, especially the naïve question of whether one stylistic vocabulary should guide all architectural production.

In one further comment with regard to New Empiricism—Richards's article in the *Architectural Review* in 1947 followed a piece published four years earlier in the same journal by the Swedish architect Sven Backström. There, he discussed the introduction of international modernism into Scandinavia around 1930 and its failure to connect with Nordic peoples. For one thing, the amount of glass used in the International Style was ill-suited for the colder climate, and then—in a strikingly paradisiacal moment—he reflected on the inability "of any new epoch-making formula" to satisfy our better understanding of the human condition. "To-day we have reached the point where all the elusive psychological factors have again begun to engage our attention," he notes, "one tries to understand them, and to adapt the building in such a way that it really serves. And there is the desire to enrich it and beautify it in a living way, so that it may be a source of joy."[6]

Far more contentious than MoMA's feeble attempts to put design in a straitjacket was the deterioration of the North American city: the growing problem of urban slums. Both the Great Depression and the war had left behind declining urban infrastructures and changing demographics. With the loss of the male labor force to the military, poorer populations from rural areas had moved into the metropolitan centers of the north in search of jobs. With the return of the war veterans, eager to reconnect with or start families, there was as well a push toward the suburbs, set in motion by governmental loan programs for veterans. Cities were becoming poorer and unsustainable with collapsing tax bases and had no real strategy for addressing the problem. And it is within this context that we can consider the feud in the 1940s and 1950s between Mumford and New York's Commissioner Robert Moses.

Moses was a political king-maker with Haussmannian pretensions, and he was also skillful at raising capital for developers. One of his concerns was routing new traffic arteries into and around

ILLUSTRATION 12.1   Aerial view of Stuyvesant Town and Peter Cooper Village, Manhattan.

Source: Photo by Alec Jordan. Wikimedia CC BY-SA 3.0.

Manhattan, such as the Triborough Bridge and freeways along the two river edges—maneuvers incidentally lauded by Sigfried Giedion in *Space, Time and Architecture*. Moses in the early 1930s had also been drawn to Le Corbusier's image of a Radiant City, predicated on large-scale housing demolition. In short, he settled on a strategy of tearing down the row houses or tenements of New York and replacing them with isolated towers spread out on grass lawns. The idea of radically reconstructing existing cities was also an understandably exciting idea to many utopian-minded designers. In 1942 Moses began the first of his large-scale urban-renewal projects on Manhattan's Lower East Side, Stuyvesant Town and Peter Cooper Village. The plan, executed with military precision on eighty acres of land, was conceived as a phalanx of 110 brick towers, fifteen stories high. The demolition removed over 600 existing buildings, several streets, and displaced 3,000 families. Here is where Mumford threw down the gauntlet.

Mumford, as we have seen, had been a strong proponent of Ebenezer Howard's Garden City, but his vision had evolved in the 1930s. He wrote two large books in this decade. In the first, *Technics and Civilization*, he argued that urbanization was now entering the neotechnic era in which the modern machine (electrification, gas engines, and new industrial materials) held the promise of creating a new social equilibrium, a simpler and more humane society capable of organizing itself around a communitarian spirit. In his follow-up study, *Culture of Cities*—in line with Howard and Wright—he proposed a plan for reducing the population of larger cities by dispersing people into smaller regional cities, designed in an ecologically sensitive way and accommodating human needs. The human race, he concludes,

> is at last in a position to transcend the machine, and to create a new biological and social environment, in which the highest possibilities of human existence will be realized, not for the strong and the lucky alone, but for all co-operating and understanding groups, associations, and communities.[7]

It was from this perspective that Mumford took on Moses. In 1948, he delivered a scathing attack in the *New Yorker* on Stuyvesant Town, which he termed the "architecture of the police state," because of its mindless parade of brick towers, its high urban density, its lack of social amenities, and its disregard for social life.[8] Moses responded with a counterattack, and Mumford rejoined by praising the low-rise housing estate of Fresh Meadows in Queens: its curving streets, open common areas, and amount of existing greenery preserved around buildings and single dwellings.[9] It should also be noted that in 1948 the atomic bomb formed a darkened background to Mumford's strategy of decentralization, the idea that a single bomb could destroy an entire city.

The feud between Mumford and Moses would continue for another dozen years, but then in 1961 a third disputant appeared: Jane Jacobs and her book *The Death and Life of Great American Cities*. It also took a strong sociological approach to the problem and similarly abhorred the "block-busting" projects of Moses, as well as the priority he gave to the almighty automobile. Yet she also contested Mumford. Although born in Scranton, Jacobs was a gritty and hardened New Yorker living in Greenwich Village without the slightest inclination to take a moment of solace in nature; density in the metropolis was something to be celebrated. Mumford was an intellectual, yet as a native New Yorker, he was far more comfortable walking the pathways of Morningside Park than Tenth Street in the Village.

Jacobs opened her book with a frontal assault on "the pseudoscience of city rebuilding and planning," which she likened to the medieval practice of bloodletting.[10] Under the condensed and ironic rubric "Radiant Garden City Beautiful," she challenged Le Corbusier, Daniel Burnham, Howard, and Mumford at one stroke. Le Corbusier's towers in the park, with their "fantastically high city density," were little more than a "social Utopia," albeit one lacking any possibility of social life.[11] Howard's idea of a garden city aspired toward a new urban environment and social life but within "a paternalistic political and economic society," whose

> aim was the creation of self-sufficient small towns, really very nice towns if you were docile and had no plans of your own and did not mind spending your life among others with no plans of their own. As in all Utopias, the right to have plans of any significance belonged only to the planners in charge.[12]

She re-shelved Mumford's *Technics and Civilization* with similar dispatch. The book "was largely a morbid and biased catalog of ills. The great city was Megalopolis, Tyrannopolis, Nekropolis, a monstrosity, a tyranny, a living death."[13] Planners, Jacobs argued more generally, were simply uninformed about how cities function. As Peter Laurence has shown, Jacobs drew upon the libertarian legacy of Friedrich Hayek and Karl Popper, who, from an economic perspective, were similarly dismissive of "Utopian social engineering."[14] She constructed an energetic defense of Manhattan and emphasized the importance of streets with a spontaneous pedestrian life of their own. The ideal urban neighborhood should have a residential and commercial mixture of buildings of different ages, and short blocks to allow residents alternate walking routes. She even cited Kevin Lynch's recent book, *The Image of the City*, which had shown that the edges created by urban freeways and rail tracks forever divide the city into islands with little or no social interaction.[15]

By the late 1950s, large federal housing programs were underway, and the government's significant stacks of chips were placed on the strategy of Moses—the now-notorious "projects." The bulldozer became the principal tool of urban design, admittedly with no strategy for reconstructing the displaced, often ethnic neighborhoods. The liberal optimism of the Lyndon Johnson administration, as voiced by Sargent Shriver in 1966, even suggested that urban poverty could be eliminated within a decade.[16] The opposite of course proved to be the case, and it would only take a few more years before one of the more egregious examples of urban renewal, the Pruitt-Igoe housing project in East Saint Louis, was given its "final *coup de grâce*" by dynamite, according to Charles Jencks, "on

July 15, 1972 at 3:32 pm (or thereabouts)."[17] Jencks, not entirely correctly, aligned the moment with the death of modern architecture.

The anti-utopian character of Jacobs's book of 1961 nevertheless stood in the forefront of a contrarian movement that, although somewhat ephemeral, nevertheless had its moments of inspiration. Colin Rowe had in fact preempted Jacobs in 1959 with his essay "The Architecture of Utopia," in which he similarly condemned the penchant of architects and planners for thinking big with its inevitable urban monotony.[18] The idea of the metropolis was also being challenged from another direction. In the early 1960s the urban theorist Melvin Webber published two influential papers, which espoused the idea of "community without propinquity"—that is, the suggestion that the urban "downtown" had itself become obsolete because of emerging technologies.[19] People living in the Bay Region of California, he noted, are as likely to have their social and professional connections with others in Washington, New York, and Hong Kong, as with someone in the metropolitan region. Many people were now working at a distance from any urban or semi-urban location, which he referred to as the "Nonplace Urban Realm."

A strong countermovement to modern city planning was also emerging in Britain. In 1963, the art historian Ernst Gombrich presented a lecture to the Architectural Association, titled "Old Towns," in which he lauded the organic or "secret magic" of older towns with their slow, piecemeal growth—in contrast to the "mechanical, cold and cheerless" character of most modern cities."[20] Christopher Alexander, in his essay "A City Is Not a Tree," contrasted such "natural" cities as Siena and Kyoto with the "artificial" cities of Levittown, Chandigarh, and the British New Towns. Even architects, he noted, prefer to live in older buildings than in newer ones, and "I trust this conservatism."[21] The critic Reyner Banham took the argument one step further. If the 1920s had created the first machine age with its widespread use of electricity and the combustion engine, a second machine age was dawning in the 1950s with the new household appliances—everything from hair dryers to hi-fi equipment.[22] Thus, in the 1960s, he began to put modern architecture "On Trial."[23] As the phenomenon of a nascent hippiedom was erupting in all its psychedelic glory, Banham proposed to give up the fixed abode of the city altogether for the "power-point homesteading in a paradise garden of appliances"—that is, living in the wild in a transportable polyethylene air bubble with

> a properly set-up standard-of-living package, breathing out warm air along the ground (instead of sucking in cold along the ground like a campfire), radiating soft light and Dionne Warwick in heartwarming stereo, with a well-aged protein turning in an infrared glow in the rotisserie, and the icemaker discretely coughing cubes into glasses on the swing-out bar—this could do something for a woodland glade or creekside rock that Playboy could never do for its penthouse.[24]

Banham was not alone, as others of this "dropout" generation were building geodesic domes and forming rural communes. In another essay, "The Great Gizmo," Banham even noted the paradisiacal instinct of Frank Lloyd Wright's Broadacre City: "You have only to go up to the Cloisters or Fort Tryon and look around you, to realize that Manhattan Island would be the most paradisal of American Gardens if only they would get New York off it."[25] Banham would eventually abandon the woodland glade and Dionne Warwick for Santa Barbara and the "four ecologies" of Los Angeles—Surfurbia, Foothills, the Plains of Id, and Autopia—yet Banham was not alone in his irreverence. Kevin Lynch, the toast of academic counter-theorists, also came round to Wright's idea of decentralization, as he expressed himself in 1975:

> Imagine an urban countryside, a highly varied but humanized landscape. It is neither urban nor rural in the old sense, since houses, workplaces, and places of assembly are set among trees, farms, and streams. Within that extensive countryside, there is a network of small, intensive urban centers. This countryside is as functionally intricate and interdependent as any contemporary city.[26]

Lynch's vision of paradise is set in the near future. Land is owned only for a lifetime and then reverts to a land trust, which can resell it or return it to a natural condition. Countries have given way to special regional trusts, which ecologically and logistically regulate a free and open society. Depopulated older cities are "pruned and shaped" to enhance their beauty with greenery and smart buildings. Each territory is different in character, and families are free to live anywhere they please. Natural landscape features are preserved and even improved upon with gardens and crops. Sound land management is the rule, the arts are supreme, and people learn to enjoy their surroundings with all of their senses: "Everyone is trained to read a place, just as everyone is trained to read a book."[27] The idea of Eden was thus redeemed, at least momentarily.

Cosmologies of Design

If I have thus far painted a bleak picture of modernism with respect to urban planning and its strategies, it is also important to note that many talented designers during these same years were attempting to prepare a more humane grounding for modernism. In the pre-war years we have Pierre Chareau and Bernard Bijvoet's exquisite Maison de Verre with it its attached Parisian garden, Maxwell Fry's Sun House in Hampstead, and Leendert van der Vlugt's designs for the Van Nelle Factory and Sonneveld House in Rotterdam. My disquiet is not with modernism as a stylistic vocabulary or with its materials and forms, but rather with the way in which it continued to narrow the compass of human concerns, particularly after the war. No one can seriously contend that all buildings in the past were designed with human needs in mind, but the majority of buildings and their cities were at least designed to a human scale and from native biological and psychological sensibilities. The psychologist Robert Sommer, in a book of 1974 subtitled *Hard Architecture and How to Humanize It*, noted that "there is no behavior apart from environment even *in utero*." Responding to the modernism of the 1960s, he defined hard architecture as buildings with a uniformity of design that resist a human imprint, buildings that are cold and inhospitable to its users, and buildings that lack any emotional or sensory appeal. "The result," he concludes, "may be somatic disorders, anxiety, and irritation, but the probable outcome will be numbness to one's surroundings, with psychological withdrawal substituting for physical avoidance."[28] He captures the essence of many cities today. The glass towers crammed into every square foot of lower and central Manhattan differ not the least from those scattered along the exceedingly wide avenues of the Pudong district of Shanghai. Local newscasts use urban skylines as backdrops, presumably out of a sense of urban pride, but these same glass canyons are experienced on the ground by pedestrians in very different ways. Moreover, the hard surfaces of glass, metal, and concrete have in their ubiquity simply become monotonous. They are an affront to the human heart because they offer nothing to the social, recreational, and emotional dimensions of human life. As a society, we in many countries seem to have lost the idea of urban culture, a sense of place, and most importantly an anthropological understanding of our own species. "Architects and urbanists," as one architect noted some years ago, "have become true specialists in the art of organizing the meagre. The result draws very close to crime."[29]

This architect was Aldo van Eyck, who was born in Holland, schooled a few blocks from Hampstead Heath, and took his architectural studies in Zurich beginning in 1938. He was thus shielded from the war, but his stay in a neutral country also allowed him into the orbit of Carola Giedion-Welcher, the wife of Sigfried Giedion. Carola had taken her doctorate in art history under Heinrich Wölfflin and Wilhelm Wörringer. She was a prominent historian of European avant-garde movements, and she tutored the young architect on the new artistic trends by introducing him to several of the leading modern artists. It was through their fascination with early human cultures that Aldo and his wife Hannie, also an architect, cultivated their anthropological interests. It was a compelling pursuit for a young architect. After the war the van Eycks, with six others, drove 4,000 miles deep into the Sahara Desert to explore the villages of isolated tribal societies. It was an arduous journey, which involved numerous vehicular problems and almost did not end well.

Aldo and Hannie returned to Algeria the following year, but their most important venture came eight years later, in 1960, when the van Eycks, together with the architect Herman Haan, made their way to sub-Saharan Mali to explore Dogon culture. Van Eyck wanted to see architecture in its original form, and he was convinced that the Dogon huts with their "laboriously fashioned bricks of sandy mud" could not have been very different from the huts of Ur five millennia ago. The Dogon villages were small urban settlements, isolated by the terrain from outside influences and culturally the people had retained their timeless rituals grounded in the belief of a higher cosmic order. On the last leg of the trip into the area, the van Eycks met the Swiss psychiatrist Fritz Morgenthaler, who, together with Paul Parin, were studying the conceptual framework of the Dogon's religious beliefs. It was a propitious meeting. The two were living among the Dogon people, knew the language, and shared their understanding of the culture with the Dutch visitors, who were deeply impressed with the basic insight into humanity they encountered. There, Aldo learned that the Dogon view of paradise was almost identical to being on earth:

> The villages are like those in which the living dwell, the rich are rich, the poor are poor. All live with their families, planting millet and onions as they did on earth. In the dry brush the same trees stand, though the fruits they bear are more beautiful in color, more lustrous, so that the dead can tell they are in paradise and no longer in the land of the Dogon.[30]

Van Eyck studied the ingenuity of their designs, and many of the koan-like expressions that he used in his writings—twin phenomena, labyrinthian clarity, the shape of the in between, a house is a tiny city—can also read as recitations of Dogon cosmology. When Aldo was co-editor of the journal *Forum* between 1959 and 1963, he published many of his photographs and offered anthropological interpretations.

It was also through the auspices of the Giedions in Zurich that Van Eyck, in 1946, received his appointment to the Amsterdam Public Works Department, under the leadership of Cor van Eesteren. Holland had been devastated by the war. Rotterdam was almost entirely destroyed by bombing and Amsterdam had been ravaged by the forcible removal of tens of thousands of Jews to concentration camps. The city was in shambles and housing was the first priority. Van Eyck, however, made his reputation not with housing but with the 700 or so minimalist playgrounds he designed over the course of a dozen years, which in fact still today attract scholarly analyses for their insights into the creative imagination.[31] The sociologist Richard Sennett has considered these playgrounds as a social exposition on the idea of ambiguity, whereas the historian Liane Lefaivre has cast them against the backdrop of Dutch Renaissance paintings and the ludic celebrations of Johan Huizinga.[32] Van Eyck placed the playgrounds on abandoned or leftover sites, in gaps between rowhouses, or by extending sidewalks into the street, and the elements he employed in a postwar economy were few: a rectangular or circular sandbox molded and rounded along the edges, raised groupings of circular stepping stones offering options for jumping or sitting, and one or two tubular structures for climbing, either arches or domes. The intention, realized with a deft artistic touch, was not to dictate how children should play but to encourage the child to be imaginative in play.

In 1955 van Eyck received a major commission. The director of the Amsterdam orphanage (himself an orphan) brought the designer a thoughtful program for building an anti-institutional orphanage outside of the city. Van Eyck could not have been more sympathetic, and both agreed it should be an open, one-story building with direct access to light and play. Soon thereafter Aldo, over several months, explored and refined dozens of plan variations. The essence of the final floor plan was a "home" for each family of children connected along two diagonal formations, intersecting at right angles. The most important aspect of the design was, however, the articulation of each of the houses. They differed with age groups and gender and van Eyck labored over individual nuances. The common features were a kitchen, dinette, living room/play area (large enough for a

ILLUSTRATION 12.2   Aldo van Eyck, Municipal Orphanage, Amsterdam. 1960. Photo by Violet Cornelius.

Source: Courtesy of the Aldo+Hannie van Eyck Foundation.

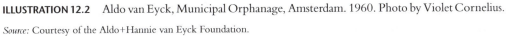

piano), and sanitary and sleeping areas. A solid masonry screen wall along the north side of each home provided a place for nesting, but he used glass walls and open courtyards along the south to feature the prospect of a green meadow. Furnishings were largely built-in, and floor levels within the common areas further differentiated the rooms spatially. All of the areas were scaled to their occupants, with toddlers, for instance, having individual places to explore while older children had places for social contact.

Another major feature of the design was its tectonic sophistication. Beams supported on columns and walls in turn supported large precast domes over the eight common areas of the homes, and the 328 small domes, one-third in size, over other areas. Francis Strauven describes the roof elements as soft domes, "mildly biomorphic," allowing a shallow articulation in a vertical direction, and likely recalling the subtle curves of the Sahara structures he had seen.[33] The larger domes have a concentric ring of circular portals providing light, whereas some of the small domes have a single central portal. Inside were many other touches by the designer's hand: the sconces in the street-like hallways, the glass globes of the table lamps, the safety worked into the design of the kitchenette. Most importantly, the "streets" were not corridors but the leftover interior spaces formed from rectangular elements arrayed diagonally, once again places for exploration and spontaneous play. Notwithstanding the building's labored and sociological design, van Eyck struggled to overcome the interference and opposition of the building trades and city authorities—all the while, the children loved their humanly scaled homes and gardens.

It was at a design conference in Belgium in 1959 that Louis Kahn first came into contact with the talent and passion of van Eyck. Kahn, seventeen years older, was impressed with his humanistic approach to design, in particular the Dutchman's desire for a building to engage emotionally with people, what van Eyck had referred to as "vernacular of the heart." Kahn toured the orphanage after the conference, and in the following year he invited van Eyck to lead a design studio at the University of Pennsylvania, where Kahn had recently joined the faculty.

Kahn himself had traveled a different road. The Estonian-born architect had emigrated to Philadelphia in 1906 at the age of five. His musically inclined mother, said to be a relative of Felix Mendelssohn, trained Kahn on the piano, but she also saw that he had drawing lessons.[34] In 1924, Kahn enrolled in the architecture program at the University of Pennsylvania, where he studied the Beaux-Arts curriculum that had been established by the French architect Paul Philippe Cret. Kahn next worked in several offices before embarking in 1928–29 on an extended tour of Europe. The trip allowed him to assimilate the recent developments on the continent and to study and sketch medieval and classical works within their native landscapes. When he returned to the United States in 1930, young and fresh with ideas, he was greeted with the Great Depression and then the war. Effectively, he lost the middle two decades of his professional years, his office surviving on only a few federal housing projects. After the war he joined the faculty at Yale, and a stay at the American Academy in Rome three years later allowed him to revisit his classical roots. By the end of the 1960s, when he was in his late fifties, he would become the world's busiest architect with a score of major commissions.

There are perhaps a half dozen designs of Kahn that house paradisiacal aspirations. The largest of his commissions, the design of the Bangladesh National Capital in Dhaka, can be characterized in such a way. The finished works consist of dozens of buildings framing the capital's vast Assembly Hall complex set within a man-made lake. Two works from the mid-1960s, the Library at Phillips Exeter Academy in New Hampshire and the Kimball Art Museum in Fort Worth, also rise to such a level. The former reverses the way in which a library is conceived, with its dramatic central atrium, supported on a squared concrete framework carved out with a massive circle at the center of each side, allowing the bookcases to be the focus of the design. The student carrels have access to natural light along the perimeter walls, a gesture he borrowed from the cloister of Santa Maria della Pace in Rome. Conversely, the natural light of the Kimball Art Museum in Fort Worth filters through the center of its sixteen cycloid vaults over ninety feet in length, only to be reflected upward by curved transoms to wash the undersides of the vaults. It is also his most refined production in terms of finishes and detailing, and it is said by many to be the best museum of the twentieth century.

Yet the one complex that best displays his design cosmology is the Salk Institute of Biological Studies in La Jolla, California, built in the 1960s. Jonas Salk had developed his polio vaccine in 1955, and with the proceeds of its success he decided to build a research institute that would house the top biologists from around the world, for which he purchased a scenic twenty-seven-acre site along the Pacific coastline. He had visited Kahn's Research Laboratories at Penn, where he found someone of a very similar mind. Salk's ideal for a place of scientific research was the monastery of Saint Francis of Assisi, a place of contemplation yet also one allowing casual contacts among scientists. Kahn knew the complex well from his travels, and he was especially happy when Salk gave him no "dictatorial program," but allowed the design to flow directly from their conversations. As Kahn himself characterized the project's development, "The simple beginning requirement of the laboratories and their services expanded to cloistered gardens and Studies over arcades and to spaces for meeting and relaxation interwoven with unnamed places for the glory of the fuller environment."[35] Salk told Kahn that he wanted a place where Picasso could be invited.

The site itself was idyllic. It was perched on a tall escarpment above the Pacific, and a craggy canyon partially snaked its way into the middle of the land. Kahn located the research labs along the eastern ridge of the intruding canyon, and he proposed houses for the scientists along the southern arm extending toward the ocean. He placed the meeting center at the western rim of the northern arm of the escarpment. It took the form of an acropolis with a figurative temple ruin to be seen

ILLUSTRATION 12.3   Louis Kahn, preliminary model for the Salk Institute for Biological Studies looking east.

Source: Photo courtesy of The Louis I. Kahn Collection, The University of Pennsylvania and the Pennsylvania Historical and Museum Collection.

from the sea. The ruin was, in fact, a grouping of freestanding columns set within a town square, which Kahn referred to as the "garden." Within was a basin fed by a narrow channel of water running down the plaza, an idea likely taken from the Court of Lions at the Alhambra. The fountain at its source was located near the entrance to the courtyard, next to the amphitheater. The garden was to be planted with trees and vegetation, and north of it was the grouping of buildings forming the meeting center with a cloister-like courtyard. The main building was the library, which was placed at the western edge of the acropolis. On the other three sides were apartments for the director and visiting scholars, kitchen, dining rooms, and a gymnasium. Both the dining room and library had the best views of the ocean, and Kahn exploited the fact by sprouting square and circular rooms toward the ocean for individual reading, seminars, and smaller groups of diners. It was for these smaller rooms that Kahn conceived the strategy of "wrapping ruins around buildings"—that is, employing expansive glass for the rooms to allow sea views but then protecting them from direct sunlight by enveloping, freestanding screen walls.

The meeting center of the Salk Institute could very well have been one of the grandest paradises of the century, but it was also its unearthly expense that caused its delay and ultimately its cut from the construction budget. Undeterred, Kahn redoubled his efforts on the laboratories themselves, which he separated into two groupings of buildings instead of four, set perpendicular to the ocean and separated by a "cloistered garden." The eighteen individual studies of the scholars are pulled out from their laboratories behind with an extension, so that each biologist has one window on the court and another turned at a forty-five-degree angle to provide a shielded view of the ocean. The garden also underwent changes. After Kahn became frustrated with his landscaping ideas, he invited the Mexican architect Luis Barragán to visit and consult. When the latter arrived, he offered the advice to "put not a tree or a blade of grass" into the garden, but to transform it into a "facade to the sky"—the idea that Kahn embraced. It actually returned the courtyard to the founding inspiration of the paved cloister at Saint Francis at Assisi.[36] To soften its appearance, however, Kahn moved

ILLUSTRATION 12.4   Louis Kahn, Courtyard of the Salk Institute for Biological Studies, completed 1965.

Source: Photo by Codera23. Wikimedia CC BY-SA 4.0.

the narrow channel of water from the unbuilt acropolis to the center of his new courtyard, precisely aligned to the setting sun of each autumnal and spring equinox. It too proved to be an idea empyreal in its own way, for in approaching the courtyard from the entrance grove at the east, all one sees are the tall, angled concrete partitions of the scientists' studies (the tonality of the mix softened and crafted by meticulously detailed formwork), teak wall panels, the ocean, and the sky complimented by the facial underpayment of the travertine plaza. The latter, once fittingly described as "a form of metaphysical meditation," presents itself as a celestial garden by virtue of the trickling sound of water and the waft of salt air blowing off the ocean.[37] With his paradisiacal ambitions and dramatic sense of play, Kahn had no peer.

Gardener of Nervous Growth

Until very recently, California has never lacked migrations of people moving into the state. And why not? Its sunny attraction has always been its scenic landscape, warm climate, semitropical vegetation, and abundant beaches, the last of which popularized surfboards, bikinis, beach-blanket parties, and the mellifluous music of the Beach Boys. Its architecture, as well, has had its unique qualities. For a while at least, the presence of the San Andreas Fault discouraged tall buildings, and the casual and relaxed "Bay Region Style" that Mumford championed in 1947 had a longer ancestry going back to Bernard Maybeck, Irving Gill, and the Greene brothers. Wright also left a trail of inspired houses in Los Angeles in the early 1920s, beginning with his "sanctuary for the arts" for Aline Barnsdall, a complex to be situated in Los Angeles on thirty-six acres of high ground between Sunset and Hollywood Boulevards. Wright's assignment was to create an Edenic estate with a mansion, two theaters, artist residences, shops, a rooftop restaurant, groves, and a lake. Only the mansion, the Hollyhock House, came to fruition. When Wright left the country to manage the building of the Imperial Hotel in Tokyo, he left the supervision of the Hollyhock House to his employee

Rudolph Schindler, who would, with his wife Pauline, soon entertain their own Edenic fantasies down the road in West Hollywood. "Schindler's Paradise," as it later came to be called by the press, was a colony of four studios built for two families. In its overall ambience, the pavilions, inspired by a Yosemite campsite, were formed with a series of L-shaped concrete walls into which were inserted redwood frameworks. They opened onto private patios and gardens, the latter well-grown today, and sleeping was originally relegated to "baskets" on the roofs under canvas. Schindler would go on to enjoy a successful career within a developing modernism.

His erstwhile university classmate Richard Neutra would join Schindler in his paradise in 1925. Neutra, like his friend, had vowed back in Vienna to work for Wright, but whereas Schindler graduated before the war and left the city, Neutra's studies were incomplete and he was drafted into the Habsburg military. Serving as an artillery officer, he came down with malaria and tuberculosis during the conflict, and later circumvented a veritable bureaucratic odyssey before arriving in Chicago in 1923. Neutra met Wright at the funeral of Louis Sullivan in the following year and soon joined him in Taliesin, where his wife Dione's cello talents were much appreciated at Wright's musical soirées. Schindler and Neutra partnered on the League of Nations Competition of 1926, yet the professional relationship soon soured. The end came as Schindler was finishing the Lovell Beach House in Newport Beach. The wealthy physician Lovell, who wrote a weekly column for the *Los Angeles Times Sunday Magazine*, titled "Care of the Body," was a proponent of sleeping porches, strict vegetarianism, regular exercise, and nude sunbathing. He had decided to build a new house in Los Angeles, a few blocks north of the Barnsdall house. Schindler was the obvious choice to design it, but Lovell instead chose Neutra. It is possible that Lovell was fascinated with Neutra's interest in psychiatry, the fact that Richard was a childhood friend of Ernst Freud and had spent some of his summer holidays with the Sigmund Freud family. Or perhaps Lovell had heard of Schindler's rumored dalliance with his wife. In any case, Neutra won the commission for what became the much-publicized "Health House," carved into two sides of a canyon just south of Griffith Park. It was a lightweight steel structure intended to epitomize a healthy modern lifestyle, with a ground-floor swimming pool and exercise area, abundant natural light and ventilation in the living areas above, and sleeping porches on the third level. The kitchen even had large cutting and washing areas for trimming fresh vegetables. The furniture and lighting were either built-in or specially designed, the detailing was dust-free, and the extensive gardens with their ameliorative aromas and visual repose were immaculate. It was, with its physiological, psychological, and environmental concerns, one of the most refined designs of the 1920s—seemingly within the formalistic confines of the International Style yet radically alien in some of its design premises and concerns.

Neutra continued to experiment with alternative housing strategies in the 1930s, such as with his own VDL Research house on Silver Lake. Partially financed by the interested Dutchman Cees H. van der Leeuw, the design demonstrated how the principles of the Lovell House—natural light and gardens—could be used in a modest house with inexpensive materials. He similarly experimented with an "all-metal" and "self-cooling" house of 1934, the earthquake-proof house in Pasadena, which he designed for the seismologist Charles Richter, and the "Plywood Model House" for an exhibition of low-cost housing in 1936. During the war, he designed a multitude of open-air schools, health clinics, and hospitals in Puerto Rico. He did all of this while maintaining a wealthy clientele, which would culminate in the majestic Kaufmann House set in the Palm Springs desert in 1946, surrounded by a landscape of massive rocks and cacti. This was the same Kaufmann who had earlier commissioned Wright to design Fallingwater, and it is easy to characterize the house, made famous by the photographs of Julius Schulman, as nothing short of a paradise. Yet Neutra, in southern California's climate, integrated gardens and water into the interiors of virtually every house he designed; he never acknowledged the divide between interior and exterior.

Neutra wrote several books stressing the importance of gardens, but his masterpiece is his broader study *Survival through Design*, published in 1954. It remains an up-to-date analysis of our ecological and biological limitations, despite our much-expanded knowledge. The overarching theme is that our biological and emotional health is bound with our physical environments, and that designers play a dangerous genetic game by creating environments that are hostile to the needs and limitations of the human organism. Neutra offers various strategies to overcome this problem. One is to repair the environment in which we are reared, which he believed was becoming increasingly polluted by poor design, poor air quality, and our ecological insensitivity to the planet. Another theme is the need to reform the education of the architect, who is in many ways the guardian of the earth as well as of the human species. The future architect, in fact, should be trained to be "a gardener of nervous growth," and should therefore be knowledgeable about how the built environment affects our biological and psychological health and happiness.[38] We must recognize that architecture, far from being a "visual art," is a multisensory experience, taking place on multiple levels, from a building's temperature, humidity, air currents, and heat loss to its aromas, tactile qualities, gravity, and musculoskeletal responses to space. All modulate or affect our optical, acoustic, chemical, muscular, and other metabolic responses.

To address these issues, Neutra argued that the designer should become familiar with human biology, in particular research related to illumination, color perception, comfort, habituation, and the limitations of the nervous system. The future designer should also understand that we are born into the world with social needs and psychological proclivities. Ritualistic behaviors that in our evolutionary past may have had survival values remain with us long after these needs have passed. Music, for instance, is not simply a cultural affectation but a necessary "acoustical decoration," whereas a fireplace retains its social and symbolic meanings. These multiple dimensions of design should be addressed through research, and to do this we must dispense with "the pure aesthetics of a bygone brand of speculation."[39] Neutra's design philosophy is to some extent summarized in one passage:

> A house, then, can be designed to satisfy "by the month," with the regularity of a provider. Here it satisfies through habituation. Or it may do so in a very different way, "by the moment," the fraction of a second, with the thrill of a lover. The experience of a lifetime is often summed up in a few memories, and these are more likely to be of the latter type, clinging to a thrilling occurrence, rather than of the former, concerned with humdrum steadiness. Here is the value of a wide sliding door opening pleasantly onto a garden.[40]

A few lines later, Neutra even recommends opening the sliding door "before breakfast or on the first warm and scented spring day."

Regionalism

The global unrest of the late 1960s—Soviet tanks in Prague, political assassinations, the Civil Rights movement, opposition to the Vietnam War—had all left behind an anxious generation of designers coming of age with few thoughts of paradise. And with the Oil Embargo of 1973 curtailing building activity, anxiety soon gave way to a sense of ennui. The awkwardly dubbed "postmodern" era ensued—a period of feigned drama, histrionic debates, and revolutionary pretensions that every generation feels called upon to express. It is true that the luster of modernism had worn off, but behind the languor was a sense of cleverness bordering on malice. Yet for many of the younger generation, as well as the popular press, the postmodern era was salad days. One of its founding premises was that somehow, somewhere, architectural "meaning" had been lost—lost, that is, to everyone save José Ortega y Gasset's "mass-man," the sophisticated individual both disdainful of culture and subversive toward the status quo.[41] The movement was also buffered with the quaint belief that this misplaced "meaning" could be found by some kind of semantic disambiguation posing as a game show of stylistic posturing. With such laxity, it was therefore little wonder that the postmodern fervor rather quickly succumbed to the "deconstructionist" currents of the mid-1980s, which sought to reduce architectural theory to a cerebral mix of dark metaphysics, based on the premise that meaning, through the writ of philosophical decree, could in fact be expunged altogether.

Of course, modernism never really went away, but this was not the issue. What the dead-end of postmodern polemics revealed, however, was that "meaning" should never have been the primary issue of design in the first place, for to elevate (or deconstruct) meaning presumes that architecture is largely a visual exercise explainable only through the critical process of rational reasoning or conceptualization. And to view design as a semantic exercise is to overlook the rather obvious fact that at the end of the design process—experientially—lies a flesh-and-blood human outfitted with multiple sensory and visceral capacities and with profound social and emotional needs. The mind-meld of Spockian theology deprives the human nervous system of its natural body, and within these six degrees of separation came forth the cautionary voices of Maurice Merleau-Ponty and Martin Heidegger. The former pointed out that we experience our environments not on some mental plane apart from us but only through our bodies.[42] We construct our reality with both exterior and interior horizons, the latter through the particular emotions and experiences that we bring to the perception itself. Our lived reality, then, is substantially corporeal and pre-reflective; consciousness is always a kinesthetic activity of our making. Heidegger, in an essay first translated into English in 1971, made an etymologically more subtle point. Thinking cannot be divorced from dwelling, and neither can it be separated from building. In his words, "The nature of building is letting dwell. Building accomplishes its nature in the raising of locations by the joining of their spaces. *Only if we are capable of dwelling, only then can we build.*"[43]

The Columbia professor Kenneth Frampton brought Heidegger's point home to architects in 1974 in a forceful tone. He used Heidegger's notion of dwelling to attack the conceptual underpinnings of postmodernism, among them "our pathological capacity for abstraction," our "prized mobility," and our indulgence of "the proliferation of roadside kitsch—in the fabricated mirage of 'somewhere' made out of billboard facades and token theatrical paraphernalia—the fantasmagoria

ILLUSTRATION 12.5   Carlo Scarpa, Detail from the courtyard garden of the Foundazione Querini Stampalia, 1961–63.

Source: Photo by author.

of an escape clause from the landscape of alienation."[44] The architect Christian Norberg-Schulz followed him to the well in a less subtle but equally profound way. Regarding the International Style or its postmodern pretender, he pointed out that the *genius loci* and cultural ambience of Prague, Khartoum, and Rome differ dramatically from one another, and designers might want to take these differences into account.[45] Suddenly in the late 1970s, there sprouted forth the idea of regionalism, three decades after Lewis Mumford had made precisely the same point with his Bay Region Style.

Some architects, momentarily at least, experienced a sense of relief. They could now, in good conscience, move past the narrow aesthetic confines of their academic trade-school razzing and take a day off from theorizing. They could, for instance, savor an espresso in Carlo Scarpa's paradise garden at the rear of his renovations to the Foundazione Querini Stampalia in Venice and enjoy the paradise of its vegetation, pools, and water channels. They could even venture outside of the city and stroll through the labyrinthian pathways of Scarpa's garden of Brion Cemetery in San Vito d'Altivole, where the Venetian brought together concrete, metals, marbles, stone, colorful glass tiles, and pockets of denticulated outcroppings. Here, in the abode of the dead, one might find the meaning of life oddly uplifting. After Scarpa had completed his funerary masterpiece, he once wondered, after investing so many years of his life into the project, if it might not have been better simply to have planted a thousand cypresses. His student Marco Frascari, however, responded by noting that Scarpa's projects were not decorated sheds but genuine creations hard-won through his lifelong dealings with the "stonecutters, masons, carpenters, glassmakers, and smiths of Venice"—real things.[46]

The incomparable work of the Mexican architect Luis Barragán also came to light with an exhibition at the Museum of Modern Art only in 1976, only after his real estate development of the 1940s, the "Gardens of Rocky Place," had been overrun with later development.[47] The 865-acre housing community, in a lava field south of Mexico City, possessed a spectacular outcropping of large rock formations and wild vegetation formed by the eruptions of the Xitle volcano. Barragán embraced the landscape as if it were Eden itself, preserving every feature possible. In the 1970s, his two residential communities of the 1960s, *Las Arboledas* and *Los Clubes*, were still in full flower in the 1970s. Both were founded as communities for horsemen and both had riding schools, which Barragán treated as gardens scaled to horses, outfitted with water troughs, grand pools, brilliantly painted stucco wall planes, all sheltered from the sun with eucalyptus and other native trees. Barragán built several other stunning buildings, including his own house, but his focus was always on the garden as the starting point of design. "Architects must have gardens to be used as much as the houses they build," he once wrote, not only to cultivate beauty but also to acquire "other spiritual values." He goes on to add,

> Such a garden leads a man to the common use of beauty as much as the use of our daily bread, and causes man unconsciously to fall into an atmosphere of spontaneous meditation without any effort and with reduced nervous tension.[48]

By the mid-1980s, Japan had emerged as a major center of regional design, drawing upon its rich history of materiality, detailing, and spiritualized landscapes. One of the many talented designers was Tadao Ando, who generally expressed his inwardly poetic and austerely meditative treatment of form and landscape through his use of water and light. One of his most blissful creations is the Water Temple situated on the Japanese island of Awaji. It is a shrine to Tantric Buddhism, and here the objective seems to be enlightenment by the journey to the temple itself, an ordeal of purification of sorts. The labyrinth involves ascending a hill along a winding gravel path through vegetation and a series of walls. What one finds at the hill's crown is not a building but a large oval pond filled with lotus blossoms. The vermillion temple of intricate fretwork actually lies beneath the pond and is accessible by a staircase leading down into the pond. At the center of the shrine is the statue of the

ILLUSTRATION 12.6   Balkrishna Doshi, Sangath, Ahmedabad, India, 1979–81.

Source: Photo courtesy of the Vastu Shilpa Foundation Archives.

Amida Buddha, who is believed to convey the message of heavenly paradise. The only question is whether in fact the message has already been understood.

The same regionalist spirit infuses the studio paradise of the Indian architect Balkrishna Doshi, located on the outskirts of Ahmedabad. Doshi began his practice in the office of Le Corbusier in the early 1950s and he later worked with Kahn on the Indian Institute of Management. Known as Sangath, Doshi describes his creation as inspired by a "revelation." The entrance is the keynote, because one enters the compound not through a building but through a garden. One must first navigate across the lawn, past the hedges, trees, flowers, statuary, pools (perhaps with a peacock or two), water channels, and grass amphitheater, before climbing a few steps to the office. The garden also functions as a public space, an invitation for all residents to sit and take recreation. Two of the five elongated barrel vaults of the complex hovering over the idyllic landscape are partly sunken into the ground to find the cooler earth, and beside all the vaults are troughs that move water from one side of the site to collection pools at the other. The skin of the concrete vaults is made from recycled fragments of white porcelain to reflect the strong sunlight away. It is a place of quietude, and the complex has been described by Kazi Khaleed as conceived from "an openly oneiric and mythopoeic way of working."[49] In his acceptance speech for the Pritzker Prize in 2018, Doshi noted that good architecture should serve only as a backdrop—that is, a building "proactivates life when in tune. It heightens all the events to their ultimate sensations such as light, space, form, structure, texture, colour, rhythm and heightens our skills and catalyses events and rituals."[50]

Tale of Two Cities

When Marshall McLuhan spoke of the global village in 1962, he did so within the context of the Gutenbergian medium of print and of its modern-day successor, the television. Those "tactile qualities" that he saw being elided by the printing press, and that new cinematic, sequential, and pictorial "sense of time of typographic man," has today morphed into the silicon screens viewed inside our faceless towers, which perfectly mirror the sensory void of so many of our global cities. Who will occupy these gray-glass offices when the virtual workplace becomes more and more a reality? Will the sense of community or social roots of the pre-global villages return in some form? Unlikely, it seems. It is more probable that our present-day utopian elitists, trapped within the censorious echo chamber of social media and corporate virtue signaling, will no longer—as the novelist Max Frisch precociously intuited—have any place, identity, or community to come home to.[51]

The question of how we build our cities is a difficult one to answer, if only because there is no one solution that fits all sizes and cultures. Therefore, the question should be recast in regional and cultural terms, and the issues before us are really not that complicated. In the late 1980s, one alternative approach materialized in the movement of "New Urbanism." It emphasized the social life of a city, and the poster child for the new movement was the sunny beach town of Seaside, Florida, fathered by the developer Robert Davis and the architects Andrés Duany and Elizabeth Plater-Zyberk. They studied the historic town plans of Frederick Law Olmsted, Raymond Unwin, and John Nolan, and the scale of Seaside allowed the focus of design to be the town square and pedestrians. Seaside's city ordinance prescribed minimal housing setbacks, narrow streets, natural vegetation, and colorful house designs—all to counter the bright sunlight of the American South. Critics scoffed, as diehard urbanists tend to do, but the design conception, like some of its successor projects across the South, was sufficiently successful in its conception to be victimized by its own success. The town soon evolved from the middle-class, human-centered community of its inception into a beach resort with pricey rentals. Nevertheless, enacted here were principles of considerable merit.[52]

There remains, however, legitimate questions of what such strategies offer the metropolis, the global cities with the mushrooming populations of Mexico City, Mumbai, San Paolo, or Shanghai. Utopians might ask, do we ban urban towers or encourage them? Paradisiacal-minded people, however, cannot be so bold. I would like to consider this question by considering two differing planning approaches of two cities—Copenhagen and Singapore—and my interest lies with their livability, culture, and health.

ILLUSTRATION 12.7 Street in Seaside, Florida.

Source: Photo by Michael E. Arth. Wikimedia CC BY-SA 4.0.

In the last few decades Copenhagen, a town that began as a late Viking fishing village in the eleventh century, has become something of an economic leviathan. The first university was founded in 1479 by King Christian I, yet it was still a modest town in the seventeenth century during the reign of Christian IV when it underwent a period of growth. Perhaps the most interesting period of its cultural development came in the mid-nineteenth century, when Hans Christian Andersen and Søren Kierkegaard walked its streets. Necessity became the mother of invention. The city was experiencing problems with pulmonary diseases and high morbidity rates when along came the devastating cholera outbreak in 1853. City officials decided to alleviate the crowded conditions by taking down parts of the confining northern ramparts, and in 1866 they adopted a plan to expand the city northward toward the ring of old defensive moats. This decision allowed the creation of a continuous band of lakes and parks to be joined to the city with new boulevards and promenades.[53] Several smaller (and now larger) parks were also spread over the city. These decisions established the very important precedent of having nature always in proximity to living areas, a strategy also employed in Norway—and much of northern Europe, in fact.

The so-called Finger Plan of 1947 set out further parameters for development. If the historic city lies within the palm of the hand, the fingers represent mass-transit or train lines that extend north and west. In this way, suburban development was directed linearly and the wedges between the fingers became green areas: nature preserves, agricultural land, and the topography's abundant lakes. Even with these natural amenities and sound planning decisions, the city, like so many other European capitals, went through difficult years during the 1980s, with budget deficits, high unemployment, pollution, gnarled traffic, and people leaving the city for the suburbs. One solution turned out to be a publicly owned, privately managed corporation to develop city-owned land in keeping with the city's existing building fabrics. Another element was the creation of a tunnel and bridge across the Øresund, or Sound, connecting Copenhagen to the Swedish city of Malmö. It spawned a regional economy and aided corporations such as Maersk, with its ever-expanding line of container ships. High-quality education for the populace also became a high priority here and throughout Scandinavia.

It was at this point that the planning efforts of Jan Gehl began to take root. He had graduated from the Royal Danish Academy of Fine Arts in 1960 and, after a few years in practice, he and his psychologist wife Ingrid received a grant to study street-life in Italian cities. He brought the results back to the Royal Academy where, as a professor, he began extensive studies of street life in Copenhagen, supported by an enlightened city council. In Gehl's first book of 1971, *Life between Buildings*, he put his finger on the root cause of many of the failed urban strategies of both then and now. It was a black-and-white photograph of city planners huddled over a scale model of city streets with tiny blocks representing buildings.[54] The image displayed the privileged primacy of logistics, or the automobile to move about the city. The buildings themselves were little more than abstractions— red and green pieces on a Monopoly board. Gehl countered this strategy with the rather startling suggestion that the principal focus of urban planners should be on people and their environments. Priority should be given to places of socialization, or the way in which residents actually experience urban life.

As his ideas have evolved over the years, his message has been condensed into the argument that cities should be lively, safe, sustainable, and healthy.[55] The last attribute is aided not only by cleaner air but also by the "green" mobility of the human foot, the daily exercise of walking or bicycling to and from work. The ideal city for Gehl, in fact, is Venice, where automobiles are restricted from crossing the lagoon and entering the city. Gehl's research over many years has been impressive. Similar to Sitte's work of more than a century ago, his teams have studied the dimensions of personal, social, and public space, distances for reading facial expression and conversation, and angles of peripheral vision. Their general conclusion is that the "shattered scale" of large spaces and large buildings leads to "cool" urban environments with little pedestrian use or social interchange.

Drawing upon his favorite example of the Piazza del Campo in Siena, his counter-thesis is that urban planners should invite people into public spaces with the instrument of "soft edges," which are created when the lower two stories of squares or major public streets are delineated facades with public amenities and inviting commercial windows. Edges should also have colorful textures, together with widened sidewalks containing benches, trees and flowers, balconies, and outdoor cafés. He also instituted a number of interconnecting, pedestrian-only streets, with the greatest attention given to their material quality and detailing. Based on his research, he has made a case that the ideal overall height for buildings should be six to eight stories, similar to the urban fabric of Copenhagen, which of course flies in the face of the scale of the global metropolis. Moreover, if automobiles cannot be eliminated from streets entirely, he argues that their lanes should be narrowed and vehicular movement slowed. Bicyclists and pedestrians should have demarcated streets or defended lanes; in short, the architectural quality, scale, and rhythm of the environmental experience for the pedestrian is paramount. These criteria do not necessarily rule out taller residential towers, but Gehl believes that these can be reserved for a few selected areas of the city, such as along the borders of waterways or parks.

Copenhagen perennially ranks at or near the top of the EU's "happiest" or "most livable" cities, but there is one other feature of the city, beyond its human scale, that should be noted, which is the widespread presence of gardens. In his book *Cities for People*, Gehl sums up the argument with an anecdote—a photograph of one inner-city neighborhood, known historically as "potato rows," depicting row after row of narrow parallel streets filled with nineteenth-century townhouses, with small front and rear gardens. American urban strategies of the 1960s would have bulldozed them. "These Copenhagen row houses," Gehl observes, "look boring and uniform seen from the air. However, seen at eye level the row houses have so many qualities and function so convincingly that the city's largest concentration of architects and their families live here."[56] Aside from their small gardens, what also contributes to this neighborhood's appeal is its location. The former potato fields, as part of nineteenth-century urban expansion, came to be wedged between Sortedam Lake along the north and Østre Park to its south, and today the rowhouses are within easy walking distance of the Art Museum, Natural History Museum, and Botanical Garden. They are also situated in proximity to many of the 3,500 outdoor café tables of the city, where Copenhageners sit and enjoy a cappuccino—in the winter with the aid of wind screens and heat lamps. Perhaps these architects and their families know what planners elsewhere are slow, if not hesitant, to admit, which is that it is possible, with the simplest urban texture, to create a community and a lifestyle approaching the urban ideal simply by allowing them access to natural and cultural amenities.

Copenhagen, nevertheless, is a relatively small, affluent, and culturally homogenous city with a population of a little more than a million people, as some critics might say. Yet Singapore, founded as a British trading post in 1819, is today an ethnically diverse metropolis of almost six million residents, of whom only 60 percent are citizens. The rest are foreigners working largely within the financial and commercial industries. When the country became a republic in 1965, Singapore was an equatorial island largely consisting of shanty towns with a relatively small colonial quarter. The rivers were mosquito infested and heavily polluted, cows grazed the town's main park, and nearly the entire city lacked sanitation. Moreover, the main island, with its sixty-three satellites, is subject to strong sunlight, high humidity and temperatures, and monsoon rains. Yet today, the maritime city-state has one of the world's longest life expectancies and a primary and secondary school system perpetually at or near the top in educational ranking. Its economy generates a per capita gross domestic product larger than the United States, and corruption is non-existent. How was this possible to transform a city so dramatically over just a few decades?

Singapore's first prime minister, Lee Kuan Yew, has recounted his efforts to raise both living habits and standards, and to build the country into a financial hub through its banking systems and international trade.[57] His successors since the 1990s have transformed the country into a major tourist destination in addition to building exceptional educational and health-care systems, seriously cutting pollution, building a modern mass-transit system, and shrinking the private use of the auto-mobile by limiting auto permits. Architecturally, the approach taken in Singapore is very different from that of Copenhagen. If the latter city has a nineteenth-century fabric of continuous low- or medium-rise housing, Singapore is an ad hoc creation of the late twentieth century. It is a city com-prised almost entirely of towers: modestly tall residential towers and tall commercial towers. A few are well designed, whereas the majority of older ones are decidedly less so. And there is a reason for this disparity. Its older towers present the image of a "hard architecture," glass coming down hard to the sidewalks below. In response, the city's Urban Redevelopment Authority has passed a statute known as "LUSH" (Landscaping for Urban Spaces and High Rises). It stipulates that the landscaped areas of each building project should be equivalent in size to the area of the developmental site. This statute has led to new buildings being wrapped with garden balconies, garden walls, and garden rooftops—in fact, to some of the most creative and high-quality buildings of any city in the world.

This statute fits in with Lee's original vision of the city, which was to transform it into a "green oasis." Early on, a fifteen-square-mile sector of the island was set aside as a system of nature preserves, water-catchment areas, and reservoirs. Lee cleaned up the basins of the Kallang and Singapore Riv-ers and allowed fish to spawn for the first time in decades. He extended sanitation lines to every part of the city and created green hospitals and green schools—that is, complexes planted within exten-sive gardens. With schools, the gardens are maintained by students as part of the cultural curriculum. Lee also began the process, as Timothy Beatley has noted, of transforming fragile ecological areas of the city into a system of naturalized parks, many connected with elevated pedestrian walkways.[58] The largest of these systems are the Southern Ridges, consisting of three linear parks along a six-mile, mostly elevated path, weaving under and through the canopies of rainforest vegetation. The route also features one of the more enchanting pedestrian bridges in the world: the Henderson Waves Bridge.

ILLUSTRATION 12.8   Forest Walk, Southern Ridges.

Source: Photo by Kars Alfrink. Wikimedia CC BY 2.0.

Although buildings today occupy 75 percent of the land, gardens abound. One of the most attractive of these is the very large Botanical Garden, which is classified as a UNESCO World Heritage Site. Other gardens have been gained with land-reclamation projects along the shoreline. The most recent additions to the city's park system are the three "Gardens by the Bay," begun in 2005 and stretching along 250 acres of waterfront. Both the Bay Central and Bay East Gardens are linear gardens that hug three miles of shorelines. The heart of the project, however, is the Bay South Garden spread over 130 acres, now one of the world's top tourist destinations. Its horticultural landscape supports two colossal greenhouses—the Flower Dome (largest in the world) with its exotic plants, and the Cloud Forest with its interior "mountain" blanketed with orchids, ferns, and mosses. The park also possesses a series of theme gardens: Serene Garden, Silver Garden, Colonial Garden, Malay Garden, Chinese Garden, Indian Garden, World of Palms, and Children's Garden. The most imaginative aspect of Bay South, however, are the eighteen Supertree Groves. These are metal structures, 80–160 feet tall, shaped into tree-like forms. Their lattices support 200 varieties of exotic ferns, vines, and orchards, but they also house an aerial skyway and observatory for viewing the gardens from above. The metal trees are more than ornaments; they collect water, take in and exhaust air, and contain photovoltaic cells to run their complex lighting systems. In the evening, they present light shows known as the Garden Rhapsody, accompanied by music.

Overlooking the park is one of the more unique architectural projects of its kind—the Marina Bay Sands, designed by Moshe Safdie. It consists of three hotel towers, fifty-five stories high, hovering over a shopping mall, theater, art-science museum, convention center, and casino. Blocks of hotel rooms, from the side, create the profile of a curving X that lightly touch in the center. The feature of the design, however, is that the three towers support, like the legs of platter, a horizontally curving, continuous Sky Park at the top, 650 feet above the ground and a thousand feet in length. It too serves up gardens, restaurants, bars, a children's play area, and a linear swimming pool along the

ILLUSTRATION 12.9   Gardens by the Bay.

Source: Photo by Dietmar Rabich/Wikimedia Commons/"Singapore (SG), Gardens by the Bay—2019–4752"/CC BY-SA 4.0.

concave edge, 500 feet long. The pool, reserved for hotel guests, is a remarkable feat of engineering in that it sits atop three swaying towers with an intricate series of expansion and contraction joints. On the opposite side of the island, fittingly, is a port for cruise ships to dock.

The Marina Bay Sands is definitely more Las Vegas than Edenic, but its saving grace is that it, like the taunting apple tree, resides in a garden. Few will deny that Singapore's intelligent pursuit of the biophilic instinct—the theme of this book—has allowed it to become one of the most economically successful and attractive cities in the world. Gardens, in addition to their ecological roles as global carbon banks, have this persuasive power of enchantment. Many years ago, the city embraced the motto of "Garden City." Today the epithet has been put aside for something more appropriate to the new reality: "City in the Garden." Other cities, particularly those today beset with fleeing residents and an abundance of social ills, might do well to take note.

Notes

1. Lewis Mumford, "Skyline: Status Quo," *The New Yorker*, 11 (October 1947), 108–10.
2. J.M. Richards, "The New Empiricism: Sweden's Latest Style," *Architectural Review* (June 1947), 199–200.
3. "What Is Happening to Modern Architecture?" *The Bulletin of the Museum of Modern Art* 15:3 (Spring 1948), 6.
4. Ibid., 8.
5. Ibid., 18.
6. Sven Backström, "A Swede Looks at Sweden," *Architectural Review* 94 (September 1943), 80.
7. Lewis Mumford, *The Culture of Cities* (San Diego, CA: Harcourt Brace Jovanovich, 1938), 492.
8. See Robert Wojtowicz, *Lewis Mumford and American Modernism: Eutopian Theories for Architecture and Urban Planning* (Cambridge: Cambridge University Press, 1996), 151–3.
9. Lewis Mumford, "From Utopia Parkway Turn East," reprinted in *From the Ground Up* (New York: Harcourt Brace Jovanovich, 1956), 5.
10. Jane Jacobs, *The Death and Life of Great American Cities* (New York: Random House, 1961), 13.
11. Ibid., 21–2.
12. Ibid., 17–18.
13. Ibid., 20–1.
14. Karl Popper, *The Poverty of Historicism* (New York: Harper Torchbooks, 1964), 67. Peter Lawrence, *Becoming Jane Jacobs* (Philadelphia, PA: University of Pennsylvania Press, 2016).
15. Jacobs, *The Death and Life of Great American Cities* (note 10), 267.
16. Sargent Shriver, cited from Steven Hayward, "Broken Cities: Liberalism's Urban Legacy," in *Urban Society* (New York: Guilford; McGraw-Hill, 1999), 117.
17. Charles Jencks, *The Language of Post-Modern Architecture* (New York: Rizzoli, 1977), 21.
18. Colin Rowe, "The Architecture of Utopia," in *The Mathematics of the Ideal Villa and Other Essays* (Cambridge, MA: Massachusetts Institute of Technology Press, 1982). In a later postscript, however, he acknowledged that the idea of utopia might persist as a "social metaphor" rather than as a "social prescription."
19. Melvin Webber, "Order in Diversity: Community Without Propinquity" (1963), in David Banister et al. (eds.), *Environment Land Use and Urban Policy* (Northampton, MA: Edward Elgar, 1999), 62–93; "The Urban Place and the Nonplace Urban Realm" (1964), in Melvin Webber et al. (eds.), *Explorations into Urban Structure* (Philadelphia, PA: University of Pennsylvania Press, 1965), 139–47.
20. Ernst H. Gombrich, "The Beauty of Old Towns," published in *Arena: The Architectural Association Journal* (April 1965), 60.
21. Christopher Alexander, "A City Is Not a Tree," *Architectural Forum* (April–May 1965), 58.
22. Reyner Banham, *Theory and Design in the First Machine Age* (New York: Praeger Publishers, 1960).
23. A six-part series of essays written for *Architectural Review*, January to August 1962.
24. Reyner Banham, "A Home Is Not a House," *Art in America* (April 1965), 75.
25. Reyner Banham, "The Great Gizmo," in *A Critic Writes: Essays by Reyner Banham* (Berkeley: University of California Press, 1996), 117.
26. Kevin Lynch, *Good City Form* (Cambridge, MA: Massachusetts Institute of Technology Press, 1981), 294. The original title was "A Place Utopia."
27. Ibid., 313.
28. Robert Sommer, *Tight Spaces: Hard Architecture and How to Humanize It* (Englewood Cliffs, NJ: Prentice-Hall, 1974), 19.
29. Aldo van Eyck, *Forum* 3 (1960), 121. Cited from Francis Strauven, *Aldo Van Eyck: The Shape of Relativity* (Amsterdam: Architectura & Natura, 1998), 360.

30. Paul Parin, "The Dogon People: 1," in Aldo van Eyck (ed.), *Miracles of Moderation* (Zurich: Eidgenössische Technische Hochschule, 1976), 13.

31. See Liane Lefaivre and Alexander Tzonis, *Aldo van Eyck: Humanist Rebel* (Rotterdam: 010 Publishers, 1999), and Anja Novak, Debbie Wilken, and Liane Lefaivre, *Aldo van Eyck: Designing for Children: The Playgrounds and the City* (Amsterdam: Nai Publishers, 2002).

32. Richard Sennett, *The Craftsman* (New Haven: Yale University Press, 2008), 232–5; Liane Lefaivre + Doll, *Ground-Up: City Play as a Design Tool* (Rotterdam: 010 Publishers, 2016).

33. Strauven, *Aldo van Eyck* (note 29), 288.

34. Joseph A. Burton, "The Aesthetic Education of Louis I. Kahn, 1912–1924," *Perspecta* 28 (1997), 204–17.

35. Louis Kahn, "Form and Design: (1960–61)." Cited in Robert McCarter, *Louis I. Kahn* (New York: Phaidon Press, 2005), 469.

36. McCarter, *Louis I. Kahn* (note 35), 204–5.

37. Juhani Pallasmaa, "Lived Space: Embodied Experience and Sensory Thought," in Peter MacKeith (ed.), *Encounters 1* (Helsinki: Rakennustieto Publishing, 2012), 133.

38. Richard Neutra, *Survival Through Design* (London: Oxford University Press, 1954), 245.

39. Ibid., 118.

40. Ibid., 229.

41. José Ortega y Gasset, *The Revolt of the Masses* (New York: W. W. Norton & Company, 1932).

42. Maurice Merleau-Ponty, *Phenomenology of Perception*, trans. by Colin Smith (London: Routledge & Kegan Paul, 1962).

43. Martin Heidegger, "Building Dwelling Thinking," in Albert Hofstadter (trans.), *Poetry, Language, Thought* (New York: Harper Colophone Books, 1975), 160.

44. Kenneth Frampton, "On Reading Heidegger," Editorial, *Oppositions* 4 (October 1974), n.p.

45. Christian Norberg-Schulz, *Genius Loci: Towards a Phenomenology of Architecture* (New York: Rizzoli, 1979).

46. Marco Frascari, "The Tell-The-Tale Detail," in *Via* 7 (Cambridge, MA: Massachusetts Institute of Technology Press, 1984), 30. Carlo Scarpa, "A Thousand Cypresses," Lecture given in Madrid in 1978.

47. Emilio Ambasz, *The Architecture of Luis Barragan* (New York: Museum of Modern Art, 1974).

48. Luis Barragán, "Gardens for Environments: Jardines del Pedregal," *Journal of the A.I.A.* 17 (April 1952), 169–70.

49. Kazi Khaleed Ashraf, "Sangath: Balkrishna Doshi," in *Twentieth-Century Architecture* (note 38), 604.

50. Balkrishna Doshi, "Ceremony Acceptance Speech for the Pritzker Prize." www.pritzkerprize.com/sites/default/files/inline-files/2018_BalkrishnaDoshi_CeremonySpeech.pdf. Accessed May 29, 2020.

51. The problem was long ago imagined in Max Frisch's novel *Homo Faber*, trans. by Michael Bullock (San Diego, CA: Harvest Book, 1959).

52. See in particular the analyses of Robert A. M. Stern, David Fishman, and Jacob Tilove, *Paradise Planned: The Garden Suburb and the Modern City* (New York: The Monacelli Press, 2013).

53. See Jes Fabricius Møller, "The Parks of Copenhagen 1850–1900," *Garden History* 38:1 (Summer 2019), 112–23.

54. Jan Gehl, *Life Between Buildings: Using Public Space* (Copenhagen: Danish Architecture Press, 1971); English translation: (Washington, DC: Island Press, 1987).

55. See Jan Gehl, *Cities for People* (Washington, DC: Island Press, 2010).

56. Ibid., 206.

57. Lee Kuan Yew, *From Third World to First: The Singapore Story, 1965–2000* (New York: Harper Collins, 2000).

58. Timothy Beatley, *Handbook of Biophilic City Planning & Design* (Washington, DC: Island Press, 2016), 51–66.

EPILOGUE

The Garden Ethic

Since the postmodern excesses of the late twentieth century, design schools everywhere have conceded that theory can only be approached with a sense of dread. By the century's close, architecture's once vaunted historicity had been shredded, and local cultures and national expressions had been upstaged by globalist economies that inevitably unravel the relationship of people with their surroundings. In the wake of these developments the business of design nevertheless flourished, yet this boom has also come at a price. The architecture of the metropolis has been reduced to the ubiquitous and monochrome glass box with all of its digitally induced geometry and feigned novelty. These gray or mirrored markers pollute our skylines, snarl our traffic arteries, fill our sidewalks with shadows, and deplete the planet's resources—all with the likelihood that with our increasingly virtual workplaces they will never achieve full occupancy. When squeezed together in cities, they offer not the slightest gesture to human dignity or quality of life. Moreover, design studios in themselves are largely powerless to challenge the economic norms and minimal standards of present building practices.

Meanwhile, a host of problems loom. Planners, educators, and environmentalists sound alarms. Leaders of industry and state assemble a few times each year to place their bets on the *deus ex machina* of new green technologies to solve our current problems, yet there is one important question that no one seems willing to raise. Is it not time to consider what our present building methods, materials, and creeds, predicated on outmoded aesthetic standards, contribute to our social and ecological crises? Is it not time to rethink in some small way how we build?

There seem to be two aspects to the depressed state of design practice today. One is simply our failure to heed more seriously our interdependence with the ecosystems of our planet and design accordingly. The second is to acknowledge that the purpose of design is not to reduce every city in the world to what Yevgeny Zamyatin has referred to as "divine parallelepipeds of transparent dwellings."[1] Should not the art of design rather lie in enriching human culture and thereby elevating human happiness?

What we seem to lack is a superintending garden ethic. Such an ethic may appear to be a small gesture in the face of so many large and difficult problems, but I believe there is more to the idea than what meets the eye. It is the desire to stop thinking of design as making "objects" and accept the larger social responsibility of nurturing a vital and sustainable culture. The Latin root word *cultura*, after all, refers to growing or cultivating something in the soil of a prepared medium, and in design terms, culture can be viewed as tending to the human organism within its built, natural, and social environments.

The garden ethic is actually little different from the inspiration that governs all of the arts. It is the gesture reflected in a poetic play of words or the musical skill exhibited in a string quartet. It is an ethic acquired through years of patience, practice, and deliberation. It is an aesthetic but a different kind of aesthetic, one that—like the Japanese teahouse—is manifested in the conduct of one's life, the courtesy we pay to ourselves as well as to others. The garden ethic concerns itself not with where we live but with *how we live*. It offers no utopian pretensions. It is, at a small scale, the making of places that are both meaningful and delightful for those who dwell within them. Culturally, the garden ethic seeks to nourish the human spirit.

We often pretend to have outgrown our biology, sometimes greatly to our detriment, and the garden ethic begins with the simple recognition that we are organisms largely shaped by our physical and cultural environments. Our surroundings condition our behaviors and contour our bodies. Their ambiance can be baneful or benefic to the senses, to our health, and indeed to the course of human evolution. And if we earlier had intuitions about how environments impinge upon our physical and mental development, the biological and human sciences of the last few decades have brought home this point in an irrefutable way. That anonymous "building occupant" of design's sociological past is now being painted between the lines, and it is time to tack this colorful portrait on the walls of our design studios. A garden ethic, in this sense, will free architecture from its antiquated values of design.

One of the more profound insights of this new knowledge is the realization that we are embodied beings—complex organisms within environments with dynamically integrated genetic, nervous, sensory, visceral, endocrine, and emotional systems.[2] Moreover, these systems are intricately embedded within larger ecosystems. We can no longer think of our minds as independent of a body or as spirits floating above the material world. We enact or create our worlds, our conduct, our cultures, and every interaction with the world is a whole-body event. The twentieth-century belief that design was a "visual art" operating through its symbols is today woefully narrow-minded and outmoded, yet it has not gone away. Our designed environments may at a basic level offer shelter and conditioned air, but more importantly they provide us with the existential field in which our lives unfold. Poor environments, we have known for many years, diminish human vitality and vitiate one's health. Good environments, as we are learning today, enhance biological and neurological growth and provide the affordance of sensory engagement, pleasure, and the exercise of social propriety.[3]

Our new knowledge of ourselves has also brought to the fore our emotional attunement with the environment. If earlier psychological models detached cognition from emotion, current affective models are founded on very different premises. Mood is not something disquieting or perturbing to cognition; it is rather a "postural attitude" that pervades cognition through and through.[4] The idea that every room has an emotional resonance, or that every city possesses a particular atmosphere, has of course long been a creative underpinning of the literary and visual arts, but only recently has the idea returned to the practice of design. Mood testifies to the primal resonance we have with a particular place or room, the way that we engage with it, and with those within it. Atmosphere is fashioned by living presences, by natural light, climate, prospects, forms, detailing, and the qualities of materials—their pleasing textures, tactile qualities, colors, sounds, aromas, and scale. Atmosphere is the very palette of pigments that a good designer wields.[5]

We are also beginning to understand how we engage the environments in which we live. If Mondrian had his chromatic realms to explore, we too have ours. The nineteenth-century notion of "empathy" that we noted earlier—the way in which we feel ourselves into the environments we inhabit—has been documented by the discovery of transmodal "mirror systems" in the 1990s. Mirror systems are connecting groups of neurons mainly in the sensorimotor regions of the brain that become active during every sensory engagement we have with the world. The sound of a piano excites the area of the motor cortex related to the movement of fingers, and a ballet dancer sympathetically engages our leg muscles. We simulate the feeling of someone across a room being touched, as we do with the arrows afflicting Saint Sebastian in the Uffizi. We even respond to inanimate objects touching one another—the force of a raindrop falling on a leaf or the weight of a beam resting on a column. We now know that we connect in visceral ways with every aspect of the physical and social environments. One general theory to explain this connection is referred to as embodied simulation—that is, we perceive and understand the actions of people, spaces, and forms around us by simulating them with our own bodies.[6] A rubble-rock wall appeals to us because we can simulate the weight of the stone and enjoy the texture and physical labor of the wall. We describe steel and glass as cold materials, because they are cold to the touch.

This new knowledge of how we engage with the world stands at the command of the creative designer. Functionalist design theory of the twentieth century was predicated on the belief that architectural forms, materials, and spaces were neutral or isotropic events. Studies today have shown that the space in the immediate vicinity of our bodies is processed neurologically in a different way than the spatial zone beyond it. The materials and shapes that we use in our buildings also mean something. Viewing a twisted column in a monastery cloister may induce a feeling of attentive tension in prayer. We imbibe the music in a concert hall through our auditory systems but also through the harmonic vibrations within our bodies. One experiment has even revealed that we simulate the force of a brush stroke applied to a canvas of an abstract painting.[7] And if this is true for the lines of a two-dimensional painting, then how much more do we internalize the three-dimensional field of our buildings and cities, which offer a multisensory continuum of visual, haptic, auditory, olfactory, and spatial sensations?

Design should and will always remain a playful and creative exercise, but professionally it should also be an informed one. A knowledge of human ecology, in its social and encultured sense, cannot be relegated to others; it must remain central to the designer's education because, as we are now learning, our buildings shape the culture in which we live. Perhaps the most capacious principle for the garden ethic, highlighted by this new knowledge, is that just as we design our physical and cultural environments, these environments in turn alter the genetic, cognitive, and behavioral patterns of who we are.

Of course, what cannot be omitted from the garden ethic is our hopeful return to the garden itself, one stretching from the bluebells in the meadow to the complex ecosystems of the great sequoias. Research has recently shed new light on nature. It has shown us that trees in a forest share water and nutrients among a community of other trees through their roots and underground fungal networks. When gnawed upon by herbivores, trees can alert their neighbors to shoot toxic tannins into their leaves. When attacked by caterpillars, elms and pines can release pheromones to attract parasitic wasps who feed on caterpillars. And of course, we have long known that through the process of photosynthesis, trees transform carbon dioxide into the oxygen that sustains all life on the planet.[8]

There is a lesson to be learned here, because nature does much more. Over the last few decades, we have amassed a trove of studies documenting that regular human contact with nature reduces rates of human morbidity; fends off various diseases; lowers stress; improves mood, sleep patterns, cardiovascular health, and memory; and boosts the immune system with anti-cancer protein production.[9] Our yen for the garden, it is now clear, is not a fanciful or romantic one; it is embedded deep within our biological genome. And the emergence of a now quite visible biophilic movement in design—introducing nature directly or indirectly into buildings and cities—has been a direct response to this gathering knowledge.[10] The environmentalist can plead the case that bringing nature into our cities will partially offset our carbon footprint, but there is a stronger argument to be made. Trees, plants, and flowers are more beautiful to live among than steel, glass, and concrete.

When Alvar Aalto, in his talk cited in the preface, noted that the "only purpose" of architecture was to create a paradise, he was not specifically alluding to the design of gardens or parks. Nor was he being utopian by suggesting grand plans to change the world. He made these remarks in a talk given to builders, and his point was that designers and planners should embrace humanism because "even a small increase of happiness is welcome." Yet to achieve this small increase of happiness, he goes on to say, we need "to throw away as much as possible of the ballast that prevents us from creating human architecture."[11] The garden ethic challenges us to discard this ballast once and for all. For too many years now, we have viewed design largely as a structural, material, technological, economic, and logistical exercise dressed each season with a new aesthetic gown. The garden ethic allows us to ennoble our lived world in a more organic way. Let us, for a moment, ponder the role that an ecologically responsive, beautiful, well-crafted, and poetically conceived living environment can play in satisfying the paradisiacal instinct.

ILLUSTRATION P. 1   *Little Garden of Paradise*, Upper Rhenish Master, Stadtel Museum/Historical Museum Frankfurt.

Source: GNU Free Documentation License, Yorck Project.

Notes

1. See the section "A Brief Excursus on Dystopias" in Chapter 11.
2. For a philosophical grounding of this new perspective, see Evan Thompson, *Mind in Life: Biology, Phenomenology, and the Sciences of Mind* (Cambridge, MA: Belknap Press, 2007).
3. For sources on environments and neurological development, see my *From Object to Experience: The New Culture of Architectural Design* (London: Bloomsbury, 2018), 55–9.
4. Two important studies in this regard are Maxime Sheets-Johnston, "Emotion and Movement: A Beginning Empirical-Phenomenological Analysis of Their Relationship," *Journal of Consciousness Studies* 6 (1999), 11–12, and Giovanna Colombetti, *The Feeling Body: Affective Science Meets the Enactive Mind* (Cambridge, MA: Massachusetts Institute of Technology Press, 2014).
5. The classic study is Peter Zumthor, *Atmospheres: Architectural Environments: Surrounding Objects* (Basel: Birkhäuser, 2006). See also Gernot Böhme, Tonino Griffero, and Jean-Paul Thibaud, *Architecture and Atmosphere* (Helsinki: Tapio Wirkkala-Rut Bryk Foundation, 2014).
6. See Giacomo Rizzolatti and Corrado Sinigagila, *Mirrors in the Brain: How Our Minds Share Actions and Emotions*, trans. by Frances Anderson (Oxford: Oxford University Press, 2008); B. Calvo-Merino, "Towards a Sensorimotor Aesthetics of Performing Art," *Consciousness and Cognition* 17 (2008), 911–22; Marc Bangert et al., "Shared Networks for Auditory and Motor Processing in Professional Pianists: Evidence from fMRI Conjunction," *NeuroImage* 30 (2006), 917–26; Sjoerd J. H. Ebisch et al., "The Sense of Touch: Embodied Simulation in a Visuotactile Mirroring Mechanism for Observed Animate or Inanimate Touch," *Journal of Cognitive Neuroscience* 20:9 (2008), 1611–23; Vittorio Gallese and Corrado Sinigaglia, "What Is So Special About Embodied Simulation," *Trends in Cognitive Sciences* 16:11 (November 2011), 512–19.
7. See Beatrice Sbriscia-Fioretti et al., "ERP Modulation During Observation of Abstract Paintings by Franz Kline," *PLoS ONE* 8:10 (October 2013). See also David Freedberg and Vittorio Gallese, "Motion, Emotion and Empathy in Esthetic Experience," *Trends in Cognitive Sciences* 11:5 (2007), 197–203.
8. See Peter Wohlleben, *The Hidden Life of Trees: What They Feel, How They Communicate* (Vancouver: Greystone Books, 2016).
9. For a few examples, see Marc G. Berman, John Jonides, and Stephen Kaplan, "The Cognitive Benefits of Interacting with Nature," *Psychological Science* 19:12 (2007), 1207–12; Qing Li, *Forest Bathing: How Trees Can Help You Find Health and Happiness* (New York: Viking, 2018); Clare Cooper Marcus and Naomi A. Sachs, *Therapeutic Landscapes: An Evidence-Based Approach to Designing Healing Gardens and Restorative Outdoor Spaces* (Hoboken, NJ: Wiley, 2014).
10. Stephen R. Kellert, Judith H. Heerwagen, and Martin L. Mador, *Biophilic Design: The Theory, Science, and Practice of Bringing Buildings to Life* (Hoboken, NJ: John Wiley & Sons, 2008); Timothy Beatley, *Biophilic Cities: Integrating Nature into Urban Design and Planning* (Washington, DC: Island Press, 2011).
11. *Alvar Aalto in His Own Words*, ed. by Göran Schildt (Helsinki: Otava Publishing Company, 1997), 215–17.

INDEX